Vienna

timeout.com/vienna

Penguin Books

PENGUIN BOOKS

Published by the Penguin Group
Penguin Books Ltd, 80 Strand, London WC2R ORL, England
Penguin Group (USA) Inc., 375 Hudson Street, New York, New York 10014, USA
Penguin Books Australia Ltd, 250 Camberwell Road, Camberwell, Victoria 3124, Australia
Penguin Books Canada Ltd, 10 Alcorn Avenue, Toronto, Ontario, Canada M4V 3B2
Penguin Books (NZ) Ltd, cnr Rosedale and Airborne Roads, Albany, Auckland, New Zealand

Penguin Books Ltd, Registered Offices: Harmondsworth, Middlesex, England

First published 2000

Second edition 2003
10 9 8 7 6 5 4 3 2 1

Colour reprographics by Icon, Crowne House, 56-58 Southwark Street, London SE1 1UN
Printed and bound by Cayfosa-Quebecor, Ctra. de Caldes, Km 3 08 130 Sta, Perpètua de Mogoda, Barcelona, Spain

Edited and designed by
Time Out Guides Limited
Universal House
251 Tottenham Court Road
London W1T 7AB
Tel + 44 (0)20 7813 3000
Fax + 44 (0)20 7813 6001
Email guides@timeout.com
www.timeout.com

Editorial

Editor Sarah Guy
Consultant Editor Geraint Williams
Deputy Editor Phil Harriss
Listings Editors Simone Coll, Isabel Fofana Coll,
    Cathy Limb
Copy Editor Sally Davies
Proofreader John Pym
Indexer Jackie Brind

Editorial Director Peter Fiennes
Series Editor Ruth Jarvis
Deputy Series Editor Lesley McCave
Guides Co-ordinator Anna Norman

Design

Group Art Director John Oakey
Art Director Mandy Martin
Art Editor Scott Moore
Senior Designer Tracey Ridgewell
Designers Astrid Kogler, Sam Lands
Digital Imaging Dan Conway
Ad Make-up Charlotte Blythe
Picture Editor Kerri Littlefield
Acting Picture Editor Kit Burnet
Acting Deputy Picture Editor Martha Houghton
Picture Desk Trainee Bella Wood

Advertising

Group Commercial Director Lesley Gill
Sales Director Mark Phillips
International Sales Manager Ross Canadé
Advertisement Sales (Vienna) Alexandra Meran
Advertising Assistant Sabrina Ancilleri

Administration

Chairman Tony Elliott
Managing Director Mike Hardwick
Group Financial Director Richard Waterlow
Group Marketing Director Christine Cort
Marketing Manager Mandy Martinez
US Publicity & Marketing Associate Rosella Albanese
Group General Manager Nichola Coulthard
Guides Production Director Mark Lamond
Production Controller Samantha Furniss
Accountant Sarah Bostock

Features in this guide were written and researched by

Introduction Geraint Williams. **History** Nicholas Parsons (*Celebrity Strauss* Robin Lee). **Vienna Today** Florian Klenk, Geraint Williams. **Literary Vienna** Oona Strathern. **Accommodation** George Hamilton. **Sightseeing** Geraint Williams (*A trot through time: Vienna's fiakers* Linda Lodding), Rory O'Donovan. **Restaurants** Geraint Williams. **Cafés & Coffee Houses** Geraint Williams. **Shops & Services** Christine Boggis. **Festivals & Events** Christine Boggis (*Having a ball* Robin Lee). **Children** Isabel Naylon, Delia Meth-Cohn. **Film** Katje Seebohm, Adrian Garcia-Lande (*The austere Austrian* Geoff Andrew). **Galleries** Lorenz Seidler. **Gay & Lesbian** Hal Rock, Chris Halls. **Music: Classical & Opera** Robin Lee. **Music: Rock, Roots & Jazz** Joe Remick. **Nightlife** Gertraud Gerst. **Sport & Fitness** Isabel Naylon, Deborah Klosky. **Theatre & Dance** Diane Shooman. **Trips Out of Town** Linda Lodding, Andrena Woodhams. **Directory** Simone Coll, Isabel Fofana Coll (*Further reference* Geraint Williams, Joe Remick).

The Editor would like to thank: Maite Bachero, Kevin Ebbutt, Karl Fluch, Jürgen Janger, Stefan Jena, Gethin Geraint Jones, Chris Leach, Lucie Roberts, Georg Schneider, Damien Wayling, Pablo Williams.

Maps by JS Graphics (john@jsgraphics.co.uk).
Vienna Street Map based on material supplied by APA Publications Gmbh & Co.

Photography by Elan Fleisher except: pages 6, 7, 13, 65, 153, 122, 123, 125, 126, 127 Austrian National Tourist Office; 11, 14, 17, 18, 21, 26, 53, 147, 148, 169, 170, 175, AKG London; 166 AFP.

Contents

Introduction

ABOUT THE TIME OUT CITY GUIDES

This is the second edition of the *Time Out Vienna Guide*, one of our ever-expanding series on the world's most crucial cities. A dedicated and enthusiastic team of writers who live and work in the Austrian capital sweated and fretted to provide you with everything you might need to know to make a visit to Vienna as rewarding as possible. While detailing the main sights and major attractions, we also direct you to Vienna's coolest cafés, sharpest shopping opportunities and finest new places to lunch and dine.

THE LOWDOWN ON THE LISTINGS

We've striven to make this guide as useful and accurate as possible. Addresses, phone numbers, transport details, opening times and admission prices were all checked before going to press. However, please bear in mind that owners and managers can change their arrangements at any time. If you are going out of your way, it's a good idea to phone before setting out. While every effort has been made to ensure the accuracy of the information contained in this guide, the publishers cannot accept responsibility for any errors it may contain.

PRICES & PAYMENT

In this guide the euro is denoted by €. Where we have listed prices, they should be treated as a guideline rather than gospel. Should they vary wildly from those we have quoted, ask for an explanation. If there isn't one, go elsewhere – but please write and let us know.

Although most hotels in Vienna take credit cards, many restaurants, cafés and museums do not. The following abbreviations have been used: **AmEx** American Express; **DC** Diners' Club; **MC** Mastercard; **V** Visa.

THE LIE OF THE LAND

Vienna is divided into 23 districts. In our listings the first number of each address is the district and the second the street number. So, for example, Café Central in the 1st district is listed: *1, Herrengasse 14*. The district number is denoted by the second and third digits in the postcode, thus for Café Central it is 1010. For maps of the city, see pages 232-243.

TELEPHONE NUMBERS

At first glance some phone and fax numbers listed may seem confusing. While there can be as many as ten or as few as three or four digits to each number, there is also the *Durchwahlen*

Following the Amsterdam Hilton bed-in way back in 1969, John and Yoko made a lightning trip to Vienna, then a grey and unlovely outpost of western values. On this stage of their adventures, later chronicled in the memorable ballad that bears their name, they did little apart from stuff their faces with chocolate cake in a suite at the Sacher. Back in Britain, John remarked in passing to David Frost that 'they're a bit square over there'. Even today Lennon's observation remains essentially true. For every Kruder & Dorfmeister, Coop Himmelb(l)au or Michael Hanneke projecting the image of a city flexing its cultural muscles, there are thousands more traditionalists who silently concur with the stodgy blend of monarchic nostalgia and deferential manners propagated by Vienna's omnipotent tourist industry.

When the first *Time Out Vienna Guide* went to press in February 2000, a new coalition government had just been formed between the conservative Austrian People's Party (ÖVP) and Jörg Haider's xenophobic Freedom Party (FPÖ). By the time the guide was on

sale, the EU had announced diplomatic sanctions against Austria, and suddenly everyone from DJs to visiting academics was cancelling engagements in Vienna.

Much of the positive energy generated through the 1990s by the city's musicians, architects and filmmakers was initially dissipated in the furore, but three years on, the shock of international outrage has in many ways made Vienna a more open city. It has prompted a long overdue assessment of the numerous skeletons lurking in the cupboards of its grandiose public buildings and heralded an upsurge in grass-roots politics after decades of cosy yet stultifying cohabitation between Austria's two main parties: the ÖVP and the social democratic SPÖ.

Vienna is now a far friendlier, more vibrant city to live in and visit than back in the time of the Beatles. Admittedly, many of the improvements were already under way in the late 1990s when inspired local government tarted up the city's smutty façades and made its public spaces accessible to a greater public. Following the events of 2000, Vienna

Advertisers

We would like to stress that no establishment has been included in this guide because it has advertised in any of our publications and no payment of any kind has influenced any review. The opinions given in this book are those of Time Out writers and entirely independent.

(direct dial extension numbers) system. This means some numbers are followed by a hyphen and then a digit (usually a 0); this tells you there are a number of extensions. Dialling the main number plus those following the hyphen will connect you to an extension. So, if you know the extension you want, dial the relevant digits after the hyphen. Extension 0 will usually get you through to the main desk/operator who will then transfer your call if necessary. Likewise, if you dial all the numbers up to the hyphen you will still get through to the same main desk/operator. If there are figures other than a 0 after the hyphen we recommend you dial the whole number, as that will be the extension you'll need to book a room, make enquiries, and so on.

ESSENTIAL INFORMATION

For all the practical information you'll need for visiting the city – including visa and customs information, disabled access, emergency telephone numbers, a list of useful websites and the lowdown on the transport network – turn to the **Directory** chapter at the back of this guide. It starts on p212.

LET US KNOW WHAT YOU THINK

It should be stressed that the information we offer is impartial. No organisation has been included because it has advertised in any of *Time Out*'s publications, and all opinions given are wholly independent. Rigorous impartiality and cosmopolitan critical assessment are the reasons our guides are so successful. But if you disagree with our opinions, please let us know; your comments are always welcome. You'll find a reader's reply card at the back of the book.

There is an online version of this guide, as well as weekly events listings for over 35 international cities, at **www.timeout.com**.

vocally rejected the rise of the far right with demonstrations that called for resistance.

That summer a remarkable piece of agitprop took place on the city's streets, promoted by Vienna Festival director Luc Bondy and sanctioned by the city council. Maverick German performance art prankster Christoph Schlingensief goaded the prejudices of Vienna's good burghers in a parody of the then wildly popular *Big Brother* series. By placing an industrial container emblazoned with the legend '*Ausländer Raus!*' ('Foreigners out') beside the Staatsoper and filling it with asylum seekers, Schlingensief invited the Viennese to select a candidate for deportation via telephone and the internet. For eight days, the square became the scene of virulent but ultimately fruitful dialogue among passers-by that set the tone for a freer Vienna.

Occasions such as these, the flourishing of the city's arts scene – symbolised by the Museumsquartier arts complex – and the opening of a plethora of new bars and restaurants have taken the edge off Vienna's apparent crustiness, providing sprightly modern alternatives to the city's habitual programme of high arts and its historic treasures. A single day in Vienna offers a wealth of splendid contrasts – pop out of baroque churches and into modern galleries exhibiting cutting-edge contemporary art; digest a meal in one of the city's traditional wood-panelled eating houses followed by an espresso and schnapps on a pavement terrace; or end a night at the opera with digital beats and glitches in the city's burgeoning club scene. Or just wander the streets of a magnificently appointed European city whose every corner breathes history.

Uncannily, work on this second edition coincided with the early elections of 2002 that gave the controversial coalition a few new innings. This time around, however, the war in Iraq relegated news of the FPÖ's continuing presence in the government to the marginalia of the international press and has brought a little of Lennon's spirit back to the city. On the facade of Vienna's Westbahnhof, the words 'Imagine Peace' blaze from an illuminated billboard.

In Love with Vienna

A short visit to Vienna, just the two of you. Why? Pure joie de vivre and the opportunity to take a bit of Vienna home with you. The city from its loveliest side, with all its treasures laid out in the shop windows: delicate Augarten porcelain, Lobmeyr crystal, enamel bracelets by M.Frey-Wille and tiny works of petit-point art. The city's finest shopping street, the Kohlmarkt, is full of Viennese tradition and trends and has the Hofburg Palace for a backdrop. Vienna is one huge, sweet temptation: from Heindl confectionery to the Originial Sacher-Torte. "Haben schon Gewählt (Have you made your selection)?" is the question at exclusive Café Demel. Then it's time to write postcards. "I have to run a  quick errand!" he says, in a bit of subterfuge designed to disguise a golden surprise. And the choices are almost unlimited at jewellers such as Anton  Heldwein, A. E. K ö c h e r t , K i e b a c k , Golden Genius , F. Halder or Art Deco. Isn't it w o n d e r f u l ? Walking hand in hand down the Graben, past the Trinity Column and on to St. Stephen's Cathedral. Zur Schwäbischen Jungfrau has wonderful bedding and linens, while Palmers is famous for its seductive lingerie. And souvenir-hunters love the Österreichische Werkstätten on Kärntner Strasse, a paradise of arts and crafts to please anyone back home. But which bag deserves a place in your hand-luggage? A Ver Sacrum from Schneiders Vienna or one by Robert Horn from the tradition of the classic Viennese avant-garde? "Why not take both?" he asks in burst of generosity. "What 's this all about? Is he in love?" "Yes. With you - and with Vienna."

In Context

Features

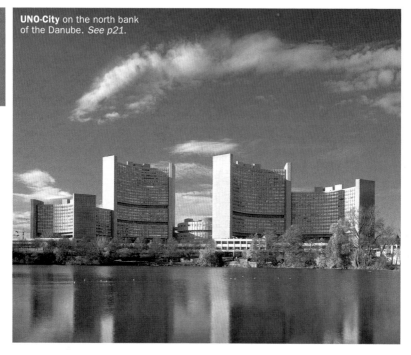

UNO-City on the north bank of the Danube. *See p21.*

History

Vienna's waltz through the centuries saw it become the hub of the Habsburg Empire, and a mecca for music.

Early in the first century AD, the settlement of *Vindobona* was only a subsidiary outpost of *Carnuntum*, the capital of the Roman province of Pannonia Superior. Vindobona, 40 kilometres (25 miles) west of the capital along the Danube, was centred on what is now the **Hoher Markt** in old Vienna, with a squadron of cavalry based nearby in the modern 3rd district. Carnuntum and Vindobona were part of a Roman defensive line, known as the *Limes*, built along the Danube to keep out the Germanic barbarians.

From the end of the third century AD the failure of the Romans to subdue the Germanic tribes, and the constant aggression of Vandals and Goths in particular, made the situation of Vindobona increasingly precarious. At the end

of the following century (probably in 395), a fire destroyed the military camp and led to the withdrawal of its Roman Legion. Roman influence lingered on, though, until the Eastern Emperor Theodosius II formally ceded Pannonia to the Huns in 433.

THE DARK AGES

When the Roman legionaries withdrew southwards, they left behind a small residue of veterans and Romanised inhabitants. These were now at the mercy of repeated waves of invaders, often themselves in flight from powerful adversaries. Despite such disruptions, there was evidently some continuity in organised administration. From at least the eighth century a governor dispensed justice from the **Berghof**, which was at the western end of today's Hoher Markt (now recalled by a plaque on the wall). The earliest recorded church in Vienna, the **Ruprechtskirche**, was built just to the east, probably in the ninth century. Its dedication to Saint Rupert indicates its association with the shippers of salt from the Salzkammergut; the missionary Saint Rupert, who died around 710, was the first Bishop of Salzburg, and the patron saint of salt miners. The eastward spread of Christianity also brought with it Bavarian settlers, the ancestors of the German-Austrians who would form the core population of the region.

By the ninth century Vindobona had disappeared, and the city's modern name – which first appeared as *Wenia* in the Salzburg annals of 881 – had become current. It is supposedly derived from the Illyro-Celtic word *Vedunja*, meaning a woodland stream. Wenia was situated at the eastern edge of the Carolingian Empire, in a buffer zone periodically overrun by the Magyars from the east. Following the defeat of a Bavarian army at Pressburg (Bratislava) in 907, Wenia was under Magyar control for several decades, but the decisive victory of the German King Otto the Great on the Lechfeld, near Augsburg, in 955 marked a turning point. The Magyars would eventually be pushed back to the River Leitha, now in the Austrian province of Burgenland, which became the permanent frontier.

This hotly disputed border territory between 'West' and 'East' – a role to which it reverted during the Cold War over 1,000 years later – came to be known as Austria. The name first occurs in an imperial document of 996 bestowing lands on the Bishop of Freising, described as being 'in a region popularly known as *Ostarrichi*' ('Eastern Realm', the origin of *Österreich*). Even before then, in 976, Emperor Otto II had awarded the 'Ottonian Mark' established by his father, between Enns and Traisen, to the Bavarian Margraves (Counts) of Babenberg. This ambitious dynasty, whose members combined shrewd diplomacy with ostentatious piety, would dominate the expanding territories of 'Austria' for 270 years.

THE BABENBERGS

When Leopold I of Babenberg (976-94) first took charge of his new possessions, the seat of his power was in Melk on the Danube. He managed to extend his lands to the east, probably as far as the Wienerwald, but Wenia itself remained in Magyar hands for some time yet. The Magyars contented themselves with occupation of the Berghof and maintaining a military presence

(setting up a camp on what is now the Schwarzenbergplatz), without establishing any permanent settlement.

The Magyars were finally forced back to the Leitha by Adalbert 'the Victorious' (1018-55). The Babenbergs still had to impose their authority over local lords, powers in the area since the Carolingian era. Like their successors the Habsburgs, the Babenbergs reinforced their territorial claims by astute marriages into rival dynasties. Their expansionist ambitions were generally projected eastwards, and the Babenberg seat was moved progressively along the Danube from Melk to Klosterneuburg, and then Vienna.

Saint Leopold III of Babenberg (1096-1135) would become the patron saint of Austria (his canonisation went through in 1485). He was a man of piety, a peacemaker who refused an offer of the German crown, devoting himself instead to founding or refounding abbeys and churches (Heiligenkreuz and Klosterneuburg among them). In 1137 his successor Leopold IV (1136-41) agreed with the bishopric of Passau to build a new church in Vienna, just outside the town boundary. Ten years later this Romanesque predecessor of the **Stephansdom** cathedral was completed.

Maria Theresia. *See p14.*

The most significant Babenberg for the history of Vienna was Heinrich II Jasomirgott (1141-77), so-called because of his favourite oath ('So help me God!'). He was prevailed upon to renounce the dukedom of Bavaria, acquired by his predecessor in 1139, but was handsomely rewarded by the upgrading of Austria itself in 1156 to a dukedom, entirely independent of its western neighbour. Equally important was Heinrich's decision to move his court to Vienna in the same year, to the area still known as Am Hof ('At the Court'). In 1155 Irish monks were summoned from Heinrich's former seat at Regensburg to found the **Schottenstift** ('Monastery of the Scots', so-called because in medieval Latin Ireland was *Scotia Maior*).

The town's economic expansion continued under Heinrich's successor, Leopold V (1177-94), who benefited from two windfalls: he inherited much of Styria and Upper Austria in 1192 when their ruler died childless; and he received a handsome share of the huge ransom paid to Emperor Heinrich VI for the release of Richard the Lionheart. (The Crusading King of England had insulted Leopold and the Emperor's representative during the siege of Acre in Palestine, and in 1192 was making his way back to England overland after being shipwrecked on the Adriatic coast. He was recognised in Vienna, and imprisoned in the castle at Dürnstein until March 1193.) Leopold's share was enough to found Wiener Neustadt and extend the fortifications of Vienna and the border town of Hainburg.

Late 12th-century Vienna was booming economically and culturally. Under Leopold VI 'the Glorious' (1198-1230), troubadours, known as *Minnesänger*, were prominent at the Babenberg court, singing the praises of noble ladies and celebrating the magnificence and virtue of the duke. Leopold VI encouraged trade, making himself popular with the burghers by allowing guilds to be formed and, most importantly, awarding Vienna its 'staple right', in 1221. This obliged foreign merchants trading on the Danube to sell their goods to local traders within two months of their being landed, effectively guaranteeing the lion's share of the downstream trade to the Viennese. It was virtually a licence to print money.

The reign of the last Babenberg, Friedrich II 'the Warlike' (1230-46) saw a decline in the fortunes of the city and the dukedom. After a fierce dispute with the German Emperor, Friedrich was killed in 1246 fighting the Hungarians, leaving no male heirs. The resulting power vacuum was filled by the ambitious Ottokar II of Bohemia, who reinforced his claim by marrying Friedrich II's widow at Hainburg in 1252.

THE COMING OF THE HABSBURGS

Ottokar cultivated the Viennese burghers – as well as executing a few who tried to oppose him – and most of the town swung behind him. He gave generous support to the rebuilding of the Stephansdom and other buildings after a fire in 1258, and founded a hospital for lepers as well as the famous **Wiener Bürgerspital** almshouse. He also initiated the building of the **Hofburg**, Vienna's future imperial palace, originally as a fairly simple fortress.

The increased sensibility towards the poor and sick that was revealed in the endowment of hospitals coincided with a great wave of religious fervour – a recurrent phenomenon in Viennese history. The uncertainties of the age were also reflected in outbreaks of religious fanaticism: processions of flagellants appeared in the streets of Vienna, complementing the more orthodox campaigns against impiety by the Dominicans, whose first church in Vienna was consecrated in 1237.

Ottokar's ambiguous position was made precarious by a failed attempt to become King of Germany (King-Emperors were elected from among the lesser princes). He was further undermined when Rudolf of Habsburg was chosen as king in his place in 1273. Rudolf, whose original, small domain was in modern Switzerland, was initially seen as a compromise candidate deemed harmless by the other electors, but he soon proved himself far-sighted and shrewd. He set out to challenge Ottokar's power, and by 1276 had occupied Vienna. They made a temporary peace, but in 1278 Ottokar was killed in the battle of Dürnkrut, on the Marchfeld north-east of Vienna. His embalmed body was displayed in the Minorite monastery, a reminder to the people that those who aspire to climb highest also fall furthest.

The arrival of Rudolf began 640 years of virtually unbroken, if sporadically resisted, Habsburg rule in Austria; Vienna was to be the *Residenzstadt* of every Habsburg ruler except Maximilian I (1493-1519), whose main seat was Innsbruck, and Rudolf II (1576-1612), who preferred Prague. From 1283 Rudolf left the government of Austria in the hands of his son Albrecht, who made himself unpopular by challenging some burgher privileges, and had to put down a rebellion in the city in 1287-8. In 1298 Albrecht I became the first Habsburg to add to the title of German King that of Holy Roman Emperor, which like Vienna would in later centuries become virtually consubstantial with the dynasty. To accommodate Vienna's new ruling house, the Hofburg would expand continuously through the centuries; and extensions to it were still being planned when war broke out in 1914.

Problems beset the Habsburgs in the first half of the 14th century. In 1310 there was a rising in Vienna against Friedrich 'the Handsome', which had two significant consequences: one of the properties confiscated from the conspirators was handed over to become the first City Hall (**Altes Rathaus**), and the city's rights and privileges were codified for the first time in the so-called *Eisenbuch* (1320). During the reign of Albrecht 'the Lame' (1298-1358), plagues of locusts ravaged the Vienna Basin (in 1338 and 1340); and hardly had they disappeared than Vienna was hit by the Black Death, at the height of which, in 1349, 500 people were dying each day. The plague was then followed by a terrible fire.

Vienna's Christian population blamed the Jews for the plague (they were said to have poisoned the wells), and Albrecht had to struggle to prevent major violence. A Jewish community had been established in Vienna since Babenberg times, and had reached a considerable size. It was mainly concentrated close to Am Hof, on and around today's Judenplatz. Its location was not accidental, for Jews traditionally enjoyed the ruler's protection; even this, though, was not always enough to spare them from persecution at times of crisis.

DYNASTY BUILDING

Duke Albrecht achieved a shrewd dynastic alliance in 1353, when his son, the future Rudolf IV, married the daughter of Karl IV of Bohemia, Holy Roman Emperor since 1346. Advantageous marriage was thereafter the principal pillar of Habsburg expansionism, aphoristically described in a 16th-century adaptation of a line from Ovid: 'Others make war; you, fortunate Austria, marry!' The magnificence of the Prague ruled by his illustrious father-in-law was a spur to Rudolf's ambitions: masons who had worked on the great cathedral of Saint Vitus in Prague were summoned to work on the Stephansdom, and Rudolf founded a university in Vienna in 1365, clearly inspired by Karl's earlier foundation of the Prague Carolinum.

In the same year Rudolf died in Milan, aged only 26. He had reigned for a mere seven years, but his ingenious policies ranged from social and monetary reform to the promotion of urban renewal through tax holidays and rent reform. Not for nothing was he known as 'the Founder' (as well as, equally aptly, 'the Cunning').

As a moderniser, Rudolf clashed with vested interests, such as the guilds and the Church. But his attempts to advance the claims of the dynasty over the title of Holy Roman Emperor were embarrassingly ill-judged. A diligently produced forgery known as the *Privilegium*

Maius invented a picturesque lineage and even more picturesque titles for the earlier Habsburgs. It was magisterially rubbished by the poet Petrarch, who had been asked to verify its authenticity by the Emperor. Even more disastrous was Rudolf's institution of a system of power sharing among the male Habsburg heirs (the *Rudolfinische Hausordnung*). This resulted in a Habsburg equivalent of the Wars of the Roses between the 'Albertine' and 'Leopoldine' lines (named after Rudolf's two quarrelling brothers and joint heirs), which lasted intermittently for four generations.

In 1411 Albrecht V, of the Albertine line, came of age and entered a Vienna under threat from Moravian knights and the Protestant Hussites of Bohemia, who laid waste parts of Lower Austria for several years. Bad harvests and the loss of the wine trade to German merchants contributed to a rancid atmosphere, in which the Jews were, once again, scapegoats.

> **'Having overrun Hungary, the Ottomans were by 1529 at the gates of Vienna, a vulnerable city with old-fashioned defences.'**

This time the ruler himself was the instigator of a horrifying pogrom, the *Wiener Geserah*. He was enthusiastically backed by the Church, which claimed the Jews were aiding the Hussites. In 1420-1 Albrecht stripped Vienna's poorer Jews of their belongings and dispatched them on a raft down the Danube. Richer members of the community were tortured until they revealed where their wealth was hidden, and then burned alive on the Erdberg. Many others opted for mass suicide to escape torture. The centuries-old ghetto by Am Hof was demolished. The reasons for Albrecht's ethnic cleansing have never been fully explained, for it represented a break in a long tradition of Jewish protection by rulers, and also removed an important source of ducal finance.

In foreign policy, however, Albrecht V showed the usual Habsburg adroitness. He married the daughter of Emperor Sigismund, and on the latter's death inherited the crown of Hungary. In the same year, 1438, he was also elected Holy Roman Emperor. Excluding a brief lapse of three years in the 18th century, the Habsburgs would retain this title (protected by bribing the other electors) right up until its abolition under pressure from Napoleon in 1806.

Only a year later, though, Albrecht died while fighting the Turks in Hungary. His heir, born

Pestsäule (1679 plague monument). *See p12.*

the Emperor's survival, the extinction of the Albertine line and the removal of the Hungarian threat meant that the way was open to a real concentration and expansion of Habsburg power. Friedrich's son, Maximilian, was to take up his inheritance in a context of expanding wealth and power, and at a time when the seeds of humanist learning planted in Vienna in earlier decades were beginning to bear fruit, amid the pan-European cultural blossoming of the Renaissance.

EMPIRE AND COUNTER-REFORMATION

Maximilian was accorded the nickname of 'the Last Knight', an indication that he lived between two worlds, that of medieval chivalry and that of the Renaissance. Possessed of astonishing energy, he performed feats of endurance as a hunter, soldier and athlete. Inspired by the spirit of the Renaissance, he encouraged the new learning at Innsbruck and Vienna, the home of such humanist scholars as Konrad Celtis and Johannes Cuspinianus. The study of pure science, medicine and cartography all began to flourish, although disproportionate attention was dedicated to the history of Austria and the genealogy of the Habsburgs (the 'House of Austria' was traced back to Noah). In 1498 Maximilian made one of his most memorable contributions to Viennese history when he founded the *Hofmusikkapelle*, the forerunner of the Vienna Boys' Choir.

Maximilian brought Habsburg marriage diplomacy to its apogee. Through his first marriage to Maria of Burgundy, one of the richest territories in Europe (including modern Holland, Belgium and Luxembourg) came under Habsburg control. His son, Philip the Fair, married Joanna 'the Mad', the daughter of Ferdinand and Isabella of Spain, thus acquiring Castile, Aragon, southern Italy and all the Spanish possessions in the New World for the dynasty. In 1515 Maximilian stood proxy for the marriage of his two young grandchildren to the male and female heirs of the joint throne of Bohemia and Hungary, then ruled by the Jagellonian dynasty. These realms too would fall to the Habsburgs after the last Jagellonian King, Lajos II, was drowned fleeing the Turks after the disastrous Battle of Mohács, in 1526.

Philip the Fair died before Maximilian, who was thus succeeded by his grandson Karl V, better known in English as Emperor Charles V. On his accession to the imperial throne in 1519 he ruled over an empire 'on which the sun never set' – much too large for one man to direct, and already beset by a stream of problems. The Ottoman advance in South-east Europe seemed unstoppable, and equally

after his father's death, was known as Ladislas Posthumus (1440-57). Ladislas' guardian was Friedrich, of the Leopoldine line, and so the dynasty immediately sank back into its chronic inheritance disputes. Friedrich was crowned Holy Roman Emperor himself in 1452, but his position at home was weak, especially in Vienna. Furious at what they saw as the favouring of other towns by Friedrich, the Viennese merchants forced the release of Ladislas, and declared their loyalty to him. Poor Ladislas died aged only 17 in 1457, whereupon fighting continued between Friedrich and his own brother Albrecht, the latter supported by the Viennese. This culminated in a seven-week siege of the Hofburg in 1462, when Friedrich was holed up in the castle together with his three-year-old son, the future Maximilian I. He was rescued by the intervention of the Hussite Bohemian king, Jiriz Podebrad, but then had to agree to share power with Albrecht. Only when Albrecht died in 1463 did Friedrich regain control of Vienna.

Friedrich III's ultimate triumph – he effectively ruled for 53 years, dying in 1493 – is often attributed to the fact that he outlived all his rivals, including the much younger Hungarian king, Matthias Corvinus, who occupied Vienna from 1485 to 1490. Moreover, ominous, after 1517, for the dynastic upholders of the true, Catholic, church, was the gathering momentum of the Reformation.

Vienna saw nothing of Karl, who ceded his Austrian possessions to his brother Ferdinand in 1521. The latter was immediately faced with the rapid success of Lutheranism, especially in the towns, coupled in the case of Vienna with demands for more self-government. Ferdinand solved this last difficulty by the simple expedient of executing Mayor Siebenbürger and six councillors in Wiener Neustadt in 1522, and subjecting the Viennese to absolutist control. He was less successful against the Lutherans and the more radical Anabaptists, despite the punishments meted out to leading Protestants (men were burned at the stake and their wives drowned in the Danube). The increasingly Protestant nobility began to make religious freedom a condition of military assistance against the advancing Turks. Having overrun Hungary, the Ottomans were by 1529 at the gates of Vienna, a vulnerable city with old-fashioned defences. The morale of the city's religiously divided population had been lowered by Ferdinand's vicious rule and a major fire in 1525. Only the heroism of the city's defender, Count Salm, and the early onset of winter prevented Vienna from falling.

The Turks left behind much devastation, but lessons were learned from the siege. Most important was the need to modernise the city's fortifications, which were rebuilt in 1531-66 using the well-proven Italian model of star-shaped bastions. Vienna became a heavily fortified imperial seat, entirely subordinate to the court, but it was also cosmopolitan, as functionaries and petitioners came from all over Europe on imperial business.

HEARTS AND MINDS

From 1551, when Ferdinand summoned the Jesuits to the city, it also became a testing ground for the Counter-Reformation. Proselytisation was led by scholars and preachers such as Peter Canisius, who compiled the catechisms of the Catholic faith to be used in the struggle for hearts and minds in a Vienna that was still 80 per cent Protestant. This struggle was characterised by dogma and paranoia; the Jewish community, which had gradually re-established itself since 1421, was again a convenient target, suffering prohibitions on property owning and trade, as well as the obligation to wear an identifying yellow ring on clothes. This oppressive atmosphere was relaxed a little under Maximilian II (1564-78), who stuck to the letter of the Peace of Augsburg of 1555, which recognised both the Catholic and Lutheran

faiths in the Empire, provided that subjects followed the faith of their princes. Lutherans flooded out of Vienna each Sunday to hold services in the chapels of nearby Protestant lords, but as the screw of the Counter-Reformation tightened under Rudolf II (1576-1608) and his brother Matthias, many migrated to more sympathetic parts of Europe.

The dominant figure of the Counter-Reformation in Vienna was Cardinal Khlesl, a Vienna-born convert from Lutheranism, who purged the university of Protestantism, and whose great *Klosteroffensive* (monastery offensive) led to the second great wave of Catholic foundations in the city (1603-1638).

Protestantism was by no means dead among the nobility, however, and as late as 1619 a group of them forced their way into the Hofburg and delivered a list of demands to Ferdinand II (1619-37). The following year saw the defeat of the Bohemian Protestants at the Battle of the White Mountain, the first major engagement of the Thirty Years War (1618-48). This war and the triumph of Catholicism in southern Germany and Austria would mean the end for Lutheranism in Vienna, even though a Swedish Protestant army threatened the city as late as 1645. In the course of the war, the Jesuits gained control of the university, in 1622, and in 1629 Ferdinand issued his 'Edict of Restitution',

Ferdinand I by Friedrich von Amerling. *See p16.*

restoring to the Catholic Church 1,555 properties under Protestant control since 1552. In Vienna Protestant laymen were also effectively expropriated by an ingenious Catch-22 – only Catholics could become burghers of the city, and only burghers could own property. This was Habsburg religiosity at its most ruthless, with cynical greed and oppression cloaked by a fig leaf of piety.

BAROQUE VIENNA

The positive side of the Counter-Reformation in Vienna is embodied in the great flourishing of the visual arts, architecture, music, drama and literature in the 17th and 18th centuries. Leopold I (1640-1705), known as 'the first Baroque Emperor', spent lavishly on huge operas and ballets. The gifted could usually expect patronage, whether they came from the Empire or beyond it. Italians long held sway in all the fine arts, music and architecture. Local architects such as Fischer von Erlach and Hildebrandt only came to the fore a generation later – and even they were Italian-trained. The music preferred at court, similarly, was for two centuries Italian-influenced, dominated by a series of Italian composers and librettists from Cesti (1623-69), through Caldara (1670-1736) and Metastasio (1698-1782), to Mozart's great rival Antonio Salieri (1750-1825).

> 'The shrewd diplomacy of Franz's Chancellor, Prince Metternich ensured Austria emerged from the wars with dignity intact and a generous territorial settlement.'

Leopold was not an attractive figure: the Turkish traveller Evliya Celebi describes his 'bottle-shaped head', with a nose 'the size of an aubergine from the Morea', displaying 'nostrils into which three fingers could be stuck'. His character was hardly more appealing, even if his deviousness was sometimes dictated by the need to fight wars on two fronts, against the French and the Turks. Educated by bigots, he married an even more bigoted Spanish wife, Margarita Teresa, who blamed her miscarriages on Jews. In 1669, egged on by Christian Viennese burghers, Leopold ordered a renewed expulsion of the Jews from their settlement on the Unteren Werd. The area was renamed the Leopoldstadt (now Vienna's 2nd District), and Jewish property was given to Christians.

Ironically, this district again became a Jewish quarter in the 19th century.

This move so weakened the imperial and city finances, however, that in 1675 the richer Jews had to be invited back. Troubles multiplied with a major outbreak of plague in 1679, whereupon the Emperor and nobility scurried off to Prague, leaving the Church authorities to organise relief for the stricken people.

THE SAVING OF CHRISTENDOM

After the plague came the Turks, who besieged Vienna for the second and last time in 1683. The city was rescued only at the last minute, after 62 days, by an army led by Jan Sobieski, King of Poland. 'Christendom' was saved. The Emperor, who had prudently retreated to Passau for the duration, returned to his *Residenz* to give public, if grudging, acknowledgement to his saviours, and the court artists got to work on bombastic depictions of 'Leopold, the Victor over the Turks'.

Leopold's reign lasted 47 years, during which the Empire survived a considerable battering. After an interlude under the promising Joseph I (1705-11), who died of smallpox aged 33, Leopold's younger son Karl became Emperor. By this time, the Habsburgs' enemies were in retreat. After a string of victories by Prince Eugene of Savoy, the Peace of Karlowitz of 1699 had restored Hungary, Transylvania and Slavonia to Habsburg rule, and in the War of the Spanish Succession the alliance of Austria, Britain and Holland effectively fought Louis XIV's France to a standstill. Even then, Leopold's duplicitous and cynical treatment of the 'liberated' Magyars managed to provoke a Hungarian war of independence (1704-11) led by Prince Ferenc Rákóczi, whose troops devastated the outskirts of Vienna in 1704.

Afterwards, Prince Eugene advised the erection of a new defensive line, the *Linienwall*, along the route today followed by Vienna's beltway, the Gürtel. Vienna began to assume the profile it has today, with outlying villages (*Vororte*) beyond the Gürtel, suburbs (*Vorstadt*) between the Gürtel and the bastions (replaced by the Ringstrassen in the 19th century), and finally the medieval core of the *Altstadt*.

After the Hungarian threat had receded, the reign of Karl VI (1711-40) saw a building boom in Vienna: existing churches were baroque-ised (all 30 Gothic altars of the Stephansdom were replaced), and new baroque churches were built, notably Hildebrandt's **Peterskirche** and Fischer von Erlachs' **Karlskirche**. The nobility, with new, undisturbed sources of revenue, were determined to compete with the ruling house, and built magnificent winter and summer palaces – at least 15 between 1685 and

Celebrity Strauss

A brief guide to one of the most prolific names in music.

Johann Strauss Senior (1804-49) was well known in his time as a composer and conductor, but is now most famous for two things: having the title of *Hofballmusikdirektor* (director of the imperial dance orchestra), and for fathering Johann Junior. His best-known and, in Vienna, most beloved piece of music is the *Radetzky March*, written in celebration of one of the Habsburgs' most successful military commanders.

Johann Strauss, Sohn (or Junior, 1825-99), is the one you should go for when faced with any tricky Strauss question. He wrote 16 operettas, over 150 waltzes, and more than 300 other dances. Known as 'The Waltz King', he's the one whose picture has been painted on Austrian Airlines jets, the one who has a coffee named after him. His father forbade him to go into music, but with his mother's support Johann Jr did it anyway: and became the world's first modern musical superstar. He made the dance music of Biedermeier Vienna universally popular, and his ten-year European tour (1856-66) produced 'Strauss hysteria', which was repeated on his American tour in 1872. His masterpiece is *Die Fledermaus*, but other important works are the operettas *Zigeunerbaron*, *Wiener Blut* and *Eine Nacht in Venedig*, as well as, of course, *An der schönen blauen Donau*, the Blue Danube Waltz, the unofficial Austrian national anthem.

There were two other Strauss boys: Josef (1827-70) was co-director with his brother Johann Jr of that Strauss touring orchestra, while Eduard (1835-1916) was the youngest Strauss son, which is his only claim to fame.

Richard Strauss (1864-1949) was born in Garmisch, Germany, and although not Austrian, had strong connections with both Vienna and Salzburg. He was one of the founders of the Salzburg Festival (with Hugo von Hofmannsthal and Max Reinhardt) and Vienna Staatsoper director from 1919 to 1924.

His most recognisable tune is the main theme of *Also Sprach Zarathustra*, inescapable since Stanley Kubrick's film *2001*, but aficionados would probably prefer to cite his operas, *Der Rosenkavalier*, *Elektra*, *Salome* or *Ariadne auf Naxos*, or his brilliant Lieder such as *Befreit* or *The Four Last Songs*. One of his favourite hangouts was Café Griensteidl, where he met his friends Hofmannsthal, Gustav and Alma Mahler, and Oscar Kokoschka.

Last but certainly not least is the silver-age operetta composer **Oscar Straus** (1870-1954). His biggest success came in 1907, with the operetta *Ein Walzertraum*, but his music is still very popular in Vienna today. Straus's 1908 operetta *Der Tapfere Soldat* was based on *Arms and the Man* by George Bernard Shaw; the translated version, *The Chocolate Soldier*, later became a hit on Broadway. Forced to emigrate to the USA in the 1930s, Oscar Straus returned to Austria at the end of World War II.

Johann Strauss's *Donauwaltzer*.

Praterstern in 1890, during the **Gründerzeit** (Founders' Period). *See p16.*

1720, the greatest Hildebrandt's **Belvedere**, for Prince Eugene. It was a time of triumphalism, bombast and conspicuous consumption by both the ruling class and the Church, not balanced by job creation for the rest, although Prince Eugene took care to re-employ his war veterans as labourers and gardeners.

The whey-faced Karl VI showed no interest in the plight of the poor. Much of the time that he did not devote to hunting was frittered away on efforts to ensure that one of his daughters could inherit the Habsburg throne, going against all the precedents that allowed only a male heir to succeed. To bolster the position of his eldest daughter, Maria Theresia, he touted a document known as the 'Pragmatic Sanction' round the courts of Europe, where it was politely signed by princes who had not the slightest intention of honouring it.

As soon as Karl died, to general rejoicing in Vienna, the Empire was attacked by Friedrich II of Prussia, who invaded Silesia and launched the War of the Austrian Succession. Encouraged by Friedrich's initial success, Karl Albert of Bavaria then invaded Bohemia, with French support. The situation was only saved by good luck, when Karl Albert died in 1745 and Maria Theresia's husband, Franz Stephan of Lothringen, was elected Holy Roman Emperor in his place. Another major factor, though, was the remarkable steadfastness of Maria Theresia herself, which so impressed the Hungarian nobles when she appeared before

them to seek support in 1741 that they offered their 'life and blood' for their 'King' – since constitutionally she could officially be neither 'Queen' of Hungary nor 'Empress', even though she has often been described as such.

THE AGE OF ABSOLUTISM

Maria Theresia, one of the greatest of the Habsburgs, had one of the most important qualities in a ruler: an ability to choose wise advisers and able administrators. With her support, men like Wenzel von Kaunitz, Friedrich von Haugwitz (a converted Protestant from Saxony), Joseph von Sonnenfels (a converted Jew from Moravia) and Gerard van Swieten (a Dutchman) reformed key elements in the ramshackle machinery of imperial government, including the army. This new approach was labelled 'enlightened absolutism' – although some parts were more enlightened than others: Maria Theresia wouldn't tolerate Jews, unless they converted, and was only with great difficulty persuaded by Sonnenfels that torturing suspects did not contribute to law and order. Motivated perhaps by her Jesuit education, she also introduced a risible 'Chastity Commission' in 1752, which caused Casanova a lot of grief on his visit to Vienna.

Despite such aberrations Maria Theresia was generally held in affection by the Viennese. She abandoned the stiff Spanish protocol of her forebears and lived relatively informally, if incongruously, in the great Schönbrunn Palace built for her, in emulation of Versailles, by Nikolaus Pacassi. Her encouragement of local manufacturing, the creation of a postal service and even the introduction of house numbering (originally to aid recruiting) were all signs of new thinking. After the death of Franz Stephan in 1765, she ruled jointly with her son, Joseph II (1765-90), who was to take enlightened reforms much further when he ruled alone after Maria Theresia died in 1780.

Joseph had travelled widely, and fallen under the influence of the French Enlightenment and even Masonic ideas. His most lasting achievement was his Tolerance Patent of 1781, granting religious freedom to Protestant and Orthodox Christians, which was followed in 1782 by a more limited Patent for the Jews. In the same year Joseph also dissolved nearly one in five of Austria's monasteries, on the grounds they weren't engaged in activities useful to the state. Also important for Vienna was his foundation of the Allgemeinen Krankenhaus, or General Hospital, in 1784, and his opening of the imperial picture gallery and parks, such as the Augarten and Prater, to public view.

The age of absolutism had seen the last flourishing of the baroque style and the transition to a classicism preoccupied with purity of form, although in architecture this did not really emerge until the following century. The change of direction in music was already evident 40 years earlier, in Gluck's ground-breaking 1762 opera *Orfeo*, considered the first opera to subordinate its music to the requirements of the drama, in place of the florid baroque operas of the Italians. Gluck was followed by the great names of the *Wiener Klassik* – Haydn (1732-1809) and Mozart (1756-91), who was based in Vienna for the last ten years of his life, which thus almost exactly coincided with the reign of Joseph II. Just as Mozart and Haydn learned from each other, so Ludwig van Beethoven, who lived in Vienna from 1792 to his death in 1827, was influenced by both of them, and in turn had a huge impact on Franz Schubert (1797-1828). This unbroken line of genius, nurtured by the patronage of Austrian aristocrats, the dynasty and the Church, and encouraged by the musical enthusiasm of the Viennese, has not been equalled by any other European city.

NAPOLEON AND *BIEDERMEIER*
The 19th century began badly for the Habsburg Empire. Joseph's promising successor, Leopold II, died unexpectedly in 1792 after reigning only two years, and was succeeded by his narrow-minded son Franz II (1792-1835). Franz's reactionary views were fuelled by events in France, where his aunt, Marie Antoinette, was executed by revolutionaries the year after he ascended the throne. The rise of Napoleon then subjected him to further humiliations, including the occupation of Vienna twice by French troops (in 1805 and 1809), the enforced marriage of his daughter to the upstart French Emperor and finally the bankruptcy of the state.

The French behaved quite graciously as conquerors (a guard of honour was placed outside Haydn's house as he lay dying, and officers crowded in to hear the première of Beethoven's *Fidelio*), but these setbacks caused the Habsburgs to lose their aura. Conscious of the absurdity of being titular Emperor of territories that had been overrun by Napoleon, Franz gave himself the new title of 'Emperor of Austria' in 1804; in 1806, a herald on the balcony of Vienna's Kirche Am Hof announced that the title of Holy Roman Emperor, founded by Charlemagne in 800, no longer existed.

Napoleon was eventually defeated in 1814, and the Habsburg capital became the venue for the Congress of Vienna, in which the allied powers – Austria, Prussia, Russia, Britain and many others – sought to agree the frontiers of post-Napoleonic Europe. The shrewd diplomacy of Franz's Chancellor, Prince Metternich – as well as the advantage of being hosts – ensured Austria emerged from the wars with dignity intact and a generous territorial settlement.

On the other hand, it now required the repressive apparatus of Metternich's police state to keep the lid on aspirations unleashed in the wake of the French Revolution. Strict censorship meant that even Franz Grillparzer (1791-1872), Austria's greatest dramatist and a Habsburg loyalist to the core, could get into trouble; disrespect for the authorities could only be voiced indirectly, as in the brilliant ad libbing of the comic genius Johann Nestroy (1801-62). Denied any political voice, Viennese burghers were driven into internal exile. They retreated into a world of domesticity, 'in a quiet corner', the characteristic features of the *Biedermeier* culture (so-called after a satirical figure of a solid, middle-class citizen portrayed in a Munich magazine) which predominated from 1814 to 1848.

Painters like Friedrich von Amerling evoked the idealised family life of the bourgeoisie, Ferdinand Raimund conjured an escapist fairy-tale world on the stage, and Adalbert Stifter cultivated a quietist philosophy of resignation in his celebrated novel *Indian Summer*. In architecture, Josef Kornhäusel designed neo-classical buildings with a stripped-down, unobtrusive elegance. In music, the revolutionary fervour of Beethoven's

Fidelio and Ninth Symphony gave way to the melodious romanticism of Schubert's introspective *Lieder*, first performed at intimate soirées known as *Schubertiaden*.

While such a life was possible for the property owning and professional class, the burgeoning working-class population of Vienna was at the mercy of the industrial revolution. Overcrowding, unemployment and disease were rife, aggravated by a decrepitly inadequate infrastructure and water supply. A cholera epidemic in 1831-2 prompted some remedial measures, but not before typhoid fever from infected water had claimed the life of Schubert, in 1828. Meanwhile, the population of Vienna exploded by 40 per cent between the beginning of the century and 1835, to reach 330,000. Many of the new migrants were former peasants, who had been driven off the land and were searching for work.

The desperation of the famine-stricken working class and the frustrations of the politically impotent middle class erupted in the Revolution of March 1848. At first it seemed as if the old order was doomed: almost the whole Empire was in revolt, the hated Metternich had to flee Vienna and the simple-minded Ferdinand I, who had succeeded Franz in 1835, was forced to concede a new constitution and lift censorship. In Vienna, a provisional city council was set up, freeing the burghers from noble control, and a Civil Guard recruited from local citizens was formed, with the grudging consent of the authorities.

As elsewhere in Europe, in this tumultuous year of revolutions, it was the army that put an end to the uprisings. The great Marshal Radetzky won major victories in northern Italy; the Croatian General Jellacic moved against Hungary (helped by the intervention of Russian troops); and Marshal Windischgraetz subdued Vienna. Habsburg authority seemed to have been restored, but not all the achievements of the Revolution could be rescinded: serfdom was abolished throughout the Empire forever, and the mere existence of liberal constitutions, however briefly they had been in force, supplied a new theoretical basis for discussion.

FRANZ JOSEF

Ferdinand had abdicated, and was succeeded by his 18-year-old nephew Franz Josef I (1848-1916). Franz Josef began his reign with summary executions and savage repression of former revolutionaries. Yet, by the end of his 68-year rule, he had presided over a gradual emancipation of his people. By 1900 the seemingly anachronistic Habsburg monarchy was in practice no more oppressive than most western European states. In 1867 he approved

the *Ausgleich* or 'Compromise' with Hungary, granting it equal rights in a new 'Dual Monarchy', to be called Austria-Hungary. Universal adult male suffrage was introduced in 1907, earlier than in Britain. What couldn't be controlled, however, were the forces of nationalism, which eventually tore his multi-ethnic empire apart, plunging Europe into war.

For Vienna, Franz Josef's most significant measure was the demolition of the old city bastions in 1857, and the approval of a plan for the area beyond them to be occupied by a magnificent boulevard, the **Ringstrasse**, on the Parisian model of Baron Haussmann. A symbol of burgeoning civil society, the Ring was to be lined with imposing public buildings, each built in a historicist style symbolic of its place in society. This great project, which took shape over some 26 years, was to be completed with an 'Imperial Forum' linking the last part of the Hofburg to be built (the **Neue Burg**) with the museum quarter. This part of the plan was never carried out, but the Ring, with its new museums, city hall, opera, theatres and stock exchange, still transformed Vienna into a modern metropolis.

> ## 'Freud's novel treatment for 'hysteria' and new-fangled technique of hypnosis were viewed with indifference or suspicion by colleagues in the medical establishment.'

Much of the finance for this reconstruction came from the high bourgeoisie, whose tastes in the arts were conservative. The most generous patronage was given to Hans Makart, who painted overblown historical canvases. Statues of Habsburg rulers and generals peppered the city. The burghers' preference for the now-entrenched musical tradition of the late Wiener Klassik was satisfied by Johannes Brahms, who lived in Vienna from 1878 until his death in 1897. In contrast, Anton Bruckner, strongly influenced by Wagner, was subjected to abuse and even ridicule by the critical establishment in Vienna.

The decades from 1860 to 1900 make up the so-called *Gründerzeit* or 'Founders' Period' (also called the Ringstrassen era), and saw the construction of a modern state, economy and society. The administration of Vienna was dominated from 1861 by the liberal bourgeoisie, with money made in industrial development, land speculation and banking. The Liberal City

The **Secessionists,** including Gustav Klimt (back row, second left). *See p18.*

Council, elected by a property-based electoral roll of only 3.3 per cent of Vienna's 550,000 inhabitants, followed its own interests, but for a while these coincided in many respects with those of most citizens. Huge investment in the infrastructure resulted in an improved water supply, new bridges across the Danube and the much-needed channelling of the river itself. In 1870 Vienna acquired its first trams.

Unbridled capitalism had, of course, its `downside. In the catastrophic year of 1873 the stock market crashed, and many financiers were ruined or committed suicide. The death toll among businesses was equally dramatic, as 60 companies, 48 banks and eight insurance societies went bust. The crisis ensured that Vienna's World Exhibition of that year was a financial disaster, worsened by an outbreak of cholera. For Vienna's Liberals, it was 'never glad confident morning again'; their standing fell, despite the many achievements of the mayor of 1868-78, Cajetan Felder (he spoke nine languages, including Czech and Hungarian). The catastrophe of 1881, when the Ringtheater burned down killing 386 people, was almost the final straw. Felder's successor was held responsible, and had to resign.

FIN DE SIECLE AND END OF EMPIRE

Turn-of-the-century Vienna, as the Habsburg Empire struggled on into its last decades, has become almost a cliché of sensuality, eroticism and an overripe aestheticism. It generated some of the most conflictive movements of the modern era, including both militant anti-semitism and Zionism. It also produced psychoanalysis, and several of the greatest masters of early modernism in all the arts.

A new star rose in city politics in the 1880s, a renegade Liberal called Karl Lueger, who founded his own Christian Social party and built up a power base by exposing corruption (of which there was plenty) and stirring up anti-semitism in a vicious scapegoating of Jews (a theme that has run like a dark thread through Viennese history). Many of the wealthy Liberal magnates were Jewish, and Lueger adroitly focused popular resentment upon them.

His support was boosted by the extension of the franchise to those who paid only five *Gulden* in taxes, in 1885, and the incorporation of the peripheral settlements (Vororte) into the city in 1892. Vienna more than tripled its area and increased its population by over half a million, to 1,364,000. Immigrants poured into the city (especially Czechs, and Jews from the East), another factor in creating a climate beneficial to Lueger's politics. 'Handsome Karl' was a shrewd populist and gifted administrator, who understood how to turn the envy and discontent of Vienna's petit bourgeoisie to his advantage. The young Adolf Hitler, living in Viennese dosshouses in the 1900s, greatly admired him. Franz Josef, though, did not. Lueger's faction

Sigmund Freud, founder of psychoanalysis, who fled Vienna in June 1938. *See p19.*

won a majority on the City Council in 1895, but his election as mayor was vetoed three times by the Emperor, who among other things feared a flight of Jewish capital if he was elected. The Emperor, though, had to give way in 1897, and Lueger remained in office until 1910.

Lueger was strongly supported by the lesser Catholic clergy, although the more senior churchmen denounced his radical and anti-semitic views in 1895. Pope Leo XIII, however, upheld Lueger's claim that he was merely adhering to the social doctrines of the Church, and that his objections to Jews were doctrinal, not racial. Papal support was decisive, and the Viennese hierarchy gradually backed him. Lueger's policies may be influencing the world indirectly even today: just as the Christian Social majority was being established in the city, the Budapest-born Viennese journalist Theodor Herzl published the first Zionist agenda, *Der Judenstaat* (1896), arguing that the persistence of anti-semitism in Central Europe showed that Jews, however assimilated, could not be safe without their own state. This was received with incomprehension and even anger by the highly assimilated Viennese Jewish establishment, but it began the process that led to the foundation of Israel.

In contrast to social tensions, the emollient side of the pleasure-loving Viennese of the 19th century was revealed in the general passion for theatre and music, which made possible the astonishing careers of musicians such as Josef Lanner and the Strauss dynasty (*see p13* **Celebrity Strauss**). The Viennese waltz was a commercialised and refined version of folk dances, chiefly the *Ländler* of Upper Austria. The dance became emblematic of hedonistic escapism. Its critics pointed out that the Viennese were too busy waltzing to heed the news of the catastrophic defeat of the Habsburg army by the Prussians at Königgrätz (Sadowa) in 1866, a defeat that marked the beginning of the end for the Habsburg Empire.

Even more censorious things were said about the craze for operetta, which began with an Offenbach-influenced work by Franz von Suppé (*Das Pensionat*, 1860) and continued into the 20th century (its last major figure, Robert Stolz, died in 1975). But the operetta was the first, and perhaps the only, successful multicultural product of the Austro-Hungarian monarchy.

In the 1890s, Vienna and its peculiar atmosphere generated several new trends. The secession movement displayed a galaxy of talent. One of the most important figures was the architect Otto Wagner, who departed from the ponderous historicism of his youth to create early-modernist buildings of great functional integrity. A trenchant critic of Wagner, Adolf Loos, rejected secessionist ornamentation and carried the idea of functionalism still further. The artist Gustav Klimt broke existing taboos to produce masterpieces of sensual eroticism, combined with a pessimistic emphasis on the inevitability of death, a preoccupation he shared with the next generation of expressionists such as Egon Schiele. Gustav Mahler took over the Imperial Opera and swept away generations of shibboleths he described as *Schlamperei* (sloppiness), to the indignation of the players. The most successful playwright was Arthur Schnitzler, whose bleak depictions of sexual exploitation, societal cynicism and personal trauma won the admiration of Sigmund Freud.

Freud's own *Interpretation of Dreams* appeared in 1900, and caused not a ripple. His novel treatment for 'hysteria' and new-fangled technique of hypnosis were viewed with indifference or suspicion by colleagues in the medical establishment. The author Karl Kraus wrote that 'psychoanalysis is the disease of which it purports to be the cure'. Kraus edited the journal *Die Fackel* (The Torch), which became an effective counterblast to the belligerent mood that overtook the city after the Empire slithered into war in 1914. Many other modernist writers, such as Hermann Bahr (the self-publicising leader of the *Jung Wien* literary circle), became ranting war propagandists.

WAR AND 'RED VIENNA'

World War I killed off the coffeehouse milieu of turn-of-the-century Vienna, in which Bahr and Kraus had flourished. The brilliant *feuilletons* (meandering cultural essays) perused over the coffee cups, the interminable feuds, the narcissism, the head waiters who acted as unpaid secretaries, the unpaid bills – in short the whole bohemian existence seemed anachronistic after Austria and her allies lost the war and the Empire was dismembered in 1918-19. The assassination of the heir apparent, Archduke Franz Ferdinand, lit the fuse that led to war, and old Emperor Franz Joseph finally died in 1916. Franz Joseph's inexperienced great-nephew Karl I (1916-22) took over the throne, but was unable to end the war on honourable terms. This sealed his fate, and he went into exile in March 1919.

Vienna's situation was desperate. Deprived of its empire, it had become a *Wasserkopf*, a diseased 'hydrocephalus', in a state reduced from over 50 million to three million people overnight. One third of the population was in Vienna, including a huge number of bureaucrats, many of whose jobs no longer existed, plus unemployed refugees and ex-soldiers. A 'Republic of German Austria' (*Deutschösterreich*) was proclaimed on 12 November 1918. The name reflected the desire of most Austrians – of all political parties – for an *Anschluss* or union with Germany. This proposal, though, was firmly knocked down by the Allies, who had not fought a war so that Germany could actually increase in size. So the First Austrian Republic began its peculiarly unwanted existence.

In 1919 the Social Democrats swept to power in the Vienna City Council. The party had been founded in 1889 by Viktor Adler, a Jewish doctor with a strong social conscience, and rapidly expanded its support among workers living in horrific conditions. By 1900, the socialists were able to win 43 per cent of the votes in local elections, although the absurdly discriminatory electoral system meant they had only two seats on the City Council. After the war, though, the party's moment had come. Adler died in the flu epidemic of 1918, but he and gifted Marxist theoreticians such as Otto Bauer had laid the foundation for the period known as *Rotes Wien*, 'Red Vienna', which followed. It was the first example in the world of a city administered by socialists.

A major difficulty was that Vienna was still officially part of Lower Austria, which was conservative dominated. This mismatch was resolved in 1922, when Vienna became a *Bundesland* (Federal Province) in its own right. The Social Democrats were able to embark on one of the most intensive programmes of housing, welfare and cultural initiatives ever seen in Europe. The 63,736 apartments built between 1923 and 1934 naturally had to be paid for, as did the new leisure facilities, schools, colleges and child benefits. The Council's director of finance Hugo Breitner found the money by imposing taxes on unearned income (such as rents), luxuries (such as champagne), property and businesses. His critics called him the 'tax vampire', but few would quarrel with the achievements of 'Red Vienna'.

The City Council's socialist measures and its uncompromising *Kulturkampf* (cultural struggle) with the Church was a major factor in the growing polarisation between socialist Austria (principally Vienna) and conservative Catholic Austria (much of the non-urban rest of the country). For most of the 1920s power was held at national level by a Christian Social government led by a priest, Ignaz Seipel. His greatest achievement was rescuing the country from hyper-inflation in 1922, but differences between right and left widened inexorably during his rule. Both sides had their own militias (the conservative *Heimwehr* and socialist *Schutzbund*), and a crisis occurred in 1927 when a conservative jury acquitted Heimwehr soldiers who had shot and killed members of the Schutzbund. An enraged mob burned down the Palace of Justice, ignoring pleas for restraint from socialist leaders. Matters worsened as the world economic crisis deepened post-1929, and unemployment rose.

Tensions climaxed in a brief civil war in 1934, in which the relatively well-armed forces of the right easily overcame the socialist militias. During the fighting, Karl Ehn's huge housing block the Karl-Marx-Hof, a bastion of red support, was shelled into submission. Authoritarian rule was then imposed on Austria, and Vienna's administrative independence ended, by the regime of Engelbert Dollfuss, a peculiar mix of extreme reactionary Catholicism and home-grown fascism.

THE ANSCHLUSS AND WORLD WAR II

In 1933 Hitler came to power in Germany. Very soon he began a drive to increase his influence in the land of his birth, Austria. Shortly after the civil war the Nazis attempted a coup d'état in Vienna, killing Chancellor Dollfuss. Though an extreme right-winger, he had not been ready to follow Hitler's orders. Dollfuss's successor, Kurt Schuschnigg, soon found himself under pressure from Hitler and local Nazis to accept the *Anschluss* of Austria to the German Reich (the 'Greater German' solution most Austrians had wanted at the end of World War I). Schuschnigg tried to rally support by calling a referendum on Austrian independence for 13 March 1938. In order to pre-empt this (which would almost certainly have endorsed independence) German troops crossed the border at dawn on 12 March.

In Vienna the Nazis lost no time in hounding their opponents and stigmatising Jews. Hitler was ecstatically received when he addressed a crowd of 200,000 in the Heldenplatz. The Church hastened to make its accommodation with him – Cardinal-Archbishop Innitzer gave a Nazi salute on his way to meet the *Führer*, and urged the faithful to vote for the *Anschluss* in the subsequent Nazi plebiscite (when he later had second thoughts, Nazi thugs trashed his residence). One of the first events of Nazi rule was the *Reichskristallnacht* on 9 November 1938, when mobs attacked Jews, synagogues and Jewish property. Adolf Eichmann (who, like many of the most virulently anti-semitic Nazis, was Austrian-born) opened an office on Prinz Eugen Strasse, where Jews were 'processed': those with sufficient resources could buy their freedom; the rest were sent to the concentration camps. Some 120,000 Jews emigrated, while 60,000 were either to be executed or to die through forced labour. Leading non-Jewish opponents of the Nazis were also interned in camps. On 1 April 1938 the first batch of prominent Austrian politicians (including Leopold Figl and Franz Olah) left for the camp at Dachau.

More than 30 concentration camps were built in Austria. The most notorious is Mauthausen, on the Danube east of Linz, where 35,318 out of 197,000 prisoners were executed between 1938 and 1945. The main activity at the labour camp was hacking out the stones for the cobbles of Vienna. Mauthausen is now a memorial.

As the catastrophe of World War II unfolded, a kernel of resistance appeared in Vienna, partly spurred by the Allies' Moscow declaration that Austria's status at the end of the war would depend on her willingness to rebel. This was the origin of the notion of Austria as 'Hitler's first victim', rather than an equal participant in Nazism, which became a stylised political discourse during the post-war four-power occupation of Vienna, the period sharply captured in the film *The Third Man*.

Because Vienna lay to the east, quite a lot of war industry was moved to the area. This proved fateful, after 7 March 1944, when the Allies could reach the city with bombers from Italy. In one air raid over 400 people died in the cellars of an apartment behind the Opera. They were never exhumed, and a monument, *Against War and Fascism*, was erected on the site in 1988.

In spring 1945, the Soviet army arrived in Vienna, and the city was taken after fierce fighting. The war's end saw a devastated city: there had been 8,769 deaths from Allied bombing, and 2,226 from fighting on the ground; 1,184 resistance fighters had been executed, 9,687 died in Gestapo prisons; 36,851 apartments had been destroyed and thousands of other buildings damaged. Over 50,000 Viennese Jews had been slaughtered by the Nazi regime, and a quarter of a million Austrians had died in German uniform.

Some of these statistics could support the notion of Austria as 'victim' of the Nazis, but on the other hand this idea – politically convenient for the occupying powers, as they sought to detach Austria from Germany – also meant that in Austria the 'de-nazification' process only stigmatised the most prominent Nazis, allowing huge numbers of passive, opportunistic or enthusiastic participants in Hitler's regime to present themselves as mere patriots. This confusion between image and reality in dealing with the Nazi era (which wasn't allowed to exist in Germany) has returned to haunt post-war politics.

POST-WAR AUSTRIA

In the short term the 'victim' thesis was beneficial, assisting Austrian leaders in their negotiations to end the occupation. This became a real possibility after the death of Stalin, and in 1955 the *Staatsvertrag* (Austrian State Treaty) was signed in the Belvedere. Austria became free and independent, and also neutral, in a manner that was convenient to both the West and the Soviets. Neutrality, vital to Austria's security during the Cold War, is another issue that has become divisive since 1989.

Supported by UN aid and the Marshall Plan, Austrians displayed great resourcefulness in rebuilding their devastated country: especially considering the Soviets had dismantled most of

A motorised unit of the Red Army in front of Parlament in April 1945.

Austria's industry and shipped it eastwards as war reparations. The rebuilding of Vienna's burned-out Stephansdom was complete by 1952, and by 1955 both the Burgtheater and the Staatsoper reopened. With cultural renewal self-irony also returned and cabaret flourished, notably Helmut Qualtinger's brilliant satirical portrait of the typical Viennese petit-bourgeois opportunist 'Herr Karl', who joined the Nazis because they offered free sandwiches and beer. Conspicuous by their absence were the leading lights of the literature, stage and music of pre-war Vienna – most of whom had been Jews.

Vienna voted consistently for Social Democrat mayors, and in 1970 the national government itself became socialist under the charismatic if imprudent Bruno Kreisky, Chancellor until 1983. It was his achievement that Vienna became a third seat of the United Nations, when the UN Development Organisation moved to a custom-built **UNO-City** on the north bank of the Danube. The city had already hosted the Atomic Energy Commission since 1956, and was to add OPEC (1965) and the monitoring commission for the Helsinki Agreements (OSCE) to its portfolio. This much sought-after world profile also made Vienna a target: the OPEC conference was stormed by Arab terrorists in 1975, Palestinian terrorists murdered a City Councillor and launched a grenade attack on the Vienna synagogue in 1981, and in 1985 there was a bloody attack on the El Al desk at Schwechat Airport.

Vienna has enjoyed stable government and constant investment in its infrastructure (notably the steadily expanding U-Bahn), even if there have always been mutterings about corruption. The new-broom Mayor Helmut Zilk, elected in 1984, made both the political and the cultural life of the city more lively, and controversial: the enfant terrible of German theatre, Claus Peymann, took over the Burgtheater in 1986, scandalising audiences with provocative productions of plays by Thomas Bernhard, tackling taboo themes such as Austrian complicity in Nazi rule.

Zilk himself committed the city to a gesture of reconciliation with the Jews, and a new Jewish Museum opened in 1993. Major exhibitions, such as those celebrating *fin de siècle* Viennese culture, have attracted growing numbers of tourists, while Habsburg nostalgia and Kaiser-Kitsch have been marketed with ever-greater ruthlessness. The fall of the Iron Curtain, followed by Austria's entry into the EU in 1995, has brought new challenges, and new conflicts. Fears of a flood of cheap labour and 'foreign takeovers' have been ably and notoriously exploited by the Freedom Party. Vienna thus entered the 21st century with its usual ambivalence, 'moving forwards with its head turned towards the past'.

Key events

AD 8 Vindobona becomes part of the Roman province of Pannonia.
212 The civil settlement at Vindobona is raised to the rank of Municipium.
881 'Wenia' appears in the Salzburg annals.
996 First occurrence of the name Ostarrichi (Austria) in an imperial document.
1298 Albrecht I is the first Habsburg to be elected Holy Roman Emperor.
1338-49 Vienna hit by disasters: locust swarms, plague and fire.
1420-1 The Wiener Geserah: the first notorious pogrom against the Jews.
1529 First Turkish siege of Vienna.
1551 The Jesuits are summoned to Vienna. The Counter-Reformation begins.
1577 Protestant worship forbidden in Vienna.
1658-1705 Rule of the 'first Baroque Emperor', Leopold I.
1669 Second expulsion of Jews from Vienna.
1679 Plague in Vienna.
1683 Second Turkish siege of Vienna.
1704-11 Hungarian War of Independence against Habsburg hegemony.
1740-80 Maria Theresia reforms government, education, law and the army. The age of enlightened absolutism.
1781 Tolerance Patent offers toleration to non-Catholic faiths and later (1782) also to Jews.
1780-91 Mozart in Vienna.
1805-9 Vienna occupied by Napoleonic troops.
1811 The Austrian state is declared bankrupt.
1814-15 Congress of Vienna settles post-war map of Europe.
1848 Revolution all over the Empire.
1848-9 Franz Josef I becomes Emperor. Defeat of the revolution.
1857 Demolition of city bastions. Building of the Ringstrassen boulevard begins.
1860-1900 Founders' Period (Gründerzeit). Liberal political hegemony, industrial expansion.
1861 Liberals take over city hall. Infrastructural investment by Mayor Cajetan Felder (1868-78).
1866 Austrian defeat by the Prussians at Königgrätz (Sadowa).
1870 Vienna Tramway Company set up.
1873 World Exhibition in Vienna. Cholera outbreak. Stock Exchange crash.
1881 Ringtheater burns down.
1888-9 Viktor Adler founds the Social Democratic Party.

1897-1910 Karl Lueger's term as Mayor of Vienna. Communalisation of public services, anti-semitic populist politics.
1889 Crown Prince Rudolf commits suicide.
1898 The Vienna Secession is founded.
1900 Freud's *Interpretation of Dreams* published.
1914 Franz Ferdinand assassinated.
1914-18 World War I.
1916 Death of Franz Josef I.
March 1919 Franz Josef's successor, Karl I, resigns and leaves the country.
May 1919 Social Democrats take power in Vienna City Council. Period of 'Red Vienna'.
12 Nov 1919 Proclamation of the Republic of 'Deutschösterreich'.
1919 Treaty of St Germain fixes the new borders of Austria, shorn of her Empire.
1922 The Christian Social Chancellor, Ignaz Seipel, rescues the country from hyper-inflation by means of foreign credits.
1927 The Palace of Justice is burned down.
1934 'Civil War' between Catholic Conservative government forces and the Social Democrats ends in victory for the Conservatives and the founding of the Fatherland Front. Corporate State set up by clerico-fascist regime.
1934 Attempted Nazi putsch results in assassination of Chancellor Dollfuss.
1938 *Anschluss* with Hitler's Reich. Hitler welcomed in Vienna by jubilant crowds.
9 Nov 1938 *Reichskristallnacht* – Jewish properties burned and looted, Jews beaten up.
1939-45 World War II.
1945-55 Occupation by the Allies. Vienna under four-power control.
1955 Austrian State Treaty liberates the country, which becomes neutral.
1956 The Atomic Energy Commission is set up in Vienna.
1965 OPEC offices located in Vienna.
1970 Social Democrats take power under Bruno Kreisky, who is Chancellor until 1983.
1981 Vienna becomes the third seat of UNO.
1984 Helmut Zilk becomes Mayor of Vienna.
1989 Fall of the Iron Curtain.
1995 Austria joins the European Union.
2000 Formation of controversial ÖVP-FPÖ coalition leading to announcement of EU sanctions against Austria.
2002 Coalition collapses – new elections – victory for ÖVP without overall majority.
2003 Start of a new ÖVP-FPÖ coalition.

Vienna Today

A city with two faces.

Vienna has long had the reputation of a provincial town with a streak of global importance. As late as the 1970s, the social life of the Viennese rotated around a handful of turgid bars and cafés. Apart from the now over-subscribed Café Hawelka, focal point of the post-war art scene, nocturnal life was confined to Jazzland, the only venue to feature international musicians. Despite the city becoming the UN's third seat, cosmopolitanism was conspicuously absent. 'Vienna is an old crone/forgotten/in whose mouth her teeth have rotten,' Arik Brauer, a Jewish songwriter sang in the '70s. At the weekends the Viennese fled to the bucolic silence of the Vienna Woods, or got hammered at Nussdorf or Grinzing's numerous *Heurigen*.

However, since the parting of the Iron Curtain in 1989 and European Union membership in 1995, Vienna appears to have created the semblance of an open society. The Social Democrat-led city council of Red Vienna realised that Austria's capital was no longer on Europe's periphery, but slap in its centre. The city dressed up, its grey façades were given a coat of paint, private cars were banned from the historic centre and the area declared Europe's most extensive pedestrian zone. Austria's most celebrated architect, Hans Hollein, miraculously infiltrated his futuristic Haas Haus right in front of the nose of the city's beloved cathedral – a clear sign that Vienna was refusing to go the way of Salzburg and Innsbruck and descend to the level of a moth-eaten imperial theme park.

Particularly in the late 1980s and early 1990s, when the election of former SA member Kurt Waldheim to the presidency unleashed an international outcry, Red Vienna did its best to welcome back those expelled during the Nazi era. Intellectuals and artists were invited to such bourgeois institutions as the venerable Burgtheater, where German-born director Claus Peymann successfully goaded its tremendously conservative audience by substituting the habitual diet of period classics with works by Austrian dissidents Thomas Bernhard, Peter Turrini and Elfriede Jelinek. Belated tributes to the city's Jewish community, both the annihilated and the survivors, finally arrived in the form of a Jewish Museum and the Judenplatz Holocaust memorial.

The city also invested in the 'man in the street'. Red Vienna's public housing tradition was perpetuated with the construction of thousands more municipal flats that keep Vienna's living and housing costs moderate. On a strip of Danube wetland, the city council converted the 20-kilometre (12.5-mile) Donauinsel into a huge natural leisure area. Home to joggers, skaters and bathers by day, on warm nights its centre see a crowd of young Africans and South Americans dance samba in the shadow of the neighbouring hyper-modern district that shot up beside the Danube in the late 1990s.

The central districts of the city witnessed the opening of many excellent, moderately priced restaurants that are gradually altering Vienna's eating habits. The quaint Spittelberg quarter, whose lively prostitution scene once petrified Hitler, survived property speculation to become the epicentre of the city's bourgeois eco-bohemians. Art galleries and chic bars blossomed here in the 7th district and in the streets bordering the Naschmarkt, Vienna's magnificent open-air food market, which also narrowly survived demolition in the 1960s. Today Vienna's art set goes there to sip macchiato and purchase rocket and lemongrass.

In art and public life, Vienna's investments are so huge that the city may well be reaching saturation point. Karlsplatz houses an array of artistic institutions – from the brand-new Kunsthalle Project Space to the Secession, home of the city's original art dissidents. Just a step away, the vast cultural hypermarket of the Museumsquartier shelters no less than ten different initiatives. Furthermore, the nearby Albertina, the world's largest collection of graphic art, reopened in 2003 after years of renovation and po-mo restyling.

Even the run-down red-light district along the Gürtel ring road is slowly getting a facelift. Separating Vienna's multicultural neighbourhoods from the wealthier inner-city districts, this traffic-clogged boulevard is currently being redesigned by a team of young architects. The arches beneath the overhead U-Bahn line are now home to new restaurants, clubs, shops and cultural centres that contrast with the area's traditional line in shady bars and sex shops.

However, this new openness is in peril. Multi-culturalism hasn't been universally embraced. In 1999, the city's Jewish community and intellectuals were shocked when right wing populist Jörg Haider's 'Freedom' Party (FPÖ) took 27.2 per cent of the vote. Haider's attacks on 'foreigners' and 'African drug dealers' struck a nerve with both the inhabitants of peripheral housing complexes and the good burghers of Grinzing. Regrettably, Vienna is home to a species of aggressively xenophobic cave-dwellers who insult the Turkish cook while munching his cheap kebabs. A 'real' Viennese taxi driver will frequently grumble about the *Tschuschen* (an insulting name for the city's 200,000 former Yugoslavians) and call for a new *Dolferl* (Viennese nickname for Adolf Hitler) to 'put an end to this mess'.

'Crime has been rising steadily since the early 1990s. But compared to other European cities, Vienna remains astonishingly safe.'

Crime has been rising steadily since the early 1990s. Hundreds of foreigners languish in Vienna's huge prison at Landesgerichtsstrasse. Drug dealers are a common sight in the Schwedenplatz and Karlsplatz U-Bahn stations and pickpockets operate along Kärntner Strasse. But compared to other European cities, Vienna remains astonishingly safe. Car crime is minimal and, whatever the time, no district is off-limits. 'It is the city where eastern European mafia-bosses come to wind down,' a police spokesman once remarked.

Xenophobia, however, is only one of Haider's popular campaigning tools. Despite a booming economy, he cleverly exploited the dissatisfaction many Austrians harboured against the interminable SPÖ-ÖVP coalition that ensured 'jobs for the boys' for card-carrying social democrats and conservatives. In Austria, the two parties even run rival motoring associations.

So in 2000 the Austrians got what they wanted. Wolfgang Schüssel, leader of the conservative People's Party, formed a coalition with the Haider Right to the astonishment of Europe's political classes. All 14 European member states froze diplomatic relations in protest at the presence in government of a racist party that had constantly played down the Nazi era (in 1991 Haider remarked that the Third Reich had a decent employment policy and in 1999 compared Churchill's war record to

that of Hitler). Chic, hedonistic Vienna suddenly discovered it had a political conscience and 200,000 demonstrated on Heldenplatz, scene of Hitler's triumphant Anschluss speech. An unauthorised 'Speakers Corner' was set up by artists and intellectuals in front of the Chancellor's office and for three years, hundreds of demonstrators ritually marched through the city every Thursday evening.

Fortunately the fears of the resistance movement were unfounded. With the exception of Jörg Haider insulting the foreign names of state representatives and personally visiting Iraqi dictator Saddam Hussein, the government approached race issues with caution. Some minor reforms did affect the lives of immigrants, some of whom now have to study German before being granted an unlimited residence permit. On the other hand, after nearly 60 years of struggle, compensation for the 'aryanisation' of Jewish property after 1938 finally began to trickle through.

The 'man in the street' soon tired of Haider's antics. Even devoted followers realised that comrades of the *minimo lider* enjoyed scandalous privileges. The odd minister became embroiled in political scandals and was forced to resign, all coinciding with increases in Austria's unemployment rate and tax burden.

At the 2001 Vienna City Council elections, the first big vote since Haider entered power, the FPÖ lost about 50 per cent of its votes. The social democrats of the ruling mayor, Michael Häupl, won an absolute majority and in 2002 the Haider-Schüssel coalition came to an acrimonious end, fuelled by FPÖ opposition to EU enlargement and its insulting attitude to important European political partners, particularly the Czech Republic and Slovenia. By autumn 2002 internal intrigues left Haider's party on the verge of implosion, with the moderate wing of the party refusing to cooperate with right-wing fundamentalists grouped around Haider. Several FPÖ ministers resigned.

The hotly contested 2002 elections saw the FPÖ's share of the vote plummet to 10 per cent prompting Haider's withdrawal to the southern outpost of Carinthia where he had been elected Regional Governor in 1999. FPÖ voters defected en masse to the ÖVP, showing Wolfgang Schüssel to be a brilliant tactician. With 42 per cent of the votes, the ÖVP was the outright winner, provoking the worst Social Democrat result since 1970 and scuppering plans for a German-style Red-Green coalition. The captains of industry breathed a sigh of relief and Schüssel, portrayed in the media as a dragon-slaying St George, thanked 'God'. Only one bastion offers any vocal resistance: Red Vienna.

Literary Vienna

The life stories of Austria's authors don't make for easy reading.

The roots of modern Austrian literature can be traced back to Franz Grillparzer. He was, if you are feeling generous, the Shakespeare of Austria. He was born in 1791 in the Bauernmarkt in old Vienna, when the city was the cultural capital of the German-speaking world; by the time he died in 1872 the Empire was already in decline. His celebrated 'Shakespearean' feel for tragedy was inspired not just by those turbulent times, but by his own family life. His youngest brother and mother both killed themselves, and he had a long-standing and difficult affair with his cousin's wife, before moving on to fall in love with a 15-year-old girl. On a happier note, Grillparzer was a great frequenter of the long-gone Silbernes Kaffeehaus in Plankengasse, a popular meeting point for writers and artists.

Towards the turn of the 20th century literature fed even more hungrily on the atmosphere of intoxication and melancholy that was intrinsic to the final apocalyptic spurt of the Habsburg Empire. Georg Trakl (1887-1914) has the dubious honour of being one of the unhappiest poets of this time. He was a hypersensitive alcoholic outsider, with frequent moods of 'frantic intoxication and criminal melancholy'. His training as a pharmacist offered him optimum access to drugs, and the advantage he took of this was clearly reflected in his work. A tortured sexual relationship with his sister ('the thousand devils whose thorns drive the flesh frantic') didn't help. He died of a cocaine overdose in 1914. His sister shot herself a few years later. Trakl is notoriously difficult to translate, but he was greatly admired by his contemporaries such as the great philosopher Ludwig Wittgenstein (1889-1951), who supported him for a time and hailed him a genius.

Another colourful Viennese character was the precocious Hugo von Hofmannsthal (1874-1929), or Loris, as he was known, who was already feted in Viennese intellectual circles at the age of 16. He gave up poetry following a premature mid-life crisis, and ended up writing libretti for Richard Strauss. Hofmannsthal died suddenly of a heart attack just before the funeral of his son, who had committed suicide. Another, later writer who had an even more

miserable life was the novelist Joseph Roth (1894-1939). Rediscovered in the last few years, he was born on the eastern edge of the Habsburg Empire, in modern Poland, but his work is closely associated with Vienna. Roth's father disappeared before he was born and died in a lunatic asylum, World War I curtailed his education, his wife went mad, and he himself survived on menial jobs and journalism before he died exiled, alcoholic and destitute in Paris. During the 1920s and 1930s he somehow managed to write the finest chronicles of the dying days of the Empire, *Radetsky March* and *The Imperial Crypt*, as well as the now famous *The Legend of the Holy Drinker.*

Alongside alcoholism, the literary '-isms' of the turn of the century were impressionism, symbolism and naturalism. Hermann Bahr (1863-1934) decided he was an expressionist, and became the leading spirit of the *Jungwien* literary circle, which included the likes of Schnitzler and Hofmannsthal and convened at Café Griensteidl on Michaelerplatz. Nearby, the Café Central on Herrengasse was the favoured haunt of poet Peter Altenberg (1859-1919, and now represented by a dummy).

HEDONISM & HYPOCRISY

The increasing psychologisation of writing in these years is most clearly illustrated by Arthur Schnitzler (1862-1931). He became a friend of Freud, though Freud had first avoided meeting him 'from a kind of reluctance to meet my double'. Schnitzler's 1926 *Dream Story*, filmed as *Eyes Wide Shut* by Kubrick, depends heavily on dream psychology, explores the subconscious, and for its time was, like Freud, a great taboo breaker. Despite its date it is set firmly in *fin de siècle* Vienna, and conveys a strange atmosphere of hedonism, bourgeois hypocrisy and sexual and psychological frustration. Schnitzler's other internationally renowned work is the 1900 play *Riegen*, best known in English by its French title *La Ronde*, especially through Max Ophuls' classic 1950 film (it was also the source of the 1990s adaptation *The Blue Room*). Characteristically pessimistic, it portrays a circle of sexual encounters through every class of end-century Vienna. Schnitzler, a Jew who unlike many at that time denied his Jewishness, also documented the anti-semitic climate of Vienna in the period before World War II in his novel *The Road to the Open*.

The use of aphorisms was another distinguishing feature of Austrian writing in the first years of the 20th century. This was the trademark of the Bohemian-born Jewish satirist Karl Kraus (1874-1936), author of the phrase 'If I must choose the lesser of two evils, I will choose neither', which became a motto for a whole generation of Viennese. He was the founder, editor and writer of *Die Fackel* (The Torch), the leading satirical magazine of its day.

Fellow-countryman Robert Musil (1880-1942) said of Kraus that 'there are two things which one can't fight because they are too long, too fat and have neither head nor foot: Karl Kraus and psychoanalysis'. Professional jealousy aside, Musil was a celebrated essayist, and wrote a beautiful if unusual short story *The Temptation of Silent Veronica*, about a psychotic woman who appears to have been buggered by a dog, and, more famously, his huge, unfinished three-volume novel *The Man Without Qualities*. Written after World War I, it dealt entirely with the last years of the Empire before 1914. Like many writers, he left Austria after the *Anschluss*, and died penniless and anonymous abroad.

Another casualty of the curse of Vienna was Ödön von Horváth (1901-38), a friend of Joseph Roth who fled to Paris to escape the Nazis and shortly afterwards was killed by a falling branch on the Champs-Elysées during a freak storm. Meanwhile, the 'almost over-gifted' Jewish writer Stefan Zweig (1881-1942) fled from the Nazis to South America, to kill himself with his wife in Brazil in 1942. Utterly cultured, a speaker and translator of several languages, he was a respected figure in literary circles throughout Europe, and for a time in the 1920s his hugely popular biographies and historical books made him the world's most widely-translated author. Reading Zweig's autobiography *The World of Yesterday*, it is easy to see how, as the social and political climate changed, the disillusionment that led to his suicide set in.

POST-1945

After World War II, circumstances were completely different. Austrian literature only came to life again post-1945 when it 'leapt over its own cultural shadow'. This was not easy. Novelist Heimito von Doderer (1896-1966), who had been a Nazi prior to 1938, wanted, according to one critic 'to be popular and profound and succeeded in neither'. As the full horror of the Nazi death camps emerged, poets such as the Romanian Jewish (but, again, German-speaking)

The cantankerous **Thomas Bernhard**.

Paul Celan (1920-70) – who lived for a while in Vienna – questioned whether it was possible to make the unspeakable speak. His world-famous *Death Fugue* gave the answer, as did a prose text *A Call to Mistrust*, by one of the first Austrian women writers to achieve any prominence, Ilse Aichinger. It was another woman, Ingeborg Bachmann, whose poems and short prose texts also hit hardest at the nerves of the post-war period. She set fire to herself in her bed in Rome in 1973.

Another important post-war writer is HC Artmann. Intelligent, successful, but daring to be cheerful (only relatively, of course), he was a keen member of the progressive avant-garde *Wiener Gruppe* (Vienna Group), which emerged in the 1950s inspired by Dadaism, futurism, and long sessions in the Café Hawelka.

The most talked-about and successful modern Austrian writer is Thomas Bernhard (1931-89). His mood can be summed up by the dour décor of his favourite coffeehouse, Café Bräunerhof. A compulsive melancholic, naturally a fan of Trakl, and obsessed by Wittgenstein, Bernhard can be very funny, if you have a Samuel Beckett-ish sense of humour. In his most readable book, *Wittgenstein's Nephew*, he writes about his time spent with the philosopher's clinically insane nephew. He had a love-hate relationship with his country. Bernhard's predecessors were scornful of their countrymen, and yet still wanted their applause; he went one step further, and in his will banned all productions of his plays in his homeland.

▶ *For a selection of Austrian- and Vienna-related books available in English, see p224.*

Accommodation

Accommodation

There's plenty to choose from – but book well in advance.

What's your preference? A palace where the prince still retains quarters, a simple friendly family-run pension or a laid-back hostel? All these and the full range in between are available here, depending in part on how much luxury you want and what you want to spend. Vienna is not exactly cheap, but if you pick and choose and follow the usual tips for European cities (such as the areas around the railway stations), you won't have to take out a loan to cover the cost of a decent room. You'll find hotels scattered throughout Vienna, even well into the suburbs. The larger international chains arrived late in Vienna, led by the InterContinental in the mid 1960s. This means that many hotels are small by today's standards; but it also means that hotels tend to be individually run and offer more personal service. You can check out the spectrum by visiting www.vienna.info.at or www.wien-tourismus.at.

One hurdle in Vienna, however, is the abundance of congresses and conventions that take over chunks of hotel space in the mid-price category. Last-minute rooms are always available but not necessarily at the price or in the area you'd prefer. The centre of the city fills up first, starting with the 1st district and going on to the 2nd to the 9th districts, which also has decent accommodation and where prices tend to be lower. After that you may have to sacrifice convenience, so it pays to book in advance.

Vienna's hotels are classified according to a star rating reflecting amenities and services. The five categories are also a guide to room rates. Our listings follow the following categories: **The sky's the limit** (over €320 for a double); **Expensive** (€180-€350); **Moderate** (€130-€220); **Budget** (€70-€135); **Very cheap** (under €75); **Seasonal hotels**; **Hostels**; **Camping** and **Long-term accommodation**. A single room or single occupancy will usually cost 65-70 per cent more than double-room rate although some newer hotels charge the full double rate. Hotel rates are not always solidly fixed; much depends on season and what's going on in town, and it pays to ask about special offers. If you arrive without accommodation, there are helpful offices at the Westbahnhof (west) and Südbahnhof (south) railway stations and at Schwechat airport. In town, the tourist office on Albertinaplatz, behind the Staatsoper, will make bookings for a small fee.

Some of the traditional hotels have been around for many years, if not centuries, so air-conditioning is a luxury limited mainly to the most upmarket, and Vienna can become quite hot and humid. The older, smaller hotels have often been tucked into buildings which were converted from residences or offices. Many of the older hotels have difficulty dealing with the needs of the handicapped. We have listed those with special rooms for the disabled. You can also check with the tourist office for specific information on accessibility and services. Unless otherwise noted, all rooms have en suite bathrooms and breakfast is included. A car is more a complication than a convenience. Street parking is limited to overnight (8pm-8am) and to a maximum of two hours with a normal parking ticket during the day in all nine of the inner districts. Relatively few hotels have garages or street parking.

1st District

The sky's the limit

Bristol
1, Kärntner Ring 1 (515 160/fax 16 550/ www.westin.com/bristol). U1, U2, U4 Karlsplatz/ tram 1, 2, D, J. **Rates** €385-€490 single; €385-€590 double; €880-€4,200 suites. **Credit** AmEx, DC, MC, V. **Map** p243 E8.
The Bristol easily ranks among the world's top hotels, and not just for location. Set on the Ringstrasse across Kärntner Strasse from the Staatsoper, this hotel offers nearly every service and amenity a guest could demand; the concierge is out-standing. The 140 rooms are furnished to reflect Viennese heritage, but state-of-the-art technology and elegant modern bathrooms also feature. The Bristol bar is a traditional and intimate meeting place going back to well before the 1945-55 era when the Bristol was the US military headquarters. The Korso restaurant behind the lobby is well thought of, while the more informal Sirk-Eck restaurant and café is a midday favourite.
Hotel services *Air-conditioning. Babysitting. Bar. Business services. Concierge. Conference facilities. Currency exchange. Disabled: 2 adapted rooms. Fax. Fitness centre; use of John Harris Club (see p191) free to guests. Laundry. Limousine service. Multilingual staff. No-smoking rooms. Parking (€22-€28 per day). Restaurant.* **Room services** *Hairdryer. Minibar. Dataport. Room service (24hrs). Safe. Telephone. Turndown. TV: satellite/VCR (on request).*

The **Imperial** exemplifies the traditonal luxury hotel in Vienna.

Hilton Vienna Plaza

*1, Schottenring 11 (313 900/fax 313 9 022 009/
www.hilton.com). U2 Schottentor/Universität/
tram 1, 2, D.* **Rates** €324 single; €364 double;
€530-€2,600 suite. **Credit** AmEx, DC, MC, V.
Map p242 D5.

On the positive side, nearly anything you might
want in a luxury hotel you'll find in the Hilton Plaza.
Abundant use of cherrywood in contrast to light
pastel colours adds an elegant touch. Amenities are
complete, service is outgoing, staff friendly and helpful. But you'd be hard pressed to differentiate
between this and similar accommodation in any
other major city. Even the original art is, well, foreign. The vaguely '30s-style furniture in the lobby
sets the style for the least Viennese of Vienna's top
hotels; the 218 rooms and suites are mainly upmarket standard, with marble baths. The sister Hilton
on Stadtpark is due to reopen in 2004 after total renovation; in the 2nd, the Danube Hilton (Handelskai
269, 727 770), a cleverly converted storage warehouse, offers huge Scandinavian-style rooms and a
riverside location.
Hotel services *Air-conditioning. Babysitting.
Bar. Business centre. Café. Concierge. Conference
facilities. Currency exchange. Disabled: adapted
rooms. Executive lounge. Fax. Fitness centre.
Laundry. Multilingual staff. No-smoking floors.
Parking (€3/hr). Sauna. Solarium. Restaurants.*
Room services *Hairdryer. Minibar. Dataport.
Radio. Room service (24hrs). Safe. Telephone.
TV: cable.*

Imperial

*1, Kärntner Ring 16 (501 100/fax 501 10 410/
www.luxurycollection.com/imperial). U1, U2, U4
Karlsplatz/tram 1, 2, D, J.* **Rates** €446-€656 single;
€535-€756 double; €925-€4,583 suite. **Credit** AmEx,
DC, MC, V. **Map** p243 E8.

More luxurious today than when it was built as a
town palace in 1869, the Imperial is the first address
for state visitors or anyone else seeking the ultimate
in discretion, service and accommodation. Expect the
staff to address you by name. Most of the 138 rooms
are high-ceilinged, spacious and meticulously
appointed with antiques and comfortable furnishings;
bathrooms are elegant, many as big as bedrooms in
other establishments. The bar, done up in red velvet,
is cosy if sometimes noisy; the restaurant is erratic in
quality, but the café is a justifiably popular favourite
for lunch, afternoon tea or a post-concert snack.
Hotel services *Air-conditioning. Babysitting.
Bar. Beauty salon. Business services. Butler service.
Conference facilities. Concierge. Currency exchange.
Disabled: adapted room. Fitness centre. Interpreting
services. Laundry. Limousine service. Multilingual
staff. No-smoking floor. Restaurant. Sauna. Valet
parking.* **Room services** *CD player. Dataport.
Hairdryer. Minibar. Room service (24hrs). Safe.
Telephone. TV: cable/satellite/VCR.*

Sacher

*1, Philharmonikerstrasse 4 (514 560/fax 514 56 810/
www.sacher.com). U1, U2, U4 Karlsplatz.* **Rates**
€215-€365 single; €312-€420 double; €455-€3,550
suite. **Credit** AmEx, DC, MC, V. **Map** p242 E8.

Hilton Vienna Plaza. *See p29.*

Countless films have been made here, books written about the Sacher and its legends, and the venerable 108-room hotel continues to uphold both tradition and reputation. Emperor Franz Josef dined here almost daily, on *Tafelspitz* (boiled beef). The location immediately behind the Staatsoper is superb and so is the service; the Hotel Sacher concierge can work miracles with tickets to sold-out events. Guest rooms are opulent down to the last detail, with attractive furnishings and modern baths, while retaining authentic Viennese flavour. The art on corridor walls rivals many museums. The elegant and relaxed lounge bars are popular meeting places, and the new Sacher-Eck informal coffee house looks promising.
Hotel services *Air-conditioning. Babysitting. Bar. Business services. Concierge. Conference facilities. Currency exchange. Disabled: adapted rooms. Fitness centre; use of John Harris Club (see p191) free to guests. Interpreting services. Laundry. Limousine service. Multilingual staff. No-smoking rooms. Valet Parking (€29/24hrs). Restaurant.* **Room services** *Hairdryer. Internet access. Minibar. Dataport. Room service (24hrs). Safe. Telephone. TV: cable. VCR/DVD (suites only).*

Expensive

Astoria

1, Kärntner Strasse 32-4 (515 770/fax 515 7782/ www.austria-trend.at/asw) bus 3a. **Rates** €141 single; €199-€235 double; €260 suite. **Credit** AmEx, DC, MC, V. **Map** p242 E8.

The Astoria is one of the grand old hotels dating from the 19th century, which accounts for the large high-ceilinged rooms along with the slightly musty atmosphere and original art deco accents. Renovations have brought facilities and classic period decor up to date in the 118 rooms. The trade-off for a superb central location and views over the busy pedestrian Kärntner Strasse is street noise, less evident on the upper floors or those looking on to the side streets. Front desk management is helpful.
Hotel services *Babysitting. Bar. Breakfast buffet. Conference facilities. Currency exchange. Internet point (foyer). Laundry. Limousine service. No-smoking rooms. Parking garage (€22/day). Restaurant.* **Room services** *Hairdryer. Minibar. Dataport. Radio. Room service (6am-midnight). Telephone. TV: cable.*

Europa

1, Neuer Markt 3/Kärntner Strasse 18 (515 940/ fax 515 94 620/www.austria-trend.at/euw). U1, U3 Stephansplatz. **Rates** €141 single; €199-€235 double. **Credit** AmEx, DC, MC, V. **Map** p243 E7.

Top-to-bottom renovations have swept this superbly central hotel into the 21st century with stunningly modern room decor and furnishings. The dramatic colours and styles are quite the opposite of traditional Vienna. Closets cleverly set as room dividers give rooms a suite-like atmosphere. Baths are slick and complete. Of the 116 moderately sized rooms, those on the Neuer Markt side lack the view and buzz from overlooking the busy, pedestrian-zone Kärntner Strasse. Corner rooms are more spacious and have angled windows that give a partial panorama outlook, and rooms on the eighth floor have small outside terraces. The staff are occasionally overstretched but will look after your needs fairly well. The Europa café is highly popular.
Hotel services *Air-conditioning. Babysitting. Bar. Business services. Conference facilities. Currency exchange. Interpreting services. Laundry. No-smoking floor. Multilingual staff. Restaurant. Valet parking.* **Room services** *Dataport. Hairdryer. Minibar. Room service (7am-10pm). Safe. Telephone. TV: cable/satellite.*

Marriott Vienna

1, Parkring 12a (515 180/fax 515 18 6736/ www.marriott.com). U4 Stadtpark, U3 Stubentor. **Rates** €179-€270 single; €179-€270 double; €279-€490 suite. **Credit** AmEx, DC, MC, V. **Map** p243 F7.

The glasshouse impression you get from the outside of the Marriott Vienna carries over into the open atrium lobby, café and bar, complete with greenery and waterfall. There are few intimate corners. The atmosphere is quietly busy and businesslike and definitely American, but that does translate to efficient yet friendly service. The 313 rooms are spacious and attractively furnished in modern, if somewhat standard style. Rooms on the front offer a restful view over the Stadtpark; upper rooms at the back look toward Stephansdom and the centre of the city with the Vienna woods in the distance. Rooms facing the inner courtyard are quiet, if viewless.

Hotel services *Air-conditioning. Babysitting. Bar. Business services. Concierge. Conference facilities. Currency exchange. Fitness centre. Interpreting services. Laundry. Limousine Service. Multilingual staff. No-smoking rooms. Parking: garage (€30/24hrs). Restaurant. Sauna. Solarium. Swimming pool (indoor).* Room services *Dataport. Hairdryer. Minibar. Room service (24hrs). Telephone. TV: cable/satellite. Safe.*

Radisson SAS Palais

1, Parkring 16 (515 170/fax 512 2216/www.radisson sas.com). U4 Stadtpark/tram 1, 2. Rates €260-€350 single; €260-€380 double; €350-€380 suite. Credit AmEx, DC, MC, V. Map p243 F7.
Take two elegant turn-of-the-century townhouses and a clever architect and the result can be as enticing as the 247-room Radisson SAS Palais. The former inner courtyards have been glassed over to become an atrium lobby and open café area with touches of greenery. Rooms and baths have been cleverly incorporated into the structures. Decor is a successful combination of Scandinavian modern and Viennese traditional, retaining a comfortable old-world feeling. Views are best out over the park from the upper front rooms. Service is generally good but the front desk occasionally does get harried.
Hotel services *Air-conditioning. Babysitting. Bar. Business services. Concierge. Conference facilities. Currency exchange. Disabled: adapted rooms. Fitness centre. Internet point. Laundry. Limousine service. Multilingual staff. No-smoking floors. Parking. Restaurant. Sauna. Solarium.* Room services *Dataport. Hairdryer. Minibar. Room service (6am-midnight). Safe. Telephone. TV: cable/satellite.*

Moderate

Am Opernring

1, Opernring 11 (587 55180/fax 587 551829/ www.opernring.at). U1, U2, U4 Karlsplatz. Rates €140-€170 single; €155-€185 double; €215-€280 suite. Credit AmEx, DC, MC, V. Map p242 E7.
Front rooms at the Am Opernring, a Best Western affiliate, look diagonally through the trees across the busy Ringstrasse to the classic view of the Staatsoper. The hotel shares its building with offices, but the 45 spacious rooms and baths are imaginatively integrated on separate floors. Furnishings and decor have been redone to lend a fresh, light look. Rooms on the inner courtyard are quieter but have an uninspired view of the back of another block. New apartments with kitchenette have been added for longer-term stays. The family management is helpful.
Hotel services *Babysitting. Concierge. Currency exchange. Laundry. Multilingual staff. No-smoking floor. Parking (€22/day).* Room services *Hairdryer. Internet access. Minibar. Room service (7am-6pm). Safe. Telephone. TV: cable/satellite.*

Am Schubertring

1, Schubertring 11 (717 020/fax 713 9966/ www.schubertring.at). U4 Stadtpark/tram 1, 2. Rates €99-€135 single; €128-€156 double; €218 suite. Credit AmEx, DC, MC, V. Map p243 F7.

The upper floors of two late-19th-century office buildings have been attractively converted into a friendly, central hotel. Linking the structures has created confusing hallways but directional signs are adequate. The 39 rooms have varying views, upward, outward and inward. The period-furnished rooms are appealingly decorated in light colours with touches of dark wood and fabric. Bathrooms are compact but modern. Service is good and there's an intimate bar.
Hotel services *Air-conditioning. Babysitting. Bar. Concierge. Conference room (max 8 people). Currency exchange. Laundry. Parking: garage (€13/24hrs).* Room services *Dataport. Hairdryer. Kitchenette (some rooms). Minibar. Room service. Safe. Telephone. TV: cable/satellite.*

Amadeus

1, Wildpretmarkt 5 (533 87380/fax 533 873 838/ www.hotel-amadeus.at). U1, U3 Stephansplatz/bus 1a, 3a. Rates €80-€120 single; €142-€160 double. Credit DC, MC. V. Map p243 E6.
This newish intimate hotel is wonderfully central for shopping and the smaller museums. Rooms are period-furnished mainly in white with dark red, while bathrooms are pristine white. The smallest singles are indeed compact, the doubles smallish but comfortable. Weekend packages are offered with double rooms at single rate. Staff are friendly and helpful.
Hotel services *Air-conditioning. Currency exchange. Fax. Laundry. Safe.* Room services *Minibar. Dataport. Room service (7am-10pm). Telephone. TV: cable/satellite.*

Kaiserin Elisabeth

1, Weihburggasse 3 (515 26-0/fax 515 267/ www.kaiserinelisabeth.at). U1, U3 Stephansplatz. Rates €75-€115 single; double €200-€220 double. Credit AmEx, DC, MC, V. Map p243 E7.
The venerable Kaiserin (Empress Elisabeth was Emperor Franz Josef's wife) has a lobby, all red velvet and crystal, that exudes a slightly decadent imperial atmosphere. The location is superb, on the edge of a pedestrian zone just off Stephansplatz. Many of the 63 rooms have with parquet floors and oriental carpets, with 1950s touches; the newest rooms are stunning and retain a Viennese feel. Bathrooms are attractively tiled in light colours. The front desk is a decided plus, with very helpful staff.
Hotel services *Air-conditioning (in 2 floors). Babysitting. Bar. Concierge. Conference room. Currency exchange. Laundry. Multilingual staff. No-smoking rooms. Parking: garage (€28/day).* Room services *Dataport. Hairdryer. Minibar. Room service (7am-10pm). Telephone. TV: cable/satellite.*

König von Ungarn

1, Schulerstrasse 10 (515 840/fax 515 848/ www.kvu.at). U1, U3 Stephansplatz. Rates €133 single; €188 double; apartment from €175-€296. Credit AmEx, DC, MC, V. Map p243 F7.
The 'King of Hungary', in the shadow of the cathedral, is tucked into a charming 16th-century house (Mozart lived next door). Conversion into a hotel

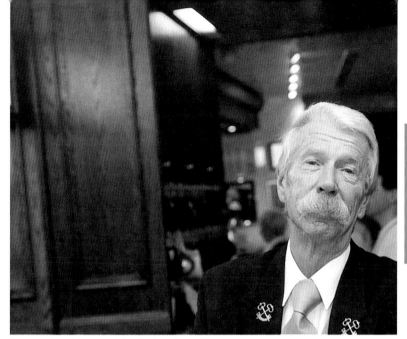

All present and correct at the **Sacher**. *See p29.*

turned the central courtyard into a captivating informal atrium lobby and lounge, complete with tree. Access to the 33 medium-sized rooms on the upper floors is via galleried hallways. Each room is individually decorated, with an emphasis on antique and country furnishings, stripped wood and colourful fabrics.
Hotel services *Air-conditioning. Babysitting. Bar. Concierge. Conference facilities. Currency exchange. Laundry. Multilingual staff. Parking (€15-22/day). Restaurant.* **Room services** *Dataport. Hairdryer. Minibar. Room service (6pm-11pm). Safe. Telephone. TV: satellite.*

Mailberger Hof

1, Annagasse 7 (512 0641-0/fax 512 064 110/ www.mailbergerhof.at). U1, U2, U4 Karlsplatz/U1, U3 Stephansplatz. **Rates** €125-€140 single; €195-€205 double; €230 junior suite. **Credit** AmEx, DC, MC, V. **Map** p243 E7.

Tucked away in a baroque palace on a pedestrian side street from the busy Kärntner Strasse, the Mailberger Hof is a favourite with opera stars and other regulars who welcome its discreet, quiet location. The lobby lounge is restful for informal relaxation and there's a business corner with desk and modem connection. The 40 rooms are splendidly decorated in co-ordinated homely style, some tending toward Laura Ashley without being overdone, some in elegant period decor. For longer stays, small apartments with kitchenettes are available. A 10% senior discount is offered. The family management is accommodating and helpful and the hotel's own ticket office is a highly useful service.

Hotel services *Babysitting. Business services. Conference facilities. Currency exchange. Garden. Laundry. Multilingual staff. No-smoking rooms. Restaurant.* **Room services** *Dataport. Hairdryer. Minibar. Room service (11am-9pm). Safe. Telephone. TV: cable/satellite.*

Mercure Wien Zentrum

1, Fleischmarkt 1a (534 60-0/fax 534 60-232/ www.mercure.com). U1, U4 Schwedenplatz, U3 Stephansplatz/tram 1, 2, N. **Rates** €125-€150 single; €145-€170 double; €190-€225 apartment suite; €23 breakfast. **Credit** AmEx, DC, MC, V. **Map** p243 F6.

Central indeed is this Mercure, one of six in Vienna. You're only steps away from the assortment of restaurants and bars known locally as the 'Bermuda Triangle'. The 154 rooms tend toward the chain's standard look: neat and attractive, with furniture in light natural wood. A 49-room annexe is geared to the needs of business travellers. Nearby, across the canal, is the slightly newer Mercure Wien City with 123 rooms (Hollandstrasse 3, 213 13-0). Rates and amenities at both facilities are much the same.

Hotel services *Air-conditioning. Babysitting. Bar. Business services. Conference facilities. Currency exchange. Disabled: adapted room. Laundry. No-smoking floors. Parking: garage (€21.50/day). Restaurant.* **Room services** *Dataport. Hairdryer. Minibar. Telephone. TV: cable.*

Rathauspark

1, Rathausstrasse 17 (404 12-0/fax 404 12-761/ www.austria-trend.at/rhu). U2 Rathaus. **Rates** €128-€140 single; €178-€210 double; €290-€310 junior suite. **Credit** AmEx, DC, MC, V. **Map** p242 D6.

DOROTHEUM

SEIT 1707

An upmarket residence, once the home of author Stefan Zweig, has been painstakingly restored and converted into this attractive 117-room hotel close to city hall and the university. Elegant touches are still evident in the plaster-ornamented ceilings of rooms on the lower floors. Rooms are welcoming and decorated in light colours. The American-style full breakfast buffet is highly recommended.
Hotel services *Babysitting. Bar. Business Services. Concierge. Conference facilities. Laundry. Fax. Internet access. Multilingual staff. No-smoking floor. Parking (€18/day).* **Room services** *Dataport. Hairdryer. Minibar. Telephone. TV: cable.*

Römischer Kaiser

1, Annagasse 16 (512 7751-0/fax 512 7751-13/ www.hotelroemischerkaiser.at). U1, U2, U4 Karlsplatz/bus 3a. **Rates** €129-€159 single; €159-€199 double; €198-€238 junior suite. **Credit** AmEx, DC, MC, V. **Map** p243 E7.
Now a family-managed Best Western Premier affiliate, the 'Roman Emperor' is set in a former private town palace centrally located on a quiet sidestreet off Kärntner Strasse. The 24 rooms are on the smallish side as are the bathrooms, but the light-coloured decor is pleasant (although the new Versace-designed baths are a bit overdone). Staff are courteous.
Hotel services *Air-conditioning. Babysitting. Concierge. Conference room. Currency exchange. Laundry. Fax. Multilingual staff. No-smoking rooms. Parking (€17/day).* **Room services** *Dataport. Hairdryer. Fax. Minibar. Room service (7am-9pm). Safe. Telephone. TV: cable/satellite.*

Starlight Suiten

1, Salzgries 12 (535 9222/fax 535 9222 11/ all locations: www.starlighthotels.com) U2, U4 Schottenring/tram 1, 2/bus 3a. **Map** p243 E6.
1, Renngasse 13 (533 9989/fax 533 9989 11). U2 Schottentor/tram 1, 2, D. **Map** p242 E6.
3, Am Heumarkt (710 7808/fax 710 7808 11). U4 Stadtpark. **Map** p243 F7.
Rates *all locations* €135 single; €165 double.
Credit AmEx, DC, MC, V.
These three hotels, with 45-50 suites each, offer a welcome variation to the Vienna scene. All are new and suites are similar in concept, with living room, bedroom and tiled bathroom, a working area and minibar. The furnishings and decor are decidedly modern, with natural woods and bright colours. The locations, totally renovated former apartment buildings, are relatively quiet, yet convenient for transport and the city centre. Staff are outgoing, and helpful with services such as theatre tickets.
Hotel services *Air-conditioning. Babysitting. Bar. Currency exchange. Fax. Laundry. Multilingual staff. No-smoking rooms. Parking (€15/day).* **Room services** *Dataport. Hairdryer. Iron (on request). Minibar. Microwave. Telephone. TV: cable/satellite.*

Wandl

1, Petersplatz 9 (534 550/fax 534 55 77/www.hotel-wandl.com). U1, U3 Stephansplatz. **Rates** €82-€105 single; €135-€170 double; €180 suite. **Credit** AmEx, DC, MC, V. **Map** p242 E6.

If location is everything, the Wandl has it, centrally situated just off the pedestrian Graben, the heart of the city's most elegant shopping district. This has been a family-owned hotel for over 150 years. Renovations have led to baths for most but not all rooms, and have added bright, wide corridors. Decor in most rooms is on the simple side, but comfortable; for a treat take one of the old-style rooms. Staff are accommodating; ask for special rates for a longer stay.
Hotel services *Bar. Concierge. Currency exchange. Fax. Laundry. Multilingual staff. Parking (€20/day).* **Room services** *Dataport. Room service. Safe. Telephone. TV: satellite.*

Budget

Austria

1, Wolfengasse 3/Fleischmarkt 20 (515 230/fax 515 23-506). U1, U4 Schwedenplatz/tram 1, 2, 21, N/ bus 2a. **Rates** €74-€95 single; €106-€136 double.
Credit AmEx, MC, V. **Map** p243 F6.
This older hotel is located on a blissfully quiet cul-de-sac, convenient for the city centre and transport. Period furnishings, decor and new baths have brought most of the 46 rooms up to a modern standard, but the hotel still has a few rooms without baths which would fit in our 'budget' price range. Despite such touches as oriental carpets and crystal chandeliers, the general atmosphere is one of informal relaxed comfort. Staff are particularly friendly and will help with theatre and concert tickets.
Hotel services *Babysitting. Currency exchange. Internet access. Laundry. Multilingual staff. No-smoking rooms. Parking (€19/day).* **Room services** *Hairdryer. Iron (on request). Minibar. Dataport. Room service (24hrs). Telephone. TV: cable/satellite.*

Pension Christina

1, Hafnersteiggasse 7 (533 2961 0/fax 533 2961 49/ www.pertschy.com). U1, U4 Schwedenplatz/tram 1, 2, 21, N/bus 2a. **Rates** €60-€70 single; €95-€120 double. **Credit** AmEx, DC, MC, V. **Map** p243 F6.
The 33 rooms are somewhat on the small side but attractively decorated and comfortably furnished. Amenities are few, but the main draw here is a quiet yet central location on a tiny sidestreet just steps away from Schwedenplatz. The Christina is part of the local Pertschy group, so if the pension here is full, there may be rooms either at the slightly more expensive Pension Pertschy (*see p36*) or slightly cheaper Pension Baronesse (Lange Gasse 6, 1405 1061-0) near the university.
Hotel services *Currency exchange. Day permit (€3.60) street parking; €16/day garage. Fax. Multilingual staff. No-smoking room.* **Room services** *Kitchenette (1 room). Minibar. Safe. Telephone. TV: cable.*

Hotel Orient

1, Tiefer Graben 30 (533 7307/fax 535 0340/ www.hotelorient.at). U2, U4 Schottenring. **Rates** *maximum 3hrs* €52 double; €65-€77 suite. *Night* €105 double; €160 suite. **Credit** AmEx, DC, MC, V. **Map** p242 E6.

Suites are sold by the hour and the night (Saturdays and Sundays only) for furtive philanderers and clubbers who want to keep the party going in this 'love hotel' with its authentic overtones of early art deco. Choose from the Kaisersuite, the new Rosa Rosa Rosa room with whirlpool, the Red Room, Mona Lisa or the Taste of Africa room. Former guests have included Orson Welles and Kenneth Anger. The Orient also has a branch, Domizil, a family-oriented 40-room pension behind Stephansdom (Schulerstrasse 14, 513 3199-0, www.hotelpensiondomizil.at).
Hotel services *Bar (hotel guests only).* **Room services** *room service (24hr).*

Kärntnerhof

1, Grashofgasse 4 (512 1923/fax 512 19 23-39/ www.karntnerhof.com). U1, U4 Schwedenplatz/tram 1, 2, 21, N/bus 2a. **Rates** €72-€92 single; €95-€143 double. **Credit** AmEx, DC, MC, V. **Map** p243 F6.
A small cul-de-sac only three blocks from Schwedenplatz hides this hotel discovery from general notice. But the guests who know it return regularly for the 43 attractive modernised rooms and exceptional personal service; no tour groups here. The location is wonderfully quiet, despite the fact that Kärntnerhof is also central to public transport, restaurants, shopping and nightlife.
Hotel services *Bar. Concierge. Currency exchange. Disabled: adapted rooms. Fax. Garden. Internet access. Iron. Parking (€16/day). Laundry. Multilingual staff.* **Room services** *room service 24hrs. Hairdryer. Telephone. TV: cable.*

Pension Nossek

1, Graben 17 (533 7041-0/fax 535 3646/www.pension-nossek.at). U1, U3 Stephansplatz. **Rates** €46-€88 single; €105-€130 double. **No credit cards.** **Map** p243 E7.
The family-owned and managed Pension Nossek on the three middle upper floors of a late-19th-century apartment/office block has been a favourite for generations, both for its friendly service and its superb location in the heart of the city amid the top shops. The pedestrian area ensures relative quiet. The 28 rooms range from fairly spacious to compact, and oriental carpets and crystal chandeliers grace the period-style furnishings. Many guests book their stay up to a year in advance.
Hotel services *Fax. Laundry. Multilingual staff. Parking (€10/day). TV lounge.* **Room services** *Hairdryer. Minibar. Room service (7am-10pm). Telephone. TV: cable/satellite.*

Pension Pertschy

1, Habsburgergasse 5 (534 49-0/fax 534 49-49/ www.pertschy.com). U1, U3 Stephansplatz. **Rates** €67-€77 single; €97-€162 double. **Credit** AmEx, DC, MC, V. **Map** p242 E7.
You might easily overlook this town palace just off the Graben in the heart of the city. But the once-elegant stairway (which you hardly notice when you take the lift to the first floor reception) gives a clue to the history of this friendly pension. The inner rooms look on to a quiet central courtyard. Most of

the 50 rooms are spacious, done up in comfortable period furniture, including some antiques; a couple still have their original tiled heating stoves as showpieces and some have kitchenettes. Baths, of course, were later additions, not luxurious, but generally satisfactory. New rooms on the top floor front are elegant with parquet floors, crystal chandeliers and decor in rose and cream. Staff are unusually helpful. The Pertschy group includes the slightly cheaper Pension Christina (*see p35*).
Hotel services *Fax. Internet access. No-smoking rooms. Parking: garage (€16/day).* **Room services** *Hairdryer. Minibar. Telephone. TV: satellite.*
Branch: **Pension Baronesse** 8, Lange Gasse 61 (405 1061).

Post

1, Fleischmarkt 24 (515 83-0/fax 515 83-808/ www.hotel-post-wien.at). U1, U4 Schwedenplatz/tram 1, 2, 21, N/bus 2a. **Rates** €72 single; €111 double. **Credit** AmEx, DC, MC, TC, V. **Map** p243 F6.
Location is the main attraction here, steps from public transport at Schwedenplatz and convenient for shopping and nightlife. The 107 rooms are a bit on the dated side with standard furniture and occasional oriental rugs on the parquet floors. The few rooms without baths are real bargains. Staff are accommodating if sometimes overstretched.
Hotel services *Café-restaurant. Fax. Parking (€16/day).* **Room services** *Dataport. Hairdryer. Iron. Laundry. Room service (6.30am-10pm). Telephone. TV: cable/satellite.*

Pension Suzanne

1, Walfischgasse 4 (513 2507/fax 513 2500/ www.pension-suzanne.at). U1, U2, U4 Karlsplatz/ tram 1, 2, D, J/bus 3a. **Rates** €72 single; €90-€111 double. **Credit** AmEx, DC, MC, V. **Map** p243 E7.
Most of the 25 rooms in this 1950s building were originally small apartments, meaning that many rooms are complete with mini-kitchenettes; a few even have small outside terraces. Rooms are comfortable with compact bathrooms. Rooms on the courtyard or those in the back building are the quietest, although all have soundproof double-glazing. The central location within moments of shopping and the opera could not be better. The family-managed Suzanne has a host of regulars, so book early.
Hotel services *Concierge. Cooking facilities. Currency exchange. Fax. Internet point.* **Room services** *Hairdryer. Telephone. TV: cable.*

Zur Wiener Staatsoper

1, Krugerstrasse 11 (513 1274-0/fax 513 1274-15/ www.zurwienerstaatsoper.at). U1, U2, U4 Karlsplatz/ tram 1, 2, D, J/bus 3a. **Rates** €76-€100 single; €109-€135 double. **Credit** AmEx, MC, V, DC. **Map** p243 E7.
The colossi supporting the bay above the entry door give the outward impression of more elegance than this older hotel offers. The trade-off inside is smallish yet comfortable rooms with undistinguished decor. But rates are remarkable for a location just off Kärntner Strasse and literally within a baton's

throw of the Staatsoper. Don't expect much in the way of facilities, but the staff are willing and do their best. The sister Hotel Schweizerhof has 55 rooms at still lower prices.

Hotel services *Currency exchange. Drinks at reception (24hr). Fax. Multilingual staff. Parking (€16/day).* **Room services** *Hairdryer. Safe. Telephone. TV: satellite.*
Branch: Hotel Schweizerhof 1, Bauernmarkt 22 (533 1931).

3rd District

The sky's the limit

Im Palais Schwarzenberg
3, Schwarzenbergplatz 9 (798 4515/fax 798 4714/ www.palais-schwarzenberg.com). U1, U2, U4 Karlsplatz/tram D. **Rates** *€255-€330 single; €330-€400 double; €350-€925 suites.* **Credit** AmEx, DC, MC, V. **Map** p242 E8.
For the sheer elegance of a county estate with city convenience the Schwarzenberg is a unique experience. You truly are a guest in regal quarters. Ignore the drab car park in front and revel in the relaxed elegance of the hotel. At the back are formal gardens, great for jogging or strolling. The 44 rooms and suites easily sustain the standards of the palace, built in 1720 and still owned by the Schwarzenberg family (see p78) whose art and antique furnishings contribute to the authenticity and style. For the ultimate in luxury, take one of the duplex suites overlooking the gardens. Six newly converted rooms in the wing at the back (to which you'll be taken by golf cart) are stunningly Italian contemporary, light and appealing. For a special treat, arrange dinner in the glass-enclosed restaurant or outdoor terrace, both looking out at the garden.
Hotel services *Air-conditioning. Babysitting. Bar. Business services. Concierge. Conference facilities. Currency exchange. Fax. Fitness: use of John Harris Club (see p191) free for guests. Garden. Interpreting services. Laundry. Limousine service. Parking (free). Multilingual staff. Restaurant.* **Room services** *CD player. Dataport. Disabled: adapted rooms. Hairdryer. Minibar. Room service (24hrs). Safe. Telephone. TV: cable/satellite/VCR.*

Expensive

InterContinental Wien
3, Johannesgasse 28 (711 220/fax 713 4489/ www.vienna.intercontinental.com). U4 Stadtpark. **Rates** *€210-€290 single; €240-€320 double; €380-€2,620 suite.* **Credit** AmEx, DC, MC, TC, V. **Map** p243 F7.
The 453-room InterContinental was Vienna's first chain hotel when it went up in the mid 1960s. It has worn well, from the velvet and crystal lobby to the more modern, but still comfortably individual style of the rooms. For service and accommodation, the hotel remains one of InterContinental's flagships.

The best Hotels

For stylish luxury
The elegant atmosphere is understated and relaxed, but guests at the **Im Palais Schwarzenberg** (*see p37*) immediately sense that they are indeed sharing accommodation with nobility.

For echoes of old Vienna
The incomparable **Sacher** (*see p29*) reflects a lavish bygone era without misplaced nostalgia and at no sacrifice to modern comforts.

For affordable charm
It's easy to picture a more elegant era at the **Kaiserin Elisabeth** (*see p32*).

For intimacy and style
The **König von Ungarn** (*see p32*) radiates a sense of relaxed comfort far removed from the usual hotel atmosphere.

For location, location, location at low prices
An address more central than that of **Pension Suzanne** (*see p36*) is hard to find, and especially difficult at prices such as these.

For backpackers
Hop across the street from the Westbahnhof rail station into the **Fürstenhof** (*see p41*); backpackers are welcome, staff accommodating and the price is fair.

For sheer craziness
Wombat's City Hostel (*see p43*) is about as wonderfully off-the-wall as the utterly non-Viennese name would suggest.

The city centre is about a ten-minute walk away. Rooms at the back overlook the city, those on the front, the Stadtpark. Both the relaxed lobby café and adjacent bar are open and hardly private. The restaurants lean toward Mediterranean cuisine of a satisfactory, if undistinguished standard (although the range of breakfasts is impressive). Staff are excellent and accommodating.
Hotel services *Air-conditioning. Babysitting. Bar. Barber. Business services. Concierge. Conference facilities. Currency exchange. Fitness centre. Garage (€17/24hrs). Hairdresser. Health & beauty centre. Interpreting services. Laundry. Multilingual staff. No-smoking floors. Restaurant. Sauna. Solarium.* **Room services** *Dataport. Hairdryer. Iron. Minibar. Room service (24hrs). Safe. Telephone. TV: cable/satellite.*

One of the new breed – **Das Triest**. *See p39*.

Moderate

Dorint Biedermeier

*3, Landstrasse Hauptstrasse 28 (716 71-0/fax 716
71-503/www.dorint.com/wien). U3, U4 Landstrasse,
then bus 74a/tram O.* **Rates** €150-€180 single;
€180-€300 double. **Credit** AmEx, DC, MC, V.
Map p243 G7.

This jewel of a hotel resulted from the skilful conversion of 19th-century residential buildings into
modern accommodation. Here you'll have an instant
sense of old Vienna; the 203 rooms are done up in a
period style and decor that emphasises comfort
with simplicity. The only problem for individual
travellers is the tour groups which are also drawn
by the authentic Viennese charm. The location is
about 20 minutes' walk from the centre, although
transport is convenient and frequent. The picturesque narrow alley that divides the hotel is home
to boutiques and galleries.

Hotel services *Air-conditioning. Babysitting.
Bar. Beauty salon. Business Services. Concierge.
Conference facilities. Conservatory. Currency
exchange. Disabled: adapted rooms. Laundry.
Multilingual staff. No-smoking rooms. Parking
(€15/day). Restaurant.* **Room services** *Hairdryer.
Minibar. Safe. Telephone. TV: satellite/pay-TV.*

Very cheap

Etap Hotel Wien St Marx

*3, Franzosengraben 15 (798 4555/www.etap
hotel.com). U6 Erdberg, then bus 78a, 79a.*
Rates €39 single; €46 double; €4.90 breakfast.
Credit AmEx, MC, V. **Map** p241 K10.

The new Etap offers about the cheapest overnight
stay going (children under 12 stay free). The 271
rooms are identically decorated in blue and white.
Beyond that, furnishings and services are spartan.
The hotel is on the airport side of the city in a former dreary factory neighbourhood now slowly
being rehabilitated; access by car is fairly easy. The
underground direct to city centre is a ten-minute
walk or short bus ride away. Shops, restaurants, cinema, bars and clubs are at the nearby Gasometer
complex (*see p76*), about a seven-minute walk.

Hotel services *Air-conditioned. Disabled: adapted
rooms. Internet access. Multilingual staff. No-
smoking rooms. Parking: garage (€6.60/day).*
Room services *TV: satellite.*

4th District

Expensive

Das Triest

*4, Wiedner Hauptstrasse 12 (589 180/fax 589 1818/
www.dastriest.at). U1, U3, U4 Karlsplatz/tram 62,
65.* **Rates** €190 single; €245 double; €299-€502
suite. **Credit** AmEx, DC, MC, V. **Map** p242 E8.

Once a stagecoach station on the route south to
Trieste, Das Triest was totally rebuilt in 1995 as a

luxury hotel in slick modern Italian style. The concept developed by designer Sir Terence Conran
reflects and retains touches of the building's origin.
Attractively smart rooms and stylish bathrooms
have been cleverly fitted into available spaces, individually different while preserving views toward the
city centre and the quiet inner courtyard. In keeping
with the theme, the restaurant favours northern
Italian cuisine, moving outdoors into the courtyard
in summer. The 'American' Silver bar is ranked
among the best for selection and ambience.

Hotel services *Air-conditioning. Babysitting.
Bar. Business services. Conference facilities.
Currency exchange. Fitness centre. Laundry.
Limousine service. Multilingual staff. No-smoking
floors. Parking garage (€21/day). Restaurant.
Roof-garden (garden suites). Sauna. Solarium.*
Room services *Dataport. Hairdryer. Minibar.
Room service (24hr). Safe. Telephone. TV:
cable/satellite/VCR.*

Budget

Carlton Opera

*4, Schikanedergasse 4 (587 5302/fax 581 2511/
www.carlton.at). U1, U2, U4 Karlsplatz/U4
Kettenbrückengasse/tram 62, 65.* **Rates** €59-€90
single; €75-€130 double. **Credit** AmEx, DC, MC, V.
Map p239 D8.

The façade reveals the 1904 origins of this hotel;
fortunately, many of the art deco touches inside are
preserved as well. The 52 rooms are mostly high-
ceilinged, many with parquet flooring. Furnishings
are comfortable if undistinguished, the white tiled
bathrooms likewise. Single rooms are compact but
adequate. The location, about a 15-minute walk from
the city centre, puts you close to the Naschmarkt
with its bustle of spice shops, greengrocers, food
stalls and restaurants.

Hotel services *Air-conditioning. Currency
exchange. Concierge. Cooking facilities. Fax.
Internet access. Iron. Laundry. Multilingual staff.
No-smoking rooms. Parking (€12/day).* **Room
services** *Coffeemaker. Hairdryer. Kitchenette.
Minibar. Room service (8am-6pm). Safe. Telephone.
TV: cable/satellite.*

6th District

Moderate

Das Tyrol

*6, Mariahilfer Strasse 15 (587 5415/fax 587
54159/www.hotel-tyrol-vienna.com). U2
Museumsquartier/bus 2a.* **Rates** €110-€180 single;
€140-€230 double. **Credit** AmEx, DC, MC, V.
Map p242 D8.

This cosy 30-room hotel has been totally renovated
from top to bottom with a refreshingly appealing
result. Rooms have been cleverly fitted into unusual
spaces but with no sacrifices to comfort or convenience. Decor is modern, with inviting colours and

original art; the bathrooms are gleaming white affairs. The museum quarter is across the street, the most popular city shopping district at the doorstep and city centre only a short bus or underground ride away. Staff are charming.

Hotel services *Air-conditioning. Babysitting. Bar. Business services. Concierge. Internet access. Laundry. Multilingual staff. No-smoking rooms. Parking: garage (€15/day). Sauna. Solarium.* **Room services** *Dataport. Hairdryer. Minibar. Room service (noon-11pm) Safe. Telephone. TV: cable/satellite.*

Mercure Wien Europaplatz

6, Matrosengasse 6-8 (599 010/fax 597 6900/ www.mercure.com). U3, U6 Westbahnhof (exit Millergasse)/tram 6, 18. **Rates** €108-€118 single; €138 double; €178-€200 studio; €13 breakfast. **Credit** AmEx, DC, MC, V. **Map** p238 B9.

It's just a few minutes' walk from the Westbahnhof station or the underground (take the Millergasse exit) to this newish Mercure at the head of the Mariahilfer Strasse main shopping district. Transport to the museums and city centre is fast and frequent. Decor in the 210 rooms is colourful with natural wood much in evidence. The tiled baths are bright and complete. This is the French chain's flagship hotel in Vienna, so service is particularly attentive.

Hotel services *Babysitting. Bar. Business services. Café. Conference facilities. Currency exchange. Disabled: adapted rooms. Internet access. Laundry. Multilingual staff. No-smoking floors. Parking: garage (€13/day). Restaurant.* **Room services** *Hairdryer. Minibar. Room service (6.30am-10.30pm). Safe. Telephone. TV: cable/satellite.*

Budget

Ibis Wien Mariahilf

6, Mariahilfer Gürtel 22-4 (599 98-0/fax 597 9090/ www.accorhotels.at). U3, U6 Westbahnhof/U6 Gumpendorferstrasse/tram 6, 18. **Rates** €64-€69 single; €79-€84 double. **Credit** AmEx, DC, MC, V. **Map** p238 B8.

Rooms at the newish Ibis are among the best value in town. You're about eight minutes on foot from the Westbahnhof (use the Millergasse exit from the underground or hop tram 6 or 18 one stop), even closer to Vienna's main Mariahilfer Strasse shopping thoroughfare. The 341 rooms are bright and contemporary, if furnished on the simpler side. Rooms on the upper floors of the Wallgasse side have magnificent views over the city. You will have to fight tour groups at breakfast and check-out, so plan accordingly.

Hotel services *Air-conditioning. Bar. Conference facilities. Currency exchange. Disabled: adapted rooms. Internet access. Iron. Laundry. Multilingual staff. No-smoking rooms. Parking: garage (€10.50/day). Restaurant.* **Room services** *Dataport. Telephone. TV: cable/satellite.*

Moderate

K+K Hotel Maria Theresia

7, Kirchberggasse 6 (521 23/fax 521 2370/ www.kkhotels.com). U2, U3 Volkstheater/tram 49/bus 2a. **Rates** €155 single; €205 double; €240-€400 suite. **Credit** AmEx, DC, MC, V. **Map** p242 D7.

The location of this newish K+K hotel is ideal for the museums and shopping and has convenient transport to the city centre, about 20 minutes' walk away. Nearby is the quaint Spittelberg district with narrow streets and 18th-century houses now home to restaurants, artists and galleries. The

The lobby at **Das Tyrol**. *See p39.*

hotel is spacious and informal, its 123 rooms standard in decor and furnishings. You may find tour groups here. Staff are friendly and helpful. The sister K+K Palais Hotel offers 66 rooms in a former town house on a quiet square. Rates for both hotels are the same.

Hotel services *Air-conditioning. Babysitting. Bar. Conference facilities. Currency exchange. Fitness centre. Interpreting services. Laundry. Multilingual staff. No-smoking rooms. Parking (€14/day). Restaurant. Sauna.* **Room services** *Dataport. Hairdryer. Minibar. Room service (6.30am-10pm). Safe. Telephone. TV: cable.*

Branch: **K+K Palais Hotel** 1, Rudolfsplatz 11 (533 1353).

Pension Altstadt Vienna

7, Kirchengasse 41 (522 6666/fax 523 4901/ www.altstadt.at). U2, U3 Volkstheater/bus 48a. **Rates** €99-€139 single; €129-€149 double; €149-€249 suite. **Credit** AmEx, DC, MC, V. **Map** p238 C7.

A one-time residential building close to the main museums has been lovingly converted into a highly personal, intimate pension. Each of the 36 rooms and suites is individually decorated, mostly in a period style, some with a few antiques; there's a fireplace in the main lounge. Upper rooms and suites look out over the city centre. Management is unusually helpful and customer satisfaction is pretty much guaranteed.

Hotel services *Airport service (€30). Babysitting. Bar. Bike storage room. Currency exchange. Parking: street (day permit €7). Garage (€18/day). Laundry. Limousine service. No-smoking rooms.* **Room services** *Dataport. Hairdryer. Minibar. Safe. Telephone. TV: cable/satellite.*

Budget

Fürstenhof

7, Neubaugürtel 4 (523 3267-0/fax 523 3267-26/ www.hotel-fuerstenhof.com). U3, U6 Westbahnhof (exit Westbahnhof)/tram 6, 18. **Rates** €44-€92 single; €108 double. **Credit** AmEx, DC, MC, V. **Map** p238 B8.

Walk diagonally left out of the Westbahnhof, across the thick traffic on the Gürtel (or take the pedestrian tunnel to Innere Mariahilfer Strasse) to get to this family managed hotel. The historic façade identifies the building as about a century old. Most of the 58 rooms are large with comfortable, if undistinguished furnishings and decor. Windows are now soundproofed, but rooms at the side have less traffic noise than those on the front. If you can cope with toilet and shower down the hall, the few rooms without baths (but with sinks) are two-thirds the price of the others. Staff are friendly and supportive if occasionally harried.

Hotel services *Currency exchange. Fax. Iron. Parking (€10.50/day). Laundry. Multilingual staff.* **Room services** *Dataport. Internet access. Minibar. Room service (24hrs). Telephone. TV: cable.*

Very cheap

Kugel

7, Siebensterngasse 43 (523 3355/fax 523 3355-5/ www.hotelkugel.at). U2 Volkstheater, then tram 49. **Rates** €33-€56 single; €45-€86 double. **No credit cards. Map** p238 C8.

The Kugel is in a shopping area (that has ample restaurants) and is only a couple of tram stops away from the main museums. The 37 attractively decorated rooms with their modern fourposter beds are a real bargain; a few rooms without bath or some just with shower but no toilet are cheaper still. Booths in the breakfast room are reminiscent of a modest country restaurant and offerings are ample, or you can start your day instead at one of the nearby coffee houses. Family management is outgoing and helpful.

Hotel services *Bike storage room. Parking: garage (€9). Fax.* **Room services** *Hairdryer. Minibar (in some rooms). Telephone (some with dataport). TV: satellite.*

8th District

Budget

Hotel Zipser

8, Lange Gasse 49 (404 54-0/fax 404 54-13/ www.zipser.at). U2 Rathaus/tram 5, 33. **Rates** €63-€69 single; €74-€124 double. **Credit** AmEx, DC, MC, V. **Map** p242 C6.

This one-time apartment block near city hall and the university dates to 1904 but the 47 fair-sized rooms are fresh and inviting, in contemporary restful colours and furnishings. Some rooms on the back have splendid tree-shaded balconies. The staff are unusually friendly and accommodating, in part accounting for the long list of returning guests. The district is interesting for its small shops and many restaurants.

Hotel services *Bar. Business services. Currency exchange. Fax. Internet access. Laundry. Parking (€13.50/day).* **Room services** *Hairdryer. Safe. Telephone. TV: cable.*

Very cheap

Pension Lehrerhaus

8, Lange Gasse 20 (403 2358-100/fax 403 2358-69/ www.lhv.at). U2 Lerchenfelder Strasse/tram J. **Rates** €27-€44 single; €49-€73 double. **Credit** DC, MC, V. **Map** p242 C7.

A modest 40-room hotel, with high-ceilinged rooms of various sizes; toilet and bath facilities vary accordingly, but rooms are welcoming and immaculate. Decor is mainly in lighter colours with light wood furniture. Rates vary depending on facilities; rooms without bath or toilet are real bargains. Breakfast is not included; pay for what you want from coin machines in the breakfast room.

Hotel services *Fax. TV lounge.* **Room services** *Hairdryer. Iron. Telephone. TV (some rooms): cable/satellite.*

Pension Wild

8, Lange Gasse 1 (406 5174/fax 402 2168/
www.pension.wild.com). U2 Lerchenfelder
Strasse/tram 46. **Rates** €37-€65 single;
€45-€89 double. **Credit** AmEx, DC, MC, V.
Map p242 C7.
Combine a relaxed family-managed environment
(one that's gay-friendly) with a convenient location
and it's not surprising that this pension is usually
fully booked. The 22 rooms are attractively modern
with colour co-ordinated fabrics and light wood furniture. Most rooms are recently redecorated. Buffet
breakfast is offered in a cheerful front room and
small kitchenettes on each floor are handy for snack-
ing or light meals.
Hotel services *Fax. Internet access.* **Room**
service. *Hairdryer. Minibar (some rooms). Room*
service (6am-10pm). Telephone (some rooms). TV:
cable (some rooms).

Seasonal hotels

During the summer vacations, student
residences are turned into reasonable if modest
hotels. All have single or double rooms, with
bath or shower. Furnishings are what you'd
expect in a better-class dorm, adequate but
nothing fancy. There's central booking via
the Academia (401 76-55 or 401 76-77, fax
401 76-20, www.academia-hotels.co.at) for
three hotels grouped in Pfeilgasse; and
Albertina group (512 7493, fax 512 1968,
www.albertina-hotels.at) with three locations,
two of which are quite central.

2nd District

Accordia

2, Grosse Schiffgasse 12 (212 1668/fax 212
1668-697). U2, U4 Schottenring/tram 1, 2/bus 5a.
Rates €45 single; €70 double. **Credit** AmEx, DC,
MC, V. **Map** p243 F5.
Newest of the seasonal hotels and belonging to the
Albertina group, this 122-room three-star hotel is
across the Danube canal, but only a short walk to
the city centre.
Hotel services *Bar. Bike storage room. Garden.*
Room services *Telephone. TV: cable.*

4th District

Haus Technik

4, Schäffergasse 2 (587 6569-0/fax 586 8505). U1
Taubstummengasse/tram 62, 65/bus 59a. **Rates**
€45 single; €70 double. **Credit** AmEx, DC, MC, V.
Map p239 D9.
Newly refurbished and reopened in 2003, this three-
star 99-room Albertina facility is within fairly easy
walking distance to the opera, city centre and trans-
port to other sights.
Hotel services *Bike storage room. TV lounge.*
Room services *Telephone. TV: cable.*

7th District

Atlas

7, Lerchenfelder Strasse 1-3 (521 78-0, 401 7655/
fax 401 7620). U2 Lerchenfelder Strasse. **Rates**
€58 single; €80 double. **Credit** AmEx, DC, MC, V.
Map p242 C7.
Location makes the difference at this 182-room
three-star Academia group facility; museums are
nearby and the underground is literally at the door.
Hotel services *Bar. Bike storage room. Garden*
café. Restaurant. **Room services** *Dataport.*
Telephone.

8th District

Academia

8, Pfeilgasse 3a (401 76-0/fax 401 76-20). U2
Lerchenfelder Strasse, then tram 46. **Rates** €46
single; €62 double. **Credit** AmEx, DC, MC, V.
Map p238 C7.
With 300 rooms, this is one of the larger and better
of the seasonal hotels and headquarters of the
Academia group. Double rooms are the same size as
singles with a second bed added, and adequate if not
overly spacious. The adjacent Avis (Pfeilgasse 4)
offers 72 somewhat larger rooms at the same rates
and shares a coffee bar and breakfast room facilities
with the Academia.
Hotel services *Bar. Concierge.* **Room services**
Dataport. Iron. Telephone.

19th District

Aramis

19, Döblinger Hauptstrasse 55 (369 8673/fax 369
2420). U2 Schottentor/tram 1, 2, D, then tram 37.
Rates €45 single; €70 double. **Credit** AmEx, DC,
MC, V. **Map** p234 C1.
Set back from the street in a quiet park-like area, this
58-room Albertina group hotel offers three-star facilities. The neighbourhood is upmarket, residential
and surprisingly convenient (about 15 minutes by
tram) for the city centre.
Hotel services *Bar. Bike storage room. Garden.*
TV room. **Room services** *Telephone. TV: cable.*

Hostels

The city's *Camping* leaflet will give you the
addresses and critical details of the youth hostels
and other similar ultra cheap accommodation.
Schlossherberge am Wilhelminenberg is the
most elegant of the hostels, but it's a long bus
ride from the city centre to reach this 41-room,
164-bed hilltop castle.

Jugendherberge Wien-
Myrthengasse

7, Myrthengasse 7 (523 6316 /fax 523 5849/
www.oejhv.or.at/www.jugendherberge.at).
U2, U3 Volkstheater then bus 48a to Neubaugasse.

Rates per person €14.50-€17.50. **Credit** AmEx, DC, MC, V. **Map** p238 C7.

The closest of the hostels to the centre, with 68 rooms and 270 beds.

Hotel services *Internet access. Laundry (self-service). TV lounge.*

Jugendgästehaus der Stadt Wien/Hütteldorf-Hacking

13, Schlossberggasse 8 (877 0263/fax 877 0263-2/ www.hostel.at). U4 Hütteldorf. **Rates** *per person* €12-€13.90; €14-€14.50 incl breakfast. **Credit** AmEx, DC, MC, V.

The location of the hostel is on the fringe of the city, but transport is easy and frequent. The place has 60 rooms and 285 beds.

Westend City Hostel

6, Fügergasse 3 (597 6729/fax 597 6729-27/ www.westendhostel.at). U3, U6 Westbahnhof (exit Innere Mariahilfer Strasse-Millergasse)/ tram 6, 18. **Rates** *per person* €16-€23 incl breakfast. **No credit cards. Map** p238 B9.

Once both a bordello and a hotel, this 27-room, 211-bed hostel three minutes from the Westbahnhof rail station was totally transformed in 2002. Rooms at the Westend City Hostel are modestly furnished, but attractive nonetheless, in white and natural press-board. Each has a shower/toilet module. All rooms are no-smoking. A deal with a nearby restaurant allows cheap meals.

Hotel services *Fax. Garden courtyard. Internet access. Laundry. Multilingual staff. Parking garage (€13/day). Safe. TV lounge.* **Room services** *Lockers.*

Wombat's City Hostel

15, Grangasse 6 (897 2336/fax 897 2577/ www.wombats.at). U3, U6 Westbahnhof, exit Gerstnerstrasse/tram 52, 58. **Rates** *per person* €19; €38 single/double; €3 buffet breakfast. **No credit cards. Map** p238 A9.

Wombat's City Hostel is very cool, from the London phone booth in the lobby to the cluttered front desk, casual lounge and bar. The neighbourhood just back of the rail station is a tangle of streets dreary with car repair garages but the rooms here are immaculate and bright, if spartan. All rooms are no-smoking and include shower and toilet. Movie nights and other in-house entertainment are occasionally organised.

Hotel services *Bar (welcome drink is free). Bike rental and storage room. Disabled: adapted rooms. Fax. Internet access. Laundry. Multilingual staff. Safe. TV (cable) lounge.* **Room services** *Lockers.*

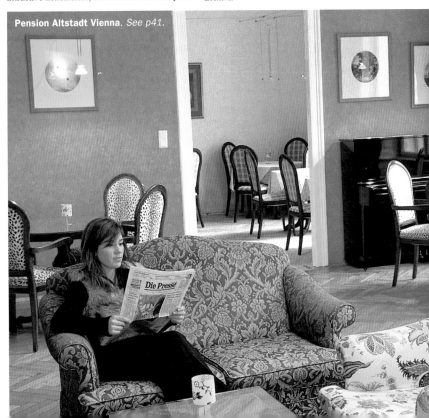

Pension Altstadt Vienna. See p41.

Camping

Facilities at Viennese campsites are first-class, particularly at prime locations such as Neue Donau and Schlosspark Laxenburg, and experience extreme demand during the summer peak season – so book early. Check out the sites at www.wien.camping.at.

14th District

Camping Wien West
14, Hüttelbergstrasse 80 (914 2314/fax 911 3594/ www.wiencamping.at). Tram 49 then bus 148, 152 to campsite. **Rates** *per person* €5-€5.50; €3-€3.50 4-15s; €3.50 tent; €6-€6.50 camper van; €3 electricity hook-up; €21-€25 1-2 person bungalow; €31-€35 3-4 person bungalow. **Open** Mar-Jan. **Credit** AmEx, DC, MC, V.

The site is on the edge of the Wienerwald, 8km (5 miles) west of the city centre. Facilities include lounges, kitchen with cooking facilities, supermarket, buffet, washing machines and dryer. Disposal facilities for chemical toilets and motor van service centre. Gets packed in midsummer.

22nd District

Aktiv Camping Neue Donau
22, Am Kaisermühlendamm 119 (202 4010/ fax 202 4010/www.wiencamping.at). U1 Vienna International Centre, then bus 91a to campsite Kleehäufel. **Rates** *per person* €5.50; €3 4-15s; €3.50 tent; €6.50 camper van; €3 electricity hook-up. **Open** May-Sept. **Credit** AmEx, DC, MC, V.

This location is just north of the 'New Danube' recreation area parallel to the main Danube, and there are hiking, cycling, swimming, boating and nude bathing areas nearby. It's about 4km (2.5 miles) north-east of the city centre. Facilities at Aktiv Camping include lounges, kitchens with cooking facilities, a supermarket, a buffet and washing machines. In addition, there are disposal facilities for chemical toilets and a camper van service centre.

23rd District

Camping Rodaun
23, An der Au 2, Vienna-Rodaun (888 4154/ fax 888 4154). Schnellbahn S-1, S-2, S-3 to Liesing, then bus 253, 254, 255. **Rates** *per person* €5.45; €3.27 3-13s; €4.36 tent; €5.01 camper van. **Open** end Mar-early Nov. **Credit** V.

This campsite is about 10km (6 miles) west of the city centre in the Rodaun suburb. It is on the fringes of the Wienerwald, adjacent to an artificial lake created by a dam across the Liesing river, and so feels pretty rural. Facilities include electricity outlets and a restaurant.

Long-term accommodation

1st District

Sacher Apartments
1, Rotenturmstrasse 1 (533 3238/fax 533 3238). U1, U3 Stephansplatz. **Rates** *up to 9 days* €68-€88 single; €88-€108 double. *10 days or longer* €48-€66 single; €67-€88 double. Monthly rates by agreement. **No credit cards. Map** p243 E6.

This eight-room apartment hotel occupying the upper floor of a post-war office block offers compact but comfortable accommodation. It's in the very heart of the city and there is public transport (and even horse-drawn carriages) literally at the door. **Hotel services** *Air conditioning. Fax. Laundry.* **Room services** *Dataport. Hairdryer. Kitchenette. Microwave. Refrigerator. Safe. Telephone. TV: cable/satellite.*

Singerstrasse 21-25
1, Singerstrasse 21-5 (514 49-0/fax 513 1617/ www.singerstrasse2125.at). U3 Stubentor/U1 Stephansplatz/tram 1, 2, bus 1a. **Rates** *studio* €595-€700/€2,105-€2,522 per wk/mth. *Executive suite* €945-€1,050/€3,362-€3,800 per wk/mth. Reception available 8am-8pm Mon-Fri. **Credit** AmEx, DC, MC, V. **Map** p243 F7.

The 77 serviced apartments in this multi-floored purpose-built complex look fresh in their attractive livery of light grey walls and contrasting natural wood floors. Two sizes each of studio and two-room executive accommodation offer every convenience a longer-term guest could want, from elegantly outfitted bathrooms to compact full kitchenettes complete with glassware, tableware, dishes, pots and pans, toasters, coffee machine, microwave oven and even a dishwasher.
Hotel services *Air-conditioning. Concierge. Fax. Laundry. Multilingual staff. Parking: garage (€11/day).* **Room services** *CD player. Dataport. Safe. Telephone. TV: cable/satellite.*

19th District

Kaiser Franz Joseph Apartments
19, Sieveringer Strasse 4 (329 00-0/fax 320 7355/ www.deraghotels.de). U2 Schottentor/tram 1, 2, D, then tram 38 or U4 Heiligenstadt, then bus 39a. **Rates** €92-€138 single; €117-€175 double; 2-wk and longer rates by agreement. **Credit** AmEx, DC, MC, V.

Kaiser Franz Joseph is a newish facility with 95 hotel rooms and 344 serviced apartments. The decor is attractively modern with comfortable furnishings. Set on the fringe of an upmarket residential district close to the wine gardens, the location nevertheless has good transport to the city centre.
Hotel services *Bar. Business services. Currency exchange. Fax. Fitness centre. Hairdresser. Laundry. Massage. Multilingual staff. No-smoking rooms. Parking: garage (€12/day). Restaurant. Sauna. Shopping service. Solarium.* **Room services** *Dataport. Kitchenette. Minibar. Telephone. TV: cable.*

Sightseeing

Introduction

Paradise for pedestrians, Vienna combines a seductive grandeur with exemplary urban planning.

Bearing in mind the upheavals Vienna endured and inflicted on itself throughout the 20th century, it is surprising to see how pristine the city has remained. Despite the loss of the vast Habsburg empire, civil war and a disastrous pact with National Socialism, Vienna has miraculously preserved an extraordinarily beautiful and coherent architectural heritage acquired over many centuries. Amid the baroque palaces and churches, imposing 19th-century apartment buildings and art deco façades, the only thing that irks the eye is the heavy-handed kitsch wrought by a tourist industry intent on exploiting Vienna's status as former imperial metropolis and European capital of classical music – an industry that thrives on busloads of trippers rather than independent backpackers.

However Vienna has plenty more to offer the independent traveller with a liking for the arts, intellectual and geopolitical history and carefree self-indulgence. Blessed with a user-friendly quality that owes much to over a century of rigorous urban planning and enlightened municipal government, Vienna is helpfully divided into 23 clearly delineated *Bezirke* (districts) that surround the historic centre in two concentric circles. The kaleidoscopic central core of the Innere Stadt is hemmed in by the Danube Canal to the north and by the east–west horseshoe formed by the monumental Ringstrasse and contains the vast majority of the city's best-known sights. Once you're finished with the inner city, access is easy to districts 2-9, where the remainder of Vienna's most worthwhile sights are located. When you finally tire of the asphalt, take any of the trams heading north and west and you'll find yourself in the legendary **Vienna Woods** (*see p200*) or among the vineyards that line the city's northern fringe.

Tourist-Info Wien

1, Albertinaplatz (211 14-222). U1, U2, U4 Karlsplatz. **Open** 9am-7pm daily.
The main tourist information agency. It has tickets for almost all groups and venues as well as maps, city tours and a currency exchange.

Museums & galleries

Despite considerable municipal and state largesse in matters of the arts, free entrance to museums is virtually unknown. Those intending to see Vienna's bewildering, eclectic selection of museums and art galleries from the inside should purchase the **Vienna Card**, which offers entrance discounts to over 170 museums and sights and 72 hours' free public transport for €16.90. The card is sold from hotels, tourist offices and stations.

Tours

Vienna's multi-layered history is reflected in the vast number of specialised walking tours. There are walks taking in Jewish Vienna, architecture and Viennese erotica. Times and details appear in the monthly *Wien Programm* leaflet (www.wienguide.at), available from the tourist office and hotels. Of particular interest is the **Third Man** tour (usually 4pm Mon-Fri, but phone Dr Brigitte Timmermann on 774 8901 to check – or look in the monthly *Wiener Spaziergange* brochure, available from the tourist office). The two-and-a-half-hour tour in English and German takes you down the canals and to all the places that featured in the Orson Welles film. Classical music fans will enjoy **Music Mile Vienna** (bookings 588 30-0/ www.musikmeile.at). Starting from Theater an der Wien, just follow the stars embedded in the pavement for a classical music 'Walk of Fame'. Both audio guides and guided tours are available in English.

Top five — Experiences

- A spin round the Ringstrasse on trams 1 or 2 with Kruder & Dorfmeister's 'High Noon' on the headphones.
- Coffee, cake and the papers in Café Sperl.
- Saturday at the flea market with Otto Wagner's flamboyant facades in the sunlight.
- Roast pork and Budweiser at the Schweizerhaus in the Prater.
- A headful of white wine spritzer at a Heuriger among the vineyards.

The Innere Stadt

A Viennese whirl around the stately elegance of the city centre.

Functional and decorative, Adolf Loos' public conveniences on the **Graben**. *See p54.*

Maps p242 and p243

The Romans founded the garrison town
Vindobona in 15BC along the banks of the
Danube, but the present inner city was
developed through the patronage of the
Babenberg dukes and, more importantly,
the Habsburgs. Yet the area's growth was
stunted by the monarchy's fear of the invader;
it is one of Vienna's idiosyncrasies that its
city walls were maintained long after other
European cities had expanded and integrated
their historic centres into the surrounding
suburbs. Rated a UNESCO World Heritage
Site in 2001, the area is an outstanding
testimony to the baroque age, 19th-century
liberalism and, to a lesser extent, the Middle
Ages. Modernism in the form of the local strain
of art deco, Jugendstil, or Adolf Loos' austere
functionalism is also part and parcel of the
Innere Stadt's architectural texture.

Bisected by the north-south axis of
Kärntner Strasse and Rotenturmstrasse,
the Innere Stadt centres on **Stephansdom**,
Vienna's magnificent Gothic cathedral. From
Stephansplatz the broad elegant thoroughfare
of Graben eventually leads to the vast, rambling
Hofburg, the Imperial Palace, headquarters of
the Habsburg Empire until its demise in 1918.
These are the busiest streets of the Innere Stadt,
where tourism is most palpably present.

The Innere Stadt's 3.6 square kilometres
(1.39 square miles) are now one of Vienna's
prime shopping and leisure districts. You'll
also encounter an appetising array of coffeehouses, beer cellars and other watering holes.
Indeed the pavement-café ambience is akin to
that of the Mediterranean. There's a lot to pack
in here, but with its gentle pace and relative
serenity, central Vienna is one of the most
remarkable, yet liveable city centres of any
major European capital.

Stephansplatz

Situated at the junction of two U-Bahn lines
(U1 and U3) and two of Vienna's most famous
pedestrian streets, Kärntner Strasse and Graben,
Stephansplatz and the cathedral are useful
landmarks from which to start an exploration
of the Innere Stadt, as well as providing a fine
vantage point for getting an impression of
Viennese street life. Visitors are often struck
by the sheer emptiness of Vienna's streets,
yet whenever a door is pushed open, bars and
restaurants are packed, the clientele seemingly
having been beamed in. But Stephansplatz,
dominated by the imposing bulk of the
cathedral, is rarely empty. Street performers,
political protesters, office workers, tourists,
costumed students hawking tickets for Strauss
evenings of dubious merit, throng the square,
providing a variety of visual entertainment. The
buildings surrounding Stephansdom on three
sides are a mixture of baroque and 19th-century,
housing various agencies of the church.

On the north side of Stephansplatz is the
Dom- und Diozesanmuseum (Cathedral and
Diocesan Museum). Facing the main entrance
to the cathedral the buildings are nondescript
post-war edifices, with some, such as the
corner of Rotenturmstrasse, frankly shoddy.
The demolition of one such monstrosity made
way for Hans Hollein's curvaceous Haas
Haus (1990), once the city's most controversial
modern building due to its proximity to the
venerable cathedral. It now houses a variety
of humdrum high-street retailers, but the upper
floors are occupied by two restaurants and a
bar run by society gastronome Attilla Dogudan.

For all the fuss, the Haas Haus is not actually
situated on Stephansplatz, but on the adjacent
and often overlooked Stock-im-Eisenplatz
('iron in wood' is a rough translation) where
journeymen would hammer a nail into a log to
ensure safe passage home after a trip to Vienna.
A glass case protecting a stump of larch studded
with nails is on the side of the Equitable Palace
building (on the corner of Kärntner Strasse), the
neo-baroque 19th-century seat of the famous
insurance company. It's worth taking a peek
inside at the sumptuous marble cladding of
the entrance hall and the courtyard tiled in
Hungarian Zsolnay ceramics. To gain access to
a locked palatial building in Vienna it usually
suffices to ring the bell of any corporate-
sounding address and push open the door.

Dom- und Diozesanmuseum

*1, Stephansplatz 6 (515 52 35/60). U1, U3
Stephansplatz.* **Open** 10am-5pm Tue-Sat.
Admission €5; €4 concessions; €2.15 children.
Credit AmEx, DC, MC, V. **Map** p243 E6.

Located in the baroque Archbishop's Palace, the
pricey Cathedral- and Diocesan Museum can only
be truly recommended to devotees of baroque painting. Highlights are works by Austrian masters such
as Anton Kraus, Franz Maulbertsch and Michael
Angelo Unterberger. However, there is a hotch-potch
of curiosities typical of ecclesiastical museums: the
first European portrait on panel, that of Rudolph IV
(1360); a Giotto-esque stained-glass window (1340)
with Jugendstil ornamentation (restored 1900); and
the blackened remnants of the cathedral's Gothic
carved choir stalls (destroyed 1945 in a bombing
raid). Another attraction is the massive Nürnberg
iron treasure chest (1678), displayed open to reveal
the mechanics of its complex multi-lock system. The
artist's inscription reads: 'The art [of construction] I
have from God the Highest so I can mock my
enemy', dating from the days of the Turkish
onslaughts. The lock itself was never broken.

Stephansdom

*1, Stephansplatz (5155 23767). U1, U3
Stephansplatz.* **Open** 6am-10pm daily. **Map** p243 E6.
Although originally located beyond the medieval
city walls, St Stephen's Cathedral forms the epicentre of the present Innere Stadt and dominates the
city's skyline. No other building is so unanimously
loved and revered by the Viennese as their dear
Steffl ('little Stephen' in the local dialect). It is certainly a symbol of endurance, having undergone
numerous phases of building and repair due to the
ravages of the Turks, the Napoleonic French and the
Allies. The last restoration was finished in 1948 after
fire, reputedly started by hungry looters sacking
nearby shops, destroyed the roof of the nave. From
the outside the cathedral appears divided into three
distinct parts. On a sunny day the geometrically
designed tiled roof of the nave, depicting the
Habsburg crown protected by chevrons, is magnificent. Dating from the late 13th century, the oldest
existing feature is the Romanesque Riesentor
(Giants' Gate), the main entrance to the cathedral.
The origin of the name is unclear, but the most
attractive explanation is that mammoth bones dug
up during the building work were taken by the good
burghers of Vienna to be the remains of a race of
giants killed in the biblical flood. The entrance is
flanked by the impressive Heidentürme (Pagan
Towers), so-called because of their tenuous resemblance to minarets, forming a façade peppered with
references to the city's history past and present.

Look out for the circular recess to the left of the
entrance, which enabled citizens to check that their
local bakers weren't peddling undersized loaves, and
on the other side the inscription O5 – capital O and
the fifth letter E – representing the first two letters
of Oesterreich, a symbol of the Austrian resistance
in World War II. Now protected by plexi-glass, this
symbol used to be regularly highlighted in chalk
whenever Nazi collaborator and ex-Austrian president Kurt Waldheim attended Mass. The icing on
the cake is undoubtedly the 137m (450ft) high south

tower, a magnificently hoary Gothic finger completed in 1433 after 74 years of work. A north tower of similar dimensions was projected in the early 16th century, but austerity measures imposed during the first Turkish siege of 1529 sadly put paid to the idea.

The interior with its beautiful high vaulting is surprisingly gloomy yet often packed with visitors. Still, it very much remains a place of worship, and during Mass, access is denied to most of the nave. It is worth going inside to see the extraordinary carving of the Pilgram pulpit at the top of the nave, where the sculptor, contravening the usual stonemasons' code of practice, has depicted himself looking out of a window to admire his own work. This motif is repeated under the organ loft on the north side of the nave. Other highlights include the tomb of war hero Eugène of Savoy in the Tirna Chapel, also located to the north of the nave just inside the main entrance. Visibility is, however, poor. The cathedral's catacombs are home to the entrails of the principal Habsburgs, while, bizarrely, their hearts dwell in the Augustinerkirche and what was left of their bodies in the Kaisergruft. Unless you have an overriding interest in contemplating piles of bones and skulls, give the catacombs a miss.

A lift operates from the north side of the nave to the top of the north tower where the cathedral's enormous bell, the Pummerin ('Boomer'), is housed. For the sense of achievement and to enjoy the splendid views, you could take the 553 steps that lead to the top. Access is from the outside on the south side.

East of Stephansdom

The two principal streets to the east of Stephansdom, Singerstrasse and Domgasse, lead towards Vienna's only remaining medieval quarter. The lack of top-rated monuments means this small but charming labyrinthine network of streets is practically free of tourists and must be one of the most desirable residential areas of any European inner city. The area directly behind the cathedral is known as the Blutviertel (Blood Quarter), which supposedly derives from a massacre of renegade Templar Knights in 1312 on Blutgasse, connecting Singerstrasse and Domgasse. In contrast the house at Blutgasse 7 has a fine example of the tranquil, airy inner courtyards that abound in this area.

Look out for the exterior walkways that give access to the flats – at Blutgasse 3 for example, a so-called *Pawlatschenhaus* (gallery house – deriving from the Czech *pavlac*) that are found throughout the city. On Singerstrasse are several 17th-century palaces such as the Neupauer-Breuner (No.16) housing the Vienna branch of Sotheby's and the Woka lighting company (responsible for repros of modernist classics by Josef Hoffmann and Adolf Loos).

One block east at the junction of Singerstrasse and Grünangergasse is the imposing Palais Rottal, and in the delightful Grünangergasse (at No.4) there's Palais Fürstenberg with two finely carved stone greyhounds over the portal.

Schatzkammer des Deutschen Ritterordens

1, Singerstrasse 1 (512 1065/www.deutscher-orden.at). U1, U3 Stephansplatz. **Open** *Church* 7am-6pm daily. *Treasury* May-Oct 10am-noon Mon, Thur; 3-5pm Wed, Fri; 10am-noon, 3-5pm Sat. **Admission** €3.60; €2.20 concessions; free under-11s. **No credit cards. Map** p243 E7.

The building on Singerstrasse and those of the adjoining courtyard belong to one of the most powerful orders to emerge from the Crusades. The fearful sounding Teutonic Knights ('Deutschen

The best | Major sights

Belvedere
Baroque doesn't get any more elegant.
See p77.

Hofburg
Europe's largest family residence breathes history. *See p55.*

Kaisergruft
The imperial crypt is the key to the Viennese way of death. *See p53.*

Karlskirche
Baroque with a Byzantine touch. *See p81.*

Museumsquartier
Early days yet, but Vienna's cultural theme park entertains at all levels. *See p72.*

Ringstrasse
Europe's most extravagant boulevard and potted guide to architectural history. *See p68.*

Schönbrunn
Gorgeous gardens despite the imperial overkill. *See p88.*

Secession
Temple to the city's long-gone modernity. *See p81.*

Staatsoper
Europe's music capital has venues to match. *See p170.*

Stephansdom
Vienna's short on Gothic, but this is the city's hoariest steeple. *See p48.*

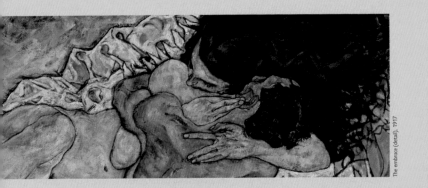

The embrace (detail), 1917

e.g. «Egon Schiele»
Österreichische Galerie
Belvedere

Upper Belvedere
Prinz Eugen-Str. 27, 1030 Vienna
Tue – Sun, 10 am –18 pm

ÖSTERREICHISCHE GAL
BELVEDERE

1903
2003
1OO JAHRE
ÖSTERREICHISCHE
GALERIE BELVEDERE

T +43/1/79 557-134 · www.belvede

Blutgasse courtyards. *See p49.*

Ritterordens') had the Schatzkammer (church and treasury) constructed in the 14th century as a place for the care of the sick and needy: good works that began during the Crusades and continue to this day. The church is recognisably Gothic, but apart from the 16th-century altarpiece and the coats of arms and the tombstones of its illustrious members, the point of interest here is an eclectic collection in the Treasury – everything from arms and armour to bizarre household objects picked up during the Crusades. Not to be missed is the tiny, beautifully painted 18th-century Sala Terrena, Vienna's earliest concert hall, where Mozart reputedly played, located at the foot of the staircase to the treasury. The two cobbled inner courtyards are also worth strolling through and there is a shady terrace bar, a godsend in the summer heat.

Figarohaus

1, Domgasse 5/Schulerstrasse 8 (513 6294). U1, U3 Stephansplatz. **Admission** €1.80; 70¢ concessions. **No credit cards.** **Map** p243 F7.
Mozart lived here between 1784 and 1787, his happiest years in Vienna, when he wrote *The Marriage of Figaro*. The house is now a museum, but it contains none of his personal effects – those are all in his home town of Salzburg. Here you can view copies of famous manuscripts. Visitors can listen to his works on headphones, but really this is only for Mozart devotees.

In & around Kärntner Strasse

A pedestrian street since the 1970s, Kärntner Strasse connects Stephansplatz with another of Vienna's major tourist attractions, the **Staatsoper** (Opera House, *see p170*), so is always clogged with visitors. Luxury shops used to trade here, but the street is now awash with chainstores and takeaways. An occasional glimpse of former glories is offered by such establishments as Lobmeyer at No.26, a famous glassmaker with a museum containing some original items by the Wiener Werkstätte design firm. Near the corner of Stock-im-Eisenplatz is the Kärntnerdurchgang with the fabulous Adolf Loos American Bar (1908) – *see p182*. Weihburggasse leads down to one of the most pleasant squares in Vienna, the Italianate Franziskanerplatz, probably better known in Vienna for the Kleines Café (*see p182*) than for the good works of the Franciscans. Sit here in summer and admire the baroque houses of Weihburggasse and the delightful Moses Fountain (1798) by JM Fischer.

The other streets to the east of Kärntner Strasse – Himmelpfortgasse, Johannesgasse and Annagasse – all have a number of splendid baroque houses and a sprinkling of minor sights, the most notable being the Winter Palace of Prince Eugène of Savoy in the first of the three, at No.8. Conceived by perhaps the most important architect of this era JB Fischer von Erlach, and completed by his great rival JL von Hildebrandt in 1709, this fine baroque palace is now used by the Ministry of Finance. Although the rooms are out of bounds, the most arresting features, the vestibule and the staircase propped up by four atlantes and the statue of Hercules on the landing, can be seen during office hours. On the corner of Annagasse and Seilerstätte, another baroque mansion houses the recently opened multimedia music museum, **Haus der Musik**.

Franziskanerkirche

1, Franziskanerplatz (512 4578). U1, U3 Stephansplatz. **Map** p243 E7.
The Habsburgs had a penchant for austere monastic orders such as the Franciscans and Capuchins, a tradition that goes back to Rudolf of Habsburg, the founder of the dynasty. The present Church of the Franciscans dates from 1611, but the order was given possession of the neighbouring house some 20 years earlier, itself an establishment for the reform of the city's prostitutes, where townsmen were encouraged to take them as wives. Today, by contrast, the church feeds the homeless. The façade is an odd mixture of Gothic and German Renaissance dotted with curious roundels that used to contain portraits of saints. The

Thievery corporation

After receiving Hitler's invading troops in 1938 with jubilation, many Viennese embarked on a brutal six-month orgy of intimidation of the city's Jews that eventually led to over 65,000 Jewish people perishing in Nazi concentration camps. The property of both the assimilated rich and the poorer Eastern community was either simply stolen or acquired by coercion for derisory sums. This form of institutionalised robbery, known as 'aryanisation', led to the expropriation of around 60,000 Jewish-owned dwellings, as well as numerous businesses, shops and places of entertainment. Few of the owners of these assets lived to demand their restitution, while those who survived were fobbed off with an insulting cocktail of obstructionism and indifference. Part of the reason for this lies in the Allies' geopolitical interest in restoring Austrian nationhood. At the 1943 Moscow summit, they officially designated Austria the 'first victim of Nazi aggression', inadvertently providing the post-war authorities with a convenient alibi for ignoring Jewish claims for property restitution.

After the war Austria got down to the task of reconstruction and until the Waldheim Affair in the 1970s and the rise of Jörg Haider hit the headlines, Austrian attitudes to this tenebrous period of its history remained unchallenged. In 1998, the coalition government of the SPÖ-ÖVP announced the founding of a 'Historians' Commission' to investigate 'the expropriation of property in the period of Nazi rule (1938-

1945)'. In 2003, five years' research revealed that Austria's record on restitution had been 'half-hearted'.

The Commission's findings were, however, pre-empted in 2002 when two young Viennese journalists published an astonishing little volume that, unusually for Austria, provided precise details as to what was aryanised and who profited from it. Taking its title from Vienna's tourist board newsletter, *Unser Wien* (Our Vienna) dryly argues that much of what fuels Austria's lucrative tourist industry is in fact stolen property. In a lengthy chapter entitled 'The Topography of Robbery', some of the city's best-known attractions are shown to be expropriated Jewish property. Two of the city's flagship hotels, the **Imperial** (*see p29*) and the **Sacher** (*see p31*), were partly owned before 1938 by Samuel Schallinger who died in the Theresienstadt camp in 1942. Two of the city's best-known coffee houses, Cafés **Mozart** (*see p125*) and **Bräunerhof** (*see p122*), were among 25 similar establishments to be aryanised – either handed over to wholly incompetent successors (ice-hockey players, chimney sweeps) or liquidated and used for other purposes. Many of the car showrooms along the Ringstrasse, for instance, were formerly Jewish-owned coffee houses. Even that great icon of post-war Vienna, the Prater Big Wheel was stolen from its Jewish owner Eduard Steiner, who was later murdered in Auschwitz.

In recent years the growing interest in Vienna's fin de siècle modernist heritage has

---

interior is rather more luxurious than you might expect from the Franciscans and the trompe-l'oeil, by Jesuit lay brother and painter-architect Andrea Pozzo (1707), surrounded by an arched high altar, is worth a look. Also check the enormous green curtain with fleurs-de-lis rendered in stucco that hangs from the north wall.

Haus der Musik

1, Seilerstätte 30 (516 48 10/www.hdm.at). U1, U3 Stephansplatz. **Open** 10am-10pm daily. **Tickets** €8.50. **Credit** AmEx, DC, MC, V. **Map** p243 E7.
Zubin Mehta called it 'a Disneyland of sound', but don't worry: there are no robotic dolls singing 'It's a small world after all'. Instead, the Haus der Musik gives you 5,000sq m (53,820sq ft) of pure musical experience – everything from a prenatal listening room where you can re-experience what the embryo hears in the womb, to the Future Music Blender where the Sensor Chair turns your gestures into

music. It's a hands-on museum for the most part; you can even create your own sound composition to take home on CD: for an extra €7.

West of Kärntner Strasse

Directly west of Kärntner Strasse lies Neuer Markt, a large traffic-clogged rectangular square, formerly the medieval flour market. Architecturally, the square is a dreadful hotch-potch; however, amid the parked cars is a copy of Donner's splendid Providentia Fountain (1739). The naked figures of the original – allegorical representations of the four main Austrian rivers – proved too much for Maria Theresia's Chastity Commission and were removed in 1773. Since 1921 they have been in the **Barockmuseum** in the Lower Belvedere. Notable among the square's commercial

given the tourist industry a lucrative alternative to the monarchic fare habitually fed to visitors. Much of this too was either stolen or acquired by means of dubious purchases. Prominent landmarks such as the so-called **Loos Haus** (*see p55*) on Michaelerplatz became the property of the Opel company in 1938 which vandalised the building's original entrance. Several Otto Wagner buildings suffered a similar fate; his magnificent **Majolika Haus** (*see p81*) on Wienzeile was acquired by having its Jewish proprietor certified insane. In the late 1990s the seizure by US customs of a Schiele painting on loan to New York's Museum of Modern Art from the Leopold Collection highlighted the fate of many works of art previously owned by Jewish collectors.

Alerted by New York attorney Ed Fagan's successful 'class actions' on behalf of US claimants against Switzerland, an important agreement was reached in Washington in 2001 whereby the Austrian government agreed to finance a General Settlement Fund for resolving outstanding claims. Too little, too late, many would say. *Unser Wien* has the merit of alerting today's visitors to the omnipresence of these ghosts of the past – half the city's pharmacies, including the Jugendstil **Engelapotheke** (Bognergasse 9), were aryanised. Whenever you attend a screening of *The Third Man* at the **Burgkino** (*see p155*), buy a Topfengolatsche at an Anker bakery or drink the odd pint of Ottakringer beer, spare a thought for the fate of their former owners.

establishments is the baroque façade of former court jewellers Koechert and the vaulted cellars of organic grocers and restaurant **Culinarium Österreich**. To the south, behind an unassuming grim façade is the **Kapuzinerkirche** and the **Kaisergruft**, the crypt containing the spectacular tombs of the Habsburgs.

Kaisergruft & Kapuzinerkirche

1, Neuermarkt (512 6853-12/www.kaisergruft.at).
U1, U2, U4 Karlsplatz or U1, U3 Stephansdom/
tram 1, 2, D, J/bus 3a. **Open** 9.30am-4pm daily.
Admission €3.60; €2.90 concessions; €1 under-14s.
No credit cards. Map p242 E7.
From 1633 onwards, the Habsburgs were laid to rest in the crypt of the Church of the Capuchins. Each funeral was preceded by a belittling ritual consisting of the reigning Emperor announcing his name to the waiting prior who then proceeded to deny knowledge of his person and refuse him entry. Finally the

Emperor was forced to identify himself as 'a humble sinner who begs God's mercy' and the cortege would be granted permission to enter. Today an admission fee and silence ('Silentium!' reads the inscription over the entrance) is all they ask. Many of these early tombs are decorated with skull and crossbones, weapons and bats' wings, progressively increasing in size until you reach the gigantic iron double tomb of Empress Maria Theresia and her husband, Franz Stephan. For sheer size and representational extravagance – above the tomb the couple appear to be sitting up in bed embroiled in a marital tiff – this has to be the highlight of the show. In stark contrast, their son Josef II, whose reforms tried and failed to popularise the drop-bottom reusable coffin, lies in a simple copper casket. Further along is the New Vault with its bizarre, diagonal concrete beams where major Habsburgs like Maximilian I of Mexico and Napoleon's second wife, Marie Louise, are to be found. Their son, the Duc de Reichstadt, was moved from here to Paris in 1940 by the Nazis in an attempt to ingratiate themselves to their new subjects. People tend to dwell a little longer in the Franz-Josef Vault as here lie the Habsburgs who still touch hearts: Franz Josef I, the last Emperor, his wife, the eternally popular Empress Elisabeth, and their son, the unhappy Prince Rudolph, victim of the Mayerling suicide pact. Sissi's tomb is invariably covered in flowers and small wreaths with ribbons in the colours of the Hungarian flag commemorating her sympathy for that country's national aspirations. The vault itself is simple with elegant wall lights in the Jugendstil manner. The last room contains the remains of Empress Zita, buried with full pomp in 1989, and a bust of her husband, Emperor Karl I, who died in exile in Madeira.

West of Neuermarkt

The area bounded by Neuermarkt to the east, Graben to the north and Hofburg to the west consists of a network of narrow streets ideal for strolling and replete with antique shops and galleries, unmissable *Kaffeehäuser* such as the Bräunerhof and Hawelka, plus the **Jüdisches Museum** and the **Dorotheum** auction house.

Dorotheum

1, Dorotheergasse 17 (515 600/www.dorotheum.com). **U1, U3 Stephansplatz**. **Open** 10am-6pm Mon-Fri; 9am-5pm Sat. **Admission** free. **No credit cards**. **Map** p242 E7.
In the past, a 'visit to Auntie Dorothy's' was a popular euphemism for hard times. Set up in 1707 by Emperor Josef I as a pawn shop for the wealthy, the Dorotheum is now Vienna's foremost auction house with small branches throughout the city. The building is a bit of neo-baroque bombast built in the late 1890s. Auctions are held daily, with regular specialised sales. The Glashof on the ground floor is full of interesting, and more affordable, bric-a-brac. Affluent fans of modernist furniture should try the Franz-Josef Saal on the second floor.

Jüdisches Museum

1, Dorotheergasse 11 (535 0431/www.jmw.at). **U1, U3 Stephansplatz**. **Open** 10am-6pm Mon-Wed, Fri, Sun; 10am-8pm Thur. **Admission** €5; €2.90 concessions. **No credit cards**. **Map** p242 E7.
Vienna has the distinction of being home to the world's first Jewish museum, opened in 1895 and closed, its exhibits confiscated by the Nazis, in 1938. The museum has been housed in the Palais Eskeles since 1993; the building was re-worked in 1995 by far-out architects Eichinger oder Knechtl, and now serves as a study centre, archive and library, with three floors of exhibition space. The ground floor has an important collection of Judaica, displayed amid fragmented frescoes by Nancy Spero reworking images such as those of a medieval matzo bakery, Gustav Mahler conducting and the smoking remains

of a synagogue razed by Nazis. The first and second floors hold temporary exhibitions, often linking general historical, political and artistic themes of the city with the role of Jews and their interaction with the Gentile community. The second floor also has a permanent historical exhibition using 21 holograms to depict aspects of Jewish culture in Vienna. A combined ticket for the museum, the synagogue and the new Museum Judenplatz costs €7.

Graben & Kohlmarkt

Graben and Kohlmarkt are remarkable in that they are entirely made up of baroque 19th-century and belle epoque buildings, without a single post-war pre-fab besmirching either. Graben ('ditch') today is a broad pedestrian thoroughfare built along what was the southern moat that defended the Roman camp established a few streets to the north. Commerce harks back to imperial times with innumerable shops bearing the k.u.k. (*kaiserlich und königlich*) royal warrant, among them gentlemen's outfitters announcing branches in Prague and Karlsbad.

Architecturally, the buildings on Graben are either historicist or Jugendstil but the street's most exuberant flourish, the Plague Monument, is resoundingly baroque. The most noteworthy historicist edifice is the neo-classical Erste Österreichisches Sparkasse (First Austrian Savings Bank – built in 1836) on the corner of Tuchlauben, emblazoned with an enormous gilded bee symbolising thrift and hard work. The only remaining baroque building is the Bartolotti-Partenfeld Palace (1720) at No.11. Jugendstil is represented by the monumental Grabenhof (1876) at Nos.14-15, built by **Otto Wagner** (*see p70*) to another architect's plans, and the Ankerhaus at No.10 which Wagner designed, built and for a time used as his studio. Where Habsburgergasse crosses Graben there are some delightful (and useful) Jugendstil-inspired public conveniences, and between the two flights of steps leading to the ladies and the gents, the fine Josef Fountain built by JM Fischer.

Pestsäule/Dreifaltigkeitssäule

1, Graben. U1, U3 Stephansplatz/bus 1a, 2a, 3a. **Map** p242 E6.
Between the Josef Fountain and the other fountain that JM Fischer designed to commemorate Leopold III soars Graben's centrepiece, the Pestsäule or Plague Monument (also known as the Trinity Column or Dreifaltigkeitssäule). Dating from 1692, this is probably the best example of the many that were erected throughout the Empire to mark the end of the plague of 1679 and also to celebrate deliverance from the spiritual 'plagues' of the Turks and the Reformation. The baroque stone carving, primarily by Fischer von Erlach, depicts a gorgeously ephemeral mass of cherubs and saints swathed in clouds.

Peterskirche

1, Petersplatz. U1, U3 Stephansplatz/bus 1a, 3a.
Map p242 E6.
Built on the site of what was probably Vienna's oldest Christian temple dating from the late fourth century, the Church of St Peter was built by Lukas von Hildebrandt and completed in 1733. Undoubtedly the finest baroque church of the Innere Stadt, it has a green copper dome that echoes the more bombastic Michaelertor in the Hofburg. The dome's fresco has faded badly but the interior remains spectacular due to a wealth of trompe-l'oeil effects around the choir and the altar. Today the church is a focus of Opus Dei activity in Vienna.

Neidhart-Fresken

1, Tuchlauben 19 (535 9065). U1, U3 Stephansplatz.
Open 9am-noon Tue-Sun. **Admission** €1.80;
70¢ concessions; free Fri. **No credit cards.**
Map p243 E6.
This private house/museum contains the oldest secular frescoes in the city (1400-20). A cloth merchant, Michel Menschein, commissioned this *Four Seasons* cycle depicting scenes of lively medieval jollity inspired by the songs and verse of Neidhart von Reuental (1180-1240), an aristocratic minstrel.

Designer or designed shops

Unlike Vienna's rudimentary standards of window dressing, many of its shopfronts are works of art in themselves. The Graben-Kohlmarkt axis is dotted with minor modern masterpieces of the genre. From the magnificent Klimt-like mosaic angels on the Engel Apotheke, a chemist's in the adjoining Bognergasse, through Loos' exercise in minimalist clarity for the Manz bookstore at Kohlmarkt 16, to designs by Austria's most famous contemporary architect Hans Hollein on both Kohlmarkt and Graben – shops can be enjoyed as simple artefacts. Knize, a bespoke outfitter's at Graben 11, was designed by Loos too, and still has many of its original fittings in the interior.

In the early 1970s the jeweller's Schullin had Hollein render the façade of its premises at Graben 26 in bluish marble with a trickle of gold running through. Hollein was given another opportunity on Schullin's shop at Kohlmarkt 7, where he came up with a striking axe-like form in sheet metal over the door supported by thin wooden uprights. Messrs Schullin have clearly prospered and in the mid-1990s they had Italian designer Paolo Piva convert a small shop space in the **Loos Haus** at Kohlmarkt 18 into a specialised watch department. Piva's work must have struck a chord as his designs were later selected for the extensions to the Knize store.

Designer shops also pepper this district; Kohlmarkt itself, the city's former coal and charcoal market, is Vienna's Bond Street. There are, too, several eye-catching indigenous establishments such as map-makers Freytag & Berndt (*see p133*) in Max Fabiani's Jugendstil building, the Artariahaus (No.9); and Demel (No.14) one of the most ornate cafés in the city (*see p122* and *p140*). Although the elegance of the shop-fronts is diverting, it is the view of the Michaelertor and its magnificent dome that dominates the street, leading you inexorably towards the labyrinth of the Hofburg.

Loos Haus

1, Michaelerplatz 3. U3 Herrengasse/bus 2a.
Map p242 E7.
The stir caused by the Haas Haus was minor in comparison with the outrage unleashed by the building of Adolf Loos' modernist masterpiece opposite the baroque Hofburg. Built between 1909 and 1911, the Loos House immediately received the nickname of 'the house without eyebrows' in reference to the absence of window cornices. Work was even stopped at one point until Loos agreed to add ten window boxes. The story goes that the Emperor was so appalled by the unseemly nakedness of its façade that he ordered the curtains to be drawn on all palace windows overlooking the new neighbour. Art critic Robert Hughes sees in Loos' abandoning of ornamentation the seeds of German architect Mies van der Rohe's now-popular dictum 'less is more'. In the words of the architect himself: 'The evolution of culture is synonymous with the removal of ornamentation from utilitarian objects.' Today the building is a bank and has exhibition space on the upper floors.

Hofburg

The vast area of the Imperial Palace and its adjoining parks and gardens occupies most of the south-eastern part of the Innere Stadt, from the **Burgtheater** round to the **Staatsoper**. Within its confines are two of Vienna's universally known institutions – the **Spanische Reitschule** and its famous Lipizzaner horses, and the **Burgkapelle** where the Vienna Boys' Choir sings Sunday Mass. Rewarding museums are the **Weltliche und Geistliche Schatzkammer** (the Secular and Sacred Treasuries) and the **Völkerkundemuseum** (Ethnological Museum).

An important public thoroughfare runs straight through Hofburg connecting the Ringstrasse to Kohlmarkt and Graben, so the whole ensemble is open 24 hours a day and is particularly atmospheric after dark. Built over a period of seven centuries up until the fall of the Empire after World War I, Hofburg owes its size to the reluctance of successive royal families to occupy their predecessors' quarters.

Sightseeing

Peterskirche, the finest baroque church of the Innere Stadt. *See p55.*

Whereas the Habsburgs' ancestors, the Babenbergs, had their court on Am Hof, the new rulers set up shop in 1275 in the Burg, a fortress originally built by King Ottokar II of Bohemia on the site of what is today the Schweizerhof. Under Ferdinand III (1521-64) two separate entities, Stallburg and Amalienburg, were added; they were eventually joined together in the 1660s by the Leopoldischer Trakt during the reign of Leopold I (1657-1705). The name Schweizerhof comes from the time of Maria Theresia (1740-80) when Swiss guards were billeted here. However, it was under her father Karl IV (1711-40) that two of Hofburg's greatest baroque edifices was built, namely the Hofbibliothek and the Winterreitschule by Fischer von Erlach, father and son. The square of In der Burg was finally completed in 1893 with the construction of the Michaelertrakt.

The sprawling seat of the Habsburgs can be roughly divided into four parts – the **Alte Burg**, the oldest section containing the Schatzkammer (treasury) and the Burgkapelle (chapel); **In der Burg**, where Franz Josef and Elisabeth's apartments are located; **Josefsplatz**, access point to the Spanish Riding School, the National Library and numerous minor museums; and finally the **Neue Burg** on Heldenplatz.

Alte Burg

The core of the palace is the Alte Burg, built around the original fortress (1275). The oldest part is the portion of moat running beside the Schweizertor, the entrance to this section.

Burgkapelle

1, Schweizerhof (533 9927-71). U3 Herrengasse, Volkstheater/tram 1, 2, D, J. **Open** *Jan-30 June, mid-Sept-31 Dec* 11am-3pm Mon-Thur; 11am-1pm Fri. **Mass with Boys' Choir** *3 Jan-27 June, 12 Dec-26 Dec* 9.15am Sun, Christmas Day. **Map** p242 E7.
Dating from the late 1440s, the original Gothic features of the Palace Chapel have been considerably tampered with over the years, but the vaulting and wooden statuary are still intact and visible. Unfortunately you can only visit as part of a guided tour or by attending the 9.15am Sunday morning Mass in the company of the Vienna Boys' Choir and members of the Vienna Philharmonic. Tickets cannot be reserved by phone, instead fax 533 9927-75 or try the Palace Chapel's box office (open 11am-1pm, 3-5pm daily).

Kleines Café and the Moses fountain, in **Franziskanerplatz**. *See p51*.

Weltliche und Geistliche Schatzkammer

1, Schweizerhof (525 24 363). U3 Herrengasse, Volkstheater/tram 1, 2, D, J. **Open** 10am-6pm Mon, Wed-Sun. **Admission** €7.50; €5.50 concessions; €6.50 with Vienna Card. **No credit cards.** **Map** p242 E7.

Undoubtedly the most important of Hofburg's museums, the 'Secular and Sacred Treasuries' contains the great treasures of the Holy Roman Empire, fine examples of gold and jewellery and a number of fascinating totemic artefacts. The entrance is beneath the steps to the **Burgkapelle** and is best reached through the Schweizertor. Most of the exhibits were amassed by Ferdinand I (1521-64) but assembled in the Hofburg under the reign of Karl VI in 1712. There are 20 smallish rooms with extremely subdued lighting and labelling in German; however, the entrance price includes the use of a device that gives an English commentary. In the secular section, top exhibits include the crown of Rudolph II (room 2) made in 1602 and festooned with diamonds, rubies, pearls and topped with a huge sapphire; the ornate silver cot of Napoleon's son, the Duc de Reichstadt (room 5); an amazing agate bowl once thought to be the Holy Grail, though more likely stolen from Constantinople in 1204; and opposite, the 'horn of the unicorn', a 2.4m (8ft) long narwhale's horn. In the twilight and confusing layout of the rooms, don't miss the star attraction: the Byzantine octagonal crown of the Holy Roman Empire. Finally, room 12 contains a number of relics – Karl VI was an inveterate collector – including splinters of wood supposedly from the Cross, a shred of the tablecloth from the Last Supper and a tooth of John the Baptist.

In der Burg

This section comprises the buildings around the large square of the same name opposite the Schweizertor. It is probably the busiest part of the Hofburg with buses, taxis and fiakers all allowed through and tourists swarming near the entrance to the Schatzkammer. The buildings are uniformly baroque; the square is empty but for the lone statue of Emperor Franz, the first Austrian Emperor and the last of the Holy Roman Empire.

To the south is the Leopoldischer Trakt, now out of bounds as part of the Austrian President's official residence. Opposite is the Reichskanzleitrakt, the section housing Franz Josef and Sissi's apartments. The passageway beside the Leopoldischer Trakt takes you into Ballhausplatz and the Austrian Chancellor's offices, scene of disturbances following the announcement of the coalition between the ÖVP and Haider's FPÖ in 2000.

Kaiserappartements/ Hofsilber- und Tafelkammer

1, Innerer Burghof Kaisertor (533 7570/ www.hofburg-wien.at). U3 Herrengasse, Volkstheater/tram 1, 2, D, J. **Open** 9am-5.30pm daily. **Admission** €7.50; €3.90-€5.90 concessions. **Credit** AmEx, DC, MC, V. **Map** p242 E7.

The Silver and Porcelain Collection reveals how the Habsburgs liked to entertain – for example, there's the 290-piece Sèvres dinner service given to Maria Theresia by Louis XV. The Imperial Rooms include those of Franz Josef and Sissi, which are in stark contrast to the opulence of the crockery section.

Franz Josef was a frugal old dog whose daily routine consisted of a cold wash at 4am, a spartan breakfast of bread roll and coffee, and then down to affairs of state while 'his cities snored from the Swiss to the Turkish border', in Frederic Morton's memorable phrase. Access to the rooms is by means of a splendid marble staircase. This leads first to Franz Josef's centre of operations, a series of chambers of more or less identical decoration but with the recent addition of informative plaques in English that help bring the rooms to life.

Next door in the Audienzimmer you can see the raised desk where Franz Josef stood to receive petitions, one of his favourite pastimes. His readiness to award titles to the middle classes, especially to Jews, galled the traditional aristocracy. In his study hangs a portrait of Sissi by Franz Winterhalter. In the Grand Salon there are pictures and a bust of Field Marshal Radetzky. Here too is Winterhalter's larger, oft-reproduced portrait of Sissi, exuding a glamour that is difficult to detect in her chambers, which come next. Here any parallel with Princess Diana evaporates despite the superficial common ground of marital difficulties, an obsession with the body beautiful and a violent death. In her bedroom and boudoir the fittings are just as spartan as Franz Josef's – simple iron bed, copper bathtub. A quirky note is struck by a set of wooden exercise bars.

Once you're past the Sissi section there are four rooms known as the Alexander apartments. This set of rooms is where Alexander I, Czar of Russia, stayed during the Congress of Vienna in 1815, but they are bereft of a memento of his passing. Fans of the drama of Mayerling (*see p201*) will enjoy the Small Drawing Room where there are portraits of Prince Rudolf and the lesser known, but equally tragic Karl Ludwig (1833-96), Franz Josef's younger brother who died from drinking the contaminated waters of the River Jordan.

Josefplatz

Josefplatz is named after Josef II, one of the more progressive of the Habsburgs, who in 1783 ordered the demolition of the wall that encased the square within Hofburg, thus converting it into a public thoroughfare. A large equestrian statue of the iconoclastic Emperor (1807) stands in the middle of the square. Josefsplatz is the scene of one of the key moments in *The Third Man*, when Harry Lime stages his death in a motor accident in front of the Palais Pallavicini – his sumptuous place of residence. The Pallavicini (1784) and the nearby Palais Pálffy are examples of fine 1st district baroque aristocratic palaces. Star attractions on Josefsplatz include the **Augustinerkirche**, the **Nationalbibliothek** and the **Spanische Reitschule**. Nearby is Albertinaplatz, the triangular square named after the **Albertina**.

The wedge-like Albertinaplatz contains the controversial *Monument against War and Fascism* by the Austrian sculptor Alfred Hrdlickla. This consists of four separate elements – two marble blocks symbolising the Gate of Violence; a representation of Orpheus entering Hades; the Stone of the Republic engraved with fragments of an Austrian Declaration of Independence published in 1945; and in the middle, the origin of the outrage, a small bronze statue of a kneeling Jew scrubbing the street clean.

Albertina

1, Albertinaplatz 3 (534 830/www.albertina.at). U1, U2, U4 Karlsplatz/tram D, J, 1, 2, 62, 65. **Open** 10am-6pm Tue-Sun. **Admission** €7.50; €5.50 concessions. **Credit** MC, V. **Map** p242 E7.

Peering out from above the old Hofburg ramparts on to the Burggarten and Staatsoper, these former imperial guest apartments take their name from Maria Theresia's son-in-law, Duke Albert of Sachsen-Teschen, who founded one of the world's greatest collections of graphic art in 1768. This includes 145 Dürer drawings, 43 by Raphael, 70 by Rembrandt, a large number of Schiele's and many more by Leonardo da Vinci, Michelangelo, Rubens, Cézanne, Picasso, Matisse and Klimt. Badly bombed in World War II, the Albertina was for years the most visibly dilapidated building of the Hofburg complex until it underwent a complete restoration of its exhibition space and its plush state rooms, costing over €90 million. It reopened in March 2003. Faced with the dilemma of how to exhibit a collection of some 1.5 million prints and 50,000 drawings, watercolours and etchings, the authorities have opted for non-permanent three-month exhibitions featuring stellar items from its catalogue bolstered with loans from elsewhere. The entrance ticket also provides access to the state rooms. Other novelties include a new reading room for the National Library and a café/restaurant run by top-notch caterers Do & Co serving refreshments on the ramparts. The Albertina is also home to the **Filmmuseum** (*see p156*).

Augustinerkirche

1, Augustinerstrasse 3 (533 7099). U1, U2, U4 Karlsplatz, U3 Herrengasse/tram 1, 2, D, J. **Map** p242 E7.

The Gothic church of St Augustin, dating from the early 14th century, is an important stop for those on the quest of the Habsburgs' entrails. Here in the Herzgrüftel ('Little Heart Crypt') lie their hearts, part of a Spanish imperial tradition to create several focal points of devotion to the Crown. Viewing is only by appointment, though. Free for all to see is Canova's impressive marble memorial to Maria Theresia's daughter Maria Christina and the rococo organ on which Brückner composed his memorable Mass No.3 in F minor. Sunday morning Mass is celebrated with a full orchestra.

Nationalbibliothek

1, Josefsplatz (53410-0/www.onb.ac.at). U1, U2, U4 Karlsplatz, U3 Herrengasse/bus 2a, 3a. **Open** *May-Oct* 10am-4pm Mon-Wed, Fri-Sun; 10am-7pm Thur. *Nov-Apr* 10am-2pm Mon-Wed, Fri-Sun; 10am-7pm Thur. **Map** p242 E7.

Entrance to Austria's largest library is through the western side of Josefsplatz. The main reason to go is to see Fischer von Erlach's Prunksaal, often described as 'one of the finest baroque interiors north of the Alps'. Completed by his son in 1735, this immense space is adorned with marble pillars, an enormous frescoed dome showing the Apotheosis of Karl IV by Daniel Gran, and gilded wood-panelled bookcases containing over 200,000 works. These include a 15th-century Gutenberg Bible and the 15,000 volumes of Prince Eugène of Savoy's collection, which his spend-thrift niece sold to the Habsburgs. The library also has Museums of Globes, Theatre and Esperanto, as well as collections of papyrus and musical scores.

Spanische Reitschule

1, Winterreitschule, Michaelerplatz 1 (533 9031/ www.srs.at). U1, U2, U4 Karlsplatz, U3 Herrengasse, U1, U3 Stephansplatz/bus 2a, 3a. **Open** *Mar-June, Sept, Nov, Dec* 10am-noon Tue-Sat. **Admission** €11.50; €5 children; free 3-6s; no under-3s. **Credit** AmEx, DC, MC, V. **Map** p242 E7.

The world-famous Spanish Riding School and its Lipizzaner horses are one of Vienna's top five classic tourist attractions, but high ticket prices mean it's really only for those with a serious interest in dressage (unless you must see the splendid baroque setting). These graceful grey horses are a cross between Spanish, Berber and Arab breeds and the name commemorates the imperial stud in Lipizza, near Trieste, where they have been bred since 1570. The horses are stabled in the Stallburg (Stables), site of the Lipizzaner Museum.

Lipizzaner Museum

1, Stallburg/Hofburg, Reitschulgasse 2 (533 7811/ www.lipizzaner.at). U1, U3 Stephansplatz, U3 Herrengasse/tram 1, 2, D, J/bus 2a. **Open** 9am-6pm daily. **Admission** €5; €3.60 concessions; combination ticket with Riding School morning exercise €14.50; €11.60 concessions; children €8. **Credit** AmEx, DC, JCB, MC, V. **Map** p242 E7.

Again, only for those with an equestrian bent. The display shows the history of the famous breed, complete with baroque paintings, saddles, liveries and uniforms. Through a couple of windows you can get a glimpse of the nags themselves in their stables.

Österreichisches Theatermuseum

1, Palace Lobkowitz, Lobkowitzplatz 1 (512 8800/ www.theatermuseum.at). U1, U2, U4 Karlsplatz/ tram 1, 2, D, J. **Open** 10am-5pm Tue, Thur-Sun; 10am-8pm Wed. *Children's museum* 10-10.30am, 2-2.30pm Tue-Sun. **Admission** €4; €3 children; €3.60 with Vienna Card. **No credit cards. Map** p242 E7.

Housed in the baroque Lobkowitz Palace just off Albertinaplatz, this museum has a permanent collection of costumes, stage models and theatrical memorabilia. Jugendstil artist Richard Teschner designed an innovative convex mirror stage as a puppet theatre, where performances are held with his original figures and music score. Enquire about performances at the ticket booth.

Gedenkräume des Österreichischen Theatermuseums

1, Hanuschgasse 3 (512 2427). U1, U2, U4 Karlsplatz/tram 1, 2, D, J. **Open** 10am-noon, 1-4pm Tue-Fri; 1-4pm Sat, Sun. **Admission** €4; €3 concessions; €3.60 with Vienna Card. **No credit cards. Map** p242 E7.

The Memorial Rooms of the Austrian Theatre Museum commemorate the great and good of the Austrian stage such as Max Reinhardt, Hugo Thimig, Emmerich Kalman, Fritz Wotruba and Herman Bahr.

Neue Burg

The monumental Neue Burg overlooking the vast emptiness that is Heldenplatz (Heroes' Square) was the last section of Hofburg to be constructed. Not completed until 1926, it was never occupied by a Habsburg. Its monumental neo-classicism gives Vienna the same air that circulates in all major seats of power, past and present. One can only wonder how it would have looked had Gottfried Semper's plans for a 'Kaiserforum', with an identical edifice on the opposite side of the square come to fruition. Of the square's original features, it's worth taking a close look at Anton Fernkorn's two fine equestrian statues which face each other: Prince Eugène of Savoy, nearest the Neue Burg; and Karl IV, who vanquished Napoleon at Aspern in 1809. The building today houses the main reading room of the National Library and four museums: the collections of weaponry, ancient musical instruments and the Ephesus Museum accessible with a single ticket, and the **Völkerkundemuseum**, which has a separate entrance and ticket. There is no access to the balcony where Hitler stood, but a good view can be had from inside.

Some mutations have taken place in the Neue Burg's short history. The triumphal Burgtor on the Ringstrasse side (incorporated within the city walls in 1820) was transformed into a monument to the Austrian dead of World War I by the Austro-Fascists in 1934. The latter also built two entrances to the square on either side of the Burgtor, whose stylised eagles represent one of Vienna's rare examples of truly fascistic architecture. The square is inseparable from the memory of Hitler's triumphal declaration of Austria's incorporation into the Third Reich. It is instructive that Thomas Bernhard, the greatest dramatist and enfant terrible of post-war Austria, should have entitled his most scathing attack on his country's past *Heldenplatz*. On a

Palais aplenty

As the Habsburg Empire spread its tentacles throughout Central Europe over seven centuries, the aristocrats of its subject nations started commissioning stupendous pieds-à-terre in the vicinity of the Court. A great number are built in the baroque style, the exuberant, theatrical language of the 17th and 18th centuries consisting of intricate decoration, playful spatial organisation and sweeping vistas. Early baroque architecture in Vienna is primarily the work of Italians such as Canevale and Martinelli, but after the defeat of the Ottomans, the post-1683 building boom revealed the talents of local masters such as Fischer von Erlach, senior and junior, and Lukas von Hildebrandt who, respectively, created the city's two baroque masterpieces – Karlskirche and Belvedere.

Vienna has palaces like most cities have cinemas. After years of neglect the majority have been renovated, usually by the government, cash-rich multinationals or local real estate firms in search of prestigious premises. Many are located on and around Herrengasse (Lords' Lane), which as the name suggests, has always been a hotbed of aristocratic activity. Here are some of the most prominent and accessible.

Palais Daun-Kinsky

1, Herrengasse. U2 Schottentor. **Map** p242 E6.
Located at the end of Herrengasse, the Palais Kinsky, as it is usually named, was completed in 1716 for one of Maria Theresia's generals by Lukas von Hildebrandt. The ceremonial staircase off the inner courtyard is particularly outstanding. Its restoration is now complete and new tenants include Marqués, a gorgeous but pricey tapas bar done out in Moorish style, a fine-art auction house, and the Downkinsky, a basement club featuring 'after-work' sessions à la Ally McBeal.

Palais Esterházy

1, Wallnerstrasse 4. U3 Herrengasse. **Map** p242 E6.
This enormous late 17th-century pile has offices, shops and the chicest pizza joint in Vienna, Regina Margherita. The Palais was once home to the Hungarian Esterázy family whose coat of arms blazes in gold above the entrance. The most interesting part of the complex is the Esterházykeller, a *Bierkeller* with vaulted ceilings, dark and conspiratorial in the best Central European tradition (*see p101*).

Palais Ferstel

1, Freyung 2. U2 Schottentor. **Map** p242 E6.
The Harrach's Renaissance-style neighbour is the work of Heinrich Ferstel, architect of the Votivkirche and the Universität. Finished in 1860, Palais Ferstel is perhaps best known as the home of the Café Central. Its stoutly columned entrance leads into an Italian-style arcade lined with gift shops. Formerly the seat of the Vienna Stock Exchange, the first-floor rooms are now used as corporate banqueting halls.

Palais Harrach

1, Freyung 3. U2 Schottentor. **Map** p242 E6.
Palais Harrach was rebuilt in 1690 to Domenico Martinelli's original design after it burnt down during the Turkish siege. Today its upper floors are used for temporary exhibitions by the Kunsthistorisches Museum, while the courtyard is home to a couple of private galleries, some interesting designer shops, and Martinelli, an exclusive Italian restaurant. Take a look in Martinelli's window at the display of Roman antiquities found during restoration work.

slightly more positive note, the flags fluttering on the north side of the square mark the headquarters of the Organisation for Security and Cooperation in Europe (OSCE), a hive of diplomatic activity during the 1990s during the genocidal conflict in the former Yugoslavia.

Sammlungen des Kunsthistorischen Museums in der Hofburg

1, Neue Burg, Heldenplatz (52 524/www.khm.at). U1, U2, U4 Karlsplatz/tram 1, 2, D, J. **Open** 10am-6pm Tue-Sun. **Admission** €9; €6.50 concessions; €8 with Vienna Card. **No credit cards**. **Map** p242 D7.

The three collections of the fine arts museums in the Hofburg are an excuse to enter the imposing edifice of the Neue Burg, from the central balcony of which Hitler announced the Anschluss. The museums are located on either side of the Neue Burg's monumental central staircase.

The **Ephesus Museum** displays the spoils from 19th-century Austrian archaeological digs in Ephesus and Samothrace.

The **Collection of Arms and Armour** was originally made up of ceremonial weapons acquired by two Habsburgs (Archdukes Ernst of Styria and Ferdinand of Tyrol); this is now one of the world's most extensive displays of arms and armour from the 15th to the 17th centuries.

The **Collection of Ancient Musical Instruments**, also started by Ferdinand of Tyrol, is a chronologically arranged exhibition of the world's greatest assembly of Renaissance instruments. Together with the initiative of Austrian conductor Nikolaus Harnoncourt, it has helped rekindle worldwide interest in early music played on original instruments.

Völkerkundemuseum

1, Neue Burg, Heldenplatz (534 30-0/www.ethno-museum.ac.at). U1, U2, U4 Karlsplatz/tram 1, 2, D, J/bus 2a. **Open** 10am-6pm Mon, Wed-Sun. **Admission** €7.50; €5.50 concessions; €2 school children (groups of 10 or more); €6.50 with Vienna Card; free entry on 26 Oct. **No credit cards.** **Map** p242 D7.

While the Austro-Hungarian Empire dominated most of central Europe and the Balkans, it never got a foothold in more far-flung places. Nonetheless it managed to assemble a more than respectable collection of exotica, now housed in this Ethnological Museum. The holdings are divided into geographical sections, with China, Korea and Japan on the ground floor, and Polynesia and the Americas on the first floor. A hunter/gatherer department occupies a separate wing. The anthropologically minded will enjoy the varied exhibits, the most celebrated of which is the crown of Montezuma, a unique feathered headdress that's the most valuable specimen on display in the Central America section. A darkened adjoining room shows the best-preserved collection of these feather mosaics in the world.

In & around Herrengasse

On Michaelerplatz is **Café Griensteidl** (*see p123*), a reconstructed version of what was once one of Vienna's most famous literary cafés and second home to Arthur Schnitzler, Hugo von Hofmannsthal and others. Closed at the turn of the 20th century, it was reopened in 1990. On the opposite side of the square is the Michaelerkirche. A neo-classical façade hides the church's Gothic origins, but these can be seen from a pretty courtyard by entering Kohlmarkt 11. Notice here too the well-conserved baroque carriage houses. In the middle of the square there are also some nondescript Roman ruins, considered by locals to be the remains of a brothel. They are displayed in a designer recess by Hans Hollein.

West of Michaelerplatz runs Herrengasse – Lords' Lane – lined with innumerable palaces that are today primarily used to house government agencies. The Landhaus at No.13 was the seat of the Lower Austrian regional government until a new administrative centre was built in the regional capital St Pölten. The building witnessed the outbreak of the 1848 Revolution when troops fired on a crowd demanding the resignation of arch-reactionary Prince Metternich. Opposite the Landhaus is the **Palais Ferstel** and **Café Central**. The streets heading south off Herrengasse lead to the impressive, but lifeless, ministerial quarter around Minoritenplatz. The cobbled square is dominated by the Gothic Minoritenkirche and

Rachel Whiteread's holocaust memorial in **Judenplatz**. *See p63.*

its striking octagonal tower. Inside is a curious copy (in elaborate, minute mosaic) of Leonardo's *Last Supper*, commissioned by Napoleon in 1806.

Schottentor & the Mölker Bastei

To the west, Herrengasse narrows into Schottengasse leading eventually to the Ringstrasse at Schottentor, a busy junction overlooked by the neo-Gothic **Votivkirche** (*see p69*). To the north is a network of fine, if rather lifeless, 19th-century streets, but to the south are some of the few remaining chunks of the old city walls, the minuscule but picturesque Mölker Bastei. Take the Mölkerstieg steps beside the Spar store, near the corner of Schottengasse, that lead into Schreyvogelgasse. It is here that Harry Lime made his first appearance in *The Third Man*, in the doorway of No.8. Much has been made of the house at No.10, the Dreimäderlhaus (1803), where it was purported that Schubert had a carnal interest in all three of the daughters who lived there. Today it is probably of more interest as the premises of fashionable shoe designer Ludwig Reiter (*see p138*).

Follow the cobbled street round and you are now on the Mölker Bastei, the old rampart. Beethoven lived for a period at No.8, the Pasqualatihaus (1798). The house has a small museum (535 8905; open 9am-12.15pm, 1-4.30pm Tue-Sun; admission €1.80; 70¢ concessions; no credit cards).

Freyung

The name Schottentor (Scots' Gate) refers to the supposedly Scottish Benedictine monks whom the Babenbergs invited to run the church and monastery they had founded in 1155. The monks in fact came from Scotia Major (the medieval name for Ireland). One of the many ersatz Irish pubs that flourish in Vienna now (and throughout Europe, for that matter) has led a rather absurd campaign to have the name changed. Schottenstift (Monastery of the Scots) offered asylum to fugitives in the Middle Ages, which is the origin of the name of the broad tract that runs past the monastery, the Freyung or sanctuary. Ignore the church and pass through the adjacent entrance to the Schottenhof, a spacious neo-classical courtyard. On the opposite side is the Museum in Schottenstift, a fairly recent creation installed in the rooms of the Prelacy. It has some good 17th- and 18th-century Dutch, Flemish and Austrian paintings, but is most famed for the Schottenaltar, a 15th-century winged altarpiece featuring a superb painting of *The Flight to*

Egypt, with a view of Vienna in the background. Freyung itself, its broad cobbled pavements flanked by the palaces **Harrach** and **Ferstel** (*see p61* for both) to the south and the so-called Schubladlkastenhaus (Chest of Drawers House, 1774), is transformed on Fridays when a market of organic farmers, apiarists, schnapps distillers and various back-to-the-landers is held. Further along on the north side is the **KunstForum**, a space sponsored by Bank Austria, hosting prestigious itinerant exhibitions of modern painting (*see p159*).

Am Hof

Freyung slopes gently upwards to Am Hof, the biggest square in the Innere Stadt. Formerly the power centre of the Babenberg dynasty and scene of jousts and executions, today it is a little windswept and lifeless except on Fridays and Saturdays when an antiques and antiquarian book market operates.

Am Hof's most impressive building is the Kirche am Hof from the balcony of which the end of the Holy Roman Empire was effectively announced in 1806 when, on the orders of Napoleon, Emperor Franz II proclaimed himself Franz I of Austria. Today it's the spiritual home of Vienna's Croatian community. Its Gothic core is only seen from the lanes at the rear since the façade is resoundingly baroque, crowned by a host of angels in honour of the Nine Choirs of Angels to whom the church is dedicated.

Other buildings worth noting on Am Hof include: the Feuerwehr Zentrale, surely the grandest fire station in Christendom, with its Firefighting Museum (the Bürgerliches Zeughaus – the Citizens' Armoury, 1732) at No.10; and a couple of fine baroque houses at Nos.12 and 13. In the basement of No.12 is the tenebrous Urbani Keller, the most elaborate and possibly the gloomiest of Vienna's beer cellars.

The Engelapotheke chemist's shop at Bognergasse 9, just past Am Hof, is a small masterpiece of Jugendstil decoration. Naglergasse, a narrow street running parallel to Am Hof, is the natural continuation of Graben. The street was an extension of the same Roman fortifications and has some well-conserved baroque façades hiding original Gothic houses.

Judenplatz

As you leave Am Hof to the north, an attractive network of ancient lanes and alleyways leads to what was Vienna's medieval Jewish ghetto. Schulhof, a pretty cobbled lane beside the Kirche am Hof, is home to two of Vienna's many small museums – the **Uhrenmuseum** (Clock Museum) and the **Puppen- und**

Spielzeug Museum (Doll and Toy Museum) – as well as a string of alluring bars and restaurants. From here the magnificent baroque Kurrentgasse leads north into Judenplatz, the centre of the ghetto, dating back to the 12th century. Surrounded by a magnificent array of baroque and 19th-century buildings, Judenplatz is perhaps the most beautiful square in the 1st district. Its centrepiece is British sculptor Rachel Whiteread's austere monument to Austrian victims of the Shoah. This concrete cast of a library with the spines of the books facing inward is set on a low plinth engraved with the names of the camps. Although it was scheduled to be unveiled in 1998, 60 years after the Kristallnacht, the opening was held up until 2000 by the unexpected discovery of the remains of the medieval synagogue, burnt down in the ferocious pogrom of 1421. Virulent disputes as to the suitability of Whiteread's design also delayed matters. By converting the ground floor of the nearby Torah Jewish school into the recently opened **Museum Judenplatz**, a permanent home was made for those parts of the synagogue which could be salvaged.

Facing Whiteread's monument is a statue of Gottfried Lessing (1729-81), a major figure of the German Enlightenment whose work *Nathan the Wise* was a paean to tolerance towards the Jews. The original was destroyed by the Nazis; the sculptor Siegfried Charoux made a new cast after World War II but it was not re-erected until 1982.

At No.2 is Zum Grossen Jordan (The Great Jordan), the oldest house in the square. The relief on its façade dates from the 16th century and could not be further from the spirit of Lessing, in that it actually celebrates the events of 1421. Depicting the baptism of Christ, it has a Latin inscription that reads: 'By baptism in the River Jordan bodies are cleansed from disease and evil, so all secret sinfulness takes flight. Thus the flame rising furiously through the whole city in 1421 purged the terrible crimes of the Hebrew dogs. As the world was once purged by the flood, so this time it was purged by fire.'

Apart from the fine apartment buildings, the square's most spectacular edifice is the Böhmische Hofkanzlei (Bohemian Chancery) from which the Habsburgs ruled over the Czech lands for almost 300 years. It is now the seat of the Constitutional and Administrative Courts.

Puppen- und Spielzeugmuseum

1, Schulhof 4 (535 6860/www.puppen museumwien.com). U3 Herrengasse, U1, U3, Stephansplatz/bus 1a, 3a. **Open** 10am-6pm Tue-Sun. **Admission** €4.70; €2.35 over-6s; €3.15 per person (groups of 10 or more); €1.60 per person (children's groups). **No credit cards. Map** p242 E6.

The Doll and Toy Museum is contained within an 18th-century house adjacent to the Uhrenmuseum (*see below*). It was adapted into a private museum in 1989 for 600 dolls and toys from the 19th and 20th centuries – mostly of French and German origin.

Uhrenmuseum

1, Schulhof 2 (533 2265/www.museum.vienna.at). U3 Herrengasse, U1, U3 Stephansplatz. **Open** 9am-4.30pm Tue-Sun. **Admission** €3.60; €1.80 concessions; €1.40 6-18s; €5.40 family with two children under 19; free 9am-noon Fri (except holidays); free tours every first/third Sun of month (guides speak English if requested). **No credit cards. Map** p242 E6.

Covering three floors of the baroque Obizzi Palace, the Clock Museum houses timepieces and chronometers from the 15th to the 20th centuries (the most recent piece is a 1992 computer clock).

Museum Judenplatz

1, Judenplatz 8 (535 0431/www.jmw.at). U3 Herrengasse. **Open** 10am-6pm Mon-Thur, Sun; 10am-2pm Fri. **Admission** €3; €1.50 concessions. **No credit cards. Map** p242 E6.

Opened in 2002, the Museum Judenplatz owes its existence to the ruins of the medieval synagogue unearthed during modifications to the square. It is located in the Misrachi-Haus Torah school. Visitors descend three flights of stairs (clad in the same porous concrete as Whiteread's monument) to see an informative audio-visual re-creation in English of life in Vienna's medieval ghetto. Detailing living conditions, the role of the synagogue and relations with Gentile power, the digital re-creation of the ghetto's topography is marred by poor lighting and looks rather washed out. A tunnel leads under Judenplatz to the synagogue's foundations, which are superbly presented in subdued lighting on a raised plinth. The rest of the building continues to function as a Torah school and the ground floor now houses the Simon Wiesenthal Archive.

Maria am Gestade & around

The recently re-cobbled Jordangasse leads into Wipplingerstrasse and the Altes Rathaus, the baroque Old Town Hall, home to various municipal agencies and the interesting **Museum of Austrian Resistance**. Its courtyard encloses a beautiful fountain by Donner, the Andromeda Brunnen (1745), and the Gothic Salvatorkapelle, the town hall chapel, whose fine Renaissance portal is located in Salvatorgasse directly behind.

Wipplingerstrasse heads north-west towards the Ringstrasse, past an enormous sign showing a chimney sweep (a much-loved figure in Viennese mythology) and over the Jugendstil bridge spanning Tiefer Graben, once the course of the Alserbach Danube tributary. More atmospheric is the walk to the left of the Altes Rathaus and along the cobbled Salvatorgasse to

A trot through time: Vienna's fiakers

As romantic as the gondolas of Venice, the horse-drawn carriages of Vienna are a graceful reminder of times gone by. Known as fiakers, these carriages queue up at tourist landmarks, inviting you to trot back in time. Fiaker drivers favour the dress code of their forefathers; many of them are bewhiskered, attired in checkered trousers and topped with a bowler hat. If you don metaphorical blinkers and block out references to modern life, you can easily imagine Vienna at the turn of the 20th century.

The name fiaker was first mentioned in 1622. It came from Paris where horse-drawn cabs for hire lined up outside the 'Auberge Saint Fiacre', an inn located on a street named after the Irish monk, Saint Fiacrus. Later in the 17th century, the entrepreneur Nicole Sauvage saw the commercial potential of cabs-for-hire. Before long, cabs pursued their fares on every corner of the Continent's cities. In 1693, during the reign of Leopold I, the first Viennese fiaker licence was issued.

Rigid rules applied to the processing of fiaker drivers. Not only did every candidate for a licence have to show he had a history in the transport trade, he also had to prove he owned a certain amount of property and was of upstanding character. He was also held to a strict code of conduct. If a driver refused a ride, he was imprisoned for 48 hours and given ten lashes with a birch branch.

Over time, the role of fiakers changed from being simple taxis. Today, of course, they exist primarily as a way to engage in a spot of nostalgia. These two-horse carriages, now driven by women as well as men, are historically accurate in design. Some are lacquered black with red leather tufted interiors, others are painted fairy-tale snow white with vases of roses standing sentinel. In inclement weather, the carriage tops are closed and you can huddle under thick woollen blankets. It's hard not to be caught up in the mesmerising clippety-clop of horse hooves on cobblestones.

Despite their long history, fiakers aren't exempt from present-day controversy. Recent newspapers headlines such as 'Stop pooh bags!' pitted the city council against animal rights groups who lambasted the city's plans requiring fiaker horses to wear nappies. The whiff of contention over animal waste still hangs over Vienna.

Present day cabbies are fluent in local history and will gladly add commentary as you trot along. Be sure to enquire about the price before you depart. Both long and short tours are available, with varying fares; none is cheap. A tour of 40 minutes costs about €58 for the entire cab, which easily seats four people.

Fiaker ranks are on Stephansplatz (north side of the cathedral), in Augustinerstrasse (in front of the Albertina Museum) and on Heldenplatz (in front of the monument to Archduke Charles). For an authentic journey back in time, hire a fiaker early in the morning or on a quiet Sunday when few but you, the driver and the horses populate the streets. After your ride, head to one of the local coffee houses to top off your experience with a cherry – order a 'fiaker café' (a double espresso served with powdered sugar, heated cherry brandy and cream, served with a cherry on top). True aficionados may wish to visit the Fiaker Museum at Veronikagasse 12 in the 17th district (401 060). But opening hours are so limited (phone for details) that your best bet is to experience the real thing.

Sightseeing

where Maria am Gestade (Our Lady of the Riverbank), one of Vienna's finest Gothic churches, looks over a flight of steps leading down into Concordiaplatz. It used to have strong ties to the Danube fishermen and today attracts worshippers from Vienna's Czech community.

Archiv des österreichischen Widerstands

1, Wipplingerstrasse 8 (Altes Rathaus, stairway 3) or Salvatorgasse 7 (53 436/90319/www.doew.at). U1, U3 Stephansplatz, U1, U4 Schwedenplatz/tram 1, 2. **Open** 9am-5pm Mon-Thur. **Admission** free. **Map** p242 E6.
The Austrian Resistance Archive was founded in 1963 by ex-resistance fighters and anti-Fascist historians to chronicle the fate of the 2,700 Austrian resistance fighters executed by the Nazis (and the thousands more who died in the camps). The events pre- and post-1938 leading to Austria's disastrous pact with the Third Reich are also portrayed. Yet the exhibition reeks of neglect and underfunding. Despite a welter of fascinating material detailing the horror – mostly photos, personal effects, and propaganda – the whole thing needs a major overhaul. To gain access, visitors call at the archive and a student volunteer (military service refuseniks) is sent to open up.

Hoher Markt

Vienna's oldest square and site of Vindabona's Roman forum, Hoher Markt today is an ungainly ensemble of historicist apartment buildings and shabby post-1945 warrens. At midday tourists congregate around the Jugendstil Ankeruhr, an elaborate mechanical clock encrusted into a sort of bridge between the two monumental edifices belonging to the Anker insurance company. The figures that trundle out on the hour include Marcus Aurelius, Roman governor of Vindabona, and composer Josef Haydn. The full list and a history of the clock are given on a plaque in various languages on the insurance building. Inside the bridge beneath the clock look out for the stone brackets depicting Adam, Eve, an angel and a devil with a pig's snout. Running below is Bauernmarkt, a swish shopping street with a number of designer stores and eateries. The centrepiece of Hoher Markt is Fischer von Erlach the Younger's *Vermählungsbrunnen* (Marriage Fountain) dramatising Mary's marriage to Joseph, presided over by a high priest – undoubtedly a figment of the sculptor's baroque imagination. In the shopping arcade on the south side there's access to Roman ruins.

Römische Ruinen unter dem Hoher Markt

1, Hoher Markt 3 (535 5606). U1, U3 Stephansplatz **Open** 1-4.30pm Mon; 9am-12.15pm Tue-Sun. **Admission** €1.80; 70¢ concessions. **No credit cards. Map** p242 E6.

Hoher Markt is the core of Roman Vindabona but all that remains is this site of officers' quarters with baths and underground heating, dating from AD 1-4. The ruins beneath Hoher Markt were reopened in 2001 after much-needed restoration; there's an informative display on life in the Roman garrison.

Judengasse & Ruprechtskirche

North of Hoher Markt further traces of medieval Jewish Vienna are visible along Judengasse and Seitenstättegasse, where the Stadttempel, the main synagogue is located. Photos show Judengasse in the 19th century as bustling with second-hand clothes dealers and today the rag trade still operates in the form of small boutiques.

However, in the early 1980s the area became the hub of Vienna's nightlife scene, receiving the moniker of 'The Bermuda Triangle' – the place you can never find your way out of. Today it's all rather post-teenie and naff, but the abundance of bars and restaurants catering for a well-heeled crowd gives the area a buzz. During the day the streets are sleepy, often the only presence being the armed police who patrol permanently since the 1983 attack on the Stadttempel, which left three dead.

Built in neo-classical style by Josef Kornhäusel in 1826, the synagogue is one of the few that escaped destruction in the Nazi years, probably because setting it on fire would have endangered neighbouring houses. It can be visited with a combined ticket that includes entrance to the Jewish Museum and Museum Judenplatz. At No.2 is the so-called Kornhäusel-Turm, built by the architect as a studio and, according to local legend, a refuge from his nagging wife. Its sheer size can best be appreciated from behind in Judengasse.

Sterngasse runs off Judengasse to the west, and is worth checking out for the splendid English bookshop **Shakespeare & Co** (*see p133*). At the end of the street a flight of steps named after Theodor Herzl, the Viennese founder of Zionism, leads down to Marc-Aurel-Strasse.

At the end of Judengasse is a railed balcony overlooking the busy Franz-Josefs-Kai and the Donaukanal. Among the high-rise buildings of the 2nd district, an area especially punished by bombing, is the surprisingly modest headquarters of OPEC, scene in 1976 of one of Carlos the Jackal's most daring one-man kidnappings. While you're admiring the cityscape from here you may well overlook the ivy-clad **Ruprechtskirche** to your right, the oldest church in the city, whose existence is documented from 1137. Squat and Romanesque, it is a great tonic after Vienna's baroque excesses. The steps take you down to a broad concourse leading east to Schwedenplatz. It's all 1970s cement, but the human traffic descending into its busy U-Bahn station or waiting for trams makes it one of those bustling zones that Vienna often seems to lack. The ice-cream salon Am Schwedenplatz at No.17 is a local legend.

To the west of the steps in Morzinplatz stands the Monument to the Victims of Fascism (1985) on the site of the former Hotel Metropole, Gestapo headquarters during the war and bombed to bits in 1945. The monument is emblazoned with the yellow Star of David, the pink triangle and other symbols of Nazi enemies. Further west the streets of the 19th-century textile quarter form an extraordinarily homogeneous network of monumental apartment buildings, but have a deserted moribund air. Apart from a number of lively bars and restaurants along Salzgries, the only other attraction around here is the Rudolfsplatz park and the Black Market record store nearby on Gonzagagasse.

In & around Rotenturmstrasse

Named after the red tower that formerly capped the city wall, Rotenturmstrasse cuts through the northern section of the Innere Stadt. Lively and commercial, it is a good pointer for those unfamiliar with the city. At its most northerly point it divides the Bermuda Triangle zone from the medieval streets around Fleischmarkt, the old meat market. Among the shops and restaurants there are a few discreet sights. At No.7 for instance, there is a plaque marking Billy Wilder's home when he was a schoolboy in Vienna; opposite is a fine Jugendstil façade at No.14. Next door a pleasant courtyard houses Vienna's first vegetarian restaurant, Siddhartha, and the headquarters of the Austrian Buddhist Society. The street widens at No.11 where the narrow Griechengasse descends towards Schwedenplatz.

Visible from the steps is the late 18th-century Greek Orthodox church. It is no longer in use; services are now held at Hansen's flamboyant Griechische Kirche (1861) – full of gilt and decorative brickwork – on Fleischmarkt. Built for Greek subjects of the Habsburgs, this Byzantine fantasy is the most arresting edifice on the street, but with two carpet stores on its ground floor, it is hard to believe this is still a place of worship. Sunday is the best day to view the interior: during the rest of the week it's impossible to penetrate beyond the dark yet ornate arcaded hallway.

Adjoining the church at No.11 is another of those truly Viennese institutions, the Griechenbeisl

(*see p103*), one of the city's oldest restaurants, with connections to the Greek community and famous past patrons such as Beethoven, Brahms and Schubert.

Fleischmarkt runs directly into Postgasse and winds round into the beautiful Schönlaterngasse with its fine baroque façades, such as the Basilikenhaus at No.7. At No.5 is the vast Heiligenkreuzerhof, a fine courtyard bounded by mid-18th century outbuildings which was the city premises of the Cistercian monks of Heiligenkreuz (*see p201*). Originally an outlet for the monastery's produce, the buildings are now highly desirable apartments with the occasional ground-floor gallery. This oasis of calm is currently threatened by the opening of a waxworks promising to attract 500,000 visitors a year.

Schönlaterngasse, 'the street of the Beautiful Lanterns' (don't miss the one on No.6), comes out on Sonnenfelsgasse, which, along with the parallel Bäckerstrasse, runs from the Alte Universität (or now Dr-Ignaz-Seipel-) Platz to Lugeck, on Rotenturmstrasse.

Apart from the Renaissance portal at No.15 and the excellent Kunstbuchhandlung (one of the best art bookshops in Vienna) at No.8, the most noteworthy feature of Sonnenfelsgasse is the massive baroque Hildebrandthaus at No.3. Inside is the labyrinthine Zwölf-Apostelkeller ('Twelve Apostles Cellar'), Vienna's largest and best-loved *Bierkeller*.

Bäckerstrasse also has a handful of remarkable houses with arresting façades and courtyards, such as the marvellous Renaissance Hof at No.7, the premises of violin and piano manufacturers. The Alt Wien at No.19 is a place worth remembering for late-night drinking. Note also the bizarre patch of mural that was unearthed during restoration work at No.12, showing a bespectacled cow playing backgammon with a wolf – supposedly a parody of the tension between Catholics (the cow) and Protestants (the wolf) in 17th-century Vienna.

To the east Bäckerstrasse opens out into Dr-Ignaz-Seipel-Platz and the buildings of the Alte Universität, the Akademie der Wissenschaft (Academy of Sciences) and the Jesuitenkirche. The latter was built by an unknown architect in 1627, but both the façade and interior were substantially altered in 1703-5 by trompe-l'oeil master Andrea Pozzo who introduced a painted false 'dome'. This illusion works best from a spot on the nave marked with a white stone. The square is remarkable for an absence of modern buildings, but once you're through the tunnel on the southern side, it's back to the spaciousness of the Ringstrasse.

The Ringstrasse

The august arc of the Ringstrasse epitomises majestic Vienna in all its pomp.

Maps p242 and p243

Unlike most cities of its size and stature, Vienna kept its city walls intact well into the 1850s. Outside lay a vast area of greenbelt known as the *Glacis*, which separated the old city from the suburbs. City and suburbs became a single administrative entity in 1850, leading to huge population growth and hence an acute housing shortage. In response, Emperor Franz Josef in 1857 initiated a building programme that helped give Vienna the face it bears today.

The broad, horseshoe-shaped Ringstrasse, and an outer ring formed by the streets running from Universitätsstrasse to the Stadtpark were constructed along the Glacis over the following three decades. They were to become the equivalent of the Parisian *grands boulevards* – thoroughfares designed to quell revolt by ensuring the rapid movement of troops to scenes of unrest. Nevertheless the Ringstrasse's very existence is a testimony to the democratisation of public life in 19th-century Vienna, following the 1848 Revolution.

While the first Ringstrasse project, the **Votivkirche**, was built to reaffirm imperial absolutism, the military defeats of 1859 and 1866 and the advent of a constitutional monarchy in 1867 forced a reassessment of the entire programme. Gradually the emphasis came to be on buildings of public utility – the city hall, the university, the parliament, the museums, the opera house, the Burgtheater and the numerous parks and gardens. The array of buildings takes some beating when it comes to sheer pomp and ostentation. 'A Martian coming to earth would unhesitatingly land at Vienna, thinking it to be the capital of the planet.' Bill Bryson's observation is close to the mark. Although heralding a new age, the buildings of the Ringstrasse, apart from Otto Wagner's **Postsparkasse**, contributed nothing in the way of innovation. Instead the models of the past were preferred, to express the aspirations of the burgeoning Viennese middle classes, a style baptised as historicism.

Think of a day along the Ringstrasse as a way to refresh your knowledge of the principal European architectural styles. Each section of the road has its own name, such as the Burgring for the stretch that passes the **Hofburg**. As well as the civic edifices there are innumerable palatial apartment buildings. According to

dissident architect Adolf Loos, these enabled Viennese landlords to fulfil their wish to own a palace and their tenants' wish to live in one.

The vast majority of Vienna's temples to high art are located on the Ringstrasse or a stone's throw away. The world-famous Staatsoper (State Opera House) was the first public building to be opened on the hallowed street in May 1869. For many years the Opernball with its ostentatious show of wealth and neo-monarchist nostalgia, was the focus of virulent left-wing/anarchist demonstrations. Spirits also run high in and around the Burgtheater, possibly the most important theatre in the German-speaking world.

Down a side street off the Ringstrasse, behind the Imperial Hotel, lies Vienna's foremost concert hall, the **Musikverein** (*see p169*). It is Theophil Hansen's most extravagant work, for some the culminating work of historicist decoration.

Today the street is no longer the address of choice it once was – traffic has put paid to that. The buildings now tend to be used as offices, with shops and restaurants on the ground floors. This commercial activity is also on the decline as high rents dissuade retailers and parking restrictions make access difficult.

The best way to familiarise yourself with the Ringstrasse and get an idea of the dimensions of Vienna's inner core is to take a tram ride round the whole Ring, which includes the canal embankment too, not strictly speaking a part of the Ringstrasse. Tram 1 goes round clockwise and Tram 2 anticlockwise.

Donaukanal to Schottentor

The Schottenring ('Scots' Ring') is the least interesting stretch of the Ringstrasse. It was named after the Benedictine monks who established a church and monastery just inside the city walls in the late 12th century. Yet there are several notable buildings along this section, including Vienna's only inner city high-rise, the Ringturm (1955), which looks over the Donaukanal, cutting quite a dash with its night time illumination.

On the opposite side of the Ringstrasse, between two apartment buildings, you get a glimpse of the Rossauer Kaserne, a bizarre red-brick barracks, one of three built in the wake of the 1848 Revolution and now occupied by the

Rathaus

police. The finest public building along here, at Schottenring 20, is the Börse (stock exchange), built by one of the major Ringstrasse architects, Theophil Hansen. The subdued red of the brickwork (*Hansenrot* as it is often referred to) and the white stone of the cornices make this one of the Ringstrasse's most elegant edifices.

Schottentor to Oper

It's worth walking this section as the display of public buildings is awesome. Apart from a minor detour to take in the **Votivkirche**, it's a straight run past the **Universität**, the **Rathaus** and **Burgtheater** (*see p194*), before a rest in the **Volksgarten**. Further on come the **Parlament**, the **Kunsthistorisches Museum** and **Naturhistorisches Museum**. These last two, designed by the great German architect Gottfried Semper, were conceived as part of a grandiose plan that would link them to the Neue Burg and its planned mirror image on the other side of Heldenplatz by means of two triumphal arches across the Ringstrasse. The building of this so-called Kaiserforum was ditched after the fall of the House of Habsburg.

Votivkirche

9, Rooseveltplatz. U2 Schottentor/tram 1, 2, D. **Map** p242 D5.
The Votivkirche was built opposite the spot where Franz Josef survived an assassination attempt by a Hungarian nationalist in 1853. Work began in 1854 and wasn't completed until 25 years later, owing to the exacting craftsmanship demanded by the 27-year-old architect Heinrich Ferstel. Two monumental

steeples rendered with elaborate stone carving recall the great Gothic cathedral of Chartres. Yet there's something moribund about this church, possibly because it never had any parishioners apart from soldiers of the nearby barracks, the Rossauerkaserne. The Votivkirche is beset with restoration problems and is often draped in advertising hoardings in an attempt to raise funds.

Universität

1, Dr Karl-Lueger-Ring. U2 Schottentor/tram 1, 2, D. **Map** p242 D6.
Due to its decisive role in the events of 1848, the university was out of favour with the forces of reaction and it was not until 1870 that this site was secured. Work began in 1873 with that master of pastiche Heinrich Ferstel given command once again. His brief was to build in Renaissance style, echoing the secular universities of Italy. It is easy to gain access to the university in term time, and a walk around the arcades of the inner courtyard is very pleasant. Try to get into the Grosser Festsaal, the main hall, to see Klimt's ceiling frescoes depicting the seven pillars of wisdom. It is clearly marked via the main entrance on the Ringstrasse, but not officially open to the public. Try to mingle with the crowds attending the graduation ceremonies frequently held here.

Rathaus

1, Rathausplatz. U2 Rathaus/tram 1, 2, D. **Map** p242 D6.
Forming the centrepiece of Rathausplatz and its gardens, the town hall is undoubtedly the most imposing edifice on the Ringstrasse. Inspired by Flemish Gothic and resembling the Hôtel de Ville of Brussels, Friedrich Schmidt's building is clearly visible from the Hofburg and was a constant reminder to the court that the burghers were now running the show.

Visitors are free to wander through the seven inner courtyards, but must join a guided tour to see the elaborate interior decoration and numerous frescoes illustrating scenes from Vienna's past. Open to the public too is the vast Rathaus Keller, a touristy but impressively grand cellar serving beer and roast pork. The Rathausplatz has become something of a people's playground since the early 1990s when the socialist mayor Helmut Zilk took it upon himself to liven up the city's dreary nightlife. Throughout the summer, films of operas are shown on a giant screen in front of the town hall and the square is inundated with stands offering food and drink.

Parlament

1, Dr Karl Renner-Ring 3 (www.parlament.gv.at).
U2, U3 Volkstheater/tram 1, 2, D.
The neo-classical Parlament stares across the Ring at the Imperial Palace to the east. Built by Danish architect Theophil Hansen, it bristles with Hellenic statuary and bronze chariots. The façade of the building appears obscured by the two lateral ramps and the rather splendid statue of Athena, set in a fountain representing the Danube, Inns, Elbe and Vltava. Architecturally it is as problematic as the birth of Austrian democracy itself, and seen face-on

from pavement or tram-window level looks pitifully small. The building suffers from indifferent acoustics too. Nevertheless it is worth a walk up the ramp to take a closer look at the recently restored frontal frieze of Franz Josef I granting the first, highly limited democratic constitution.

Naturhistorisches Museum

1, Wien, Burgring 7 (52 177/www.nhm-wien.ac.at).
U2 Babenbergerstrasse, U2, U3 Volkstheater/tram 1, 2, D, J. **Open** 9am-6.30pm Mon, Thur-Sun; 9am-9pm Wed. **Admission** €6.50; €5 concessions. **No credit cards. Map** p242 D7.
One of the largest and most celebrated natural history museums in the world, this is the scientific counterpart to the Kunsthistorisches Museum across the square. It was opened in 1889 and not much has changed since; some of the display cases are over a century old, the labelling is in German and little has been done to embrace modern museum interactivity. The basis of the collection is the work of Emperor Franz Stefan, Maria Theresia's husband, an amateur scientist who collected skulls, fossils, precious stones, meteorites and rare stuffed animals. It also includes items acquired by Rudolph II and Prince Eugène of Savoy. The most valuable piece has only recently been put on display: the 'Venus of Willendorf' (found in the

Otto Wagner

Few architects – only Gaudí in Barcelona springs to mind – have left their imprint on a city like Otto Wagner has on Vienna. He was the architectural kingpin of turn-of-the-century Vienna and became a crucial link between 19th century historicism and modernism.

Born in 1841 to a family that encapsulated the bourgeois aspirations of the Ringstrasse era, Otto Wagner had the wealth and backing to be trained as an architect. His skills were later fine-tuned at the Academy of Fine Arts by the Staatsoper duo Siccardsberg and Van der Nüll. By the late 1860s Wagner was building apartments along the Ringstrasse and demonstrating himself to be a shrewd businessman in this time of unfettered speculation. He gradually acquired enough influence to dictate his own terms to the city's rich and powerful.

Central to Wagner's thinking was a firm belief in the parity of beauty and function (free from Loos' alarming, Freudian-rooted, loathing of ornamentation). This belief culminated in the one building that completely eschewed the historicist diktat of the Ringstrasse ensemble – the Postsparkasse (*see p75*), a masterpiece of 20th-century functionalist architecture.

However, it was in the 1890s via his involvement in urban engineering projects and exposure to the Secession movement that Wagner's functionalist vein first came to the fore. Advocating public transport as the key to modern urban planning, he was appointed chief architect of the new Vienna City Railway System. Between 1894 and 1901 he designed 30 stations and was instrumental in the planning and design of tunnels, viaducts and bridges. Most are still in use today, as a trip along the overground stretch of the present U6 from Spittelau to Längenfeldgasse illustrates. The U4 too is very much Wagner's baby. Out of town in Hietzing he designed the rather bombastic Kaiser Pavilion – the Emperor's own metro station (*see p92*). In contrast, his stations on the U4, U6 and S45 have an understated elegance with their delicate floral stucco and proud ironwork at the front, from the stanchions of the platform canopies to the railings between each station.

Another example of Wagner's aesthetic approach to civil engineering can be seen on the Nussdorfer Wehr- und Schleusenanlage – the weir and lock gates at the start of the Donaukanal in Nussdorf (*see p98*).

Wachau), a curvacious 11cm/4in-high limestone fertility symbol believed to be over 25,000 years old. The museum has minerals, zoological exhibits and a valuable collection of meteors. It also contains the world's largest collection of human skulls (some 43,000 – from 40,000 BC to the present). Here too is the largest single topaz known (110kg/243lb), and an ostrich given by Maria Theresia to her husband Franz Stephan studded with 761 precious stones and over 2,000 diamonds. In addition, the museum stores the oldest human sculpture, 'Fanny' from Stratzing (dated 32,000 BC), in a vault – photos of it are on display.

Kunsthistorisches Museum

1, Burgring 5 (entrance Maria Theresien-Platz) (52 524/www.khm.at). U2 Babenbergerstrasse, U2, U3 Volkstheater/tram 1, 2, D, J. Open 10am-6pm Tue, Wed, Fri-Sun; 10am-9pm Thur. English lecture tours Easter-1 Nov 11am, 3pm Tue-Sun. **Admission** €9; €6.50 concessions. *English lecture tours* (minimum of ten) €8 with Vienna Card. **No credit cards.** **Map** p242 D7.

The Museum of the Fine Arts is one of the finest of its kind in Europe, containing a huge collection of art treasures amassed by the Habsburgs. Indeed, more than a day is needed to appreciate these imperial galleries in full. The building's architecture and decoration – with its granites, marble and stucco interspersed with murals by Makart, Matsch, Gustav Klimt and his brother Ernst – produces an overwhelming effect upon entry. The main galleries on the first floor are arranged in a horseshoe plan with Flemish, German and Dutch paintings in the east wing and Italian work in the west.

Most visitors begin a tour in Room X, the busiest in the museum, with its almost unrivalled collection of work by Pieter Bruegel the Elder, acquired by Rudolph II. The nature theme of Bruegel's work can be seen in pictures such as *Hunters in the Snow* (1565). *The Peasant Wedding Feast* (1568-9) echoes repercussions of the Reformation and was the source of inspiration for Jacob Jordaens' boisterous and bawdy *The Feast of the Bean King* (c1656) in Room XI. Moving to the smaller rooms (XVI), *The Adoration of the Trinity* (1511) illustrates Albrecht Dürer's resplendent use of colour. Continuing to Room XVIII, Holbein's *Jane Seymour* (1536), his first portrait executed as Henry VIII's court painter, is crisply objective in characterisation and costume. The Flemish painter Anthony van Dyck's *Portrait of a Young Man in Armour* (c1624, Room XII) is a subtle psychological study contrasting hard, shiny metal with the softness of white lace and pale facial features.

Completed in 1898, the pillars either side of the lock gates are capped with two huge bronze lions. Wagner had hopes of transforming the whole of the Wiental into a rival to the Ringstrasse, but beyond the Gürtel little was completed apart from the railway.

Wagner lionised his contemporary Gustav Klimt as 'the greatest artist who ever walked the earth', sharing his messianic desire to do away with the dead wood of historicism. Both owed a considerable part of their fame to their participation in the shenanigans of the Ringstrasse. Unlike the tortured and obsessive painter, however, Wagner was a paradigm of the hyperactive rational artist-engineer, perfectly at home with the trappings of wealth and fame.

Wagner's villas in the Hütteldorf district and above all the revolutionary Kirche am Steinhof (*see p88*) built for the patients of a psychiatric hospital are worth the trek to the woods of the western suburbs. Otto Wagner died in 1918 and is buried in a tomb of his own design – disappointingly free of Jugendstil iconography – in the Hietzing cemetery (*see p93*).

Sightseeing

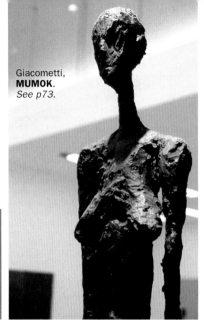

Giacometti,
MUMOK.
See p73.

Egon Schiele,
Leopold Museum. See p73.

Rooms XIII and XIV contain the museum's collection of Peter Paul Rubens; *Self Portrait* (1638-40) depicts him as a nobleman, but with tiny, tired lines around his eye. Nearby *The Little Fur* (Room XIII), the name Rubens gave to the portrait of his second wife Hélène Fourment, is a sensitively painted statement of the love of an older man for a younger woman (Hélène was only 16 when she married the 53-year-old Rubens). She also stood model for the voluptuous girl captured by a lurid satyr in the *Worship of Venus*. Some of the facets of Dutch 17th-century life are visible in Jan Steen's humorous *Topsy-Turvy World* (1663) and Jan Vermeer's reflective *Art of Painting* (1665-6) (Rooms XXIII-IV). The three Rembrandt self-portraits (1652, 1656 and 1657) in Room XV have withstood the critical survey of experts and de-attribution.

Crossing through the café takes you to Room VII and Bernardo Bellotto. He was taught by his uncle, the Venetian Antonio Canal, known as Canaletto. Here are several of Bellotto's views of Vienna, commissioned by Maria Theresia. Caravaggio's major work *Madonna of the Rosary Feast* (1606-7), in Room V, was purchased by Rubens and his friends after the artist's death in 1610. Three large rooms (I-III) are dedicated to the Venetian school: Tintoretto, Veronese and Titian. Room II has one of the few authenticated works by Giorgione, *The Three Philosophers*. Raphael's *Madonna in the Meadow* (1505) in Room IV is a serene piece, its composition influenced by Leonardo da Vinci.

On the ground floor, the east wing (the Kunstkammer) is a chamber of curiosities and exotica (Rooms XIX-XXXVII) with ornaments, glassware, clocks, globes and astrolabes. Benvenuto Cellini's gold and enamel salt cellar (1540) was a present to Archduke Ferdinand of Tyrol. The Egyptian and Near Eastern collections (I-VII) of the west wing include wall paintings, pottery, the remains of mummified bulls' heads, crocodiles and cats and examples of Books of the Dead on papyrus. The Greek and Roman collection in Rooms IX-XV includes the famous Gemma Augustea, a two-layered onyx cameo that commemorates the military victories of the first Roman Emperor.

Museumsquartier

Beyond Maria-Theresien-Platz lie the former imperial stables. Designed by Fischer von Erlach and completed by his son in the early 19th century, this charming if somewhat dilapidated collection of buildings was chosen as the site for the so-called Museum Quarter (MQ). The MQ was one of the most ambitious building projects undertaken in Vienna in the 20th century, costing approximately €145 million. It opened in 2001 and is one of the ten largest cultural complexes in the world. Spread over 60,000sq m (71,760sq yd) are brand-new art museums such as the **MUMOK** (Museum of Modern Art) and the **Leopold Museum**, the new venue of Vienna's principal contemporary art gallery, **Kunsthalle Wien** (*see p160*) as well as spaces dedicated to disciplines from architecture (**Architektur Zentrum Wien**) to modern dance (**Tanzquartier Wien**, *see p194*). Other tenants include the superbly interactive **Zoom** children's museum (*see p152*), a revitalised version of the **Tabak Museum** and the offices of the Vienna Festival.

MQ had a difficult birth. Popular pressure forced amendments to architects Ortner & Ortner's original plans, including the reduction in the size of the buildings and removal of a 56m (183.8 ft) 'reading tower'. The resulting ensemble fits so neatly and discreetly behind Fischer von Erlach's original baroque frontage that the only clue to the wonders within is the circular orange and white MQ logo burning out into the night.

As you enter via the vaulted central portal, a broad piazza stretches out to reveal the white limestone of the Leopold away to the left and the monolithic MUMOK lying at a slight oblique angle to the right. Between the two, the former winter riding hall has been modified to hold the Kunsthalle Wien concert/performance space and a restaurant. Several of the original sculpted horses' heads serve as a reminder of the building's equine past. In contrast, the windowless bunker of the MUMOK has infuriated both cutting-edgers and the forces of reaction. Plagued with structural problems from the start, it endured an embarrassing temporary closure during the first year and more recently a connecting bridge had to be built to help patrons find their way to the somewhat over-concealed restaurant/bar.

The **quartier 21** project (*see p160*) involved the rental of spaces in the front section to peripheral cultural initiatives such as electronic music, net activism, intercultural projects and video art. Resembling a mall selling bite-size pieces of culture, quartier 21 is as yet neither fish nor fowl.

Architektur Zentrum Wien

7, Museumsplatz 1 (522 3115/www.azw.at). U2 Museumsquartier, U2, U3 Volkstheater. **Open** 10am-9pm daily. **Admission** €5; €3.50 concessions. **Credit** (up to €22) AmEx, DC, JCB, MC, V. **Map** p242 D7.
Located in the vaulted section beyond the MUMOK, this is a documentation centre, archive and exhibition space that features developments in architecture internationally. Though its much vaunted permanent exhibition on 20th-century Austrian architecture has yet to be unveiled, it does produce excellent temporary displays such as 2001's 'Demolition Deutschland' that used film images of the post-war destruction of buildings in Germany as a metaphor for the transitory nature of power structures and their architectural manifestations: very cerebral, very interdisciplinary. Regular Sunday walking tours related to architectural themes in Vienna are also organised, see the website.

Art Cult Center/Tabak Museum

7, Mariahilfer Strasse 2 (526 17160/www.artcult.at). U2 Museumsquartier. **Open** 10am-5pm Tue, Wed, Fri; 10am-7pm Thur; 10am-2pm Sat, Sun. **Admission** €3.60; €2.20 concessions. **No credit cards**. **Map** p242 D8.
Reopened in 2001 on its original site, the Tobacco Museum is run by Austria Tabak, the state tobacco monopoly. There's a fine display of carved pipes, snuff boxes and cigarette packets. The museum also operates as an arts centre with concerts and exhibitions under the moniker 'Art Cult Center'.

Leopold Museum

7, Museumsplatz 1 (525 700/www.leopold museum.org). U2 Museumsquartier, U2, U3 Volkstheater. **Open** 10am-7pm Mon, Wed-Sun; 10am-9pm Fri. **Admission** €9; €7 concessions. **Credit** AmEx, DC, JCB, MC, V. **Map** p242 D7.
The Leopold Museum owes its existence to a Viennese ophthalmologist's lifelong obsession with the great Austrian expressionist Egon Schiele. In the 1950s, Rudolf Leopold acquired his first Schieles for a song. The museum's full catalogue now numbers over 5,000 works and embraces many other crucial figures of 19th-century and modernist Austrian painting. On the entrance floor are important works by Klimt and Richard Gerstl. The first floor is given over to the engrossing peasant art of Albin Egger-Lienz and mid-century Austrians such as Maria Lassnig and Oswald Oberhuber, while the top floor houses the Schiele paintings and other expressionists, most notably Oskar Kokoschka. A panoramic window offers a superb cityscape.

Museum moderner Kunst Stiftung Ludwig Wien (MUMOK)

7, Museumsplatz 1 (525 000/www.mumok.at). U2 Museumsquartier, U2, U3 Volkstheater. **Open** 10am-6pm Tue, Wed, Fri-Sun; 10am-9pm Thur. **Admission** €8; €6.50 concessions. **Credit** AmEx, DC, MC, V. **Map** p242 D7.
The forbidding confines of the Museum of Modern Art contain Vienna's premier contemporary art collection exhibited over five floors. In all MUMOK offers a rather dour tour through the -isms of 20th-century art. The space is claustrophobic, accentuated by the absence of natural light. On the menu is a fairly impressive collection of American pop art by Jasper Johns, Warhol, Lichtenstein, Rauschenberg and so on, plus examples of parallel European movements such as radical realism, arte povera, abstract impressionism and land art. Lurking in the depths of the bunker is a fine résumé of the local contribution: Viennese actionism, a heady brew of animal sacrifice, action painting and public masturbation and defecation – concocted by figures such as Herman Nitsch, Arnulf Rainer and Gunther Brus.

The Ringstrasse parks

On the south side of the Ringstrasse there are three major parks, each offering a variety of curiosities – from statues and hothouses to classical music concerts. Some of the city's hottest nightspots are located here (out of earshot of Vienna's grumpy residents). There's also a good selection snack options, including a converted botanical garden.

Sightseeing

Burggarten

Main entrance: Burgring. U1, U4 Karlsplatz/tram 1, 2, D, J. **Open** *Apr-Oct* 6am-10pm daily. *Nov-Mar* 6am-8pm daily. **Map** p242 E7.

The Palace Gardens are leafy and informal, with expanses of lawn. In the past they were the preserve of tourists who came to photograph the marble Mozart Denkmal. This statue of the boy-wonder, set on a plinth depicting scenes from *Don Giovanni*, was moved here in 1953 from Augustinerplatz. But now Friedrich Ohmann's 1901 Palmenhaus has been restored to become one of Vienna's most spectacular restaurants, and the nearby Albertina reopened, summers here will be mighty crowded.

Schmetterlinghaus

(533 8570/fax 532 2872/www.schmetterlinghaus.at). U1, U4 Karlsplatz/tram 1, 2, D, J. **Open** *Apr-Oct* 10am-4.45pm Mon-Fri; 10am-6.15pm Sat, Sun. *Nov-Mar* 10am-3.45pm daily. **Admission** €4.70; €4 concessions; €3.30 6-26s; €2.20 3-6s. **Credit** AmEx, DC, JCB, MC, V. **Map** p242 E7.

The west wing of the Palmenhaus was converted into a butterfly house after restoration in 1999. Now it's home to around 40 species acquired from butterfly farms in Thailand, Costa Rica and Brazil, none of them rare or endangered. Several hundred butterflies fly freely in 85% humidity amid a welter of tropical vegetation, large trees and a waterfall.

The Pavillon in the **Volksgarten**.

Stadtpark

Main entrance: Johannesgasse (beside Stadtpark U-Bahn station). U2 Stadtpark, U3 Stubentor/ tram 1, 2. **Open** 24hrs daily. **Map** p243 F7.

The largest of the Ringstrasse parks, the Stadtpark stretches from just east of Schwarzenbergplatz to Stubentor, going beyond the causeway of the Wien river. The main entrance is flanked by superb stone-carved Jugendstil colonnades. Just to the north is the most emblematic building in the park, the neo-Renaissance Kursalon, a venue for rather tacky Strauss concerts. Apart from tourists and snoozing office workers, the park is also the stomping ground of dope dealers. Music is very much the theme here, and the schmaltzy but nonetheless finely executed statue of Johann Strauss junior draws many amateur photographers. Scattered around the park, you'll also find busts of Schubert, Bruckner and Lehár (he of *The Merry Widow*).

Volksgarten

Main entrance: Heldenplatz (opposite the Neue Burg). U2, U3 Volkstheater, U3 Herrengasse/tram 1, 2, D, J/bus 2a. **Open** *Apr-Oct* 6am-10pm daily. *Nov-Mar* 6am-8pm daily. **Map** p242 D7.

Despite its egalitarian-sounding name, the People's Garden was originally a playground for Vienna's beau monde at the turn of the 19th century. It was built after Napoleon's troops demolished the southern section of the city walls, so the frenchified garden layout is somewhat ironic. The centrepiece is the Doric Theseus-Tempel, commissioned by Napoleon as a replica of the Theseion in Athens to house Canova's statue Theseus and the Minotaur. This statue was moved to the staircase of the Kunsthistorisches Museum in 1890. Dear to the hearts of many Austrians is the statue of Empress Elisabeth (1837-98) at the northern corner. Today the name Volksgarten is synonymous with the large semi-open-air discotheque over the Ringstrasse from the museums, and with the superb Pavillon next door: a sleek 1950s construction where the tuned-in and turned-on of Vienna drink Caipirinhas to dope beats in the shadow of the Neue Burg (*see p183*).

Oper to the Schwarzenbergplatz

South-east of the Staatsoper, the Ringstrasse takes the name Kärntnerring, acknowledging the route south to Kärnten that bisects it at this point. This is the Ringstrasse at its most bustling, with the big names of Vienna's hotel trade. From the Staatsoper to the next major junction at Schwarzenbergplatz, shoppers spill out of the Ringstrassen Gallerien, an immaculately clean shopping centre.

Where Kärntnerring turns into Schubertring the Ringstrasse opens out into a vast rectangular concourse named after Karl von Schwarzenberg, hero of the Battle of Leipzig (1813). His equestrian statue stands amid the stream of today's iron horses that make Schwarzenbergplatz a nightmare to cross on foot. Undergoing modification in 2003, with the installation of new lighting by acclaimed Catalan architect Alfonso Arribas, the square is lined with monumental buildings such as the Kasino am Schwarzenberg. At the far end of the square stands the Russen Heldendenkmal (Russian Heroes' Monument), a not universally welcomed gift from the Soviet people commemorating their liberation of Vienna. In front of this column is the Hochstrahlbrunnen (Tall Fountain), built in 1873 in honour of Vienna's first mains water supply.

On the west side is the elegant art nouveau French Embassy (1912), with its vaguely oriental façade. On nearby Zaunergasse is the Arnold Schönberg Center (see p171).

Parkring & Stubenring

Beyond Schwarzenbergplatz, the north side of the Ringstrasse is lined with more top-of-the-range hotels overlooking the **Stadtpark** to the south. On foot it is more enjoyable to cut through the park and check out its memorials to Strauss and co, or in summer, to stop and listen to the free concerts held in the afternoon in front of the Kursalon. At Stubentor things pick up a little and on this last stretch of the Ringstrasse there are a couple of top-class sights. If you're in need of refreshment, call in at the highly attractive coffee house, Café Prückel (see p125).

Directly opposite the **Postsparkasse** is the former Kriegsministerium (Ministry of War), which today houses less bellicose sections of the civil service. This neo-baroque monster was completed as late as 1912 and demonstrates how little had changed ideologically and architecturally since the first Ringstrasse building was erected in the 1850s. Walk 500m (about 550yd) east and you reach the Donaukanal with its characteristic green railings. Overlooking the canal is the curious Urania, an observatory built in 1910 by Max Fabiani. Currently being renovated, it usually functions as a cinema and puppet theatre.

Museum für Angewandte Kunst (MAK)

1, Stubenring 5 (712 8000/www.mak.at).
U3 Stubentor, U4 Landstrasse/tram 1, 2.
Open 10am-6pm Wed, Fri-Sun; 10am-midnight Thur. **Admission** €9.90; €4 concessions; free under-10s; free Sat. **No credit cards.**
Map p243 F7.
The Museum of Applied Arts is to Austria what the Victoria & Albert Museum is to England (only smaller). The building dates from 1872 and is another neo-Renaissance work by Ferstel. The permanent

The best Minor sights

Zentralfriedhof
The old Jewish cemetery here is a haunting reminder of the destruction of a whole community. *See p94.*

Karl-Marx-Hof
When the Viennese led the world in social experimentation. *See p96.*

Kirche am Steinhof
Otto Wagner goes ecclesiastic with astonishing results. *See p88.*

Heeresgeschichtliches Museum
Doesn't tell the whole story, but an engrossing view of Habsburg military might and more in a stupendous setting. *See p79.*

Fernwärme
Few cities have a such an iconic municipal rubbish incinerator. *See p84.*

exhibition features splendid displays of Jugendstil furniture and design as well as Klimt's *Stoclet Frieze*. In the course of a revamping completed in 1993, the director, Peter Noever, invited several artists working in Vienna to devise concepts for the various rooms. Some are excellent: Franz Graf's blue room, Gang Art's installation for the carpet collection, Barbara Bloom's presentation of the chair collection in silhouette. A visit is full of unexpected pleasures. Don't miss the superb café and what must be Vienna's sexiest museum shop, full of designer trivia displayed in restaurant-like cold cabinets.

Postsparkasse

1, Georg-Coch-Platz 2 (www.postparkasse.at). U3 Stubentor/tram 1, 2. **Open** 8am-3pm Mon-Wed, Fri; 8am-5.30pm Thur. **Map** p243 F6.
Built from 1904 to 1912 and crammed into a narrow gap between apartment buildings, Otto Wagner's Postsparkasse (Post Office Savings Bank) is the most monumental of Vienna's modernist buildings. However, its conception as an alternative home for middle-class savings to the powerful Jewish-dominated banking houses of the late 19th century shrouds the building in an unpleasant cloud of anti-semitism. Quite unlike anything else along the Ringstrasse, the Postsparkasse shines like a beacon of modernity with its economy of ornamentation and radical choice of materials. The façade, with its slabs of grey marble held in place by metal studs (17,000 in all), is crowned by the institution's name rendered in unmistakable Jugendstil lettering overseen by stylised angels of victory wielding laurel wreaths. The Postsparkasse still functions as a bank, so can be seen during normal business hours.

3rd-9th Districts

From stark fascist towers to florid baroque masterpieces, the southern and western districts encompass some of the city's most diverse sights.

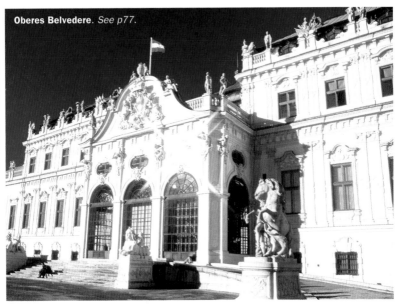

Oberes Belvedere. *See p77.*

Landstrasse

Maps p239, p240 & p241

One of Vienna's largest inner city districts, the 3rd, takes its name from Landstrasse-Hauptstrasse, the busy street heading south-east from the Stadtpark in the direction of Hungary. The district is bordered to the east by the Donaukanal with its opulent 19th-century apartment buildings. In its southern reaches the population is more markedly working class, holed up in modern flats and Red Vienna fortresses such as the mighty Rabenhof.

Landstrasse is the location of some of the city's most eclectic sights, top of the list being the magnificent **Belvedere Palace** just south of Schwarzenbergplatz. In a street facing the side entrance to Belvedere is the eccentric Bestattungsmuseum (Burial Museum) and south of the palace, beyond the Südbahnhof, is the splendid Heeresgeschichtliches Museum detailing military history. East of the palace, off Rennweg is the Vienna's main diplomatic

quarter with many fine buildings and churches. Down towards the canal, east of Landstrasse-Hauptstrasse, are the KunstHausWien and the Hundertwasser Haus, two curious buildings by the dippy-hippie Austrian artist Friedensreich Hundertwasser; despite the disapproval of the city's intelligentsia, they are becoming some of Vienna's most popular tourist attractions.

Gasometer

3, Guglgasse. U3 Gasometer. **Map** p241 K10.

Five minutes out of Vienna airport, you may catch a glimpse of four circular brick towers, each 70m (230ft) high, one of which is obscured by a glass shield indented in the middle. If cutting-edge architecture floats your boat, retrace your steps to see the Gasometer housing project close up. These obsolete 100-year-old gas tanks were briefly venues for raves before four firms of architects received subsidies of €230 million to convert them into a complex to revitalise the shapeless Erdberg area. The tanks are connected throughout the three-floor shopping and leisure area and have their own U-Bahn station. As winner of the competition, Coop Himmelblau

(Vienna's celebrated deconstructionist team) got the brief to build an external symbol in the form of the glass shield. While this looks great at a distance, the 250-room student residence it contains suffers from low ceilings and cheap materials. Jean Nouvel built nine towers around his tank, knocking huge windows into the walls and cladding the exterior with a metallic finish that creates a marvellous play of light. For Gasometer D, Austrian architect Wilhelm Holzbauer opted for a three-point star of stacked housing with the open areas grassed over as a communal garden – his is probably the most liveable option.

St Marxer Friedhof

3, Leberstrasse 6-8 (796 3613). Tram 71. **Open** *Nov-Mar* 7am-dusk daily. *Apr, Oct* 7am-5pm daily. *May, Sept* 7am-6pm daily. *June-Aug* 7am-7pm daily. **Map** p240 H10.

Located in a desolate part of the 3rd district, with adjacent motorway flyover, St Mark's was the first of Vienna's outer-limits cemeteries, built on the orders of Josef II, who decided to close all cemeteries of the Innere Stadt for hygienic reasons in the 1780s. No one has been buried here since 1874. By far the most illustrious corpse was Mozart's, given a pauper's burial in a mass grave in 1791. Mozart's death coincided with Josef II's Diktat making mass burial the norm. His wife Constanze's later attempts to pinpoint the exact place of burial, an impossible quest, led to the erection of the so-called *Mozartgrab*, featuring an angel in mourning and a truncated pillar representing his early death. A plan of the graves is available at the entrance.

Strassenbahnmuseum

3, Ludwig-Koessler-Platz (786 03 03/www.wiener-tramwaymuseum.org). U3 Schlachthausgasse/tram 18, 73. **Open** *May-Oct* 9am-4pm Sat, Sun. *Vintage tram sightseeing tours May-Oct* 9.30am, 1.30pm Sat, Sun (departs from Karlsplatz). **Admission** *Museum* €2; free under-15s. *Tram tours* €15; €13.50 with Vienna Card; €5 under-15s. **No credit cards**. **Map** p240 J8.

Housed in three brick sheds, this museum contains all forms of carriage to have graced the rails of Vienna's vast tram network, including horse-drawn trams, a working steam tram and several buses. The ubiquitous red and white tram is known as the 'Bim', aping the sound of its bell. The newest Siemens-built, Porsche-designed ultra-low platform model is also on display.

Belvedere

The palace consists of two separate entities – the **Unteres** (Lower) and **Oberes** (Upper) **Belvedere**, located at either end of an expanse of French gardens on three levels. The upper part is by far the most impressive and is considered one of the finest secular baroque buildings in Europe. The main entrance to the palace is on the southern side. Building was commissioned by Prince Eugène of Savoy,

master strategist of the defeat of the Turks. Having acquired the land in 1697, Eugène had to wait until 1714 (when he'd received his share of the booty from the Emperor) to start building. With Lukas von Hildebrandt at the helm, the two palaces were completed in record time – the Unteres Belvedere in two years (1714-16) and the Oberes Belvedere, amazingly, in only one (1721-2). The lower palace became the Prince's residence, while the monumental Oberes Belvedere served as a palace for receptions, negotiations and feasts. Eugène established various gardens on the eastern side of the grounds, which contained his aviary and menagerie – once home to the first giraffe to survive in captivity in Central Europe. To the south, the Alpine Garden and the University Botanical Gardens are well worth a visit. After the Prince's death the Belvedere passed to Viktoria, Eugène's thoughtlessly extravagant niece, who sold the contents of the library to the Habsburgs and the picture collection all over Europe. In 1752 Maria Theresia bought the Belvedere itself and in 1776 Josef II had the imperial picture collection moved there. Three years later the gardens were opened to the public.

The last resident of the Belvedere was Archduke Franz Ferdinand, later of Sarajevo fame, who set up a rival court there. The Belvedere returned to the political limelight in 1934 when Schuschnigg, Chancellor of the Austro-Fascist government, used it as his residence, and again in 1955, when the Austrian State Treaty that established Austria as an independent neutral state was signed there.

Oberes Belvedere & Österreichische Galerie

3, Prinz-Eugen-Strasse, 27 (7955 7134/www.belvedere.at). Tram D, O, 18/bus 13a, 69a. **Open** 10am-6pm Tue-Sun. **Admission** €6; €3 concessions; combicard for all collections (Upper & Lower Belvedere, Atelier Augarten, Ambrosi Museum) €7.50; €3 students. **No credit cards**. **Map** p239 F10.

The façade of the Upper Belvedere is one of Vienna's great sights and the view it commands of the city one of the best. Add to this the contents of the Austrian Gallery and it becomes clear why this is one of Vienna's biggest crowd-pullers. If you only get to one gallery during your stay, make it this one. The great attraction is the collection of paintings by Vienna's modernist triumvirate – Klimt, Schiele and Kokoschka. The country's major collection of 19th- and early 20th-century painting, both Austrian and European, is divided into nine major categories here. Highlights among the Classical collection are Caspar David Friedrich's *Sea-Shore in Mist* (1807). The Biedermeier/Romanticism section is full of pious family portraits in bourgeois living rooms, but also some interesting cityscapes of Vienna. This section has the superb *Naschmarkt in Wien* (1894) an

The *Flaktürme* in Arenberg Park, used as an art space by **MAK**. *See p79.*

example of Austrian Realism by Carl Moll, and *Steamer at Kaisermühlen* (1872) by Emil Jakob Schindler (Alma Mahler's father). There are also works by Courbet, Daumier, Delacroix and Corot. The rather patchy collection of Impressionist paintings includes Renoir's *After the Bath* (1876); there's a Van Gogh too, *The Plain at Auvers* (1890). The historicist nudes of Hans Makart in *Bacchus and Ariadne* and the *Five Senses* series are a sensual treat, in stark contrast to Egon Schiele's disturbing emaciated human forms in the Austrian expressionism section. Oskar Kokoschka's more animated, twisted brush strokes can be seen in his superb *Tiger-Lion* (1926), painted after being scared out of his wits in front of a lion's cage at London Zoo. Before reaching these treasures you'll have passed before *The Kiss* and the *Portrait of Adele Bloch* by the man who got the ball rolling in the first place, Gustav Klimt.

Unteres Belvedere & Barockmuseum

3, Rennweg, 6a (7955 7134/www.belvedere.at). Tram 71. **Open** *Gardens* dawn till dusk daily. *Museums* 10am-6pm Tue-Sun. *English highlights tour* 4pm Sun. **Admission** €6; €3 concessions; €7.50 combicard (*see Oberes Belvedere*). **No credit cards. Map** p239 F8.

Entering the Belvedere from Rennweg, you pass the Lower Belvedere and the signs direct you into the Baroque Museum. This contains a range of works by the principal Austrian baroque painters, the original lead castings from the fountain on Neuer Markt and plenty of trompe-l'oeil effects. The latter make the Marmorsaal the highlight of the visit – a two-floor extravaganza celebrating the Prince's military career and, in a fresco by Martino Altamonte, shamelessly transforming him into the god Apollo. Next comes the Groteskensaal (Hall of Grotesques), housing some incredible busts of faces in a variety of grimaces by the oddball sculptor Franz Xaver Messerschmidt (1732-83). After the Marmorgalerie, you reach the

Goldkabinett – a baroque freak-out, fuelled by oriental vases, 23-carat gold panelling and a lot of mirrors. The Museum of Medieval Art is in the Orangery; highlights include the magnificent colours of the early 15th-century Znaimer Altar attributed to a Viennese workshop. The work of Michael Pacher, a 15th-century Tyrolean painter and sculptor best known for his Gothic altar in St Wolfgang near Salzburg, is represented by five pictures that mark the transition towards a more perspective-based Renaissance art.

Prinz-Eugen-Strasse

Running parallel to the Belvedere on the western side, Prinz-Eugen-Strasse, dividing the 3rd and 4th districts, has its share of imposing edifices, many of them now embassies. Near the corner with Schwarzenbergplatz is the discreet entrance to Palais Schwarzenberg (1720), now a five-star hotel but built by Fischer von Erlach and son for Adam Franz von Schwarzenberg, Equerry to Emperor Karl VI. Its present owner reputedly thanked Elizabeth II for 'bombing my palace into a profitable hotel'.

A block further south of the entrance to the Upper Belvedere is Goldeggasse where at No.19 you can visit, by prior appointment, the **Bestattungsmuseum** (Burial Museum). At the end of Prinz-Eugen-Strasse, across the hellish Gürtel (the inner city ring road), is the depressing sight of the post-war Südbahnhof. Vienna is disappointing for railway enthusiasts since all its 19th-century stations were bombed out of existence. It is worth the trek up beyond the station to the **Heeresgeschichtliches Museum** just to admire Theophil Hansen's fantastic synthesis of Byzantine (the dome), Moorish (brickwork and window arches) and late-medieval Italian elements.

Bestattungsmuseum

4, Goldeggasse 19 (50 195/4227). Tram D. **Open**
noon-3pm Mon-Fri, by appointment only. *Group
tours* on request. **Admission** free. **Map** p239 F10.
The Burial Museum is a fitting testimony to the local
obsession with the ceremonies and paraphernalia of
death. Some exhibits are frankly comical – a coffin
with a bell pull for those mistakenly buried alive,
and a packet of undertakers' cigarettes bearing the
legend *Rauchen sichert Arbeitsplätze* ('Smoking
protects jobs'). The museum also displays historic
photographs of Emperor Franz Joseph's and
Archduke Franz Ferdinand's funerals. There's also
a touching documentary of a couple pushing their
son's coffin on a cart in 1945.

Heeresgeschichtliches Museum

*3, Hauptgebäude, Arsenal Objekt 18 (information 79
561/www.bmlv.gv.at/hgm). U1 Südtirolerplatz/tram
D, O, 18/bus 13a, 69a.* **Open** 9am-5pm Mon-Thur,
Sat, Sun. **Admission** €5.10 incl audio-guide; €3.30
over-10s; €7.30 family. **No credit cards.**
The Museum of Military History was Vienna's first
purpose-built museum (commissioned by Franz Josef
I and completed in 1856). It was designed by Theophil
Hansen as part of the Arsenal complex – one of four
large barracks built post-1848 to quell possible unrest.
Of these, only the Arsenal and the Rossauer Kaserne
remain. Access to the museum is through the
Feldherrenhalle (Hall of the Generals), which is lined
with statues of pre-1848 Austrian military leaders.
The museum is on two floors with courtyards given
over to armoured vehicles. The first floor contains mil-
itaria from the Napoleonic Wars, the Austro-Prussian
War as well as artefacts from the Thirty Years' War
(1618-48) and the second siege of Vienna (1683). The
trophies captured in these campaigns are among the
finest in the museum – Turkish standards, tents and
the Great Seal of Mustafa Pasha. The west wing of the
ground floor assembles all the uniforms of the armies
of the Crown Lands after the reform of 1867. The sheer
size and diversity of the Imperial Army is astonishing; at one time it protected an empire of over 54 million subjects. The fascinating room covering the
assassination in Sarajevo on 28 June 1914 of Archduke
Franz Ferdinand contains the car in which he was shot
and his blood-stained tunic. A recent acquisition is the
Mayor of Sarajevo's settee on which the Archduke
bled to death, brought to Vienna in 1997 during the
siege of Sarajevo by the Serbs. Further displays on
World War I and its aftermath show all the tragedy
of nationalism; Albin Egger Lienz's painting *To the
Unknown Soldier* encapsulates the butchery. The east
wing of the ground floor, recently renovated, follows
the history of the Austrian Navy.

Rennweg

Rennweg slopes up the eastern side of the
Belvedere from Schwarzenbergplatz. No.3 is an
early Otto Wagner house with fine reliefs; No.5
is also a Wagner house, where Gustav Mahler

lived from 1898 to 1909. On Sunday, opposite
the entrance to the Unteres Belvedere, a crowd
files in and out of the Gardekirche (1763), the
church of the Polish community. It's worth
taking a stroll down Salesianergasse and along
Jaurèsgasse, the heart of the diplomatic area.
Note the rather badly conserved onion-domed
Russian Orthodox church at No.2. Beyond the
S-Bahn line is Ungargasse where at Nos.59-61
is the Max Fabiani Portois & Fix building
(1900) with an Otto Wagneresque tiled façade
in shades of green with Jugendstil ironwork on
the top floor. Further north is the Neulinggasse
where there are two of Vienna's six World
War II *Flaktürme* (anti-aircraft towers) in the
adjacent Arenberg Park, one of which is now
used by the MAK.

MAK (Museum für Angewandte Kunst)

*3, Arenbergpark-Dannebergplatz/Bamherzigenstrasse
(711 36 248/www.mak.at). U3 Rochusmarkt/bus 74a.*
Open *May-Nov* 3-7pm Thur. **Admission** €4 or same-
day MAK ticket. **No credit cards. Map** p240 G8.
The MAK (*see p75*) has come up with a project
called Contemporary Art Tower (CAT) to find ways
in which art can use this tower to underline its function as a memorial to the horrors of war. CAT has
so far commissioned projects by Jenny Holzer and
James Tyrell, but it remains to be seen if MAK's limited resources can cover anything substantial.

By the Donaukanal

The area of the 3rd district bordering the Danube
Canal is quiet and residential with easy access
to the lower reaches of the Prater. A steady
stream of visitors heads for **KunstHaus
Wien** (Untere Weissgerberstrasse 13, 712
0491, www.kunsthauswien.com), a surreal
gingerbread house created by local artist and
architecture guru Friedensreich Hundertwasser.
If you've developed a taste for Hundertwasser,
pop round to nearby Löwengasse to see the
Hundertwasser Haus, a municipal housing
project that brought him into the public eye.

Hundertwasser Haus

*3, corner Löwengasse/Kegelgasse (www.hundert
wasserhaus.at). Tram N.* **Map** p240 H7.
The late Friedensreich Hundertwasser's first foray
into architecture (completed in 1985), could not be
undertaken without the aid of a genuine architect.
In February 2003, Josef Krawine, who had disasso-
ciated himself with the project, astounded the
trustees of the Hundertwasser foundation by tardi-
ly claiming part-ownership of the rights to the image
of the house. The colourful façade and gilded turrets
of this apartment building appear on virtually every
tour bus itinerary, but it isn't open to the public. Like
KunstHausWien, it features the same disconcerting
uneven floors and a communal roof garden.

'Bim!' The new Porsche-designed trams, seen on the streets and at the **Strassenbahnmuseum**. *See p77.*

Hundertwasser later used his business acumen to dream up the Kalke Village opposite, a shopping complex rendered in a similar idiom.

Wittgenstein-Haus

3, Parkgasse 18 (713 3164). U3 Rochusgasse. **Open** 9am-5pm Mon-Fri. **Admission** €3. **No credit cards. Map** p240 H7.
The house philosopher Ludwig Wittgenstein designed as a home for his sister Gretl is a minimalist tonic. Continuing his father's tradition of funding new architecture, Wittgenstein along with architect Paul Engelmann conceived a series of grey concrete cubes in the functionalist spirit of Loos. It was completed in 1926. In 1970 the premises became the Bulgarian Embassy. The house can only be visited while exhibitions or literary events are being held.

Karlsplatz

Maps p239 & p242

Heading south across the Ringstrasse from the Staatsoper, a bleak vista of post-1945 buildings opens out into the amorphous Karlsplatz. Plagued by an illogical series of pedestrian non sequiturs, the sights of Karlsplatz are best reached via the underpass on the corner of Kärntner Strasse and the Staatsoper.

This is a favourite meeting place of the city's substance abusers and other lost souls. Signs direct you to the top-priority **Secession**, the arty **Kunsthalle Project Space** or the tranquillity of Resselpark and the majestic **Karlskirche**. In an undistinguished modern building nearby is the **Museum der Stadt Wien**. Also on Karlsplatz is the neo-Renaissance Künstlerhaus (1868) commissioned by the Viennese Society of Fine Arts, a bastion of academic painters from whom the Secessionists split in 1897. Exhibitions here are, however, uncompromisingly contemporary.

Akademie der bildenden Künste

1, Schillerplatz 3 (1st floor on the right) (5881 6225/www.akbild.ac.at). U1, U2, U4 Karlsplatz. **Open** 10am-4pm Tue-Sun. **Admission** €3.63; €1.45 concessions; €2.18 with Vienna Card. **No credit cards. Map** p242 E8.
The Academy of Fine Arts – which rejected the young Adolf Hitler on two occasions – is set back from the Ring behind a statue of Friedrich Schiller. Theophil von Hansen's building houses a fine, if largely forgotten picture gallery. A porter points the way to the star of the show: Hieronymus Bosch's *The Last Judgement* (1504-6), his only monumental triptych outside Spain. The collection also includes *Tarquin and Lucretia* by Titian, Botticelli's *Madonna Tondo*, and Rembrandt's early *Unknown Young Woman*, but mostly Flemish and Dutch paintings.

Historisches Museum der Stadt Wien

4, Karlsplatz (505 8740/www.museum.vienna.at). U1, U2, U4 Karlsplatz/tram 1, 2, D, J/bus 3a. **Open** 9am-6pm Tue-Sun. **Admission** €3.60; €1.80 concessions; €5.40 family; €11.60 book of 10 tickets; free 9am-noon Fri. **No credit cards. Map** p242 E8.
This museum, though patchy, documents Vienna's history. It contains everything from scale models of the city, artefacts from the time of the Turkish siege, and reconstructions of interiors, to works by Makart, Klimt and Schiele. Numerous pieces by Wiener Werkstätte collaborators like Kolo Moser and Josef Hoffmann are displayed, as is the façade of Otto Wagner's *Die Zeit* telegraph office (1902).

Karlskirche

4, Karlsplatz (504 6187). U1, U2, U4 Karlsplatz/tram 1, 2, D, J. **Map** p242 E8.
Visible from all sides of the Karlsplatz, this masterpiece of baroque architecture has more than a hint of Rome and even a touch of Byzantium about it. For the current restoration work on the ceiling frescoes, a glass elevator ascends 47m (154ft) to give visitors a close look at the work and access to the roof.

Emperor Karl VI commissioned Fischer von Erlach to build a church to celebrate the end of the 1713 plague, dedicating the whole thing to the memory of San Carlo Boromeo, renowned for his role in tending victims of the 1576 plague in Milan. Thus Karl could celebrate the work of his selfless namesake by having the events of his life depicted on Fischer's splendid columns and then topping them with his own imperial eagles. The church was completed in 1737 by Fischer's son. The exterior is a hard act to follow but inside it is all light and airiness, showing off Rottmayr's immense fresco and Fischer's sunburst above the altar to great effect. In front of the church is a large ornamental pond with a Henry Moore sculpture (*Hill Arches*, 1978) reflecting the church's impressive façade.

Kunsthalle Project Space

4, Treitlstrasse 2 (52 189-33/www.kunsthalle wien.at). U1, U2, U4 Karlsplatz/tram 1, 2, D, J. **Open** 1-7pm daily. **Admission** €2; €1 concessions. **Credit** MC, V. **Map** p242 E8.
Occupying the former site of Kunsthalle Wien this less-is-more glass construction houses temporary installations and studio space for young artists. Its café and terrace are prime hangouts on a summer's night, while soaking up the sounds of the varied DJ programme (*see p184*).

Otto Wagner's Stadtbahn Pavillons

1, Karlsplatz (505 8747). U1, U2, U4 Karlsplatz/ tram 1, 2, D, J. **Open** *Apr-mid Oct* 9am-5pm Tue-Sun. **Admission** €1.80; €1.40 concessions. **No credit cards**. **Map** p242 E8.
Were it not for a protest by students from the Technische Universität, these splendid pavilions might have been demolished during U-Bahn construction in the 1960s. Originally located either side of the Akademiestrasse, they were reconstructed here with only a few slabs of discoloured Carrara marble being replaced. The two stations represent a distillation of Wagner's contribution to fin-de-siècle Vienna. Only one offers access to the U-Bahn. The other has cafés on different levels. The downstairs café hosts Klub Shabu (*see p184*) in the evenings.

Secession

1, Friedrichstrasse 12 (587 5307/www.secession.at). U1, U2, U4 Karlsplatz. **Open** 10am-6pm Tue, Wed, Fri-Sun; 10am-8pm Thur. **Admission** €5.50; €3 concessions. **No credit cards**. **Map** p242 E8.
Upon its centenary in 1998, the Viennese Secession building was sponge-painted in red. Now restored to pristine white, its sumptuous details can again be appreciated. Once the extravagance of the gilded globe has sunk in, turn to the legend above the entrance, which reads: 'To the age its art, to art its freedom'. Principally financed by Karl Wittgenstein, father of Ludwig, and designed by Josef Olbrich, the building was severely damaged in World War II and only restored to its present form in the mid-1980s. Even though space is at a premium, there are usually two or three exhibitions at one time, divided

between the main space, the dismal little graphics cabinet upstairs and the cellar. Many shows are rather po-faced hyper-politicised occasions, alternating between local heroes such as Florian Pümhosl or Johanna Kandl and big names on the international circuit. It is also the home of Klimt's controversial *Beethoven Friese*.

Wienzeile

Maps p239 & p242

No stay in Vienna would be complete without a Saturday morning stroll along the bustling concourse of Vienna's principal food market, the **Naschmarkt** (*see p141*). On both sides there are several sights worth taking in. At Linke Wienzeile 6 is the Theater an der Wien, today home of the Lloyd Webber-style musical, but with a history stretching back to 1801 when it opened under the directorship of Emanuel Schikaneder, author of the libretto for Mozart's *Magic Flute*. He is depicted as Papageno, the bird-catcher in the opera, in a statue above the main portico. More interesting than the modern façade is the backstage area down the adjacent side street, which eventually leads west to Café Sperl on Gumpendorfer Strasse – one of Vienna's most atmospheric coffee houses (*see p128*). Off the Rechte Wienzeile, Schleifmühlgasse and its adjoining streets are fast filling up with trendy shops and restaurants. The market operates through the week, but Saturday has the added attraction of a large flea market.

Otto Wagner Houses

6, Linke Wienzeile 38. U4 Kettenbrückengasse. **Map** p242 D8.
Built in 1898-9, these houses are the culmination of Otto Wagner's welding of Secessionist decorative vernacular with his own belief in the use of modern materials. At No.38 the gorgeous floral designs of the façade's majolica tiles (it's known as the Majolika Haus) and the clear distinction between commercial premises and dwelling make the buildings the antithesis of the Ringstrasse palace. The gilded embossing of No.40 is by Secessionist Kolo Moser.

Mariahilf

Map p238

Vienna's 6th district, Mariahilf, rises from the hollow of the Wien river valley via various steep lanes and flights of steps to Mariahilfer Strasse, the Viennese equivalent of Oxford Street. Sights are thin on the ground, but the uneven geography, human bustle and varied architecture make it pleasant to stroll. Head for the Gerngross shopping centre on the corner of Mariahilfer Strasse and Kirchengasse and take the high-speed lift to the top floor. Looking north from the café terrace, there's an excellent view of the hills of the Wienerwald, and to the south, the onion domes of the Mariahilferkirche with one of this district's two monolithic *Flaktürme* (*see below*) behind.

In Vienna shopping is resolutely low-key, so Mariahilfer Strasse comes as a shock with its international franchises and chain-stores. Dubbed the 'Magyarhilferstrasse' after the fall of the Wall when TVs and fridges were piled high on its pavements for Czech and Hungarian shoppers, the street now resembles any other Western European shop-till-you-drop zone.

Haus des Meeres

6, Esterházypark, Fritz Grünbaumplatz 1 (587 1417/ www.haus-des-meeres.at). U3 Neubaugasse/bus 13a, 14a, 57a. **Open** 9am-6pm daily. **Admission** €8.40; €6.40 concessions; €4 6-15s; €2.70 3-5s. **No credit cards**. **Map** p238 C8.
This rather dreary collection of reptiles, sea and freshwater fish, turtles and coral is housed in one of the huge fascist flak towers. It has been enlivened by the introduction of a tropical 'biotope': a mini rain forest featuring small monkeys leaping from tree to tree. Thrills too are to be had at the Wednesday snake-stroking session at 2pm. Otherwise, you're better off visiting Vienna's excellent zoo whose aquarium is far superior.

Museum für Mittelalterliche Rechtsgeschichte: Die Geschichte der Folter

6, Fritz Grünbaumplatz 1 (595 4593/www.folter.at). U3 Neubaugasse/bus 13a, 14a, 57a. **Open** 10am-6pm daily. **Admission** €6; €5 concessions; €3.50 under-16s; €4.50 with Vienna Card; €11 guided tours (phone 5 days in advance). **No credit cards**. **Map** p238 C8.
The 'Museum of Medieval Legal History: The History of Torture' is located in a former air-raid shelter below the Esterházypark Flakturm. Intended to teach rather than alarm, it uses dummies to stage torture scenes from medieval to modern times. Background sounds add to the atmosphere: gurgling water (water torture) or deep sighs (witch burning).

Neubau

Map p238

North of Mariahilfer Strasse lies Neubau, the 7th district, one of the most happening areas of Vienna in terms of nightlife, shops and alternative lifestyles. It's the only district governed by the Greens. Most of Neubau's attractions lie within the zone bounded by the pleasant, commercial Neubaugasse to the west and the Spittelberg quarter to the east where there is access to the **Museumsquartier** (*see p72*). Spittelberg's cobbled streets and heterogeneous Biedermeier architecture are pleasant strolling territory. The area was once a red-light district, but homes in its narrow streets are now among the most desirable

in Vienna. The proliferation of restaurants and antiques dealers also shows the area's gentrification. Before Christmas the whole area is transformed into an Advent market (*see p148*). Along Siebensterngasse the terraces of Shultz (*see p186*) and Siebenstern (a swish bar owned by the Communist Party), on the corner of Kirchengasse, are great hangouts.

Take a look at the splendid apartment building in Mondscheingasse with three lions' heads and a stucco tree. Down Kirchengasse beyond Burggasse is the fine baroque church of St Ulrich, in a gorgeous square sloping down to Neustiftgasse. At No.40 is one of Otto Wagner's most austere apartment buildings; round the corner at Döblergasse 4 is the house (currently closed to the public) where he lived and worked until his death in 1918.

Hofmobiliendepot

7, Mariahilfer Strasse 88, Andreasgasse 7 (524 3357-0/www.hofmobiliendepot.at). U3 Zieglergasse/ bus 13a. **Open** 10am-6pm Tue-Sun. **Admission** €6.90; concessions €4.50-€3.50. **Credit** AmEx, DC, MC, V. **Map** p238 C8.
Founded by Maria Theresia in 1747, this gigantic lock-up for the monarchy's unwanted furniture and fittings is a splendidly laid out museum guaranteed to interest anyone with a weakness for interior decoration. Entire rooms have been reconstructed on three floors, such as a bedroom from the Laxenburg palace and Crown Prince Rudolph's opium den.

Josefstadt

Map p238 & p234

The genteel 8th district of Vienna takes its name from Josef I (1705-11), during whose reign plans for this residential area were laid out. Bordering on Landesgerichtsstrasse directly behind the **Rathaus** (*see p69*) are fine examples of Biedermeier building in the cobbled streets around Lenaugasse. The area is popular with both the middle class and students and is a pleasant mix of *Tracht* and New Age. Sights are scarce, but window shopping in the antiques and second-hand stores of Lange Gasse, Piaristengasse and Lederergasse, and strolls in the many small parks make for a rewarding trip.

The section of the Gürtel that traces the northern boundary of Josefstadt is one of the city's hippest nightlife zones with several bars built into the arches of Otto Wagner's Stadtbahn, today the route of the U6. Places like rhiz and B72 have had exposure as temples of Vienna's burgeoning digital underground. The Gürtel also contains numerous peep-shows, sex shops and concomitant prostitution. With EC cash flowing in, projects such as Vienna's new public library built over the U6 near Burggasse should make the area more palatable, the new bars being just the aperitif. During the day it's worth crossing the Gürtel into the 16th for the vibrant **Brunnenmarkt** (*see p141*), in the heart of the Turkish and Yugoslav community.

The **Museum für Volkskunde** (Folklore Museum) is on the corner of Lange Gasse and Laudongasse. At No.17 is the Dreifaltigkeitskirche (Church of the Holy Trinity), the scene of Beethoven's funeral in 1827. A short walk away is **Piaristenkirche** on Jodok-Fink-Platz. In the centre of the square is a gilded column commemorating deliverance from the 1713 plague.

Museum für Volkskunde

8, Laudongasse 15-19 (406 8905/www.volkskunde museum.at). U2 Rathaus/tram 5, 33, 43, 44/bus 13a. **Open** 9am-5pm Tue-Sun. **Admission** €4.35; €2.90 concessions; €1.45 under-16s; €7.25 family ticket. **No credit cards. Map** p238 C6.
In Von Hildebrandt's early 17th-century Palais Schönborn, the Museum for Folklore deals with the customs, religious rites and secular celebrations of the Austrians. Temporary exhibitions are normally excellent, and wide-ranging in theme.

Piaristenkirche

8, Jodok-Fink-Platz (4204 2513). U2 Rathaus/tram J, bus 13a. **Map** p238 C6.
Josef I included in his plans land to be set aside for the Order of the Piarists to found a monastery. The Maria Treu or Piaristenkirche (1753) stands between the monastery outbuildings, its convex façade flanked by two elegant towers. The original design was traced by Von Hildebrandt in 1716 but it was not completed until the 19th century. The interior is notable for Franz Maulbertsch's magnificent ceiling frescoes and for its organ on which Anton Brückner took his examination for the Academy. As he played, an examiner commented, 'He should be examining us!'

Alsergrund

Maps p234, p235 & p242

Alsergrund, the 9th district, occupies a large area stretching as far as the Danube canal and is known as the medical and university district. Directly opposite the Church of the Holy Trinity is the **Altes Allgemeines Krankenhaus**, one of Europe's oldest hospitals now transformed into an attractive university campus. It is home to some curious sights such as the Narrenturm, an 18th-century lunatic asylum that has been converted into the fascinating, yet slightly grotesque **Pathologisch-anatomische Bundesmuseum**. To the north a couple of monolithic towers denote the presence of the AKH (Allgemeines Krankenhaus), the largest hospital in Europe, whose construction was shrouded in the most serious corruption scandal of the Bruno Kreisky era. Its ultra-modern installations can be visited on guided tours.

Nearby on Währinger Strasse is the **Josephinum**, Josef II's academy for military surgeons – now a medical museum. However, the district is probably most famous for Berggasse 19, now the **Sigmund Freud Museum**, where Freud lived and did most of his pioneering work on psychoanalysis.

The streets around Berggasse, the Servitenviertel, are pleasant to stroll around having the only church outside the city walls to survive the Turkish siege, the late 17th-century **Servitenkirche**. Nearby too is the small Jewish cemetery of Seegasse. Access is through the old people's home at Seegasse 9-11, built on the site of the old Jewish hospital. Like all such cemeteries in Vienna, this one bears the scars of rabid anti-semitism, with virtually every tomb

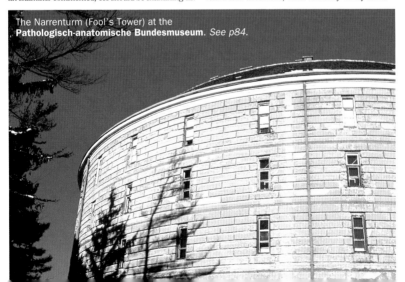

The Narrenturm (Fool's Tower) at the **Pathologisch-anatomische Bundesmuseum**. *See p84.*

desecrated. Look out for the curious mound of stones with a carved fish on top – it's not clear whether it's actually a gravestone.

Further along Seegasse you come to the congested Rossauer Lände that follows the canal embankment where various ramps and flights of steps lead to the waterside. It's worth following the path to get a fantastic view of one of Vienna's most singular buildings, the **Fernwärme**, a municipal rubbish incinerator embellished by artist Hundertwasser. The 9th district's most exuberant building is Palais Liechtenstein, a wonderful baroque summer palace. Built to a design by Domenico Martinelli between 1691 and 1711, it is still the property of the Princes of Liechtenstein, but no longer inhabited. The Liechtenstein family have announced that in 2004 the Palais will resume its former role as an art gallery to show their collection of classical painting. The impressive library will be opened to the public for the first time. From here classical music buffs may well venture to the less scenic end of the 9th district to take in the Schuberthaus, the birthplace of Schubert on Nussdorfer Strasse. The alternative is to cross the Liechtenstein Strasse and climb the magnificent Jugendstil ensemble of the Strudelhof Steps leading to Währinger Strasse.

Altes Allgemeines Krankenhaus (AKH)

9, Alser Strasse/Spitalgasse. Tram 5, 33, 43, 44. **Map** p242 C5.
There's not a great deal to see within this labyrinth of 15 or so inner courtyards, opened in 1784 as the Allgemeines Krankenhaus (General Hospital), but since the mid-1990s it has become a model conversion of existing public buildings into an inner city university campus. In the summer months it's a delightful place to hang out, as it's dotted with numerous bars and terraces; there's also a regular open-air cinema programme.

Fernwärme

9, Spittelauer Lände 45 (313 26 20 30). U4, U6 Spittelau/tram D. **Open** *Tours* by appointment. **Admission** free. **Map** p235 D2.
There can't be many cities where the municipal rubbish incinerator features in a sightseeing guide, but Friedensreich Hundertwasser's 1989 remodelling of a hideous industrial building is now one of Vienna's great visual surprises. This is mainly due to the enormous smoke stack, wrapped in vitroceramic tiles and crowned with a large golden mosaic bulb. The incinerator provides heating for over 180,000 homes and 4,000 large consumers. The plant is best observed either from the U6 line or from the banks of the Donaukanal, but for Hundertwasser devotees, two guided tours are available – one 'artistic', the other technical.

Josephinum

9, Währinger Strasse 25/1 (4277 63401). Tram 37, 38, 40, 41, 42. **Open** 9am-3pm Mon-Fri. **Admission** €2; €1 concessions. **No credit cards. Map** p235 D5.
The Josephinum museum of medical history (named after Josef II) is a Canevale building dating from 1775. Fronted by impressive wrought ironwork, the institution was intended as a school for military surgeons. The exhibits include a through-the-ages look at surgical instruments displayed in fine rosewood cabinets, but the main draw is the *Wachspräparate Sammlung*, a collection of life-size wax anatomical models made by Florentine craftsmen in 1780.

Pathologisch-anatomische Bundesmuseum

9, Spitalgasse 2 (Courtyard 13, entrance Van-Swieten Gasse) (406 8672/www.pathomus.or.at). Tram 5, 33, 43, 44. **Open** 3-6pm Wed; 8-11am Thur; 10am-1pm 1st Sat of mth. **Admission** free. **Map** p242 D5.
The so-called Narrenturm (Fool's Tower) is in the last courtyard of the former General Hospital. Commissioned by the Emperor, this house of internment for the mentally ill was built by Canevale in 1784 and was used as such until 1866. The present museum is a medical house of horrors – not for the faint-hearted.

Sigmund Freud Museum

9, Berggasse 19 (319 1596/www.freud-museum.at). U2 Schottentor/tram D, 37, 38, 40, 41. **Open** *Oct-June* 9am-5pm daily. *July-Sept* 9am-6pm daily. *Archive, library* by appointment. **Admission** €5; €3 concessions; €2 schoolchildren; €4 with Vienna Card. *Guided tours* by appointment (one day in advance). **Credit** DC, MC, V. **Map** p242 D5.
Opened in 1971 on the initiative of Freud's daughter Anna, the museum is located in the apartment where Sigmund lived and worked from 1898 to 1938, when he was forced into exile by the Nazis. On arrival, the visitor is offered a guide to the exhibits in a choice of languages and then let loose in the various rooms. The walls are filled with glass cases containing photos, letters, first editions and bits of the ethnic bric-a-brac Freud so assiduously collected. Some items, such as a photo of the house daubed with swastikas, are chilling. One room has a video set-up showing films of Freud and family. Another room is set aside for small exhibitions of contemporary art related to psychoanalysis. Staff are aficionados and extremely helpful.

Servitenkirche

9, Servitenplatz. U4 Rossauer Lände/tram D.
Servitenviertel is a charming, villagey network of streets. Belonging to the Serviten Order and designed by Canevale, this church has an oval-shaped nave said to have influenced the builders of Karlskirche. It's baroque to the marrow, with a fine interior, impressive stucco, a pulpit by Moll (1739) and a relief showing the martyrdom of a popular Czech saint, John Nepomuk. Unless you come to Mass, the church must be seen through iron railings.

2nd & 22nd Districts

Across the Donaukanal there are multifarious waterways, the UN headquarters and some of the city's best parks to explore.

Leopoldstadt

Maps p235 and p241

The barrier of the Donaukanal, with its neo-brutalist skyline, often makes the 2nd district seem grey and distanced from the Innere Stadt. Together with Brigittenau, the neighbouring 20th district, Leopoldstadt forms an elongated island between Donaukanal and the Danube. It was probably this topography that led to Ferdinand II's decision to sanction the creation of a walled Jewish ghetto in the area in 1624.

The name of the district has its origin in the anti-semitic hysteria of the post-Reformation when Leopold I was persuaded to expel the Jews in 1670, demolish their synagogue, and replace it with the Leopoldkirche. During the late 18th and early 19th century, Jews escaping from the Russian and Polish pogroms flooded into Vienna, with the majority taking up residence in Leopoldstadt. It remained an area blighted by poverty – successful Jewish families, such as the Freuds and the Schnitzlers, eventually moved to more salubrious districts. With the collapse of the Eastern Bloc the process is repeating itself. Today's Jews are overwhelmingly from ex-Soviet republics and Iran, mingling with the Turkish communities and those from former Yugoslavia, long established in the area.

The projected U-Bahn extension in 2007 should give an important impulse to an area that has its share of interesting sights, as well a markedly multicultural character. Of all Vienna's city centre districts, however, this is probably the most unkempt: full of architectural eyesores built after Allied bombing. On the positive side, its two fine, spacious parks, the **Prater** and the **Augarten**, are a joy.

Commercial activity in the 2nd district is concentrated along its two major arteries, Taborstrasse and Praterstrasse. Accessible via tram or U-Bahn from Schwedenplatz, the two roads form a triangle with Heine Strasse that contains the Karmeliterplatz open-air food market, the **Johann Strauss Haus** and the **Kriminalmuseum**, as well as numerous boho bars and restaurants. Praterstrasse eventually broadens on to Praterstern, a railway/U-Bahn station and traffic junction overlooked by the Tegetthoff column, which honours the

Habsburgs' most glorious admiral. Here the milling crowds (and general shabbiness) mark the presence of the **Wurstelprater** (see p86) Vienna's year-round luna park and home of its iconic 19th-century big wheel, the Riesenrad.

Atelier Augarten

2, Scherzergasse 1a (216 4022/www.belvedere.at). Tram N. **Open** 10am-5pm Tue-Sun. **Admission** €4.50; €2.50 concessions. **No credit cards.** **Map** p235 F4.

The atelier of Austrian sculptor Gustinus Ambrosi (1893-1975) was reopened as a museum and sculpture garden in 2002. It is run by the Österreichische Galerie; a same-day ticket to the Belvedere is valid here too. The restaurant and summer terrace are highly recommended.

Augarten

Main entrance: 2, Obere Augarten Strasse (www.augarten.at). Tram 21, N. **Open** *Nov-Mar* 6.30am-dusk. *Apr-Oct* 6am-dusk. **Map** p235 E4 to F4.

Established by Ferdinand III in 1650 and laid out in its present form in 1712, the Augarten is the oldest baroque garden in Vienna. It was opened to the public by Josef II in 1775. The park's 50 hectares (124 acres) come into their own in summer when sunbathers inundate the lawns beside the Flakturm nearest the main entrance. Summer evenings are also lively as Vienna's most popular open-air cinema, **Kino unter Sternen** (see p157), and a host of temporary restaurants set up shop in the park. Apart from its two Flaktürme, the Augarten is also home to two Viennese institutions, the **Augarten Porzellanmanufaktur** and the Vienna Boys' Choir, whose members are lodged in Fischer von Erlach the Elder's Palais Augarten. The smaller Kaiser-Josef-Stöckl (1781) is where the boys go to school. On the eastern side of the park is the **Atelier Augarten** (see above).

Augarten Porzellan Manufaktur

2, Schloss Augarten, Obere Augartenstrasse 1 (21 124-0/www.augarten.at). Tram 5, N. **Open** *Guided tours only* 9.30am daily. **Admission** €4. **No credit cards.** **Map** p235 F4.

The works of the Wiener Porzellan Manufaktur, Austria's foremost manufacturer of posh crocks, have been around since 1718. The firm's current premises, the Schloss Augarten, were constructed on the ruins of Leopold I's summer palace after it was destroyed during the Turkish siege in 1683. The building was a venue for concerts by Mozart, Beethoven and Schubert at the end of the 18th century. Augarten's florid rococo designs will probably not appeal to fans of cool understatement, but the company also does a small line in modernist designs. Temporary exhibitions are held in the foyer and wares can be purchased on the premises or at Augarten's flagship store on Graben.

Johann Strauss Haus

2, Praterstrasse 54 (214 0121). U1 Nestroyplatz.
Open 9am-12.15pm, 1-4.30pm Tue-Fri. **Admission**
€1.80; 70¢ concessions. **No credit cards**.
Map p243 G5.
Unlike most of Vienna's music museums, this one at least has a bash at period decor and does include exhibits belonging to the 'King of the Waltz', such as his grand piano, organ and stand-up composing desk. There's also a vast collection of ball-related memorabilia. Strauss lived here from 1863 to 1878.

Kriminalmuseum

2, Grosse Sperlgasse 24 (214 4678/www.kriminal museum.at). Tram 21, N. **Open** 10am-5pm Thur-Sun. **Admission** €4.50; €3.50 concessions; €2.50 children. **No credit cards. Map** p243 F5.
Exhibits at the Criminal Museum are mostly photographs and press cuttings, so a good understanding of German is needed. The museum oscillates between lionising villains such as Breitwieser (Vienna's greatest safe-breaker) and offering interesting social background to cases such as that of Josephine Luner who tortured her maid to death. The displays of Theresa Knoll murdering her husband with a hatchet (1808), and of the husband who killed his bride on their wedding night (1932) are gruesome.

Prater

Once a medieval royal hunting ground, the Prater covers a huge expanse of 60sq km (23sq miles). The famous rides, stalls and beer gardens of the Wurstelprater only make up a small part of it. The chestnut-bordered central artery, the Hauptallee, has been synonymous with the Viennese Sunday stroll since Josef II opened the park to the public in 1766. May Day festivities take place at the Prater, as does the Austrian Communist Party's annual Volksstimmefest. All year round the Prater attracts Viennese anxious for fresh air and a spot of jogging, cycling or rollerblading.
In summer, splashes from the Olympic-size Stadionbad pool can be heard on the Hauptallee. Locals flock in too for the football at the Ernst-Happel-Stadion, trap racing at the adjoining Krieau course, and flat racing at the Freudenau course, *see p187*. More leisurely pursuits include floating through the overgrown tracts of the old Danube in a rowing boat, snoozing beneath the hundreds of magnificent oaks and chestnuts, or people watching amid the hubbub of the funfair, the Wurstelprater. No entrance fee is charged as the booths, rides and restaurants are run by

many different operators. Attractions range from old-fashioned merry-go-rounds, to the cutting edge of fairground technology, epitomised by the Space Shuttle. The one ride no one should miss is the world-famous 19th-century Riesenrad, immortalised in *The Third Man*. The wheel takes 20 minutes to complete one circle; at its highest point you are 65 metres (213 feet) above the ground. In 2002, the wheel got a face-lift with a swish new café at its base and some dramatic lighting supplied by British designer Patrick Woodruffe.

Schützenhaus

2, Obere Donaustrasse 26. U1, U4 Schwedenplatz.
Map p243 E5.
Architecture is not Leopoldstadt's strong point, but Otto Wagner's Schützenhaus (Defence Tower), built 1906-7, is a charming example of Jugendstil functionalism. Constructed on the site of an old defensive fortification, Wagner's building has all the characteristics of his work: wall cladding sustained by large metal rivets, and an upper façade reflecting the waterway by means of blue tiles with a wave motif. The Schützenhaus is probably best observed from the Schwedenplatz side of the canal.

The Danube

Maps p236 and p237

No less than four waterways sport the name Danube. Most familiar to visitors will be the Donaukanal (Danube Canal), an artificial construction dividing the main part of the city from the 2nd and 20th districts. Beyond the 2nd district lies the Danube proper, a vast stretch of water divided by the **Donauinsel**, a man-made island some 20 kilometres (12.5 miles) long. Between the island and the monoliths of the UN complex is the so-called Neue Donau, a slower-flowing parallel arm dug in the 1970s. Once you reach the eastern bank, it's a relatively short walk to the Alte Donau (Old Danube), an arm of the river's original course akin to an oxbow lake, preserved for the leisure opportunities it offers. This is by far the most attractive stretch of the river, with rowing clubs and weeping willows.

Donauinsel

Over the centuries the Danube has been the cause of serious flooding, so to ensure the river's safe passage and permit the docking of larger vessels, the main causeway was dug between 1870 and 1875. The unnaturally straight course of the Danube today is rather bleak, hardly mirroring the exuberance of Strauss's famous waltz.
After the construction of the Neue Donau to the east, a long narrow stretch of land was left,

A vegetarian **Würstelstand**! *See p107.*

The Riesenrad in the **Prater**. *See p86.*

dividing it from the river's main course. For years this island, the Donauinsel, was an inhospitable, windswept tract, but with tree planting it has been transformed into a massive leisure zone to rival the Prater. While the island still falls short of being an Arcadia, the sheer space and relative cleanliness of the water make it ideal for cycling, bathing, in-line skating and picnicking during summer. Nude bathing and sunbathing are also permitted.

The area adjacent to the Donauinsel U-Bahn station has become a major nightlife area during the summer, known as the Copa Cagrana after the nearby Kagran district. It is brash and commercial, but popular with young Viennese and the South American community. In June the entire island is taken over for a weekend by the Social Democratic Party's **Donauinselfest** (*see p149*).

Vienna International Centre

(26060 3328/www.unvienna.org). U1 Vienna International Centre. **Open** *Guided tours by appointment 11am, 2pm Mon-Fri.* **Admission** €4. **No credit cards. Map** p237 K2.

Near the fleshpots of the **Copa Cagrana**, a foreboding cluster of grey semi-cylindrical towers comes into view. This is the Vienna International Centre or UNO City: a combination of conference centre and headquarters No.3 of the United Nations. Socialist Chancellor Bruno Kreisky succeeded in making Vienna the third seat of the UN in the early 1970s, running the operation from the Hofburg. The need for larger premises led to the construction of the present complex, which was finished in 1979 and houses the offices of the International Atomic Energy

Agency, the Commission for Infectious Diseases, the High Commission for Refugees (UNHCR) and UNIDO the threatened industrial organisation. Its construction almost bankrupted the city, but the complex ensures a badly needed international presence in Vienna. Bring your passport as security is tighter than ever.

Alte Donau

Two stops further on the U1 from the **Vienna International Centre** and you are in the picturesque old Danube, a pleasant area to stroll and have a few drinks or dinner at the water's edge. On the western side is the Gänsehäufel, one of the city's most popular bathing areas, comprising pools as well as the river. Many sections are the private domain of certain public workers, so you see amusing signs pointing to the Polizeibad (Police Baths) and Strassenbahner-Bad (Tram Drivers' Baths).

Opposite Gänsehäufel there is a pleasant riverside walk with several bustling restaurants among the boat houses. To the north over the Wagramer Strasse is another bathing zone, the Angelibad, which faces a quintessential Viennese summer schnitzel joint Gasthaus Birner. Take plenty of insect repellent as mosquitoes can be a problem in summer. On the north-west side of the Alte Donau, adjacent to the UNO buildings, is the Donaupark: attractive modern gardens. They are built around the Donauturm (Danube Tower), for years the tallest building in Vienna, complete with high-speed lift and revolving restaurant.

Further Afield

The outskirts – home to some of the city's greatest attractions.

West of Vienna

The main attraction on the western side of Vienna is the Habsburgs' summer palace, **Schönbrunn**, and its delightful gardens and parkland. The trip can be combined with a look round the neighbouring suburb of Hietzing, which is a treat for architecture freaks – Otto Wagner, Adolf Loos and various other Viennese Modernists built in this prosperous suburb. However, for those with a particular interest in Wagner's contribution to Jugendstil Vienna, a trip to the far-flung 14th district in the west of the city is a must. In reasonably close proximity there are two of his villas and the outstanding **Kirche am Steinhof** – Wagner's one and only stab at ecclesiastical architecture.

Kirche am Steinhof

14, Baumgartner Höhe 1 (91060 20038). U2, U3 Volkstheater/bus 48a. **Open** 3pm Sat. **Guided tours** (in German) €5. **No credit cards**.

Otto Wagner's church is located within the grounds of Steinhof, a pioneering experiment in the care of the mentally ill, set in hectares of beautiful parkland, and intended for use by patients and staff. Built in 1902, Wagner designed the layout and many of the 61 pavilions that make up the centre. In 1904 he received the commission to build the church and completed it in 1907. Take the path that runs up the hill to the left of the admin buildings and slowly the immense (32m/105ft-high) copper cupola of the church comes into view.

Set upon a huge stone plinth and clad in white marble with four Jugendstil angels by Othmar Schimkowitz aloft, the Kirche am Steinhof must be one of the world's first examples of ecclesiastical functionalism. Inside it is all light and clean surfaces. With the altar to the north, sunlight pours in through Kolo Moser's magnificent stained-glass windows depicting a procession of saints. Moser started the work on the mosaic of the altar fresco (which features St Peter with Franz Josef's head), but conversion to Protestantism led to his being dropped from the team (despite Wagner's intervention).

The architect had no truck with denominational in-fighting, envisaging his church as shrine for all religions and specifically as a place of worship for the patients of Steinhof. Wagner oversaw all the details, even designing special robes for the priests. The church was opened by Archduke Franz Ferdinand who made no attempt to hide his contempt for it, saying in his inaugural address that the architecture of Maria Theresia's time was far superior. Since the 1980s Steinhof has been an open centre with patients free to leave of their own accord. With the constant stream of visitors to the church and to performances at the Jugendstil theatre on the grounds, Steinhof has a salutary air of refreshing normality. Below the church is a memorial to the mentally ill victims of the Nazis.

Otto Wagner Villas

14, Hüttelbergstrasse 26, 28 (914 8575). Tram 49. **Admission** €11; €6 concessions. **Credit** AmEx, DC, MC, V.

The villa at No.26 is the only one of the two that can be visited, as it is now home to the Ernst-Fuchs Museum, a lamentable piece of egomania by the magical realist painter of the same name who has filled the house and garden with his gaudy oeuvre. Some credit must be given to Fuchs and his contemporary and soulmate Hundertwasser, who, in 1968, squatted the house in order to save it from the Council's demolition order. Fuchs purchased No.26 in 1972 and set about its restoration and transformation. It is an early work of Wagner's, completed in 1888, reminiscent of his Ringstrasse work, with Ionic pillars and a touch of the Palladian about it. The cube-like villa at No.28, however, is much more in the familiar Otto Wagner funcionalist tradition: a simple steel and concrete structure, completed in 1913. Sparsely adorned with characteristic blue tiles and aluminium rivets, there is also some Kolo Moser glasswork over the two entrances.

Schönbrunn

After the Hofburg, the Habsburgs' summer palace **Schönbrunn** is the major destination of the thousands of tourist buses that descend on Vienna every year. The immensity and rococo overkill of the palace and its interior will not be to everyone's taste, but the adjoining **Schlosspark**, with its zoo, palm house and acres of baroque gardens can be safely recommended. One of Vienna's best open-air baths, **Schönbrunner Bad**, lies to the east of the park (it features an Olympic-size pool and nude sunbathing zone).

Access to Schönbrunn is quick and fuss-free from the city centre with the U4 to Schloss Schönbrunn, where you should take the exit marked Grünbergstrasse and enter through the Meidlinger Tor on this street. If you want to head directly for the main entrance and access to the state rooms, leave via the other new exit.

The magnificent **Schönbrunn** has acres of baroque gardens.

Alternatively you could travel a stop further to Hietzing and enter the park through the Hietzinger Tor near the **zoo** and **botanical gardens**. The latter enables you to take a quick look at Otto Wagner's **Hofpavilion Hietzing**, Franz Josef's private U-Bahn station, before embarking on Schönbrunn.

The baroque era in Vienna is characterised by the enthusiasm of aristocrats and architects alike for building summer residences on a dramatic scale. The Belvedere, Palais Liechtenstein and Schloss Schönbrunn are the three most well-known products of the building boom that followed the defeat of the Turks. The Habsburgs' connection with what is today Schönbrunn dates back to 1569, when fear of the crescent moon was still a reality. Maximilian II acquired the land, then known as Kattenburg, in order to build a hunting lodge, which used to stand near what is today the Meidlinger Tor. At this time a natural spring was discovered on the estate, the origin of the name *Schönbrunn* ('beautiful spring').

After the siege of 1683, Leopold I went full speed ahead, commissioning a summer palace for his son, the future Josef I, from Fischer von Erlach, who also tutored the young Crown Prince on architecture. His original plans envisaged a palace on the scale of Versailles on the hill where the **Gloriette** stands today, and are considered to be one of the great unrealised works of baroque architecture. Economic considerations ruled the day and in 1696 work began on the present site where Josef himself lived for a time in an unfinished structure whose completion was interrupted by the Spanish Wars of Succession (1701-14). The present form of the palace owes its existence to the intervention of Empress Maria Theresia,

the monarch most closely associated with Schönbrunn. In order to accommodate her ever-expanding brood (she had 16 children, ten of whom lived to adulthood), she had her architect Nikolaus Pacassi add another floor to the two wings, and also supervised the work on the rococo interiors and the layout of the gardens. Her son Josef II inherited rather more of Maria Theresia's thrift than her enthusiasm for Schönbrunn and had huge uninhabited sections of the palace boarded up. He was, however, a keen gardener – completing the classical layout of the gardens and commissioning their most impressive monument, the Gloriette, in commemoration of the victory over the Prussians at Kolin in 1775, which returned Prague to Habsburg rule. Napoleon occupied Schönbrunn in 1805 and 1809, and his son, the Duc de Reichstadt, spent most of his short life within the confines of the palace. The reign of Franz Josef is intimately connected to the palace as the Emperor was born and died in Schönbrunn (1830 and 1916 respectively), but his wife Elisabeth had no fondness for the place, probably because she spent her wedding night there, reputedly staving off her husband's advances for all of two nights.

What was actually consummated in the Blue Chinese Salon at Schönbrunn in November 1918 was the dissolution of the Austro-Hungarian Empire when Karl I signed away any chance of the monarchy's survival. During the four-power occupation of Vienna, Schönbrunn was first HQ to the Russians and then to the British before it returned to the Austrian state in 1947. In 1961 it briefly assumed centre-stage when Kennedy and Khrushchev met for the first time at the palace and put the word détente on everyone's lips.

THE PARK

While the Habsburgs had done everything in their power to avoid the pernicious rationalist influence of France (Maria Theresia was the first monarch to speak French) and remain true to the Catholic ideal and Spanish court manners, the baroque gardens of Schönbrunn were their first espousal of the fashions of Paris. After this there was no going back and from Maria Theresia's time onwards the language at court was *Schönbrunner Deutsch*, a nasal upper-class twang, peppered with French expressions – the Viennese still call their milky coffee a *mélange*, refer to the pavement as the *trottoir* and take a leak in a *pissoir*.

The first gardens at Schönbrunn were laid out at the beginning of the 18th century by Jean Trehet according to Fischer von Erlach's plans, but these were greatly extended under the joint monarchy of Maria Theresia and Josef II, creating the network of avenues that intersect at two central points either side of the broad parterre that runs from the palace to the Neptunbrunnen (Fountain of Neptune), built in 1781. In the distance on the brow of the hill rises the majestic form of the Gloriette – today the rather snooty Café Gloriette with the best view of the palace and gardens. To the east of the fountain lie most of the park's follies amid the encroaching woodland: Von Hohenberg's superb Roman Ruins (1778) and his Obelisk Fountain (1777), as well as the *Schöner Brunnen* from which the palace's name derives and which was later set in a grotto by Canavale with the statue of a nymph pouring its waters into an enormous scallop basin.

Like the Prater and the Augarten, it was during the reign of Josef II (in 1779) that the gardens of Schönbrunn were opened to the public. He reputedly countered complaints at court by remarking that if he wanted to spend all his time among equals, he would have to dwell in the Kaisergruft among the tombs of the dead Habsburgs.

Schloss Schönbrunn

13, Schönbrunner Schlossstrasse (811 13-239/ www.schoenbrunn.at). U4 Schönbrunn, Hietzing/ tram 10, 58/bus 15a. **Open** *Palace* Apr-June, Sept, Oct 8.30am-5pm daily. July, Aug 8.30am-6pm. Nov-Mar 8.30am-4.30pm daily. *Gardens* 6am-dusk daily. **Admission** *Grand Tour* €10.50; €5.40-€6.80 concessions. *Imperial Tour* €8; €4.30-€7.40 concessions. *Parks and gardens* free. **Credit** MC, V.
Painted in the ubiquitous but slightly nauseating tone of yellow known as *Schönbrunnergelb*, the gigantic palace lies close to the banks of the Wien river and the main urban freeway to the west. It is the focal point of a gorgeous extension of parkland larger than the Principality of Monaco. Nowadays the administration and exploitation of the palace is

in the hands of a semi-private company that extracts as much financial mileage out of this historic monument as it can without caring unduly for its actual upkeep. In summer, concerts are held in the grounds and the outbuildings, Christmas sees the Great Court swamped with the stalls of Vienna's largest Advent market and product presentations regularly take place in its hallowed rooms.

Architecturally Schönbrunn is not particularly distinguished, but the Great Court with its impressive iron gates and obelisks topped with imperial eagles is quite a sight. Entrance to the state rooms is by way of the Blaue Stiege (Blue Staircase) on the west wing, but tickets are sold at the front of the east wing. For those who are determined to go inside, the Grand Tour covering 40 rooms (of a total of 1,441), is the best option as the Imperial Tour of 22 rooms does not include access to Maria Theresia's west wing, meaning you miss out on probably the most impressive section, from an interior-decoration angle. The ticket includes the use of a handheld device with a commentary in English; note that you are given an exact entrance time.

The circuit begins at the west wing. At the top of the Blue Staircase are Sissi and Franz Josef's nine private rooms, which are as dowdy as those of the Hofburg. Beginning with the billiard room, which served as a waiting room for petitioners, you pass into the actual audience chamber, the Nussbaumzimmer (Walnut Chamber). Next come the Emperor's study and the bedroom containing the simple iron bed on which he died, complete with a painting by Makart recreating the sombre scene of his demise. After the shared bedroom, a joyless chamber, things pick up a little with the Maria Antoinette room and the nursery, which have the original décor from Maria Theresia's time, and the breakfast room with lovely views over the park.

Here the state apartments begin with the Spiegelsaal (Hall of Mirrors) where the child Mozart played a duet with his sister Nannerl in 1792 for Maria Theresia and her daughters. This leads into the largest of the three rooms dedicated to the landscapes of the Polish court painter Josef Rosa and then out into the highly impressive Grosse Galerie aflame with the lights of chandeliers and wall appliqués illuminating three huge ceiling frescoes by Guglielmo Guglielmi to the glory of the House of Habsburg. The most easterly of the three, *The Glories of War*, is a copy, the original ironically destroyed by a bomb in 1945. Used as a ballroom during the nine-month long Congress of Vienna in 1815 (the Congress danced but didn't advance, it was observed at the time), it was also here that Kennedy and Khrushchev met in 1961. Off the Great Gallery on the park side is the Small Gallery, which also contains a fresco by Guglielmi and access to the two chinoiserie rooms. In one of these, the Round Chinese room to the west, Maria Theresia held secret meetings with her foremost adviser Prince Kaunitz. Beyond the Great Gallery you pass through the Carousel room, with a painting of the Amazonian Maria Theresia mounted on a Lipizzaner in a ladies' tournament held at the Winter Riding School in 1743, to the Ceremonial Hall with Van Metyens paintings of Josef II's wedding to Isabella of Parma in 1760. At this point the cheapskates who opted for the Imperial Tour are ushered out of the building.

The last section – the audience rooms – are only included in the Grand Tour and are undoubtedly the most worthwhile. Starting with the airy chinoiserie of the Blue Chinese room where Karl I abdicated in 1918, visitors pass into the rather stultifying Vieux-Lacque-Zimmer whose black lacquered panelling adorned with Japanese landscapes was designed by Canavale around 1770. Here too is Batoni's portrait of Maria Theresia's husband Franz I. The walnut-panelled Napoleon room is where the diminutive Corsican is thought to have slept. The elaborate Porcelain Room, the work of Isabella de Parma, with its trompe l'oeil criss-cross parasol motifs, has more painted woodwork than actual Meissen porcelain. However, no expense was spared in the subsequent Millionenzimmer where Maria Theresia reputedly spent a million silver florins on its rosewood panelling and priceless Persian and Indian miniatures.

After the Gobelinsalon with its 18th-century Brussels tapestries, you arrive at the Memorial Room dedicated to 'L'Aiglon' (the Little Eagle), the Duc de Reichstadt, Napoleon's son by Archduchess Marie Louise, who was virtually kept prisoner in Schönbrunn after his father's fall from grace in 1815 until his untimely death at the age of 21. After Maria Theresia's bedroom, the remaining rooms used to be the domain of Franz Josef's father Archduke Franz Karl and contain innumerable portraits of sundry Habsburgs. The Bergl rooms, decorated by Dutch botanist Jacquin with magnificent colourful frescoes depicting tropical birds and plantlife against idealised classical backgrounds, have finally been reopened to the public after years of neglect. Outside you have the opportunity to visit two sets of outbuildings, the Orangery and the Wagenburg, for which there is an extra charge.

Tiergarten und Palmenhaus

13, Hietzinger Tor (zoo 877 9294/www.zoo vienna.at/palm house 877 5087-406). U4 Hietzing. **Open** Zoo Oct-Apr 9am-4.30pm daily. May-Sept 9am-6.30pm daily. Palm house Oct-Apr 9.30am-5pm daily. May-Sept 9.30am-5.30pm daily. **Admission** Zoo €12; €5-€4 concessions. Palm House €3.50; €1.70-€3.10 concessions. **No credit cards**.
A large section of the western side of the gardens is taken up by the Tiergarten (zoo) built on the site of Franz Stephan's royal menagerie (1752), making it the world's oldest zoo. The first animals came from Prince Eugène's menagerie at the Belvedere. Many of the original baroque buildings and cages are still in use, but most of the zoo's 750 or so species now have more modern quarters. The cages are laid out radially in 12 units around the central octagonal pavilion (1759), all the work of Jean Nicholas Jadot.

The pavilion was originally used as a breakfast room by the imperial family and today it is a restaurant catering for visitors to one of the world's most aesthetically pleasing zoos.

The Palmenhaus (Palm House) is situated near the Hietzinger Tor entrance, beside the botanical gardens (1754). Maria Theresia's husband, Emperor Franz, was a keen botanist and gardener, financing expeditions to Africa and the West Indies to collect rare species and bring them back to Vienna. The magnificent iron and glass construction of the Palmenhaus, a replica of the one in London's Kew Gardens, is the work of Segenschmid and dates from 1882. The space is separated into three different climatic zones.

Wagenburg Imperial Coach Collection Schönbrunn

13, Schönbrunner Schlossstrasse (877 3244). U4 Schönbrunn, Hietzing/tram 60, 10, 58/bus 10a. **Open** Apr-Oct 9am-6pm daily. Nov-Mar 10am-4pm Tue-Sun. **Admission** €4.50; €3 concessions; €9 family ticket; free under-10s. **No credit cards**.
The collection has been housed in the former winter riding school of Schönbrunn Palace since the demise of the Habsburgs after World War I. The wealth of the Empire is amply illustrated by the variety of horse-drawn carriages and sleighs the family had at their disposal, the most extravagant being Emperor Franz Stephan's gold-plated coronation carriage with Venetian glass windows, weighing over 4,000 kilos.

Hietzing

With the presence of the monarchy at Schönbrunn, the process of gentrification started early in the neighbouring village of Hietzing, and today, along with the 19th district around Grinzing, it is one of the poshest areas of the city. The rapid U-Bahn connection to the city centre and a vast area of the Wienerwald on its doorstep, attracted the 19th-century business elite and successful bohemians such as Egon Schiele, who from 1912 had his studio at Hietzinger Hauptstrasse 101, the area's main drag. Today the street is not particularly charming, but once you wander into the side streets and see some of the magnificent Modernist and Biedermeier villas, it has a leafy gentility reminiscent of London's Hampstead.

Hietzing institutions include the **Café Dommayer** where Johann Strauss gave his first public concert in 1844. More to be recommended for food, drinks and atmosphere is the slightly shabby Jugendstil **Café Wunderer** on Hadikgasse. Round the corner from the Dommayer is the imposing edifice of the Parkhotel Schönbrunn (1907) where the Emperor's guests were accommodated.

Hofpavillon Hietzing

*13, Schönbrunner Schlossstrasse (877 1571). U4
Hietzing.* **Open** 1.30-4.30pm Tue-Sun. **Admission**
€1.80; 70¢ concessions. **No credit cards**.
Emerging from the ugly concrete of Hietzing station,
look east and Otto Wagner's Hofpavillon, a private
station for the imperial family, comes into view.
Built in 1899 on Wagner's own initiative (probably
to ingratiate himself with the monarchy), this copper-
domed cube adorned with decorative ironwork is a
reminder of the golden years of the railway, but
maybe a touch too ornate to form part of the
Jugendstil pantheon. This little extravagance was
used by Franz Josef on precisely two occasions. The
fine interior, designed by Wagner and Olbrich,
makes it well worth the entrance fee.

HIETZING'S VILLAS

Architecture fanatics will have a field day
wandering through Hietzing's residential streets.
There are houses by Josef Hoffmann, Friedrich
Ohmann and Adolf Loos, but unfortunately
none is open to the public. The individual
villas are widely dispersed, but there is a high
concentration along **Gloriettegasse** to the west
of the Schlosspark. Here, at No.9, Katharina
Schratt, Franz Josef's lover, was installed in a
rather modest Biedermeier villa. Further west
along the street, at No.21, is the **Villa Schopp**,
Friedrich Ohmann's fine Jugendstil house built in

1902 with floral motifs and superb decorative
iron-work. At No.18 is Josef Hoffmann's
monumental **Skywa-Primavesi Villa** (1913-5),
a rather neo-classical reading of Modernism with
four imposing central pillars on a symmetrical
frontage with two large triangular pediments
each housing a relief of a male and female figure.

Walk further west up the Gloriettegasse and
on the brow of the hill you get a stupendous view
of the Kirche am Steinhof with the woods behind.
There are five Adolf Loos villas in Hietzing.
Three of them are located in the area bounded
by Lainzer Strasse and Hietzinger Hauptstrasse
(bus 58 and 60): **Villa Scheu** at Larochegasse 3;
Villa Strasser at Kupelwiesergasse 28; and
the famous barrel-roofed **Villa Steiner** at St-
Veit-Gasse 10. Beyond Hietzinger Hauptstrasse
and close to the Kai is **Villa Rufer** at
Schliessmanngasse 11 and a great deal further
west is the **Villa Horner** at Nothartgasse 7.

A good kilometre up the nearby Veitingergasse
is the **Werkbundsiedlung**, a wedge-shaped
housing project of 70 individual homes built
between 1930 and 1932 by a group of Modernist
architects including Loos, Hoffmann and Richard
Neutra under the direction of Josef Frank. These
small geometric Bauhaus-style homes were
originally intended for sale, but even after
following strict economic criteria for their

Zentralfriedhof – the immense and fascinating central cemetery. *See p94.*

construction, they proved too expensive for prospective purchasers and were bought by the city council in 1934 and rented out. Four were destroyed in World War II, but today, after renovation in the early 1980s, there is something almost idyllic about the whole estate. In the house Frank himself designed, at Woinovichgasse 32, is a small documentation centre on the project.

Hietzinger Friedhof
Hietzing Cemetery

13, Maxingstrasse 15. U4 Hietzing, then 10-minute walk. Bus 56b, 58b, 156b. **Open** *Mar, Apr, Sept, Oct* 8am-5pm daily. *May-Aug* 8am-6pm daily. *Nov-Feb* 9am-4pm daily. **Admission** free.
The graves of many illustrious Viennese reside in this picturesque cemetery, a testimony to Hietzing's popularity among both the wealthy and the artistically inclined. Top tombs include Gustav Klimt and Otto Wagner, though the latter's is regrettably pompous. Also buried here are the composer Alban Berg, dramatist Franz Grillparzer, the leader of the Austro-Fascists Engelbert Dollfuss, and Klimt and Wagner's friend and collaborator Kolo Moser.

Lainzer Tiergarten & Hermesvilla

13, Lainzer Tiergarten – entrance on Lainzertor (804 1324). Bus 60b. **Open** *Apr-Sept* 10am-6pm Tue-Sun. **Admission** €3.60; €1.40-1.80 concessions; €5.40 family card. **No credit cards**.

To the west of Hietzing lies a vast tract of country-side bordering the Wienerwald known as the Lainzer Tiergarten, literally 'zoo', but referring more than anything to the large number of deer and wild boar that roam freely throughout its woods and meadows. The Lippizaner horses also graze here during the summer months. It's a bit of a trek from the city centre, but for those in need of greenery and peace and quiet it can't be bettered. The only major sight, apart from the wildlife, is Hermesvilla, a brick-built mansion commissioned by Franz Josef as a gift to Sissi in an attempt to save their marriage. Signposted from the Lainzer Tor, it's a gentle ten-minute walk. Hermesvilla was named by Sissi herself after her favourite Greek god, but despite interiors by Klimt and Makart and a purpose-built gymnasium she never developed any great fondness for the place.

Wotruba Kirche

13, Georgsgasse/Rysergasse (888 5003). S-Bahn 1, 2 Atzgersdorf-Mauer/bus 60a Kasernegasse. **Open** 2-6pm Sat; 9am-4pm Sun. **Guided tours** by appointment only.
To the south of Lainzer Tiergarten, near the village of Mauer, lies another of Vienna's ecclesiastical eccentricities – the Church of the Holy Trinity by Austrian sculptor Fritz Wotruba (1907-75), a rather curious conjunction of rectangular slabs of concrete illuminated by narrow, vertical glass panels. The general effect is of a voluminous brutalist sculpted

mass. Its attempt to create the atmosphere of a sanctuary within these threatening forms has been unanimously applauded by the Viennese.

Southern Vienna

The southern districts of Vienna hold little of specific interest for the visitor, but for anyone wishing to get off the beaten track and see something of the city's main working-class districts there are a handful of minor sights. The main reason people head south is to visit the vast **Zentralfriedhof**, Vienna's main cemetery, whose tombs outnumber the city's present population.

Vienna's 10th district, **Favoriten**, is the city's largest with a population of around 170,000. It was the focus of emigration by Czechs in the 19th century, and a Favoritner today is something like the Viennese equivalent of a cockney Londoner, while **Reumannplatz** is the Bow Bells of Vienna. Named after labour leader and Socialist politician Jacob Reumann,

it is a lively square with a market on the nearby pedestrian Favoritenstrasse and Vienna's best-loved ice-cream salon **Tichy**. There's a fast connection to the city centre via the U1. Right on the square is the imposing **Amalienbad** (1926), Vienna's largest public baths with room for 1,300 bathers. The main pool has an arched glass roof that can be opened and the facilities are decorated throughout with fine colourful mosaics in designs reminiscent of Jugendstil. From Reumannplatz you can take bus 68a to Urselbrunnengasse to visit the **Böhmischer Prater** (Bohemian Prater), a curiously old-fashioned mini-version of Vienna's premier fairground with antiquated rides, beer gardens and sausage stands.

Zentralfriedhof

11, Simmeringer Hauptstrasse 234 (760 410). Tram 71, 72. **Open** *May-Aug* 7am-7pm daily. *Mar, Apr, Sept, Oct* 7am-6pm daily. *Nov-Feb* 8am-5pm daily. **Admission** free (€1.80 for cars). **No credit cards**. The Central Cemetery ranks alongside Père-Lachaise and Highgate on the European graveyard

A taste for genius

After reading an obituary of Alma Mahler-Werfel, American songwriter Tom Lehrer sat down at his piano and wrote a song whose chorus asked: 'Alma tell us/All modern women are jealous/Which of your magic wands/Got you Gustav and Walter and Franz?' Even by modern standards of celeb promiscuity, Alma's marriages and affairs with four of the 20th century's intellectual giants – Gustav Mahler, Walter Gropius, Franz Werfel and Oskar Kokoschka – put 'the most beautiful woman in Vienna' in a league all of her own.

Daughter of the celebrated landscape painter Emil Jakob Schindler, Alma was born in 1879 into a privileged Viennese family and was encouraged to become a composer. She displayed an early penchant for artists, exchanging teenage kisses and fondles with Gustav Klimt and later with her composition tutor Alexander Zemlinsky. The latter never fully recovered from the shock of the announcement of Alma's forthcoming marriage to Mahler, then director of the court opera and 20 years her senior. She became Mahler's wife at the age of 22, agreeing to abandon her promising musical career, but in the words of Lehrer: 'Their marriage however was murder/He'd scream to the heavens above/'I'm writing *Das Lied von der Erde*/ And she only wants to make love'.

Eight years of dreary monogamy and two daughters later, Alma struck up with the handsome founder of the Bauhaus, Walter Gropius, following a chance meeting at a German spa. The holiday over and overwhelmed with lust, Gropius inexplicably addressed a love letter for Alma to Gustav Mahler, leading the great composer to seek advice from Sigmund Freud. Little is known of their four-hour meeting, but Freud allegedly diagnosed Alma and Gustav's relationship as one of mutual longing for a father and mother substitute: they were effectively living in the shadow of the incest taboo. Mahler became impotent and Alma flew into a fury on receiving Freud's bill for the session.

Shortly after Mahler's death in 1911, Alma married Gropius and together they had a daughter, the angelic Manon who died very young. The composer Alban Berg dedicated his violin concerto *Dem Andenken eines Engels* to Manon, but such was her mother's reputation, local pundits assumed that Alma herself had been its true inspiration. In the midst of acrimony, Alma embarked on a whirlwind romance with the enfant terrible of the Viennese arts, Oskar Kokoschka, vividly portrayed in his 1913 canvas *Die Windsbraut* (The Tempest) in which the two lovers appear to whiz round in a sort of metaphysical laundromat.

itinerary. Opened by the city council in 1870, its 2.5 million tombs, pantheons and memorials cover an area larger than the Innere Stadt. As you arrive on the tram one side of the Simmeringer Hauptstrasse is taken up with an endless line of undertakers and stonemasons (there are none on the city's high streets), as well as occasional cafés and restaurants. Of these, be sure to visit the bizarre, candlelit Schloss Concordia. The cemetery has three different tram stops: the first leaves you near the old Jewish cemetery and Schloss Concordia; the second at the main entrance; and the third by the entrance to the Protestant and new Jewish sections.

From the main entrance you can go straight to the *Ehrengräber* (the tombs of honour). Follow the main avenue past the semicircular line of tombs encrusted into arches – don't miss the memorial to mining baron August Zwang, resembling the entrance to a mine guarded by lamp-wielding dwarfs – and in sector 32A you will see the tombs and memorials to Austria's most famous composers. The centrepiece is a monument to Mozart, although his remains are lost in St Marxer Friedhof. Beethoven and Schubert were moved here from the Währing cemetery in

1899, but among those originally laid to rest here are Brahms, Hugo Wolf and most of the Strauss clan. Across the avenue features are tombs of influential Viennese such as Ringstrasse architect Hansen and the painter Makart, and towards the main church, in a circular recess is the Präsidentsgruft, the graves of the Second Republic presidents. Nearby in section 33C are some curious headstones, such as those of Bruno Kreisky and Arnold Schönberg, who lies under an extraordinary cube-like form crafted by sculptor Fritz Wotruba, himself buried in the same area.

The central monument of the cemetery is the Dr-Karl-Lueger-Kirche (1910), dedicated to Vienna's populist Mayor, 'der schöne Karl', anti-semite extraordinaire Karl Lueger. Built by Otto Wagner's pupil Max Hegele, it bears a resemblance to his mentor's Kirche am Steinhof. The areas behind the church contain several fascinating sections, such as the graves of Soviet soldiers who died during the 1945 liberation of Vienna, a monument to the victims of World War I, the graves of 7,000 Austrians who died fighting the Nazis (sector 97) and those of Austrian members of the International

Kokoschka's intensity proved too much for Alma who turned instead to the young Franz Werfel, a novelist and poet new in Vienna from Prague. Disconsolate, the painter ordered a life-size doll of Alma from a Munich doll maker featuring all her intimate details – a not entirely satisfying trophy that he kept for years before beheading it after a drunken orgy. Still married to Gropius, Alma found she was pregnant by Werfel prompting the architect to file for divorce. The child died at ten months; Werfel's diaries confess to a night of excessive passion late in her pregnancy while Alma, in one of her numerous anti-semitic asides, berated him for his 'degenerate seed'. However their love endured and in 1938 they managed to flee Vienna for Hollywood, where after some success as a screen writer, Werfel died in 1945. Alma took up residence in New York until her death in 1964.

Much has been made of Alma's ambivalent attitude to the Jews, but her relationships with Mahler and Werfel were more enduring than her marriage to Gropius whom she initially described as her 'racial equal'. For a woman enchanted by artistic creation, it is hardly surprising that she found Vienna's Jews irresistible. When she quipped 'Nothing tastes better than the sperm of a genius', she was certainly talking from experience.

Karl-Marx-Hof

Brigades in the Spanish Civil War (section 28). Numerous sections of the Zentralfriedhof are given over to non-Catholics. South of the main gate near the outer wall is the Russian Orthodox sector arranged around an onion-domed temple, and sectors 26 and 36 contain Muslim graves. The old Jewish section to the north near the first gate is the most moving, however. Overgrown and desecrated, the sheer size of it (over 60,000 graves) and the virulence of the vandalism emphasise the tragic destiny of Vienna's pre-war Jewish community. Among those buried here are members of the Austrian branch of the Rothschild family and the novelist and playwright Arthur Schnitzler.

Northern Vienna

The hills of the northern part of the Wienerwald are visible from various points along the western side of the Ringstrasse. These hills, ending abruptly at the Danube are in fact the continuation of the foothills of the Alps away to the south-west. From Schottentor you can take any number of trams to explore the four wine- growing villages that now form part of urban Vienna. **Nussdorf**, **Grinzing**, **Sievering** and **Neustift am Walde** used to be separate entities that became wealthy by supplying the city with the slightly acid white wine the Viennese drink with so much relish. With olde worlde architecture surrounded by vines and forests and impressive views over the whole city, they rapidly became home to the city's wealthier residents.

Despite a peppering of significant historical and architectural sites – numerous Beethoven memorials, the **Karl-Marx-Hof** housing complex, the Jugendstil villas of **Hohe Warte** – the chief attraction here are the many *Heurigen* or wine taverns. While many are almost universally decried as commercial or touristy by self-respecting *echte Wiener* (real Viennese), the combination of wine and views is a must for any visitor, and anyway there are still plenty of decent establishments.

Karl-Marx-Hof

19, Heiligenstädter Strasse 82-92. U4 Heiligenstadt/ tram D.
This imposing salmon-pink kilometre-long housing complex, which has become a symbol of the so-called Rotes Wien (Red Vienna) period of municipal Socialism between 1919 and 1933 (*see p97* **Red Vienna**). Built between 1926 and 1930 by Karl Ehm, a pupil of Otto Wagner, Karl-Marx-Hof originally consisted of 1,325 flats, some as small as 26sq m (280sq ft), as well as a laundry, kindergarten, library, post office, clinic, shop premises, public baths and gardens. While they are not especially innovative architecturally, they did provide hundreds of decent dwellings and facilities for working-class families in the city and have weathered considerably better than similar post-1945 projects.

During the 1934 Civil War that brought the Austro-Fascists to power, the building and many of its residents were the victims of heavy artillery fire. Patched up after World War II, a full restoration programme involving the modernisation of the flats and the building's connection to the Fernwärme district heating system was completed in 1989.

Red Vienna

The worldwide notoriety of Jörg Haider and the Austrian Freedom Party has accentuated the habitual image of Austria as a cradle of the far right. Such a view overlooks the fact that Europe's most successful experiment in socialist municipal government actually took place in Vienna in the 1920s. After World War I, Vienna was one of the five largest cities in the world, with a huge dejected proletariat subsisting in chronically insanitary and overcrowded conditions. In 1919 the Social Democratic Workers' Party (SDAP), led by Freud's intimate friend Viktor Adler, won a resounding victory in the municipal elections and over the ensuing 12 years instigated a programme of far-reaching reforms, known today as *Rotes Wien*, or Red Vienna. Although their attempts to create a proletarian culture through educational and artistic initiatives are all but forgotten, it was in the field of public housing that Red Vienna produced its most durable legacy.

Wherever you wander in the city, these vast, impressively solid tenements constantly come into view, their facades proudly emblazoned with the dates of their construction and earnest frescoes and statuary symbolising social progress and proletarian vigour. Many are dedicated to heroes of socialism, such as Rosa Luxemburg or Karl Liebknecht whose names stand out in bold red lettering. This was no empty propaganda exercise, however. For the first time a tenth of the city's population was provided with decent homes.

Financed by the *Wohnbausteuer* (home building tax), levied on wealthier citizens, the municipality scrupulously avoided social apartheid by locating these tenement blocks in every corner of the city – from the southern fringes of Favoriten to the leafy bourgeois enclaves of Grinzing and Döbling in the north. Each complex came with abundant gardens and playgrounds, nursery and health care units, communal laundry and social facilities

and of course, local branches of the party. All 400 blocks built during the period represent a lasting reminder of the SDAP's pragmatic idealism but none is more potent than Karl-Marx-Hof (*see p96*).

Obviously Karl-Marx-Hof's fame owes much to its bearded namesake, but it is also remembered as the bastion of socialist resistance during the Civil War of 1933-34 when the artillery of the Austro-Fascists almost razed the building to the ground and Red Vienna came to an abrupt end. It is by no means the period's largest housing project – both Sandleiten-Hof in Ottakring and Friedrich-Engels-Hof in Brigittenau are larger. Along the Margaretengürtel in the 5th district – the so-called 'Ringstrasse of the Proletariat' Reumann-Hof (*pictured*) – Matteotti-Hof and several others are more architecturally innovative and together form the most impressive ensemble. In the 3rd district the Rabenhof, housing one of the city's most energetic small theatres, is remarkable for its self-contained 'town within a town' asymmetric layout.

Surveying these fortresses today, it is easy glibly to dismiss them as blueprints for the disastrous public housing that later became all too familiar in the majority of industrialised nations. At the time, however, they stood for real, palpable progress. Vienna's post-war administration continued to build municipal housing on a rather less monumental scale but the names of more recent projects – commemorating the likes of Olaf Palme, Aneurin Bevan and Nelson Mandela – merely pay lip service to the idealism of the 1920s. And as neo-liberalism gains ground in Austria, aided by an increasingly benign Social Democratic Party, it remains to be seen how long Karl-Marx-Hof will remain in municipal hands.

Walking tours in English of the principal Red Vienna housing complexes are run by the Architektur Zentrum Wien (www.azw.at).

Nussdorf & Leopoldsberg

The nearest of the wine villages to the Danube, **Nussdorf** lies in the shadow of Leopoldsberg (425m/1,395ft), the second highest point of the Wienerwald, overlooking the Danube valley. Leopold of Babenberg had built a fortress on top of the hill in the 11th century, and 500 years later in 1683 an assortment of princes loyal to

the Habsburgs descended on Vienna to break the Turkish siege. The summit can be reached by bus 38a from Heiligenstadt U-Bahn along the impressive cobbled **Höhenstrasse** (*see p200*) built by a public works scheme during the Austro-Fascist regime of the 1930s. Walkers can choose between a 3km uphill trek from Nussdorf or the shorter, more intense zig-zag footpath that begins in **Kahlenbergerdorf**.

Next to **Leopoldskirche** (1693) and the ramparts there is a shady courtyard where you can have a drink and enjoy the views. Inside the church there is a display detailing the Turkish siege, and the main lookout point has a memorial to Austrian PoWs imprisoned in the USSR until the 1950s. Nussdorf's reputation is built around its wine industry and numerous *Heurigen*, especially along the narrow picturesque **Kahlenberger Strasse**. The Eroicagasse on the south side of Kahlenberger Strasse takes you to the popular **Mayer am Pfarrplatz**, more a restaurant than a *Heuriger*, located in a fine Biedermeier house where Beethoven lived for a time. Almost next door is **Heiligenstädter-Testament-Haus**. Here too you are a stone's throw from Otto Wagner's sluice gate system for the Donaukanal, but access is complicated since you must wind your way across the railway and through the industrial estate.

The area is positively bristling with Ludwig memorabilia, with street names such as Eroicagasse and Beethovengang, as well as a Beethoven monument (1910) by Robert Weigl in the Heiligenstädter Park on the south side of Grinzinger Strasse. On this street too, at No.64, is the house that Beethoven shared for a time in 1808 with the dramatist Franz Grillparzer. If you head back towards the city with tram 37 along Döblinger Hauptstrasse, you can visit the Eroicahaus at No.92 where Beethoven composed his Third Symphony, the *Eroica*. This is one of three Beethoven Museums, with identical opening times.

If you have the energy, follow Kahlenberger Strasse uphill out of Nussdorf to the north for about 2km, through the vineyards and at No.210 is the **Sirbu**, a *Heuriger* with magnificent views of the Danube and an excellent buffet dominated by roast pork (open Apr-mid Oct, 3pm-midnight Mon-Sat). If you feel like further exertions, you could attempt the **Kahlenberg** (bald mountain), the highest point of this section of the Wienerwald at 484m (1,588ft), or the more gentle option of walking downhill to Kahlenbergerdorf beside the Danube where there are buses back to the city.

Geymüller Schlössl

18, Khevenhüllerstrasse 2 (479 3139/711 36-295/ www.mak.at). Tram 41, then bus 41a. **Open** appointment only. **Admission** minimum of €56; groups of 10 or more €6.50 each. **No credit cards.** Built for Viennese banker Johann Geymüller in 1808, this summer villa in Pötzleinsdorf is used by the MAK (Museum of Applied Arts) as an annexe for its collection of fine *Biedermeier* furniture. Make the trip worthwhile, especially if you're with kids, by strolling around the delightful Pötzleinsdorfer Schlosspark with its wild deer and domestic animal zoo.

Heiligenstädter-Testament-Haus

19, Probusgasse 6 (370 54 08). Tram D, 37/bus 38a. **Open** 9am-12.15pm, 1-4.30pm Tue-Sun. **Admission** €1.80; 70¢ concessions. **No credit cards**. Virtually next door to Mayer am Pfarrplatz is the so-called Heiligenstädter-Testament-Haus, one of Beethoven's many residences in this area where, in 1802, he wrote his famous 'testament' to his brothers in which he bequeathed them his fortune, apologising for his misanthropy and spoke frankly of his oncoming deafness. Here too he wrote his Second Symphony. The house is now one of Vienna's three museums dedicated to the composer and exhibits include a copy of the testament, Beethoven's death mask and a lock of his hair. Across the courtyard is the rival Beethoven Ausstellung, belonging to the Beethoven Society, but with little to recommend it apart from the chance to see inside another wing of the house.

Grinzing & Kahlenberg

The village of **Grinzing**, the most famous of Vienna's wine villages, is the quintessence of Viennese rural kitsch, ably manipulated by inn-keepers and restaurateurs to keep the cash registers ringing. Tour groups are bussed into Grinzing for a night of white wine and *Schrammelmusik* at any one of the establishments along the picturesque main drag. The combination of villagey atmosphere and countryside makes Grinzing, like the other lesser-known nearby villages, a popular choice of the diplomatic community and the wealthy.

Mahler fans may well consider a visit to **Grinzinger Friedhof** to visit his austere Jugendstil tomb by Josef Hoffmann. Other famous residents include Ringstrasse architect Ferstel and formidable art groupie Alma Mahler (*see p94* **A taste for genius**). The daughter she had by Walter Gropius, Manon, is also buried here. The cemetery is located on Mannagettagasse off Strassergasse.

If you tire of the sickly prettiness of Grinzing, a trip on the 38a bus is one of the most spectacular routes in the city, along Höhenstrasse, taking in fine views of the forest and the city. The first possible stop is **Am Cobenzl**, a look-out point with bar and restaurant with views of Grinzing's vineyards. Further up you could descend at Krapfenwaldgasse and have a swim at the **Krapfenwaldbad**, the city's poshest swimming baths. Although the pools are fairly small, the parkland is magnificent with some of the most northerly Mediterranean pines in Europe and, of course, superb views. The 38a chugs on up to the highest point on the range, Kahlenberg. Back down in Grinzing, *Heurigen* to try are **Weingut Reisenberg** (for the food and the views), or better still **Zawodsky** (for the beautiful garden, good simple food and drinkable wine).

Eat, Drink, Shop

Restaurants

Diners no longer have to prepare for the Würst.

The pleasures of eating out in Vienna often owe more to the charms and idiosyncrasies of the city's myriad eating houses than to the weighty pork- and carbohydrate-based grub that is habitually served. The greatest of all these institutions is the *Beisl*. These wood-panelled beer houses have a melting-pot quality where all ages and social classes congregate around period formica tables near the warmth of a ceramic stove for a few drinks or a meal. The name derives from a Yiddish word meaning 'little house', harking back to when Vienna truly was the world's first multicultural city, the capital of an empire that conceived a dozen dishes that remain cornerstones of the *Beisl* repertoire to this day.

From the thick, paprika-laden Hungarian goulash to the world-famous *Wiener Schnitzel* that originated in Habsburg Milan, traditional *Beisl*-style eating owes much to Austria's once-proud empire. Pork features prominently and the pleasures of a crisp, caraway-studded *Schweinsbraten*, complemented with the tang of sauerkraut and the velvety smoothness of bread dumplings should not be missed.

Beyond the *Beisl*, Vienna's culinary horizons are broadening fast. In the late 1990s sushi was the exotica of choice; now the city is gripped by a pandemic of pan-Asian noodles. The growing interest in cooking is evident from the improved merchandise on Austria's previously dismal supermarket shelves and the opening of **Babette's** (*see p133*), Vienna's delightful first cook book shop. Even the *Naked Chef* now appears on TV, dubbed into German.

On the home front, the best news is the emergence of the neo-*Beisl*. Places such as **Wild**, **Schöne Perle** and **Tancredi** have preserved the atmosphere of extinct *Beisln*, and bolstered the menu with modern breezy Italo-oriental fusions that offer great dining in cool surroundings at knockdown prices. The enjoyable but cautious innovations served at the **Steirereck**, long Vienna's most fêted restaurant, also have their roots in *Beisl* culture; po-mo dining is yet to catch on in these parts.

On the downside, Austria continues to be McDonald's most profitable country (per capita) worldwide. Despite the corporation posting the worst financial results in its history, Austrian sales actually rose 3.6 per cent in 2002, thanks to the 14 million Big Macs and astonishing 46 million portions of fries Austrians consumed.

Yet eating in Vienna is intensely seasonal. Spring sees restaurants preparing the juicy local asparagus, or dishes flavoured with *Bärlauch*, the aromatic wild garlic leaves that grow in the Vienna Woods. Summer desserts feature strawberries from Burgenland and Wachau apricots, while in early autumn chanterelles and *Steinpilze* (porcini) become objects of devotion. Around St Martin's Day in early November, there's hardly a *Beisl* in the city that doesn't offer *Martinigansl* – succulent roast goose, served with red cabbage and potato dumplings.

1st District

Aioli

1, Stephansplatz 12, 3rd floor of the Haas Haus (532 0373/www.doco.com). U1, U3 Stephansplatz/bus 1a. **Open** 10am-1am daily. **Main courses** €16-€22. **Credit** V. **Map** p243 E6.
Do&Co's latest combines Mediterranean food in a modern setting with great views of Stephansdom. Named after the pungent garlic mayonnaise of the Spanish Levant, Aioli can trace its design and many of its ingredients back to Barcelona. Fish and seafood, Iberian hams and chorizos, manchego cheese and seasonal vegetable specialities such as pimientos de padrón (tiny green peppers fried with sea salt) and calçots (a gorgeous Catalan leek/onion hybrid) are all of the finest quality. Curiously the aïoli itself is the disappointment. Service is also a bit of a downer with staff struggling through a densely laid-out network of tables.

Barbaro's

1, Neuer Markt 8 (955 2525). U1, U3 Stephansplatz. **Open** *Bar* 8am-4am daily. *Restaurant* (bistro lounge) 11.30am-2.30pm, 6-10.30pm daily. **Main courses** €8.50-€21. **Credit** AmEx, DC, MC, V. **Map** p243 E7.
Neapolitan Luigi Barbaro became famous for feeding local politicians at his pricey La Ninfea and Martinelli. However, poor reviews in the gastro press and the closing of his Sky Bar have forced Barbaro to create this chic but informal diner/restaurant/bar on three floors. Minimal design accompanies a similarly pared-down menu featuring his superbly executed, yet reasonably priced pizzas and antipasti. The plush top-floor bar, accessible by an external lift, looks set to become a de rigueur after-work chiller for 1st-district professionals.

Bodega Marqués

1, Parisergasse (533 9170/www.marques.at). U3 Herrengasse. **Open** 6pm-1am Mon-Sat. **Tapas** €2.50-€13. **Credit** AmEx, DC, MC, V. **Map** p242 E6.

Organic delights at **Culinarium Österreich.**

Spanish food travels notoriously badly, so a tapas bar with a modicum of authenticity is always grounds for celebration. Housed in the baroque Palais Collalto on a gorgeous cobbled street a few blocks from Judenplatz, Bodega Marqués does a fine line in elaborate Basque pintxos – the Rolls-Royce of tapas – as well as great jamón ibérico with pan con tomate, fiery pimientos de piquillo and decently executed tortillas. There are also more substantial dishes such as baby lamb chops with aïoli, and a bewildering choice of 120 Spanish wines.

Cantinetta Antinori

1, Jasomirgottstrasse 3-5 (533 7722). U1, U3 Stephansplatz/bus 1a. **Open** 10.30am-2pm, 6pm-midnight daily. **Main courses** €21-€25. **Credit** AmEx, DC, MC, V. **Map** p243 E6.
The Antinori wine barons have exported their famous Florentine Cantinetta to Zurich and Vienna. Lacking the original's belle époque decor, the Vienna branch serves the same mouth-watering, essentially Tuscan fare, beginning with the olive bread placed on the table. Outstanding among first courses is the own-made ricotto ravioli; pick of the main courses is sea bass with white truffles and magnificent rosemary roast potatoes. The Antinori family's excellent Tuscan wines and olive oil all feature extensively. Like many restaurants in the 1st, the Cantinetta suffers from narrow tables cramped too close together, which can make things claustrophobic, especially for non-smokers.

Culinarium Österreich

1, Neuer Markt 10-11 (513 82 81-13/www.culinar ium.at). U1, U3 Stephansplatz. **Open** 11am-midnight Mon-Sat. *Shop* 9am-7pm Mon-Sat. **Main courses** from €15. **Credit** AmEx, DC, MC, V. **Map** p243 E7.
The former premises of Wild, Vienna's erstwhile Fortnum & Mason, is now home to Culinarium Österreich, a similar enterprise comprising restaurant, wine cellar and shop stocking the best in Austrian organic delicacies. These include fine cold cuts, bread baked on the premises, a good selection of schnapps and various types of Styrian Viagra: the divine pumpkin seed oil. Reasonably priced lunch menus featuring national classics such as *Tafelspitz* and *Gulasch* are the mainstay of the first-floor restaurant, while the bare-brick vaulted cellar should help the uninitiated tell a Welschriesling from a Gewürztraminer.

Do&Co

1, Stephansplatz 12, 7th floor (535 3969/www. doco.com). U1, U3 Stephansplatz/bus 1a, 2a, 3a. **Open** noon-3pm, 6pm-midnight daily. **Main courses** €19-€22. **Credit** V. **Map** p243 E6.
Prize-winning international cuisine from Vienna's celebrity restaurateur and caterer Do&Co. The semicircular restaurant provides views of the open kitchen and Stephansdom as you tuck into the king crab and Uruguayan steak combo, sushi or stir-fried wok creations. Further distractions are provided by the foxy young waiters and waitresses, helping to take your mind off irritating bread and butter cover charges and an uninspired selection of desserts. Rumours are abroad that a large-scale renovation is just around the corner. Not a bad thing after 12 years.

Esterházykeller

1, Haarhof 1, near Naglergasse (533 3482/www.ester hazykeller.at). U3 Herrengasse. **Open** 11am-11pm Mon-Fri; 4-11pm Sat, Sun. **Main courses** 2 buffet menus €5, €6.40. **No credit cards. Map** p242 E6.
Located in the bowels of the Palais owned by Hungarian nobles of the same name (*see p61*), the Esterházykeller became the first outlet for Hungarian wine and food in Vienna in the late 18th century. Apart from a few refrigerated cabinets for the cold cuts and dips, little has changed since. Take care on descending the steep stone steps into the gloomy vaults. Today the reasonably priced *Heurigen*-style food and rough and ready wines mostly attract locals.

Expedit

1, Wiesingerstrasse 6 (512 3313-0/www.expedit.net). U3 Stubentor/tram 1, 2. **Open** noon-midnight Mon-Fri; 6pm-midnight Sat. **Main courses** €7.50-€16. **No credit cards. Map** p243 F7.
These unassuming premises, formerly a textile warehouse, now contain one of Vienna's most original restaurants. Gone are the rolls of crimplene and instead the metallic shelving is replete with the joys of Liguria – jars of tiny olives, artichokes in oil and pesto, cases of oil and wine. Intended as a no-nonsense communal cantina, complete with blaring telly, Expedit serves a young clubby clientele with

Eat, Drink, Shop

Hofburg **Kaiserappartements**
Imperial Apartments

Imperial Apartments and Silver Collection

Myth Sisi
All rooms in the Imperial Apartments and the Silver Collection emanate the atmosphere of the Imperial family's way of life. It was here that world affairs and private lives converged and where one of history's most famous couples, Emperor Franz Joseph and the Empress Elisabeth (Sisi), lived. Sisi's dressing room and bathroom remain as lasting evidence of the beautiful Empress's eccentric lifestyle.

Opening in April 2004
"Sisi Museum" – a must for all Sisi enthusiasts

Open daily from 9 am to 5 pm
(July and August to 5.30 pm)

Kaiserappartements & Silberkammer
Hofburg Wien - entrance Michaelerkuppel
A-1010 Vienna
T: +43-1-5337570
E: info@hofburg-wien.at
www.hofburg-wien.at

Photo: F. X. Winterhalter: Empress Elisabeth © KHM

Kaiserliches **Hofmobiliendepot**
Imperial Furniture Collection

Imperial Furniture Collection
The Imperial Furniture Collection is one of the world's largest furniture museums. The museum shows Austrian furniture from the 18th to the 20th century. It is evidence of a style of living and the development of Austrian furniture-making and design.

Special exhibitions
September 2003 – January 2004
Thonet Brothers. Bentwood Furniture

January 2004 – March 2004
Experiment 70 – Design by Luigi Colani and Günter Beltzig

April 2004 – June 2004
Guided by Stars. Pilgrim routes. A photographic exhibition

Exhibition calendar: www.hofmobiliendepot.at

Opening hours: Tuesdays – Sundays 10am – 6pm

Kaiserliches Hofmobiliendepot
Andreasgasse 7, A-1070 Vienna
T: +43-1-524 33 57
E: info@hofmobiliendepot.at
www.hofmobiliendepot.at

Photo: Lois Lammerhuber © Museen des Mobiliendepots

Expedit – relaxed Italian dining in an original setting. *See p101.*

exquisitely prepared antipasti and a choice of five main courses, all with a distinctive Ligurian touch. Wines are reliable and fairly priced; a wide range of conserves can also be purchased at the bar. Booking is recommended. Alternatively you can order excellent focaccias and farinata at Expedit bar next door.

Fabios
1, Tuchlauben 6 (532 222/www.fabios.at). U1, U3 Stephansplatz, U3 Herrengasse. **Open** 10am-1am Mon-Sat; *bar only* 6pm-1am Sun. **Main courses** €18-€22.50. **Credit** AmEx, DC, MC, V. **Map** p242 E6.
The success of this absurdly luxurious designer Italian among local celebs owes something to the summer posing opportunities on pedestrian Tuchlauben. Costing millions, Fabio Giacobello's restaurant is a brave attempt to give Vienna a big city beat. He was formerly maître d' at Cantinetta Antinori and Novelli. He exploits his Italian connections to ensure a constant supply of top-of-the-range ingredients. Fish and seafood are astoundingly good: from the oven-seared octopus carpaccio with paprika to the prosciutto-wrapped angler fish on black olive mash. However, packing in 140 diners means that space between tables is minimal and the braying of neighbouring ad execs irksome.

Figlmüller
1, Wollzeile 5 (512 6177/www.figlmueller.at). U1, U3 Stephansplatz/bus 1a. **Open** Jan-July, Sept-Dec 11am-10.30pm daily. **Main courses** €6.50-€13.90. **Credit** AmEx, DC, JCB, MC, V. **Map** p243 E6.
Ask a hotel porter where to eat *Wiener Schnitzel* and chances are you'll be directed to Figlmüller. Tucked away in a narrow lane between Wollzeile and Bäckerstrasse, this cramped and slightly expensive restaurant certainly fries up excellent *Schnitzels* of alarming dimensions, but the combination of tourist trade and pseudo-rustic bonhomie is somewhat irritating. Business is evidently booming though, as a more spacious branch in Bäckerstrasse has recently opened. All wines come from the owner's own vineyards in Grinzing; no beers or hot drinks are served. **Branches**: 1, Bäckerstrasse 6 (512 1760); 19, Grinzinger Strasse 55 (320 4257).

Griechenbeisl
1, Fleischmarkt 11 (533 1977/www.griechenbeisl.at). U1, U4 Schwedenplatz/tram 1, 2, 21, N. **Open** 11.30am-11.30pm daily. **Main courses** €14-€18. **Credit** AmEx, DC, MC, V. **Map** p243 F6.
Originally an inn patronised by Greek and Levantine merchants (hence the name) and mentioned in chronicles under a variety of names as far back as 1500, the quaint Griechenbeisl suffers from an excess of historical connections. Due to its association with illustrious regulars such as Beethoven, Schubert and briefly Mark Twain, as well as its role in the Liebe Augustin legend, its maze of panelled rooms are generally occupied by residents of Omaha or Osaka. On the menu are all the traditional Austrian dishes, but you pay a supplement for the history. As you go under the arched entrance, peer down through the iron grill to see a figure of Augustin at the bottom of a well.

Hansen
1, Wipplingerstrasse 34 (532 0542/www.hansen.co.at). U2 Schottentor/tram 1, 2, D/bus 1a, 3a. **Open** 9am-8pm Mon-Fri; 9am-5pm Sat. **Main courses** €9.50-€18. **Credit** AmEx, DC, MC, V. **Map** p242 E5.
Housed beneath the stock exchange, Hansen takes its name from the building's architect. It's a sensual combination of restaurant and florist's (Lederleitner, *see p138*). Despite the subterranean location, there's an abundance of natural light, great for both the blooms and the diners. Hansen is an early closer, concentrating on unusual breakfast combinations (fennel salami with ricotta anyone?) and light lunches that change weekly. Beautifully assembled salads with strips of wild smoked salmon or guinea fowl breast can lead into fresh pasta, grilled zander or juicy calf's cheeks.

Immervoll, an updated classic.

Immervoll

1, Weihburggasse 17 (513 5288). U1, U3 Stephansplatz. **Open** noon-midnight daily. **Meals served** noon-11pm daily. **Main courses** €7.20-€15. **No credit cards**. **Map** p243 E7.

Ultra-cool, these vaulted premises were given the once-over by architect Hermann Czech. As for the food, Immervoll's owner, actor Hanno Pöschl, rightly believes that Viennese classics, cooked with care, can and do compare proudly with more fêted cuisines. The menu changes daily, offering a choice of seven starters and main courses, some of which have a more Italian bent. All are extremely good value.

Indochine 21

1, Stubenring 18 (513 7660/www.indochine.at). U3 Stubentor. **Open** 11.30am-2am daily. **Meals served** 11.30am-3pm, 6pm-midnight daily. **Main courses** €14-€22. **Credit** AmEx, DC, MC, V. **Map** p243 F7.

The French/Vietnamese fusion food here is still wowing Vienna's chattering classes. Amid whirling fans, raffia seating, potted palms and red lacquered sunshades, local society tucks into subtly spiced seafood, fish, meats and noodles, skilfully assembled by chef Wini Brugger who honed his trade over 13 years in South-east Asia. The bar and lounge area is a real colonial treat, and the cocktails superb, but there's something naff about the starchy atmosphere and the menu's descriptions of the miraculous medicinal properties of the ingredients.

MAK Café

1, Stubenring 5 (714 0121). U3 Stubentor/tram 1, 2. **Open** 10am-midnight Tue-Sun. **Main courses** €8-€15. **No credit cards**. **Map** p243 F7.

The pick of the museum cafés, the one attached to the MAK (*see p75*) has an ornate 19th-century ceiling. House speciality is pierogi – Polish ravioli stuffed with beef, cream cheese and, for carbohydrate junkies, potato. The rest is reliable bistro food. Try the garden in summer.

Markt-Restaurant Rosenberger

1, Mayserdergasse 2 (512 3458). U1, U2, U4 Karlsplatz/tram 1, 2, D, J. **Open** 7.30am-11pm daily. **Main courses** €5-€10. **Credit** AmEx, DC, JCB, MC, V. **Map** p242 E7.

If foreign-language menus bring you out in a rash, this low-priced self-service restaurant is a godsend. Arranged like a subterranean market place, the various stalls offer Argentinian steaks and grilled fish, grilled and boiled vegetables, salads, soups and sushi – all at the point of a finger. Pour your own wines and beer or mix a cocktail from the excellent selection of freshly squeezed juices. Desserts are generously sized portions of apple strudel or sachertorte. It's best to avoid jam-packed lunchtimes here.

Meinl am Graben

1, Graben 19 (from 7pm entrance around the corner on Naglergasse) (532 33 34-35/www.meinl.com). U1, U3 Stephansplatz, U3 Herrengasse. **Open** 8am-midnight Mon-Fri; 8.30am-midnight Sat. **Meals served** 8-11am, noon-6pm, 7-10pm Mon-Sat. **Main courses** €24-€29. **Credit** AmEx, DC, JCB, MC, V. **Map** p242 E6.

Better known as the city's most elegant food store (*see p140*), Meinl am Graben became Vienna's number one luxury dining experience after Christian Petz took over the upstairs restaurant. The atmosphere is laid back and the food a creative combination of simple aromatic ingredients. Grilled scallops glazed with a fine gelée on green gazpacho, or the creamiest polenta as a foil for flash-roasted kid, are representative of Petz's style. The wine cellar is famous, the staff hyper-informed and the view down Graben alone worth the price of the meal.

Novelli

1, Bräunerstrasse 11 (513 4200-0). U1, U3 Stephansplatz/bus 1a, 2a. **Open** noon-2pm, 6-11pm Mon-Sat. **Main courses** €18-€23. **Credit** AmEx, DC, MC, V. **Map** p242 E7.

This citadel of modern Italian dining is a favourite for corporate entertaining. Decked out in Tuscan russet with roaring fireplace, leather bench seating and vaulted ceiling, Novelli has an elegant yet comfortable feel. Diners can go directly to a table, or ogle the fresher-than-fresh antipasti at the rustic ceramic-faced bar. Dishes such as poached sea bass in tarragon cream are beautifully prepared and presented; from the dessert menu, plump for chocolate mousse, in three tiers, served on exotic fruit. There's also a lengthy list mostly of fine Italian wines. The clientele reflect the classy prices, but staff are pleasant.

The Best Restaurants

For intellectuals
With peeling posters and nicotined walls, **Alt Wien** (*p182*) does a pungent restorative *gulasch*, much loved by local chin-tuggers.

For vegetarians
Wrenkh (*p107*) offers Vienna's best meat-free dining in sleek, modern surroundings.

For horticulturists
Palmenhaus (*p105*) – it's a shame to waste this art nouveau hothouse on plants and shrubs.

For clubbers
Noodles at **Ra'mien** (*p112*) will build you up for doing the Charlie-Chan in the downstairs bar.

For thespians
Located in the Burgtheater, **Vestibül** (*p107*) services the palates of Vienna's luvvies.

For planning a putsch
The **Esterházykeller** (*p101*) is a lugubrious underground wine cellar ideal for plotting.

For stunning views
Weingut Reisenberg (*p120*) – the food and the vistas are worth the stiff walk.

For the gregarious
Expedit (*p101*) – where the communal tables and the Ligurian specialities soon get the chins wagging.

For fabulous fish
Land-locked Austria gets the creatures of the deep sent up from the nearby Croatian coast. **Konoba** (*see p114*) has some of the best.

For the loaded
When the sky's the limit, don't miss **Steirereck** (*p109*) or the currently kicking **Meinl am Graben** (*p104*).

For would-be-restaurant-owners
The sheer amateurish enthusiasm and solid talents of the lads at **Aromat** (*p110*) will have you scanning the property pages.

Palmenhaus
1, Burggarten (entrance Goethegasse) (533 1033/ www.palmenhaus.at). U1, U2, U4 Karlsplatz/tram 1, 2, D, J. **Open** 10am-2am daily. **Meals served** 10am-midnight daily. *Restaurant* 11.30am-midnight daily. **Main courses** €11-€15. **Credit** AmEx, DC, MC, V. **Map** p242 E7.
Located in a Jugendstil hot-house, amid mighty palms, this is one of Vienna's most spectacularly appointed bar-restaurants. A big favourite with the art crowd, the venue suffers from doubling as a drinking hole, so beware of eating beside a boozy group of chain smokers. The monthly changing menu is compact, with excellent grilled fish and pasta and the best of Austrian wines. Cakes are splendid too. The terrace overlooking the Burggarten is optimally oriented for winter sunshine: in summer you can fry. Sunday afternoons tend to resemble a riotous assembly. Occasional club nights are held.

Plachutta
1, Wollzeile 38 (512 1577/www.plachutta.at). U3 Stubentor/tram 1, 2/bus 1a. **Open** 11.30am-midnight daily. **Main courses** €12-€22. **Credit** AmEx, DC, MC, V. **Map** p243 F7.
The stately Plachutta is a Viennese institution rightly famed for one dish. *Tafelspitz* was Emperor Franz Josef's favourite Sunday lunch: boiled beef tenderloin served with rösti, puréed spinach and an apple and horseradish sauce. *Tafelspitz*'s elaborate preparation (the meal begins with the beef broth left over after cooking the meat) has probably prevented it

becoming well known internationally, so a meal here should be a high priority for any visitor to Vienna. **Branches**: 16, Ottakringer Strasse 266 (480 5730); 19, Heiligenstädter Strasse 179 (370 4125) .

Reinthaler
1, Gluckgasse 5 (512 3366). U1, U2, U4 Karlsplatz. **Open** 9am-11pm Mon-Fri. **Main courses** €5.50-€11.50. **No credit cards**. **Map** p242 E8.
An increasingly rare example of an authentic, low-priced Innere Stadt *Beisl*. Its wood-panelled rooms and green formica tables are nearly always packed with pensioners, students, and workers in overalls and suits – hunched over beers and newspapers. You'll find the usual dishes, including great *Schweinsbraten*, a stinging goulash and much offal.

Soho
1, Am Josefsplatz 1 (entrance via Burggarten) (0676 309 5161). U1, U2, U4 Karlsplatz/tram 1, 2, D, J. **Open** 9am-4pm Mon-Fri. **Main courses** €3.90-€4.60. **No credit cards**. **Map** p242 E7.
The spruced up National Library canteen is now a pleasantly designed bar-restaurant offering excellent food at true canteen prices. It is located in the basement of the imposing Neue Burg. The two lunch menus always offer a vegetarian choice and consist of Italian-inspired food with the odd wink at the Far East.

Trzesniewski
1, Dorotheergasse 1 (512 3291/www.speckmitei.at). U1, U3 Stephansplatz/bus 3a. **Open** 8.30am-7.30pm Mon-Fri; 9am-5pm Sat. **No credit cards**. **Map** p242 E7.

Eat, Drink, Shop

Visit The Renaissance Castle:

Rosenburg

Built in the 12th century, and restored in the 16th to a renaissance castle,
a visit to Rosenburg is an unforgetable journey.

Opening Hours: 1st April through 1st November, daily 9:30 - 5:00

The castle can also be rented for romantic weddings,
parties, special occassions. Contact: rosenburg@hoyos.co.at

www.rosenburg.at

The atmospheric dining room here is overseen by a troupe of rather severe ladies. The only decoration among the dark wood and granite tables are the trays full of striped egg-based canapés on rye bread. Varieties include speck (cured ham), spicy green pepper, sardine, and herring and onion. It's self-service, pay-as-you-order. The cashier will ask you to order drinks (wines or tiny beers) and give you the corresponding colour-coded counter which you exchange at the other end of the bar. Go for a mid-afternoon snack as the lunchtime rush detracts from its wonderfully gloomy *Mitteleuropa* feel. Other central branches include one in the 3rd district (Galeria, Landstrasser Hauptstrasse 97, 712 9964), one in the 6th (Mariahilfer Strasse 95, 596 4291), and one in the 7th (Kirchengasse 6-8, 523 8462).
Branches: throughout the city.

Vestibül

1, Dr-Karl-Lueger-Ring 2 (532 4999/www.vestibuel.at).
Tram 1, 2, D. **Open** 11am-midnight Mon-Fri; 6pm-midnight Sat. **Main courses** €12-€23. **Credit** MC, V. **Map** p242 D6.
Situated in the memorable neo-classical south wing of the Burgtheater, Vestibül serves everything from oysters to offal to a clientele varying from corporate to thespian. Liveried waiters work from a splendid mirrored bar, bringing out Viennese classics such as *Beuschl* (a sort of deconstructed haggis) with dumplings, as well as crisp sea bass roasted with artichokes and spring onions. It can get loud inside, but there's a terrace overlooking the Ringstrasse.

Bangers & beer

Although **Trzesniewski**'s gorgeous eggy canapés are the highlight of Viennese snack food (*see p105*), late-night grazing is dominated by the *Würstelstand*. These ramshackle sausage stands serve up countless varieties – from the spicy *Bosna* to the cheese-pumped *Käsekrainer*, fondly referred to as an *Eitriger* or puss-stick. That meat-loaf sweltering in the glass oven is *Leberkäs* (literally liver cheese), a rank local delicacy made of horsemeat. In general the *Würstelstand*'s wares are crack-in-the-mouth tubes of reconstituted meat slurry, best suited to assuaging post-beer munchies. *Bratwurst* is thinner, meatier and more suited to the British palate. Vienna's world of *Würste* was recently rocked when the Wallensteinplatz stand in the 2nd started selling vegetarian sausages. There is little to recommend them, apart from giving fleischphobes the chance to participate in a quintessential Viennese experience.

Wein & Co

1, Jasimirgottstrasse 3-5 (535 0916/www.weinco.at).
U1, U3 Stephansplatz. **Open** *Restaurant* 10am-midnight Mon-Sat; 11am-midnight Sun. *Bar* 10am-2am Mon-Sat; 11am-midnight Sun. **Main courses** €13-€18. **Credit** AmEx, DC, MC, V. **Map** p243 E6.
Austria's most visible wine merchant operates a restaurant-within-a-store concept to dodge stringent retail opening hours. This latest branch is patronised by suits and minor celebs, drawn by its cool design, pricey Italian-inspired snacks and light meals, and splendid wines. The latter are sold at shop prices, but are still costly. 'Happy Sundays' (11am-4pm) offer relief, with all open wines at half price. The chance to buy wines, spirits and gourmet delicacies until midnight seven days a week is a minor miracle in these parts. Staff are well-informed.

Wrenkh

1, Bauernmarkt 10 (533 1526/www.wrenkh.at).
U1, U3 Stephansplatz. **Open** *Restaurant* 11.30am-2.30pm, 6-11pm daily. *Bar* 11.30am-midnight daily. **Main courses** €7-€12. **Credit** AmEx, DC, MC, V. **Map** p243 E6.
Christian Wrenkh's restaurants are mercifully free of the 'nut cutlet' vegetarianism that persists in Vienna. His flagship restaurant in Bauernmarkt has long been a favourite of well-heeled fashionistas who patronise the street's pricey clothes emporia. The food is original, organic and smartly presented.
Branch: 9, Servitengasse 14 (319 7763).

Zum Finsteren Stern

1, Schulhof 8 (535 2100). *U3 Herrengasse.*
Open 5pm-1am Mon-Sat. *Restaurant* 7pm-1am Mon-Sat. **Main courses** €12-€18. **No credit cards**. **Map** p242 E6.
An excellent wine bar newly relocated to splendid premises in the baroque streets between Am Hof and Judenplatz. As well as a mouth-watering choice of small eats and wines, there are two daily menus featuring creative, Italian-oriented meat dishes. Great alfresco seating in summer is a bonus.

Zum Schwarzen Kameel

1, Bognergasse 5 (533 81 25/www.kameel.at).
U1, U3 Stephansplatz/bus 1a, 2a, 3a. **Open** *Restaurant* noon-2.30pm, 6-10pm Mon-Sat. *Delicatessen buffet* 8.30am-10.30pm Mon-Sat. **Main courses** €20-€44. **Credit** AmEx, DC, MC, V. **Map** p242 E6.
Much loved by Vienna's more conservative movers and shakers, the Black Camel has the stuffy air of a gentlemen's club but is full of ladies who lunch. Since 1618 it has operated as a delicatessen; rumour has it Beethoven used to shop here. The deli and wine merchant's still do a roaring trade, but most folk stand at the bar or lounge on the pavement terrace nibbling delicate sandwiches. These include red cabbage spread, the divine Matjesherring and even more godly smoked ham butty. In the small wood-panelled dining room, there's seriously good eating to be done: marinated goose liver with beetroot jelly, and lamb fillet on grilled fennel – sensational.

Eat, Drink, Shop

Gasthaus am Nordpol 3 – a charming example of a neo-*Beisl*.

Zwölf Apostelkeller

1, Sonnenfelsgasse 3 (512 6777/www.zwoelf-apostelkeller.at). U1, U3 Stephansplatz. **Open** 4.30pm-midnight daily. **Main courses** €5.20-€9.50. **Credit** AmEx, DC, MC, V. **Map** p243 F6.
Stacked beneath one of von Hildebrandt's most spectacular baroque houses, this cellar on three subterranean levels is the sort of place your distant Viennese Uncle Fritz would take you. Vast quantities of undistinguished food, beer and wine, along with dubious traditional music, are the tonic. Nevertheless, the labyrinth of vaulted Gothic and early baroque cellars have a Harry Potter-esque charm. Ordering is made easier by a choice of buffets. Note that there's a long walk up to the toilets from the lower ground floor.

2nd District

Bayou

2, Leopoldgasse 51 (214 7752/www.bayou.at). Tram 21, N/bus 5a. **Open** 11am-3pm, 6pm-midnight Mon-Sat; 11am-3pm, 6pm-midnight Sun. **Main courses** €7-€22. **Credit** AmEx, MC, V. **Map** p243 F5.
A Creole/Cajun diner that was one of the first of the new breed to open in the area. Gumbo stews and jambalaya sit alongside Tex-Mex dishes and the odd Indian curry – in fact anything hot and spicy is allowed in. The gumbos are rather too stodgy, so stick to lighter options such as the garlicky grilled chicken with coriander, or the salads dressed in a curious olive oil and vodka concoction. Sweet tooths should leave room for the hefty New Orleans bread pudding with butterscotch cream.

Gasthaus am Nordpol 3

2, corner Nordbahnstrasse & Nordpolgasse (333 5854). Tram 5. **Open** 5pm-midnight Mon-Sat; 11am-midnight Sun. **Main courses** €6-€10. **No credit cards**. **Map** p235 F4.
This renovated *Beisl* specialises in Bohemian (both the region and the attitude) dishes, beer and absinthe. Though its net curtains and wallpaper

have been removed, the splendidly named am Nordpol 3 has kept the bare boards and panelling of traditional Viennese eating houses. It has also retained a menu of hearty dishes: tripe soup, cured pork with horseradish, *Würst* (made in-house) and the typical Bohemian poppy-seed desserts.

Gesundes

2, Lilienbrunngasse 3 (219 5322). Tram 21, N/bus 5a. **Open** 9am-6pm Mon, Tue, Thur, Fri; 9am-5.30pm Wed; 10am-2pm Sat. **Main courses** €6.50-€8. **No credit cards**. **Map** p243 F5 to F6.
This tiny organic and wholefood store has a couple of tables where you can order from lunch menus that always include a vegan option. It's all prepared according to the principle of the Five Elements (in case you wondered). There's a good choice of organic fruit and veg, own-made desserts and teas. No smoking, no alcohol, but not as severe as it sounds.

Schöne Perle

2, corner Leopoldsgasse & Grosse Pfarrgasse (664 243 3593). Tram N, 21. **Open** 11am-midnight daily. **Main courses** €5-€11. **No credit cards**. **Map** p235 F5.
Conserving the name of its predecessor, a Chinese restaurant, this is a typical example of what local foodies call a neo-*Beisl*. It serves a menu of classic dishes in an informal, well-designed drinking and dining den. The larder is stocked exclusively with organic produce: a rarity in Vienna.

Schuppich

2, Rotensterngasse 18 (212 4340). U1 Nestroyplatz/tram N, 21. **Open** 6pm-1am Tue-Sat; noon-10pm Sun. **Main courses** €7-€23. **Credit** AmEx, DC, MC, V. **Map** p243 F5.
Lurking in the backstreets off Taborgasse, this is the address for Italian food from Friuli and Trieste. Try the €21 four-course set menu or the seasonal specialities for a good intro to a cuisine rarely seen outside Italy. The *Beisl*-style interior oscillates between gloomy emptiness and packed-to-the-gills chaos, but the food is usually reliable.

Schweizerhaus

2, Strasse Des 1 Mai 116 (728 0152/www.schweizer haus.at). U1 Praterstern then tram 21. **Open** *mid Mar-Oct* 10am-11pm Mon-Fri; 11am-11pm Sat, Sun. **Main courses** €5.40-€14. **No credit cards. Map** p240 H6.
Popular with raucous lads and lasses from many nations, this bustling establishment is loud, sweaty and beery. The restaurant is housed in and around what was the Swiss Pavilion. Run since 1920 by the Kolarik family, the Schweizerhaus is famous for serving huge portions of specialities such as *gegrillte Steltzen* (grilled pork knuckle studded with caraway seeds; 600 of which are guzzled every day), tripe soup and rivers of draught Budweiser.

Toko Ri

2, Franz-Hochedlingergasse 2 (214 8940/ www.tokori.at). Tram 31. **Open** 11.30am-2.30pm, 6-10.30pm Mon-Sat. **Main courses** €7-€16. **Credit** AmEx, DC, MC, V. **Map** p243 E5 to F5.
Sushi houses in Vienna stick to staples, with a noticeable lack of Japanese ritual. Toko Ri concentrates on quality and freshness, making it one of the city's most consistent purveyors of raw fish. The original premises, in a moribund area of the 2nd district, are tatami-cool with subdued lighting, unlike the more garish branches in the Innere Stadt and the Naschmarkt. Booking is advisable.
Branches: 1, Salztorgasse 4 (532 7777); 4, Naschmarkt, Stand 263-4 (587 2616).

3rd District

Gasthaus Wild

3, Radetzkyplatz 1 (920 9477). Tram N. **Open** 11.30am-1am Tue-Sun. *Restaurant* 11.30am-11pm Tue-Sun. **Main courses** €8-€16. **Credit** V. **Map** p243 G6.
Weinhaus Wild used to be one of Vienna's most charismatic *Gasthäuser* despite appalling food and service. Now, these monumental premises have been given a new lease of life. By conserving original features such as the beautiful wooden *Schank* (the 'bar') and removing grimy dividers, Wild has been transformed into an atmospheric neo-*Beisl* without frightening away its original clientele. The menu is rarely without an authentic Viennese offal dish, but otherwise diners can choose from inspired treatments of goat's cheese, beetroot and lamb. Service is excellent, as are the reasonably priced wines and beers.

Im KunstHaus

3, Weissgerberlände 14 (718 5152). Tram N. **Open** 10am-11pm daily. **Main courses** €6-€13. **No credit cards. Map** p240 G6.
A wacky café-restaurant located in the courtyard of Hundertwasser's Kunsthaus gallery (*see p79*). True to the artist's style, the restaurant is arrayed in bright colours, has undulating floors and is lined with fresh flowers. Compared to the setting, the menu is a bit disappointing – a mix of soups, salads and meats varying seasonally (beef soup in winter, gazpacho in summer) served by a troupe of spec-

tacularly camp waiters. A fun place to eat, then, especially in summer when you can enjoy the building's bizarre repointing from the outlandish garden.

Palais Schwarzenberg

3, Hotel Schwarzenberg, Schwarzenbergplatz 9 (798 4515/600/www.palais-schwarzenberg.com). Tram D. **Open** noon-2.30pm, 6-11.30pm (reduced menu 10-11.30pm) daily. **Main courses** €18-€30. **Credit** AmEx, DC, JCB, MC, V. **Map** p243 E8.
Part of the luxurious hotel that occupies the Schwarzenberg family's palace, this oh-so-smart dining venue offers a variety of impressive settings. The choice ranges from wood-panelled antiques-laden warmth to a gorgeous airy conservatory overlooking the hotel's splendid gardens, with an alfresco option in summer. The food generally consists of set menus featuring fussily presented Austro-Mediterranean cooking. Extravagance is the guiding principle; you might witness bizarre marriages such as poached sole with fried chorizo. But it all makes for a memorable, if costly meal.

Steirereck

3, Rasumofskygasse 2 (713 3168/www.steirereck.at). Tram N. **Open** 10.30am-2pm, 7-11pm Mon-Fri. **Main courses** €23-€28. **Credit** AmEx, DC, MC, V. **Map** p240 G7.
For most Viennese a yardstick of success is to eat at the Steirereck, long the city's leading restaurant. The establishment is currently in the throes of a move – late 2003 seems likely – to the picturesque Meierei in the Stadtpark. Superb renditions of Austrian

Schöne Perle. *See p108.*

classics with a Styrian twist, combined with a prudent attitude to innovation, are the trademark and this seems unlikely to change. Credit must go to the aptly named chef, Helmut Österreicher. Over 25 years, he has transformed the place from a suburban eating house into one of Europe's most celebrated restaurants. Diners normally choose from two set menus that change daily, but à la carte is also available. The wine list includes everything from grands crus to the south Styrian and Wachau whites. If you fancy experiencing the Steirereck's sedate belle époque rooms without breaking the bank, choose the set brunch or Wiener Gabelfrühstück ('Viennese Fork Breakfast', served 10.30am-noon). The restaurant is unusually child-friendly. Booking essential.

Taverna Lefteris
3, Hörnesgasse 17 (713 7451/www.taverna-lefteris.at). U3 Rochusmarkt/bus 4a. **Open** 6pm-midnight Mon-Sat. **Main courses** €8.50-€16. **Credit** AmEx, DC, MC, V. **Map** p240 H9.
Employees of the Greek Embassy declare this the best Greek restaurant in town. The menu has a Cretan slant, with several Turkish-influenced dishes. It's also pretty, with beautiful wooden floors, and walls painted light blue. In summer, you can eat under the trees. Greek musicians play on Tuesdays.

4th District

Amacord
4, Rechte Wienzeile 15 (587 4709). U4 Kettenbrückengasse. **Open** 10am-2am daily. **Main courses** €7.20-€12.20. **No credit cards**. **Map** p239 D8.
Amacord's smoky confines are full of bearded ecologists and earnest arty types sitting among bags of newly purchased fruit and veg, enjoying a beer or a coffee while browsing through the excellent selection of international newspapers. The food is gratifying Italian-inspired cooking but is made less enjoyable by the smoke and dearth of space.

Indian Pavilion
4, Naschmarkt, Stand 74-5 (587 8561). U1, U2, U4 Karlsplatz, U4 Kettenbrückengasse. **Open** 11am-6.30pm Mon-Fri; 11am-5pm Sat. **Main courses** €7-€10. **No credit cards**. **Map** p242 D8.
A wonderful budget Indian restaurant crammed into a tiny Naschmarkt stall, Indian Pavilion is only really an option in summer when its terrace operates. The mild curries and tasty lentil dishes are great. Indian beer and music heighten the experience.

Naschmarkt Deli
4, Naschmarkt/Stand 421-436 (585 0823/www.naschmarkt-deli.at). U4 Kettenbrückengasse. **Open** 7am-11.30pm Mon-Fri; 7am-midnight Sat. **Main courses** €6-€8.80. **No credit cards**. **Map** p242 D8.
Currently the place to hang out in the Naschmarkt. The Deli supplies booming beats along with a varied menu of pastrami sandwiches, ethno-snacks, superb salads and impeccable Italian coffee to hordes of Saturday morning slackers and dot.com worka-

holics. It is located beside Do-an (*see p126*); the terraces of both establishments become an almost indistinguishable mass on fine Saturdays. This hive of activity proved irresistible to a gang of English meatheads who trashed the place in 2002 before the European Championship qualifier in Bratislava.

Tancredi
4, Grosse Neugasse 5 (941 0048/www.tancredi.at). Tram 62, 65. **Open** 11.30am-2.30pm, 6pm-midnight Tue-Fri; 6pm-midnight Sat. **Main courses** €6.50-€15.50. **No credit cards**. **Map** p239 D9.
Tancredi produces an interesting take on traditional Viennese and provincial dishes in light, minimalist surroundings. Its menu of eight starters and 12 mains changes monthly, with a couple of vegetarian options to balance out meaty fare such as excellent roast wild boar in juniper sauce. Wines are Austrian, augmented by well-chosen foreign bottles such as Catalan Raimat reds. The Avant Garde Zweigelt is about as full-bodied as Austrian reds get.

Ubl
4, Pressgasse 26 (587 64 37). U4 Kettenbrückengasse. **Open** noon-2.30pm, 6pm-midnight daily. **Main courses** €8-€12. **No credit cards**. **Map** p239 D8.
With its ancient panelling, wood-burning stove and atmospheric sedateness, Ubl is an outstandingly conserved specimen of the Viennese *Beisl*. The usual staples such as fine Schwiebelrostbraten are here, but so too is Italian-influenced cooking such as side orders of braised fennel and other vegetable concoctions. Word has it the cooking varies greatly depending on which of the two sisters runs the show. The leafy summer terrace is a good spot to relax.

5th District

Aromat
5, Margaretenstrasse 52 (913 2453/www.arom.at). U4 Kettenbrückengasse. **Open** 11am-3pm, 6-10pm Mon-Fri. **Main courses** €6-€8. **No credit cards**. **Map** p239 D9.
Here you'll get generous portions of what the owners describe as 'international home cooking'. Located in gorgeous old shop premises and furnished with 1950s formica tat, Aromat has a curious menu featuring more soups than main courses. Classic Viennese beef broth and Tuscan pappa al pomodoro share the list with pho ga and other Vietnamese warmers. Main dishes are equally eclectic, but similarly satisfying; the fegato alla veneziana with polenta is wicked. A young, chirpy crew run proceedings, supplying moderately priced but superb Murauer beer. Only 20 diners at most can be seated.

Motto
5, Schönbrunner Strasse 30 (entrance Rüdigergasse) (587 0672/www.motto.at). U4 Pilgramgasse/bus 59a. **Open** 6pm-4am daily. **Main courses** €7-€17. **Credit** MC, V. **Map** p238 C9.
At Motto they camp it up well into the early hours. The dimly lit and beautifully appointed restaurant

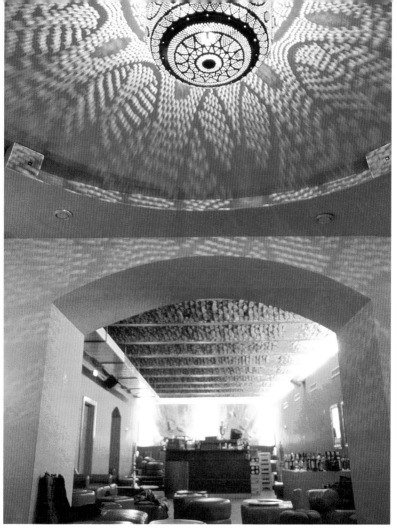

Is Vienna ready for gastro-entertainment project **Aux Gazelles**? *See p112.*

has become a magnet for models and media folk since it's one of the few places to find a reasonable meal at 3am, with a free ego massage thrown in. Specialities include Frau Helene's spectacular steak flambés (Mon, Tue, Sun). Otherwise, the menu's slightly unholy alliance of Asian, Austrian and Italian cuisines at least offers vegetarians a fair choice. And if the food's just OK, the gorgeous garden, funky bar and fine-looking waiters bitching in a variety of languages more than compensate.

Schlossgasse 21

5, Schlossgasse 21 (544 0767/www.schlossquadr.at). Bus 13a, 59a. **Open** 6pm-2am daily. **Main courses** €6.90-€19.50. **Credit** V. **Map** p242 C6.

Two restaurants share one of Vienna's best conserved Biedermeier-era inner courtyards. For this alone it's worth visiting either Schlossgasse 21 or the neighbouring Silberwirt. The former serves a fairly pedestrian mixture of Indonesian, Thai, and Indian cuisine; the latter focuses on traditional Viennese cooking. Late dining, good beers and outstanding architecture are the best reasons to pop in.

Zum Alten Fassl

5, Ziegelofengasse 37 (544 4298/www.zum-alten-fassl.at). Bus 13a, 59a. **Open** 11.30am-3pm, 6pm-midnight Mon-Fri; 6pm-midnight Sat; noon-3pm, 6pm-midnight Sun. **Main courses** €6.20-€14. **Credit** AmEx, DC. **Map** p239 D9.

Eat, Drink, Shop

Despite the appearance of rucola and lemongrass, this classic *Beisl*-style operation usually sticks to what it knows best, particularly seasonal specialities such as roast goose for St Martin's Day. Cosiness, of the wood-panelled and ceramic-stove ilk, is here in abundance. Zum Alten Fassl ('the old barrel') also stands out for its friendly service and its mastery of Viennese and Styrian classics. The back garden has lost some charm since the ancient chestnut tree was uprooted in a summer storm.

6th District

Aux Gazelles

6, Rahlgasse 5 (585 6645/www.auxgazelles.at). U2 Museumsquartier. **Open** 10am-2am Mon-Thur; 10am-4pm Fri, Sat; 10am-9pm Sun. **Main courses** €9.50-€41. **Credit** AmEx, DC, MC, V. **Map** p242 D8.
A vast North African theme enterprise, Aux Gazelles is one of the most ambitious gastro-entertainment projects to hit Vienna. It occupies the ground floor of an opulent 19th-century apartment building. You can choose between a mint tea or a tagine lunch on the café's beaten copper tables, a full-on French-Maghrebin meal in the brasserie, a cocktail in dimly lit carpeted lounges, or a dozen fines claires in the sleek oyster/caviar bar. Apart from the oyster bar, and the earthy cool of the club bar (*see p184*), the whole thing is drenched in Moroccan styling. There's even a small marble *hammam* (just steam and showers – no plunge pool). Time will tell if Vienna is ready for such extravagance.

Gastwirtschaft Steman

6, Otto-Bauergasse 7 (597 8509). U3 Zieglergasse. **Open** 11am-midnight Mon-Fri. **Main courses** €5.50-€12. **No credit cards**. **Map** p238 C8.
Despite renovation Steman has maintained its austere old-world *Beisl* charm and dark wood interior. A clouded glass wall separates the boisterous bar area from the main dining room. The menu consists of well-priced local classics: offal, game, wild mushrooms and the noble pig in all its manifestations. Staff are among the friendliest of any Viennese *Beisl*.

Kiang Noodles

6, Joanelligasse 3 (586 8796). U4 Kettenbrückengasse. **Open** 6-11pm Mon-Sat. **Main courses** €6-€19. **Credit** AmEx, DC, MC, V. **Map** p239 D8.
The agreeable Kiang chain of no-chintz Chinese restaurants was a revelation in Vienna. Kiang Noodles (inspired by London's Wagamama chain) is the best of the bunch food-wise. It specialises in many versions of the humble noodle, including fried (Singapore fried noodles with dried shrimps and mushrooms), and spicy (tan-tan noodles in soya and sesame sauce with peanut butter). Try the delicious Tza-Kiang noodles with pork and garlic sauce. There's also plenty of enjoyable vegetarian choices. As at all Kiangs, service is swift and friendly. **Branches**: 1, Rotgasse 8 (533 0856); 3, Landstrasser Hauptstrasse 50 (715 3470); 8, Lederergasse 14 (405 3197).

Nice Rice

6, Mariahilfer Strasse 45/Raimundhof 49 (586 2839). U3 Neubaugasse. **Open** 11am-11pm Mon-Fri; 11am-6pm Sat. **Main courses** €6.90-€11.60. **No credit cards**. **Map** p238 C8.
A likeable and unpretentious vegetarian restaurant, with only six tables. The cooking is creative, with an oriental touch, as in the fresh samosas or basmati rice with Persian gheimeh (a stew of yellow peas, courgettes, aubergine and soya in a saffron sauce). To drink there's organic beer. The staff are friendly and the summer terrace on Raimundhof a delight.

Orlando

6, Mollardgasse 3 (941 99 88/www.orlando.or.at). U4 Pilgramgasse. **Open** 5pm-1am Mon-Thur, Sun; 6pm-2am Fri, Sat. **Main courses** €7.90-€9.50. **Credit** MC, V. **Map** p238 C9.
Named after Virginia Woolf's gender-bending hero(ine), this popular haunt of Vienna's discreet gay and lesbian community has recently been reopened and now sports the subtitle 'straight and queer'. Orlando is low on attitude and its spacious rooms and lovely courtyard offer a warm welcome to all. Expect a menu of reliable Italian- and Asian-inspired dishes along with Viennese favourites. There are now two bars and what is called the 'cosy lounge' where you can slump on a sofa and sip cocktails.

Ra'mien

6, Gumpendorfer Strasse 9 (585 4798/www.ramien.at). U2 Museumsquartier. **Open** 11am-midnight Tue-Sun. **Main courses** €6-€15.50. **Credit** DC, MC, V. **Map** p242 D8.
Vienna's hippest noodle temple, Ra'mien has an airy designer interior that attracts a young fashionable bunch. Come here at lunchtime or early evening, when the menu features vast bowls of tasty reasonably priced la mien and Vietnamese pho noodles, along with rice dishes and gyoza dumplings. Dinner is a costlier affair, with great pan-Asian fish, seafood and tofu dishes – but it can get crowded and a little stressful. The downstairs lounge, kitted out in Hong Kong Phooey chintz, is a popular pre-club venue with DJs spinning until 4am. Booking essential.

Vinissimo

6, Windmühlgasse 20 (586 4888/www.vinissimo.at). Bus 57a. **Open** 11am-11pm Mon-Sat. **Main courses** €10-€19. **Credit** AmEx, DC, MC, V. **Map** p242 D8.
A hybrid of winery and bistro. Vinissimo's weekly changing selection of 15-20 wines is available by the glass. The full list includes some 400 labels (half of them Austrian), which can be sampled in situ or taken away. The restaurant offers Italian cuisine with a strong Viennese influence, in starters such as *Weinbeisserteller* ('wine nibble platter' – antipasti, in essence) and own-made pastas like basil and cream cheese ravioli with tomato butter, or tagliatelle with baby limes and freshwater crabs. To follow there's an excellent choice of cheeses, such as *Vorarlberger Bergkäse* (a nutty hard mountain cheese).

7th District

Chrinor

7, Kirchengasse 21 (5223236/www.chrinor.at).
U3 Neubaugasse/tram 49/bus 13a. **Open** 11.30am-
2.30pm, 6-11pm Tue-Fri; 6pm-midnight Sat.
Main courses €10-€20. **Credit** MC, V.
Map p242 E8.

Proof that Austrian cooking is on the up is provided
in this sleek diner by ex-Hansen chef Christian
Voithofer. From salads such as lamb's lettuce with
cured pecorino, truffled honey and tepid asparagus
to the audacious yellow beet soup with crispy
prawns and chilli oil – Chrinor offers a variety of
culinary and visual surprises. Try Chrinor's stupendous €8 three-course lunch menu.

Halle

7, Museumsplatz 1 (523 70 01). U2 Museumsquartier,
U2, U3 Volkstheater. **Open** 10am-1am daily. **Main**
courses €5.70-€13.50. **Credit** MC, V. **Map** p242 D7.

Halle is incorporated into the west wing of the Old
Winter Riding School whose baroque stucco occasionally peeks out among the establishment's
signature cool steel and wood. The menu caters for
an all-day clientele of museum-goers and poseurs,
including everything from breakfast to cocktails.
Food is typical art-gastro – Italian with hints of the
Orient – beautifully presented and a little expensive.

Una

7, Museumsplatz 1 (523 6566). U2 Museumsquartier,
U2, U3 Volkstheater. **Open** 9am-midnight Mon-Fri;
10am-midnight Sat; 10am-6pm Sun. **Main courses**
€6.20-€15. **No credit cards. Map** p242 D7.

The best address in the Museumsquartier. Una
occupies one of the original vaulted wings of the
imperial stables under a ceiling clad in magnificent
tiles. The bistro-style menu can feature straightforward pasta dishes, grilled fish and seasonal specialities such as game and wild mushrooms. House
wines, particularly the Zweigelt, are good value and
the desserts likewise. Refreshingly attitude-free.

Winetime

7, Zollergasse 5 (5223508/www.winetime.at). U3
Neubaugasse. **Open** from 4pm-late Mon-Sat. **Main**
courses €3.60-€8.50. **Credit** V. **Map** p238 C8.

A discreetly stylish wine bar. A small selection of
organic cheeses and cold cuts is served, plus the odd
warm dish, to accompany some 25 wines by the
glass from a cellar housing 250 varieties. Prices are
very reasonable; the accent is firmly on local produce, although the odd international name crops up.
The tiny interior is cleverly enhanced by a relaxing
blend of bare brick, unusual ironwork and natural
light from the glassed-off patio. Surprisingly for a
vinothèque, there's an eclectic soundtrack, supplied
by the neighbouring Ton um Ton (*see p143*).

Zu den Zwei Lieseln

7, Burggasse 63 (523 3282). Bus 48a. **Open** 10am-
10pm Mon-Sat. **Main courses** €4.40-€8. **No credit**
cards. Map p238 C7.

Una – a hit in the Museumsquartier.

The zwei Lieseln are a duo of imposing Viennese
matrons who fry up vast *Schnitzels* for everyone
from brickies to the Bürgermeister. The interior of
this Viennese institution is authentic *Beisl*-style spit
and sawdust with a dash of formica. In summer the
courtyard and its spreading chestnut tree are a joy.

8th District

Café Florianihof

8, Florianigasse 45 (402 4842/www.florianihof.at).
Tram 5, 43, J. **Open** 8am-midnight Mon-Fri; 10am-
midnight Sat, Sun. **Main courses** €6.70-€12.
Credit DC, MC, V. **Map** p238 C6.

You won't find a more lovingly preserved turn-of-
the-century café in all Vienna. Despite its Jugendstil
cream panelling, its aged parquet floor and its long
curved bar, this is no musty period piece. Rather, it
provides an elegant, laid-back setting ideal for
breakfast, a full meal or a quiet drink. Well-executed,
visually delightful meals come at great-value
prices. Further bonuses include international newspapers, free internet access and, once the work on
Schlesinger Platz is finished, a large summer terrace.

Heurigen

The seven square kilometres (2.7 square miles) of vineyards that lie within its boundaries make Vienna the world's largest wine-growing city. The most extensive area is on the northern fringe in districts 16-19, but the highest quality is found in the Transdanubian 21st district. On balmy summer evenings, join the Viennese for an evening in a *Heuriger*, one of the scores of rustic wine taverns dotted among the vineyards in the shadow of the Vienna Woods. Like the *Beisl*, *Heurigen* are a splendid Viennese foible, named after the tart new wine they serve. Strictly speaking, *Heuriger* owners only sell their own wines, along with a limited selection of food such as cuts of roast pork, various cheesy dips and the odd vegetable or salad. The wine is served at table; the food comes via a self-service buffet. Hard to find these days, the real McCoy even allows customers to bring along picnics. From May to September, a pine branch is hung outside to show that a *Heuriger* is open. The genre has of course been corrupted over the years and today the wine villages of Neustift, Nussdorf and particularly Grinzing are awash with macro-establishments serving full meals and full rural kitsch.

Many *Heurigen* are within easy reach of the city centre, but the further you go the higher the chances of encountering the authenticity and breathtaking views that make a real *Heuriger* so memorable. The following come highly recommended: **Hirt** (*p119*) and **Göbel**, **Sirbu** and **Zawodsky** (all *p120*).

Café Pars

8, Lerchenfelder Strasse 148 (405 8245). U6 Thaliastrasse/tram 46. **Open** 11am-midnight Mon-Sat. **Main courses** €6.40-€14.50. **Credit** V. **Map** p238 B7.
Headquarters of Vienna's Persians, the Pars cooks rice the way only Persians know – maximum fluffiness, with that wonderful crispy base. Served with butter, egg yolk and mixed fresh herbs, this is a meal in itself, but it comes with superbly spiced chicken kebabs or char-grilled beef fillet in thin strips. For the less carnivorous, there's a choice of vegetable and beany appetisers and dips. Rather heavy-handed decoration – elaborate tiling and illustrations of questionable artistic merit – is alleviated by the chance to ogle the handsome customers.

Hold

8, Josefstädter Strasse 50 (405 1198). Tram J. **Open** 8am-11pm Mon-Fri; 9am-3pm Sat. **Meals served** 11.30am-2.30pm, 6-10.30pm Mon-Sat. **Main courses** €9-€12. **No credit cards. Map** p238 B6.
A small café-cum-trattoria oozing northern Italian authenticity, Hold makes a useful pit-stop if you're exploring Vienna's noble 8th district. As well as being great for a revitalising cappuccino and almond pastry, or a quick glass of house Chianti, it also serves reasonably priced lunches and dinners featuring substantial soups, fresh antipasti and good pasta dishes. Space is at a premium, which makes communal dining de rigueur. Still, sharing a table with Hold's bohemian regulars while Paolo Conte growls over the stereo is not entirely unpleasant.

Konoba

8, Lerchenfelder Strasse 66-68 (929 4111/ www.konoba.at). Tram 46. **Open** 11am-2pm, 6pm-midnight Mon-Fri, Sun; 6pm-midnight Sat. **Main courses** €5.80-€18.90. **Credit** MC, V. **Map** p238 B7.
Once again it's down to the Croats to supply Vienna with affordable fish and seafood. In a pleasant setting of stripped-wood and po-mo ventilation ducts, Konoba imports a refreshing taste of the Dalmatian coast with dishes such as the hefty buzara – mussels in a potent wine, garlic, olive oil and parsley sauce. Garlic sometimes overpowers superbly grilled sea bass and bream, but the edge can be removed by downing plenty of fruity Dalmatian whites such as Laski Rizling and Dingac.

Más!

8, Laudongasse 36 (403 83 24). Tram J/bus 13a. **Open** 6pm-2am daily. **Main courses** €7.20-€19. **Credit** AmEx, DC, JCB, MC, V. **Map** p238 B6.
Surely one of the coolest Mexican restaurants anywhere in Europe, Más! boasts spacious designer lines and is mercifully free of Tex-Mex tat. The food may be of the usual carbohydrate-powered Mexican ilk, but it's made with good ingredients and is well presented. The real pleasure of the place lies in sipping a Margarita or a Mojito at the long bar (which has a vast illuminated tortoise-shell backdrop), taking in the formation dancing of the Latino bar staff and tapping your feet to the Fania All Stars.

On

8, Lederergasse 16 (402 6333). Tram 5, 33/bus 13a. **Open** 11.30am-2.30pm, 5.30-11pm Wed-Fri; noon-11pm Sat, Sun. **Main courses** €5.50-€15. **Credit** DC, MC, V. **Map** p238 C6.
This 24-seater 'micro designer Asian' stands out for sensational spicing and prudent prices. From the open kitchen come magnificent starters such as marinated salmon cubes with sesame ginger sauce and tuna tartar with a wasabi cress garnish. Meat fanciers will enjoy the superb marinated rabbit and a tear-jerkingly hot beef noodle soup with five spice and Thai basil. Booking is advisable.

Schnattl

8, Lange Gasse 40 (405 3400). Tram J. **Open** 11.30am-2.30pm, 6pm-midnight Mon-Fri. **Main courses** €14-€20. **Credit** AmEx, DC. **Map** p242 C6.
The stuffy Schnattl is one of bourgeois Vienna's favourite restaurants, serving Austrian dishes with a Styrian touch. Much attention to detail is paid – which may explain the long wait between courses. The wine and schnapps lists feature Austria's best.

Il Sestante

8, Piaristengasse 50 (402 9894). U2 Rathaus/tram J. **Open** 11.30am-2.30pm, 5.30pm-midnight Mon-Fri; 11.30am-11.30pm Sat, Sun. **Main courses** €7-€16. **No credit cards**. **Map** p238 C6.
Alfresco dining in the Josefstadt's Maria-Treu-Platz used to mean 'great location, awful food'. But since this Sicilian crew took over, you can ogle the Maria-Treu-Kirche while munching no-nonsense Italian food with a Sicilian/Calabrian touch. This means masterful pizzas oozing with buffalo mozzarella and fresh herbs, the fiery suppa di povero, and (not quite as reliable) pastas and risottos. The wine list features potent southern reds such as Ciró and Nero d'Avalo and the divine Amarone della Valpolicella. Brisk, friendly service is supplied by staff more at home speaking English than German.

Die Wäscherei

8, Albertgasse 49 (409 2375-11). U6 Josefstädter Strasse/tram 43, 44, J. **Open** 5pm-2am Mon-Fri; 10am-2am Sat, Sun. **Credit** AmEx, DC, MC, V. **Main courses** €4-€14. **Map** p238 B6.
Besieged by a boisterous good-looking young crowd, 'the Laundromat' does a roaring trade in competitively priced, substantial Austro-ethnic dishes, with better-than-average choices for vegetarians. Another draw is the great range of draught beers, especially bone-dry Trumer Pils and Die Weisse, a Salzburg wheat beer rare in these parts. The pleasant interior, bathed in the sound of the latest chill-out compilation, displays photographs and paintings, but by late evening, all you can see or hear is the human mass. A great summer terrace and some of Vienna's prettiest waitresses add to the allure.

9th District

Gasthaus Wickerl

9, Porzellangasse 24a (317 7489). Tram D. **Open** 9am-midnight Mon-Fri; 10am-midnight Sat. **Main courses** €4.50-€11.50. **No credit cards**. **Map** p235 D5.
Wickerl is a classic wood-panelled Vienna *Beisl*, popular with students. Apparently, the city's top chefs can be spotted here wolfing down dumplings. Food consists of the usual *Beisl* repertoire, but carefully elaborated with high-quality materials. Footie fans will appreciate the big screen TV in the back room and three beers on tap (including Budweiser).

Kim Kocht

9, Lustkandlgasse 6 (319 0242/www.kimkocht.at). *U6 Volksoper.* **Open** 6pm-midnight Mon-Fri. **Credit** AmEx, DC, JCB, MC, V. **Main courses** €11-€34. **Map** p234 C4.
Don't count on getting a table at this diminutive pan-Asian restaurant, as press hype produced an average wait of six weeks in late 2002. All the fuss is about the highly original treatment the Korean owner/chef metes out to tuna and a variety of organic produce. Kim's training as a designer comes over loud and clear in her exquisite and original presentation.

Stomach

9, Seegasse 26 (310 2099). Tram D. **Open** 4pm-midnight Wed-Sat; 10am-10pm Sun. **Main courses** €10-€16. **No credit cards**. **Map** p235 D4.

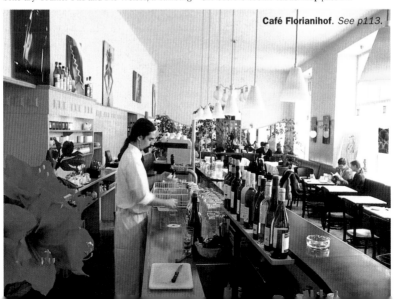

Café Florianihof. *See p113.*

Eat, Drink, Shop

Menu

Useful phrases

Do you have a table for (number) people?
Haben Sie einen Tisch für... Personen?
I want to book a table for (time) o'clock
Ich möchte einen Tisch für... Uhr bestellen
I'll have (name of food)
Ich nehme...
I'll have (name of food) with/without (ingredient)
Ich nehme... mit/ohne...
I'm a vegetarian
Ich bin Vegetarier
Can I/we have an ashtray, please
Einen Aschenbecher, bitte
The bill, please
Zahlen, bitte
Waitress/waiter
Fräulein/Herr Ober

Basics

Couvert/Gedeck Cover charge
Das Menü Fixed-price menu
Die Speisekarte Menu
Die Tageskarte Menu of the day
Die Weinkarte Wine list
Das Glas Glass
Das Messer Knife
Die Gabel Fork
Der Löffel Spoon
Die Hauptspeise Main course
Das Frühstück Breakfast
Die Vorspeise Starter
Das Mittagessen Lunch
Das Abendessen Dinner
Die Nachspeise Dessert

Menu

Almdudler Herbal lemonade
Apfelsaft (-gespritzt) Apple juice (mixed with soda water)
Bärlauch Wild garlic
Basilikum Basil
Bohnen Haricot beans
Brot Bread
Durch Well done (as in steak)
Ei (Spiegelei; Rührei; pochiertes/verlorenes Ei; weiches Ei; hartgekochtes Ei) Egg (fried; scrambled; poached; boiled, hard-boiled)
Eis Ice-cream
Eiswürfel Ice cube
Englisch Rare (as in steak)

Ente Duck
Erbsen Peas
Erdbeer Strawberry
Essig Vinegar
Fisch Fish
Fisolen Green beans
Fleisch Meat
Forelle Trout
Gans Goose
Garnelen Prawns
Gebacken Baked/fried
Gebraten Roast
Gekocht Boiled
Gemüse Vegetables
Gurke Cucumber
Hecht Pike
Hendl/Hahn/Huhn Chicken
Himbeer Raspberry
Honig Honey
Kabeljau Cod
Karfiol Cauliflower
Kartoffel/Erdäpfel Potatoes
Käse Cheese
Kichererbsen Chick peas
Knoblauch Garlic
Knödel Dumplings
Kotelett Chop
Kümmel Caraway seed
Kürbis Pumpkin
Lachs Salmon
Lamm Lamb
Lauch Leek
Leber Liver
Leitungswasser Tap water
Linsen Lentils
Lungenbraten Fillet steak
Marillen Apricots
Medium Medium-rare (as in steak)
Meeresfrüchte Seafood
Mehlspeise Pâtisserie
Milch Milk
Mineralwasser Mineral water
Obst Fruit
Öl Oil
Oliven Olives
Orangensaft/Frischgepresster Orangensaft Orange juice/Freshly squeezed orange juice
Paprika Peppers
Paradeiser Tomatoes
Petersilie Parsley
Pfeffer Pepper
Pommes frites Chips
Reis Rice
Rind Beef

Rosmarin Rosemary
Rostbraten Steak
Rotwein Red wine
Salz Salt
Sauce/Saft Sauce/Gravy
Schinken/Speck Ham
Schittlauch Chives
Schlag Whipped cream
Schokolade Chocolate
Schwein Pork
Semmel White roll
Senf Mustard
Serviettenknödel Sliced dumplings
Spargel Asparagus
Steinpilze Porcini mushrooms
Sulz Brawn
Suppe Soup
Tee Tea
Thymian Thyme
Topfen Cream cheese
Torte Cake
Trauben Grapes
Vollkorn Wholemeal
Wasser Water
Weisswein White wine
Wels Catfish
Wurst Sausage
Zander Pike-Perch
Zitrone Lemon
Zucker Sugar
Zwetschke Plum
Zwiebel Onion

Gemischter Salat Tomatoes, potato salad, green beans, lettuce and lots of onions, covered in tart wine or cider vinegar
Griessnockerlsuppe Clear beef broth with floating semolina dumplings
Heringsalat Pickled herring salad; traditionally served on Ash Wednesday
Käsekrainer Sausage filled with melted cheese
Käsespätzle Baby dumplings, covered in a powerful cheese sauce
Kraut/Schinkenfleckerl Pappardelle-type pasta with cabbage or ham
Leberknödelsuppe Clear beef broth made with liver; includes small dumplings
Rindsgulasch Beef stew spiced with paprika and served with dumplings (originally a Hungarian recipe)
Schweinsbraten Roast pork, usually served with sauerkraut and sliced dumplings
Tafelspitz mit g'röste Boiled beef served with fried, grated potatoes, covered in an apple and horseradish sauce (Emperor Franz Joseph used to eat this every Sunday lunchtime, apparently)
Tiroler g'röstl Potato and sausage hash served in a blackened skillet
Wiener Eintopf Vienna stew (vegetables, potatoes and sausage in a clear beef broth)
Wiener Schnitzel Veal or pork escalope fried in breadcrumbs
Zwiebelrostbraten Tenderloin steak in onion sauce

Eat, Drink, Shop

Typical savoury dishes

Bauernschmaus 'Peasants' treat': a plate of hot meats including smoked pork, roast pork or pork cutlet, frankfurters and a selection of ham; it's usually served with dumplings
Beuschel Chopped offal covered in sauce
Blunzn Black pudding
Brathendl/Backhendl Fried/roast chicken
Eierschwammerln Chanterelle mushrooms; served in meat sauces or over salad
Eierspeise Scrambled omelette served in a pan, sometimes with ham
Erdäpfelgulasch Potato stew; often includes pieces of frankfurter sausage
Frittatensuppe Clear beef broth with floating slivers of pancake
Gebratene Bachforelle mit Petersilerdäpfel Fried brook trout with potatoes in parsley sauce
Gefüllte Kalbsbrust Veal breast filled with several types of meat or vegetable

Dessert

Birne Helene Pear Hélène
Germknödel Sweet dumplings, filled with jam
Griessschmarrn Semolina pancake, chopped into small pieces, served with a plum compôte
Kaiserschmarrn Thick fluffy pancake, chopped into small pieces and covered in icing sugar; usually served with a plum compôte
Mohr im Hemd Rich chocolate pudding, steamed and served with a hot chocolate sauce and whipped cream
Palatschinken Thicker than the French crêpe; served sweet or savoury
Reisauflauf Rice pudding
Salzburger Nockerl Sweet Salzburg dumplings; basically a huge cloud of empty-tasting egg-white
Topfen/Marillenknödel Curd cheese or apricot dumplings, covered in breadcrumbs and fried in butter; served with a hot fruit purée

Stomach has long supplied one of Vienna's most consistently satisfying eating experiences. Don't be put off by its dilapidated façade: it hides a cosy, kitsch-free old world interior and a splendidly bedraggled inner courtyard for summer evenings. Much frequented by theatre folk, Stomach is gradually abandoning its vegetarian slant to concentrate on Styrian beef dishes such as the divine marinated *Tafelspitz* with boiled egg, chives and drizzled pumpkin seed oil. Game abounds in winter in the form of wild boar, venison, and wonderfully condimented wild trout. Reliable wines, Murauer beer and great schnapps are also to be had. The name Stomach was dreamed up by re-arranging the letters of Tomaschek, the butcher's originally located in the building.

Summerstage

9, Rossauer Lände (319 7241/www.café-stein.com/ summerstage). U4 Rossauer Lände. **Open** May-Sept 5pm-1am Mon-Sat; 2pm-1am Sun. **Main courses** €12-€14. **No credit cards. Map** p235 E4.
A loose grouping of various restaurants sets up shop along this stretch of the Danube Canal during the summer. Here you can eat and drink alfresco much later than the usual 11pm. The choice varies annually but 2002 featured the Mexican Más!, hip noodle establishment Kiang, and Die Wäscherei, as well as the bistro perennial Café Stein (*see p186*). The organisers arrange a rather lame programme of jazz, boules and exhibitions to pull in punters, but the chance to hang out late is enough to attract vast numbers nightly. Booking is therefore strongly advised.

Wok

9, Währinger Strasse 47/2 (408 0426/www.wok-vienna.com). Tram 5, 33, 37, 38, 40, 41, 42. **Open** 11.30am-2.30pm, 5.30-11pm daily. **Main courses** €8-€15. **Credit** MC, V. **Map** p242 D5.
Vienna's original Asian-fusion restaurant has this new cool branch. Behind the smoked-glass façade lies a standard minimalist interior offering finely executed pan-Asian classics such as satay, samosas, various seafood dishes and an excellent tom yang gung soup. A notable addition to Vienna's nascent ethno-dining scene. Booking is essential.
Branches: 1, Operngasse 20b (585 2102); 1, Schellinggasse 6 (512 9567).

11th District

Schloss Concordia (Kleine Oper Wien)

11, Simmeringer Hauptstrasse 283 (769 8888). Tram 71. **Open** 10am-1am daily. **Main courses** €6-€11. **No credit cards.**
This turreted folly is straight out of imperial Vienna. Located opposite the Zentralfriedhof Cemetery, the Schloss Concordia greets its patrons with a huge stone crucifix standing beside the entrance. Once the sun goes down, its ghostly rooms are lit exclusively by candlelight, creating an atmosphere of theatrical melancholy: perfect for the ageing bohemians who attend its musical evenings and readings. The over-

grown garden and glass conservatory also contribute to the feel. Less evocative is the menu, which offers predictable Viennese and international dishes, plus bizarre variations on *Schnitzel*. The popcorn *Schnitzel* is one of a kind.

15th District

Gasthaus Quell

15, Reindorfgasse 19 (893 2407/www.quell.cc). U6 Gumpendorfer Strasse. **Open** 11am-midnight Mon-Fri. **Main courses** €7.50-€11. **No credit cards. Map** p238 A0.
A good ten-minute walk from the U-Bahn, this classic Viennese *Beisl* has an atmospheric wood-panelled interior, a cracked old ceramic stove and an affable landlord. Offering the run of meaty Viennese staples, Quell also serves seasonal specials and has a leafy summer terrace.

Happy Buddha

15, Mariahilfer Gürtel 9 (893 4217/www.happy buddha.at). U6 Gumpendorfer Strasse. **Open** 11.30am-2.30pm, 5.50pm-midnight daily. **Main courses** €8-€13.90; *dim sum* €3.70-€4.30. **Credit** AmEx, DC, MC, V. **Map** p238 B9.
The 15th district has some of Vienna's best Chinese restaurants. When it comes to who serves the top dim sum, opinions are divided between here and Tsing Tao, in nearby Gerstnerstrasse. Both serve excellent Cantonese food but Happy Buddha is also chintz-free.

16th District

Café Kent

16, Brunnengasse 67 (43 1 405 9173/www.kent restaurant.at). U6 Josefstätter Strasse. **Open** 5am-2am daily. **Main courses** €5-€16. **No credit cards. Map** p238 A6.
Vienna's best-loved kebab house has extended its wonderful garden. Its popularity is unsurprising: excellent meze platters and grilled meats retail at knock-down prices, with plenty of aubergine and zucchini concoctions to satisfy vegetarians. Located amid the Brunnenmarkt, a step from the Gürtel night scene, Kent attracts shoppers, slackers and stall-holders with opening times to suit all.

Villa Aurora

16, Wilhelminenstrasse 237 (489 3333). Tram 44 then bus 46b. **Open** 10am-midnight daily. **Main courses** €6.50-€14. **No credit cards.**
Perched up in the hills of the 16th district, this 19th-century villa has a maze of rooms for informal yet candle-lit dining. The big attraction is breakfasting on the grassy meadow at the front, which is dotted with curiosities such as an old wooden fishing trawler and a glass conservatory containing a Jugendstil swimming pool. The spectacular views of Vienna make the long trek worthwhile. House specialities include different types of *Schnitzel* and game dishes; there's a limited choice for vegetarians. One warning – the staff include some real sour-pusses.

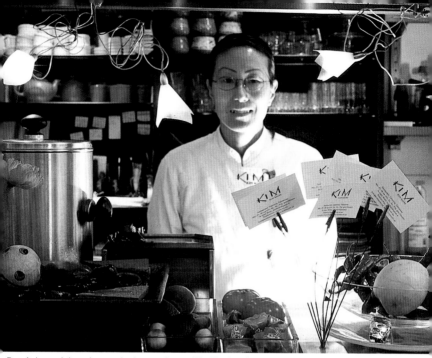

Pan-Asian cuisine given a designer edge at **Kim Kocht**. See p115.

18th District

Trattoria L'Ambasciata della Puglia

18, Währinger Strasse 170a (479 9592). Tram 40, 41. **Open** noon-3pm, 6-11pm daily. **Main courses** €8-€20. **Credit** MC, V. **Map** p234 A3.

The informal 'embassy' trades in a great selection of hearty southern Italian wines and fresh pastas. Specialities such as broad bean purée and braciola (a horse meat roulade), feature. Loud and boisterous, it's a favourite of more well-heeled members of the city's DJ clique who seem to provide the funky soundtrack.

Wirtshaus Steiererstöckl

18, Pötzleinsdorfer Strasse 127 (440 4943). Tram 41. **Open** 11am-midnight Wed-Sun. **Main courses** €10-€15. **No credit cards**.

After a walk round Pötzleinsdorfer Park, this rustic tavern is ideal for snacks, salads and more substantial meat dishes – all genuinely Styrian. Don't leave without sampling a glass of the Schilcher Most: the restorative juice of Styria's most idiosyncratic grape variety. Booking advisable.

19th District

Hirt

19, Eisernenhandgasse 165 (318 9641). S-Bahn from Franz-Josefsbahnhof to Kahlenberger Dorf. **Open** *Apr-Oct* from 3pm Wed-Fri; from noon Sat, Sun. *Nov-Mar* from noon Fri-Sun. **No credit cards**.

Probably the best way to reach this superb out-of-the-way little *Heuriger* is via a visit to Sirbu (*see p120*). After a couple of spritzers there, take the path beside Sirbu and head downhill towards the Danube. Hirt has two terraces – one overlooking the Danube and another with views of Leopoldsberg (*see p97*) – where you can feast on the usual *Heurigen* grub. The interior is rustic and cosy.

Reinprecht

19, Cobenzlgasse 22 (320 1471/1389). Tram 38. **Open** 3.30pm-midnight daily. **Credit** DC, JCB, MC, V.

A *Heuriger* housed in a 300-year-old former monastery, with a terraced garden and Europe's largest collection of corkscrews. There are grilled specialities plus a buffet, *Schrammelmusik* and decent wines by the bottle – the pinot blanc is recommended. Though it is in the tourist ghetto, Reinprecht has a lively atmosphere and is arguably the best of the Cobenzlgasse *Heurigen*.

Salettl

19, Hartäckerstrasse 80 (479 2222). Tram 37, 38 then bus 40a. **Open** 6.30am-1.30am daily. **Main courses** €5-€7. **No credit cards**. **Map** p234 A2.

Overlooking Vienna's flush 19th district, this circular Jugendstil pavilion is a haunt of the city's silver-spooned youth. Saletti is a fun place to come for breakfast, when you can choose from the substantial *Kaiserfrühstück* (the imperial breakfast), with everything from croissants to fruit salad, ham and cheese; the champagne version; or a traditional Viennese breakfast of coffee and rolls. In summer, all these are best enjoyed in the garden with its splendid views of the Vienna Woods. Inside, the pavilion often gets crowded and smoky, but it's worth taking a close look at this charming edifice.

Schreiberhaus
19, Rathstrasse 54 (440 3844/www.dasschreiber haus.at). Bus 35a. **Open** 11am-1am daily. **Credit** AmEx, DC, JCB, MC, V.
A *Heurigen* offering great food and above-average wines in a spot well-known for family parties and corporate events. The big terraced garden is pretty, and the interior comfortable and stylish, and low on kitsch. Have a post-prandial walk along the path that runs through the vineyards behind the garden.

Sirbu
19, Kahlenberger Strasse 210 (320 59 28). Bus 38a then 15min walk. **Open** *Apr-mid Oct* 3pm-midnight Mon-Sat. **Credit** V.
Sirbu has outstanding views of the Danube from a sunny terrace surrounded by vineyards. Like all *Heurigen*, it has the statutory self-service buffet consisting of various cuts of pork – try the superlative Kümmelbraten, a fatty roast belly pork studded with caraway seeds – various salads and cold cuts.

Weingut Reisenberg
19, Oberer Reisenbergweg 15 (320 9393). Tram 38 then bus 38a. **Open** *Apr* 4pm-midnight Thur, Fri; noon-midnight Sat, Sun. *May-Sept* 4pm-midnight Mon-Fri; noon-midnight Sat, Sun. *Oct-Dec* 6pm-midnight Wed-Sat. **Credit** MC, V.
The steep walk from the edge of Grinzing up to this *Heurigen*-style attraction will earn you some of the best views of Vienna. Also spectacular is the tart white wine – douse with liberal quantities of mineral water. The food is a cut above that of the average *Heurigen*, with excellent baked noodle dishes and good cheeses and salads.

Zawodsky
19, Reinischgasse 3 (320 7978/www.zawodsky.at). Tram 38. **Open** *Apr-Nov* 5pm-midnight Mon, Wed-Fri; 2pm-midnight Sat, Sun. **Credit** AmEx, DC, MC, V.
One of the best-kept secrets of Vienna's *Heurigen* culture, Zawodsky offers a tremendous view of the city and a gorgeously unkempt garden full of apple trees. There's no decor to speak of, just picnic tables and benches. The selection of cold meats and cheeses is less extensive than at most places. Opening times vary, so phone ahead.

Zimmermann
19, Armbrustergasse 5 (370 2211/www.zimmer manns.at). Tram 37. **Open** 5pm-midnight Mon-Sat; 4pm-midnight Sun. **Credit** AmEx, MC, V.
A *Heurigen* with a reputation for attracting upper-class custom. It has beautiful outdoor seating under the fruit trees and a pet zoo with rabbits and guinea pigs. Classic Viennese dishes, such as *Schinkenfleckerl* (noodles with ham) and *Butterschnitzerl*, are a cut above the usual buffet fare, but pricier.

21st District

Birners Strandgasthaus
21, An der Oberen Alten Donau 47 (271 5336/ www.noessi.at/birner). U6 Neue Donau. **Open** *summer* 9am-10pm Mon, Tue, Thur-Sun (open on Wed if weather good). *Winter* 9am-9pm Mon, Tue, Thur-Sun. **Main courses** €4.90-€12. **No credit cards**.
This spit 'n' sawdust chop house comes into its own in summer when sun-groggy Viennese cross the narrow bridge to Birners' delightful riverside terrace from the nearby Angeli baths. There are no great culinary attractions here, apart from king-size *Schnitzel* and pints of ice-cold beer.

Heuriger Göbel
21, Stammersdorfer Kellergasse 151 (294 8420). Tram 31 then bus 125. **Open** 3-10pm Mon; 11am-10pm Sat, Sun. **No credit cards**.
Architect Hans-Peter Göbel is a prize-winning vintner whose cabernet sauvignon and Zweigelt (particularly the 1993) are possibly the best red wines produced in the Vienna area. He designed this chic, *Heurigen* himself. Göbel's innovative take involves classic *Heurigen* roast pork specialities, plus exquisite nibbles prepared with organic ingredients.

Weingut Schilling
21, Langenzersdorfer Strasse 54 (292 4189). Tram 32. **Open** from 3.30pm daily. **Credit** DC, MC, V.
This large *Heuriger* has a friendly atmosphere and extensive gardens at the foot of the Bisamberg Hill. Weingut Schilling also has a good reputation for its wines – try the Cuvée Camilla. There's a copious buffet, offering such Austrian specialities as blood sausage (*Blutwurst*) and grilled pork knuckle (*Stelze*). Service is fast and efficient.

Weingut Heuriger Wieninger
21, Stammersdorfer Strasse 78 (292 4106). Tram 31. **Open** from 3pm Wed-Fri; from 2pm Sat; from 1pm Sun. **No credit cards**.
Stammersdorf is Vienna's biggest wine-producing district. This tavern features wines from Fritz Wieninger, considered one of Austria's top wine makers. Its chardonnay and cabernet-merlot come recommended. The establishment is run by Fritz's mother and brother and has a well-prepared, rustic menu.

22nd District

Strandcafé
22, Florian-Berndl-Gasse 20 (203 6747/www.strand cafe-wien.at). U1 Alte Donau. **Open** 10am-10pm daily. **Main courses** €5.40-€12. **No credit cards**. **Map** p237 M4.
On a fine afternoon in late summer, the Strandcafé is a great antidote to the city. It is situated among huge poplars and weeping willows on the banks of the old arm of the river. The big draw is racks of barbecued pork ribs served with divine roast potatoes. Tables are laid out on a floating pontoon; dinner may require lashings of insect repellent.

Cafés & Coffee Houses

These stately old-timers offer much more than just a caffeine fix.

Nothing symbolises Donald Rumsfeld's 'Old Europe' more eloquently than the traditional Viennese *Kaffeehaus*. Once the brass-handled door creaks open, you step into a world of extravagant impracticality, dogged resistance to change and often scant regard for the profit motive. These spacious interiors are bathed in sedate silence, where the tinkling of teaspoons and rustle of newspapers is dampened by thickly upholstered booths, ageing parquet floors and the disdainful glance of liveried waiters.

Often likened to London's gentlemen's clubs, there are coffee houses in Vienna to suit one's profession, pocket or political persuasion. Nevertheless, they share a common iconography of marble-topped tables, booths and bentwood chairs in varying degrees of disrepair, a bewildering selection of periodicals and a large omnipresent clock. For time and actual consumption are sublimely irrelevant, the price of a cup of coffee being the only entrance fee to this archaic theme park, often described as more a state of mind than an actual geographic location. Long waits to order and to pay are de rigueur, but the waiter's haughtiness should never be read as 'order another or move along': *Herr Ober* (as he should be addressed) is more than likely tutting at the sound of your mobile phone.

In a country known for prizing legend over historical fact, the coffee house phenomenon is shrouded in mythology. The story goes that it originated after the 1683 Turkish siege when two of the Habsburgs' most effective spies received compensation in the form of what they had first taken to be camel fodder: sacks of coffee beans. One of the two (his identity is subject to varying degrees of polemic) also earned a concession to open an establishment for the consumption of the 'Turkish drink' at Rotenturmstrasse 14, though, unusually for Vienna, no plaque commemorates this seemingly momentous occurance.

Most of the grand coffee houses still in operation today date from either end of the 19th century, when, in times of overcrowding and poor heating, they became an obligatory refuge for penniless men of ambition who often used their café of choice as a postal address and the waiters as sources of cash loans. Many such patrons were part of fin-de-siècle Vienna's extraordinary outpouring

of intellectual, artistic and political activity. Thus cafés **Griensteidl** and **Central** are associated with the comings and goings of literati and revolutionaries, the **Museum** with the shenanigans surrounding the Secessionist movement and **Sperl** with musical giants such as Gustav Mahler. The tradition continued into the post-World War II era when newer cafés such as **Hawelka** and **Bräunerhof** became second homes to bourgeois baiters such as Thomas Bernhard and the Viennese Actionists. Anecdotes and apocryphal stories abound, fuelling shelves of doctoral theses and memoirs on the subject of these legendary lounges.

So what of the coffee? Anyone conditioned to the delights of Italian varieties will not be greatly impressed. Viennese roasts from firms such as Santora, Café do Brasil and Meinl simply don't compare to the Illys and Lavazzas of this world. That said, the Vienna coffee houses do offer a kaleidoscopic range of versions on the theme, generally involving the addition of alcohol and whipped cream (*see p124* **Wien caffeine szene**).

Competing with traditional coffee houses are a variety of establishments ranging from the dirt-cheap Eduscho stores to the delightfully kitsch **Aida** chain; coffee from both is an aquired taste. The latest addition is the ubiquitous Starbucks whose arrival in 2002 prompted unfounded rumours of an imminent 'coffee house war' in the local press. True to its caring, sharing image, the first outlet on Kärntner Strasse was opened in the premises of the long-defunct Café Zum Fenstergucker, its façade lovingly restored as a 'gift to the city of Vienna'. So far though, local aversion to paper cups, non-smoking environments and West Coast chumminess has kept Starbucks expansionism to the modest level of seven stores in its first year of operation.

1st District

Café Aida
1, Stock-im-Eisen-Platz 2 (512 2977/www.aida.at).
U1, U3 Stephansplatz. **Open** 7am-8pm Mon-Sat; 9am-8pm Sun. **No credit cards**. **Melange** €2.40.
Map p243 E7.
Aida's iconic pink neon sign burns brightly at 26 branches throughout the city, making it by far Vienna's biggest café chain with the widest selection of cakes and pastries and an idiosyncratic blend

of coffee that is enduringly popular here. Although Aida's clientele hails from diverse age-groups and social classes, the branches' extraordinary interiors from the 1950s, '60s and '70s have earned the chain a cult status. Curious colour schemes where browns and pinks appear to mirror the cakes; chrome railings, plastic bucket chairs and acres of people-watching plate glass give many Aidas an air of post-modernity that contrasts vividly with their practical function. This city centre branch has all their trademark *Schnitten* (slices) and *Schüsserln* (cup cakes) as well as a splendid first-floor cake bar lined with comfortable fake-leather stools and views over the square.
Branches: throughout the city.

Café Bräunerhof

1, Stallburggasse 2 (512 3893). U3 Herrengasse/ bus 2a, 3a. **Open** 8am-9pm Mon-Fri; 8am-7pm Sat; 10am-7pm Sun. **No credit cards**. **Melange** €2.90. **Map** p242 E6.
The ironically named Café Sans Souci was one of many Jewish-owned cafés to be 'aryanised' during the Nazi-era (*see p52* **Thievery corporation**). Renamed Café Bräunerhof, its reputation as a literary café owes much to the patronage of former regular Thomas Bernhard, the irascible novelist and playwright, and philosopher Paul Wittgenstein, Ludwig's nephew, who lived in the same building. More austerely decorated than other classic Viennese coffee houses, the Bräunerhof still attracts colourful characters; blood 'n' guts performance artist Hermann Nitsch is often to be seen sketching in a corner of this atmospheric establishment. The Bräunerhof has one of the best selections of international newspapers of any *Kaffeehaus* in the city, as well as a great array of cakes and strudels, all served with a generous dollop of *Schlagobers* (whipped cream). A string trio play on Saturday and Sunday afternoons.

Café Central

1, Herrengasse 14 (533 37 63/www.ferstel.at). U3 Herrengasse/bus 1a, 2a, 3a. **Open** 8am-10pm Mon-Sat; 10am-6pm Sun. **Credit** AmEx, DC, MC, V. **Melange** €3.10. **Map** p242 E6.
When Café Griensteidl (*see p123*) was demolished at the turn of the 19th century the literary set moved to the Central, making it Vienna's principal intellectual hangout. Trotsky, or Bronstein as he was known in his clandestine years before World War I, was such an assiduous regular at the Central that an Austrian minister, on being informed of imminent revolution in Russia, supposedly remarked, 'And who on earth is going to make a revolution in Russia? I suppose you're going to tell me it's that Bronstein who sits all day at the Café Central!' Today it would require considerable suspension of belief to imagine those heady days of the Central, since the clientele is almost exclusively tourist. Pop in, though, to admire the decorated pseudo-Gothic vaulting and pay your respects to the dummy of the penniless poet Peter Altenberg

A classic Viennese waiter...

that sits just inside the door reading the paper. If you're impressed by the pastries, buy some from Café Central Konditorei (*see p139*) across the road.

Demel

1, Kohlmarkt 14 (535 1717/www.demel.at). U3 Herrengasse/bus 2a, 3a. **Open** 10am-7pm daily. **Credit** AmEx, DC, MC, V. **Melange** €3.80. **Map** p242 E6.
This 200-year-old former k.u.k. (*kaiserlich und königlich*, imperial and royal) bakery has a magnificent choice of cakes and biscuits and steep prices to match (see cost of a *Melange*). More a *Konditorei* than a *Kaffeehaus*, its grandiose interior is suitably sickly sweet with a more modern glassed-over patio at the back. A hot chocolate here is a must, as is the *Sachertorte*. Demel and Sacher (*see p125*) are the only bakeries in possession of the real recipe (so they say). A great place to buy traditional Viennese confectionery in gorgeous period-piece boxes, many with Jugendstil designs, Demel also has the most wonderful window displays. *See also p140*.

Diglas

1, Wollzeile 10 (512 57 65/www.diglas.at). U1, U3 Stephansplatz/bus 1a. **Open** 7am-midnight daily. **Credit** AmEx, DC, MC, V. **Melange** €3. **Map** p242 F7.
Plush red velvet booths give this Biedermeier café an air of intimacy. No surprise, then, that Viennese *grandes dames* reputedly come here to discuss their infidelities. Renowned for its coffee menu and good selection of teas served in bird-bath cups, Diglas offers some of the best cakes in town and possibly

...in a perfect setting – the stately **Café Griensteidl**.

the best *Apfelstrudel* going. German speakers may be able to fathom the *Wiener Schmäh* (Viennese ironic, occasionally biting, always charming humour); the waiters here are oozing with it.

Café Engländer

1, Postgasse 2 (966 86 65). U3 Stubentor/tram 1, 2. **Open** 8am-1am Mon-Sat; 10am-1am Sun. **Credit** MC, V. **Melange** €2.40. **Map** p242 F7.

Newly reopened after a brief period as an Italian restaurant, the Engländer has recuperated its former clientele of artists and general movers and shakers who also frequent the neighbouring Café Prückel (*see p125*). Modern by Viennese coffee-house standards, the Engländer has good coffee, an imaginative lunch menu and the best European newspapers. Shame about the opaque glass that obscures the view of the square.

Café Excelsior

1, Opernring 1 (585 7184). U1, U2, U4 Karlsplatz, tram 1, 2, J, D. **Open** daily 7am-1am. **Credit** AmEx, DC, MC, V. **Melange** €2.60. **Map** p242 E7.

This Turin-based coffee roaster has branches from Paris to Philadelphia, and arrived in Vienna in 2002 when it set up in the post-war monstrosity opposite the Staatsoper. Naturally they do coffee the way only Italians know, but also excellent ciabatta, bruschetta and tramezzini snacks and pasta dishes. The interior is a pleasant cocoon of teak veneeer, steel and glass and the window tables offer excellent views of the opera house and the constant human traffic around Vienna's most transited junction.

Café Frauenhuber

1, Himmelpfortgasse 6 (512 83 83). U1, U3 Stephansplatz/tram 1, 2. **Open** 8am-midnight Mon-Sat. **Credit** V. **Melange** €2.90. **Map** p243 E7.

The baroque façade of Vienna's oldest café and the neighbouring Winter Palace of Prince Eugène (*see p51*) are both the work of Johann Lukas von Hildebrandt. Operating since 1824, Frauenhuber is steeped in musical mythology, since Mozart lived in the building for a time and Beethoven occasionally performed his piano sonatas in the café itself. Today, despite its plush vaulted interior, it's a more mundane establishment, filled with shoppers and tourists from the nearby Kärntner Strasse, but one that still retains the essential coffee house attributes.

Café Griensteidl

1, Michaelerplatz 2 (535 2693). U3 Herrengasse/bus 2a, 3a. **Open** 8am-11.30pm daily. **Credit** AmEx, DC, V. **Melange** €3.10. **Map** p242 E7.

The present Café Griensteidl remains in the shadow of Hofburg on the site of the original café – a veritable battleground of such late 19th-century literary giants as Karl Kraus, Arthur Schnitzler, Hermann Bahr and Hugo von Hofmannsthal, who all decamped to Café Central after the building was demolished in 1897. Here too, Theodor Herzl is also said to have drafted *The Jewish State*, his blueprint for Zionism. The café reopened in 1990 and now attracts a mixture of civil servants from the adjoining ministries and tourists recovering from a visit to the imperial palace. Its spacious interior and numerous windows looking on to the bustle of Michaelerplatz are the principal attractions. Unusually for a Viennese *Kaffeehaus*, it's child-friendly and even has several high chairs.

Operncafé Hartauer Zum Peter'

1, Riemergasse 9 (512 8981). U3 Stubentor/ tram 1, 2. **Open** 8am-5pm Mon-Fri; 5pm-2am Sat. **No credit cards. Melange** €2.80. **Map** p243 F7.

A café for opera-lovers. Photos of opera stars, immortal and up-and-coming, adorn this quirky Jugendstil café.

Café Hawelka

1, Dorotheergasse 6 (512 8230/www.hawelka.com). U1, U3 Stephansplatz/bus 3a. **Open** 8am-2am Mon, Wed-Sat; 4pm-2am Sun. **No credit cards. Melange** €2.80. **Map** p242 E7.

Immortalised in Kraftwerk's *Transeurope Express* video, Hawelka is dark, smoky and charmingly threadbare, but no longer the intellectual hangout it became between the 1950s and the 1970s when it was a favourite of the Viennese Actionists, and Canetti, Warhol and Millers Henry and Arthur all dropped by. Still run by Leopold and Josefine Hawelka, who are well into their eighties – the lady of the house is known for her charming custom of seating single clients next to lonely members of the opposite sex. Leopold is up with the lark baking the pastries his wife feeds to a succession of German tourists on the trail of the Hawelka's former arty glory. Leopold himself is part of the Viennese furniture and his picture often crops up in tourist bumf. Despite the hype, Hawelka shouldn't be missed.

Heiner

1, Wollzeile 9 (512 2343/www.heiner.co.at). U1, U3 Stephansplatz/bus 1a. **Open** 9am-7pm Mon-Sat; 10am-7pm Sun. **No credit cards. Melange** €2.80. **Map** p242 F7.

An enticing patisserie-turned-café that has an upstairs wood-panelled room with a dolls'-house feel. The Heiner has a stack of sinfully good own-made chocolates and pastries, and diabetics are also catered for. **Branch**: 1, Kärntner Strasse 21-23 (512 6863).

Café Imperial

1, Hotel Imperial, Kärntner Ring 16 (501 10 389/ www.imperial-torte.at). U1, U2, U4 Karlsplatz/tram 1, 2, D, J. **Open** 7am-11pm daily. **Credit** AmEx, DC, MC, V. **Melange** €3.50. **Map** p243 E8.

Elegant and imposing, with gilded wallpaper and brocade draperies, the café of the Imperial Hotel is the preserve of Vienna's haute bourgeoisie and business folk. Famous regulars have included composer Richard Wagner and Karl Kraus. Piano music tinkles in the background during the afternoons and evenings.

Café Landtmann

1, Dr-Karl-Lueger-Ring 4 (24100-120/www.landt mann.at). U2 Schottentor/tram 1, 2, D. **Open** 8am-midnight daily. **Credit** AmEx, DC, MC, V. **Melange** €3.60. **Map** p242 D6.

Wien caffeine szene

In a Viennese Kaffeehaus you don't simply order 'a coffee' – it comes in a list of variations to put Starbucks to shame. It's also served on silver platter with a glass of water; a throw-back to the days when coffee was made Turkish-style and those pesky grounds had to be washed away. Know your brew:

Biedermeier Grosser Brauner with a shot of Biedermeier liqueur.

Café Maria Theresia with orange liqueur and a dash of whipped cream.

Cappuccino confusing. Unlike the Italian version, Viennese cappuccino has whipped cream on top.

Einspänner a Schwarzer (black coffee) served in a long glass with whipped cream.

Fiaker Austrian-German for the horse and carriage you can take around town (*see p65*). The coffee is a Verlängerter with rum and whipped cream.

Franziskaner made with hot milk and a topping of whipped cream.

Grosser Brauner a large cup of coffee with a dash of milk; **Kleiner Brauner** comes in a smaller cup.

Grosser Schwarzer/Mocca large black coffee.

Kaffee verkehrt more milk than coffee.

Kaisermelange with an egg yolk and brandy.

Kapuziner a Schwarzer with a shot of cream.

Kurz Viennese version of an espresso.

Mazagran cold coffee with rum and ice. To be downed in one go.

Melange most people's favourite; a milky coffee served with milk foam on top (like an Italian cappuccino).

Milchkaffe milkier than a melange.

Pharisäer strong black coffee with whipped cream on top, served with a glass of rum.

Türkische served with grounds and sugar in a copper pouring pot.

Verlängerter Brauner like the Brauner, but with a little more water in the coffee.

Verlängerter Schwarzer a watered-down Schwarzer (black coffee).

Diglas, a Biedermeier café renowned for coffee, cake and *Wiener Schmäh*. See p122.

This elegant café, opposite the Rathaus and the old university, was a favourite of Sigmund Freud where the old man regular enjoyed a slice of *Guglhupf*, the sponge cake with a hole. It's a traditional *Kaffeehaus* where hats and coats are surrendered to a frowning cloakroom dame and the liveried waiters refuse to smile. Subjected to over €500,000 of grandiose renovation, Landtmann has lost much of its authenticity but remains popular with academics, Burgtheater regulars and powerbrokers from Austrian business and politics.

Café Mozart

1, Albertinaplatz 2 (24 102-1/www.cafe-wien.at).
U1, U2, U4 Karlsplatz/tram 1, 2, D, J/bus 3a.
Open 8am-midnight daily. **Credit** AmEx, DC, MC, V.
Melange €3.60. **Map** p242 E7.
Located behind the Staatsoper, the Mozart has become another victim of the tourist trade and should be approached with scepticism. Its splendid 19th-century interior made a big impression on Graham Greene during the shooting of *The Third Man* and it became the film's Café Alt Wien. Anton Karas, composer of the immortal 'Harry Lime Theme' even wrote a Café Mozart waltz in its honour. Probably unbeknownst to Greene, the Mozart was confiscated from its Jewish proprietors after the Anschluss and handed over to one Fritz Quester, a chimney sweep by trade.

Café Museum

1, Opernring 21 (586 5202). U1, U2, U4
Karlsplatz/tram 1, 2, D, J. **Open** 8am-midnight daily. **No credit cards. Map** p242 E7.
To get a picture of the original Adolf Loos-designed interior of Café Museum, it's best to head for

the Kaiserliches Hofmobiliendepot (*see p82*) where numerous photos and items of furniture document what was a early example of elegant minimalism. Today only a few Thonet chairs serve as a reminder of the days when Café Museum was the favourite of Klimt, et al, coming from the nearby Secession. A windowless backroom is the haunt of card and chess players throughout the day and there's a small no-smoking area on the Karlsplatz side. The café closed for renovation during summer 2003, so it remains to be seen whether the atmospheric scruffiness that attracted a young bohemian crowd will be retained.

Café Prückel

1, Stubenring 24 (512 61 15/www.prueckel.at). U3 Stubentor/tram 1, 2. **Open** 8.30am-10.30pm daily.
No credit cards. Melange €2.90. **Map** p243 F7.
Originally a classic Ringstrasse café that opened in 1903, it was given its present 1950s-style look in 1989 by Viennese architect Oswald Haerdtel. Comfortable yet functional, the Prückel's understated furnishings and 6m (19ft) high ceilings adorned with magnificent Venetian chandeliers form a spacious, airy interior loved by everyone from bridge players and elderly ladies to students and bohemians. It offers a good choice of international press, plus own-made cakes and a summer terrace. There's also a small flea market in the basement and a pianist on Monday, Wednesday and Friday evenings. Ideal after a visit to the nearby MAK (*see p75*).

Café Sacher Wien

1, Philharmonikerstrasse 4 (512 1487/www.sacher.
com). U1, U4 Karlsplatz/tram 1, 2, D, J, 62, 65/bus 3a. **Open** 8am-11.30pm daily. **Credit** AmEx, DC, MC, V. **Melange** €3.30. **Map** p242 E8.

It is said that if tourists want a taste of imperial Vienna, they should stay a night at the Sacher hotel. Since this starry establishment is beyond most visitors' budgets, they make do with coffee and cake in the hotel's café. Starchy, conservative and full of monarchic clutter – Thomas Bernhard used to take refuge here from literary hoi polloi – a visit to Café Sacher today usually involves a lengthy queue (although the winter months are less busy). The café's world famous *Sachertorte* is available in a variety of formats at the hotel's shop on Kärntner Strasse round the corner. You can also have it delivered abroad.

Café Schwarzenberg

1, Kärntner Ring 17 (512 89 98). Tram 1, 2, D. **Open** 7am-midnight Mon-Fri, Sun; 9am-midnight Sat. **Credit** AmEx, DC, MC, V. **Melange** €3.20. **Map** p243 E8.

Slap bang on the Ring and perfect for posing on the summer terrace, the Schwarzenberg is another victim of overzealous renovation. The pompous pseudo belle époque interior, with mirrors gleaming from every wall, is certainly very eye-catching but once inside, the tuxedoed waiters who condescendingly serve your coffee and assume generous tips soon remove the shine. There is a piano player every night except Monday.

Café Segafredo

1, Am Graben (533 5025). U1, U3 Stephansplatz/ bus 1a. **Open** 8am-midnight Mon-Thur, Sun; 8am-1am Fri, Sat. **No credit cards. Melange** €2.80. **Map** p242 E6.

The place for wannabes to see and be seen on a summer's day or night. Of the many pavement cafés on Graben, this overcrowded establishment is undoubtedly where to watch Vienna's world and their designer dogs pass by. The coffee, however, cannot be faulted.

Café Teitelbaum

1, Dorotheergasse 11 (512 5545). U1, U3 Stephansplatz/bus 3a. **Open** 10am-6pm Mon-Wed, Fri; 10am-8pm Thur. **No credit cards. Melange** €2.50. **Map** p242 E7.

A *Kaffeehaus* in Vienna's renovated Jüdisches Museum. The Teitelbaum isn't strictly kosher, but it does serve one of the best cups of coffee in town, along with some very fine *Mohnstrudel, Linzertorte* and own-made bagels. There is also good vegetarian food, a selection of Jewish newspapers and a substantial no-smoking area.

4th District

Café Do-An

4, Naschmarkt, Stand 412 (586 4715). U4 Kettenbrückengasse. **Open** 8am-10pm Mon-Sat. **No credit cards. Melange** €2.20. **Map** p242 D8.

Adored by Vienna's bourgeois bohemians, the Do-An does wicked Illy coffee, great salads and sandwiches, and superb Kremser beer in a fishtank

location in the Naschmarkt. It's a strategic point for watching folk walk by on Saturdays when the place heaves all day long with local trustafarians inspecting their flea market trophies.

5th District

Café Rüdigerhof

5, Hamburgerstrasse 20 (586 3138). U4 Pilgramgasse/ bus 13a, 14a. **Open** 9am-2am Mon-Fri, Sun; noon-2am Sat. **No credit cards. Melange** €2.30. **Map** p239 D9.

Located in a magnificently restored Jugendstil house a stone's throw from U4 Pilgramgasse. In summer there's a pleasant terrace where you can sit and stare at the curves of the building's stucco. Inside, the Rüdigerhof is virtually a museum of retro fittings (mostly 1950s) with especially wacky fluorescent lamps. Small eats are available but most people come for a draught Budweiser or a coffee.

6th District

Bar Italia

6, Mariahilfer Strasse 19-21 (585 2838/www.bar italia.net). U2 Museumsquartier/bus 2a. **Open** 10am-2am Mon-Sun. **Credit** MC, V. **Melange** €2.50. **Map** p242 D8.

Drop in while shopping on the Mariahilfer Strasse. A choice of hearty, healthy or fatty breakfasts is served until 11.30am Monday to Saturday; 3.30pm on Sundays. The bar is modern and cool. The latest pair of sunglasses is the unofficial entrance ticket, regardless of weather or time of day. The coffee is excellent; warm up with a *café corretto con grappa* on a blustery afternoon. The brioches and focaccia sandwiches are fresh and delicious.

A landmark, and quite rightly so – **Cafe Landtmann**. *See p125.*

They're all on cake

The cakes served at Vienna's coffeehouses are often baked on the premises and usually displayed in a glass cabinet. Here are some of the more common calorific treats:

Apfelstrudel cooked apples and raisins in pastry and sprinkled with icing sugar. Usually served hot with lashings of whipped cream or a generous portion of vanilla ice-cream.

Esterházy Torte layers and layers of sponge and cream, covered in white icing and crowned with a feather emblem.

Guglhupf supposedly Freud's favourite. It can be jazzed up with pieces of candied fruit or chocolate drops, but at its most basic this is a marble cake baked in a fluted ring mould and cut into slices.

Imperial Torte a cake with a rich blend of chocolate and marzipan with a nut and butter-cream filling.

Linzertorte nutty sponge cake with a strawberry jam filling. Also try the **Linzerauge**: it's less sickly sweet, but similar to a jam tart.

Mohnkuchen sponge cake made of poppy seeds. It melts in the mouth.

Sachertorte the most famous Viennese cake. Rich chocolate sponge cake covered in apricot jam and a thick, dark chocolate layer. The cafés Sacher (*see p125*) and Demel (*see p122*) claim to be the only establishments with the authentic recipe.

Topfenstrudel like apple strudel, but with a sweet lemony curd cheese filling.

Jelinek

6, Otto-Bauer-Gasse 5 (597 4113). U3 Zieglergasse. **Open** 8am-8pm Mon-Fri. **Credit** V. **Melange** €2.80. **Map** p242 D8.

This quiet, relaxing coffee house off the Mariahilfer Strasse is mercifully free of historical or mythological nonsense but nevertheless a wonderful reminder of the pre-Starbucks era. Run by an old couple who do not allow mobile phones and frown on tipping, it has a loyal clientele of young to thirtysomethings. Only children of regulars are tolerated. There are excellent own-made cakes and a few snacks. It's worth popping into after a morning's shopping.

Café Ritter

6, Mariahilfer Strasse 73 (587 8238). U3 Neubaugasse/bus 13a. **Open** 8am-11.30pm daily. **No credit cards.** **Melange** €2.70. **Map** p238 C8.

A curious mixture between a Jugendstil and a 1950s café. In fact, it was originally opened at Prince Esterházy's summer palace in 1867. Now it lies on this busy shopping street. It gets unbearably smoky.

Café Savoy

6, Linke Wienzeile 36 (586 7348). U4 Kettenbrückengasse/bus 59a. **Open** 5pm-2am Mon-Fri; 9am-2am Sat. **No credit cards.** **Melange** €2.80. **Map** p242 D8.

Teehaus

Haas & Haas

1, Stephansplatz 4 (512 26 66/www.haas-haas.at). U1, U4 Stephansplatz. **Open** 8am-8pm Mon-Fri; 8am-6.30pm Sat. **Credit** DC, MC, V. **Melange** €3. **Map** p243 F6.

Tucked away behind Stephansdom, Haas & Haas is famed for preparing Vienna's best breakfasts. Part teashop, part café, it offers 47 varieties, all served in the appropriate china, either in the airy wicker-chaired rooms or under vines on the gorgeous summer terrace. The breakfast menu includes specialities from ten countries and ranges from British fry-ups to the Japanese miso soup, salmon, omelette and green tea option. Everything is beautifully laid out and guarantees an optimum start to the day.

High Tea

4, Paniglgasse 17 (504 1508/www.hightea.at). U1, U2, U4 Karlsplatz. **Open** 9am-10pm Mon-Fri, 9am-6.30pm Sat. **Credit** AmEx, DC, MC, V. **Map** p239 E8.

Owned by local tea importers Demmers, High Tea is a beautifully appointed mixture of shop, tea house and restaurant. Beyond the entrance area, laden with teas and associated paraphernalia, English chocolate and gift items, lie two spacious rooms with lovely distressed 19th-century ceilings and a jolly mismatched collection of armchairs and sofas where students, yuppies and ladies that lunch sip cups of char. Demmers are also up with the times and provide a sleek lunch area with glass ceiling, two free internet terminals and coffee should you want it. The breakfasts, bagels and toasties are all made with organic ingredients.

Gilded glamour, baroque-style, with full-length mirrors (reputedly the largest in Europe) and carved reliefs on the ceiling. The Savoy is frequented by an arty, camp crowd. It also has a garden and some tables outside, but traffic noise intrudes. *See also p165.*

Café-Restaurant Servus

6, Mariahilfer Strasse 57-9 (587 6392). U3 Neubaugasse. **Open** 10am-midnight Mon-Sat. **Credit** MC, V. **Melange** €2.60. **Map** p238 C8.

The Servus' Jugendstil interior soon fills with shoppers and cinema-goers. There's an excellent choice of freshly prepared dishes and a great banana milkshake. A further attraction is the cheerful pianist on Tuesday, Thursday and Saturday nights.

Café Sperl

6, Gumpendorfer Strasse 11 (586 4158/www.cafesperl.at). U2 Museumsquartier/bus 57a. **Open** 7am-11pm Mon-Sat; 11am-8pm Sun. **Credit** AmEx, DC, MC, V. **Melange** €2.91. **Map** p242 D8.

The apotheosis of the Viennese *Kaffeehaus*, the Sperl's faded grandeur is today surprisingly cosy despite its awesome dimensions. Sperl plays the role of *Kaffeehaus* in more films than any other, so don't be surprised to catch it on celluloid – or to see a film crew outside. Thought to have been a haunt of two of Alma Mahler's husbands, Gustav Mahler and Franz Werfel, it has managed to retain an atmosphere of stately silence, in part due to a ban on mobile phones. Most Viennese have a soft spot for Sperl with its tuxedoed, grumpy waiters and mousy waitresses, velvet booths and expansive windows. It also has two billiard tables. Approach the own-made cake display with care: it's uncovered.

7th District

Café Westend

7, Mariahilfer Strasse 128 (523 3183). U3, U6 Westbahnhof. **Open** 7am-midnight daily. **Credit** DC, MC, V. **Melange** €2.90. **Map** p238 B9.

Conveniently located opposite the Westbahnhof, this café provides new arrivals with everything that is authentic in a Viennese coffee house – grubby stucco, chandeliers, ceiling sunbursts, marble-topped tables and extremely generous portions of strudel and chocolate cake from ancient display cabinets. And to cap it all, the coffee is actually very good and the waiters uncommonly friendly.

8th District

Café Eiles

8, Josefstädter Strasse 2 (405 3410). U2 Rathaus/tram J. **Open** *Winter* 7am-11pm daily. *Summer* 8am-10pm daily. **Credit** AmEx, MC, V. **Melange** €2.70. **Map** p242 C6.

A favourite haunt for lawyers and politicians because of its proximity to the Parliament and Rathaus, Eiles is also a practical stop before taking on the delights of Vienna's 8th district. It has booths and high tables and serves a hearty Viennese breakfast from 7am to 11.30pm.

Café-Restaurant Hummel

8, Josefstädter Strasse 66 (405 5314/www.cafehummel.at). Tram 5, 33, J. **Open** 7am-2am Mon-Sat; 8am-2am Sun. **Credit** AmEx, DC, MC, V. **Melange** €2.30. **Map** p238 B6.

This extremely busy bar-restaurant-coffee house is the focal point of Josefstadt. The waiters are notoriously rude and take particular exception, understandably, to people who consume Big Macs from the nearby McDonald's on their terrace. However, it's great for people-watching, and it has the *Guardian* every day.

13th District

Café Dommayer
13, Auhofstrasse 2 (877 5465/www.dommayer.at).
U4 Hietzing. **Open** 7am-midnight daily. **Credit**
AmEx, DC, MC, V. **Melange** €3.10.
Café Dommayer is one of the city's best-known
traditional *Kaffeehäuser*, and is just a stone's throw
from the Palace of Schönbrunn. Johann Strauss
Junior made his debut here in 1844. Concerts still
take place on the third Saturday of the month. The
restaurant has a huge garden where different theatre companies perform on the third Sunday in the
month, from May through to September. Strauss
concerts by the Vienna Strauss Ensemble are held
from 2 to 4pm every Saturday throughout the year.
The café holds a Christmas market in its garden
throughout December.

Café Gloriette
13, Gloriette, Schönbrunn Schlosspark (879 1311/
www.gloriette-cafe.at). U4 Schloss Schönbrunn.
Open *May-Sept* 9am-1hr before the park
closes daily. **Credit** AmEx, DC, MC, V.
Melange €3.
Although beautifully situated high up on the hill
overlooking the Palace of Schönbrunn, this café is
little more than an unimaginative slice of wedding
cake housed in the Gloriette, an impressive neo-
classical arcade erected in 1775 during the reign of
Maria Theresia. The view is the café's redeeming
feature, so it's best to book ahead to make sure you
secure a window table.

16th District

Café Club International
16, Payergasse 14 (403 1827). U6 Josefstädter
Strasse. **Open** 8am-2pm Mon-Sat; 10am-2am Sun.
No credit cards. Melange €2. **Map** p238 A6.
Part of a local initiative to integrate the Ottakring
district's various immigrant communities through
housing advice and language courses, Club
International runs a cheerful little café with the
sunniest terrace on Yppenplatz. It's particularly
worth a visit here on Saturdays when the nearby
Turkish/Balkan-flavoured Brunnenmarkt (*see*
p141) is accompanied by an excellent farmers'
market selling flowers, vegetables, wine and other
country produce.

Café Weidinger
16, Lerchenfelder Gürtel 1 (492 0906). U6
Burggasse. **Open** 7am-12.30am Mon-Fri; 8am-
12.30am Sat, Sun. **No credit cards. Melange**
€1.90. **Map** p238 B7.
With its threadbare upholstery and amber nicotine-
stained ceilings, the roomy L-shaped Café
Weidinger is one of those magnificent Viennese
establishments that used to occupy every major
junction in the city. Today the majority of these
places have been turned into Admiral betting
shops, so it's worth doing your bit to preserve the

historic genre. Here the clientele is a pleasant mixture
of switched-on slackers and tubby early-retired
males who drop in for a coffee or a beer and a game
of cards or billiards. The green baize and ageing
wood-panelling are magnificently lit by a line of
suspended white globes.

18th District

Café Wilder Mann
18, Währinger Strasse 85 (405 4704). U6 Volksoper.
Open 9am-7pm Mon-Fri. **No credit cards.**
Melange €2.50. **Map** p234 C4.
Worth a visit just for the name, the Wild Man's spacious post-war interior has a slightly melancholic
air of *Brief Encounter* about it. Ideal for a quiet
afternoon's ruminating, the café has some good
cakes and small snacks, if rather substandard coffee. Take a look at the statue of the cudgel-wielding
Wild Man – a story from the Turkish siege – on the
building's façade.

Wiener Konzertcafé Schmid Hansl
18, Schulgasse 31 (406 3658). Tram 40, 41.
Open 8pm-4am Tue-Sat. **Credit** V. **Melange** €3.
Map p234 B4.
A hybrid café/small *Heuriger*. Original owner
Schmid Hansl was renowned for bursting into song
in front of his clientele, and became so famous that
professional singers flocked to the café to accompany him in a duet. Hansl's son, a former member
of the Vienna Boys' Choir, now runs the café and
opera stars still perform here unannounced. True
to the plaque outside the café that reads 'Home of
the Viennese song', so-called *Wienerlieder* and
operetta are played here every evening.

19th District

Blaustern
19, Döblingergürtel 2 (369 6564/www.blaustern.at).
U6 Nussdorfer Strasse/tram 37, 38. **Open** 7am-
1am Mon-Thur; 7am-2am Fri; 8am-2am Sat;
9am-1am Sun. **No credit cards. Melange** €2.20.
Map p234 C2.
Located on the Gürtel, close to Spittelau and
Hundertwasser's Fernwärme (*see p84*), this large,
modern café-restaurant pulls in the posh youth from
the nearby economics faculty with a combination
of chic design, Becks on tap, own-brand coffee and
great meals and snacks. There's a large terrace in
summer, but the traffic noise is overwhelming by
local standards.

Cobenzl
19, Am Cobenzl 94 (320 5120/www.cobenzl.at).
U4 Heiligenstadt, then bus 38a. **Open** 10am-10pm
daily. **No credit cards. Melange** €2.40.
This pavilion café offers a fantastic view over
Vienna from the top of Cobenzl hill from its round
terrace or window seats. The drink to go for here is
the excellent hot chocolate.

Eat, Drink, Shop

Shops & Services

High-street names dominate the main shopping areas, but treasures lie in the back streets.

The face of shopping in Vienna has changed visibly over the past few years, with big names and high-street giants moving into understated shopping centres and dull streets turning bright and shiny with new businesses. The two main shopping centres are still **Mariahilfer Strasse** and **Kärntner Strasse**, where more H&Ms seem to join an already packed market almost every month, and European fashion chains open ever more outlets. But the real gems are to be found in the back streets. Almost every street in Vienna has a few shops in it – many are dingy, unappetising establishments you might walk past without really noticing, but at any time you could stumble upon an incredible shop like Teuchtler Alt&Neu record store, or Blumenkraft florist. Big designers are now moving into the main shopping streets around Stephansdom, with Armani and Salvatore Fergamo joining Chanel, Dior and Louis Vuitton in Kohlmarkt, but they are never very far from quirky specialised places such as knife shops or little art stores.

Off the main drag, keen window shoppers should visit **Josefstädter Strasse** in the 8th district, a traditional Viennese high street with lots of little shops selling anything from trendy lamps to flowers; **Neubaugasse** in the 7th, a haven of second-hand and offbeat shops, and **Weihburggasse** (just off Kärntner Strasse in the 1st), which features Vienna's Prada store just steps from tiny arty and religious boutiques.

You can also find Vienna's greatest commercial attraction, its antique and bric-a-brac emporia, lurking in the back streets. Much of the stuff you come across in the junk shops is the legacy of the fine craft tradition that flourished in Vienna under the patronage of the Habsburgs and many shops still sport the stamp of quality, the royal k.u.k. (*kaiserlich und königlich*) warrant.

Austria and the Alpine region as a whole has a reputation for being pricey, but as capital cities go Vienna offers very cheap living, especially when it comes to eating, drinking and buying clothes. Opening hours, once very restricted with half-day Saturdays, are loosening up a little now, with several supermarkets as well as more and more little bakers opening on Sundays and public holidays, and talk of Sunday opening floating around political circles. Most shops are open from 9am to 6 or 7pm, and on Saturday from 9am to 5pm. Service isn't always the friendliest and uppity shop assistants (as well as waiters) are legendary in Vienna.

So what is there to spend your dosh on in Vienna? Most of the high streets are filled with foreign goods and even many of the products touted in souvenir shops are not actually Viennese – the famous chocolate *Mozart Kugeln* (Mozart balls) are a speciality of Salzburg, and Loden's traditional dark green weaves and the cutesy Swarovski glass figures (*see p144*) both originate from the Tyrol. Chocolate is not an Austrian speciality, but the pâtisserie is excellent. Those with extra cash to splash can acquire a Woka lamp, a pair of Reiter trainers or some fab '60s or '70s design from Es Brennt… Lichterloh.

One-stop

Gasometer
11, Guglgasse (www.g-town.at). U3 Gasometer. **Open** 10am-7.30pm Mon-Fri; 9am-5pm Sat. **Credit** varies. **Map** p241 K10.
A massive three-storey complex with a cinema, bars, a big Spar supermarket and loads of high-street stores and boutiques, Gasometer is worth a visit even if you hate shopping. Four massive cylinders which once stored gas have had their insides pulled out and replaced by luxury flats and a shopping mall, and windows have been punched into the original brick outsides in an amazing architectural feat.

Generali Center
6, Mariahilfer Strasse 77. U3 Neubaugasse. **Open** 10am-7pm Mon-Fri; 10am-5pm Sat. **Credit** varies. **Map** p238 C8.
A two-storey shopping centre with a big supermarket in the basement, Generali is home to lots of Asian furniture shops as well as trendy young clothes stores and a few gift shops. It also houses the **Pan** discount store (*see p137*).

Gerngross
7, Mariahilfer Strasse 38-40 (52180-0). U3 Neubaugasse. **Open** 9.30am-7pm Mon-Fri; 9am-5pm Sat. **Credit** varies. **Map** p238 C8.
A five-floor complex of various franchises, including a massive branch of electrical shop Saturn (which sells everything from computer equipment

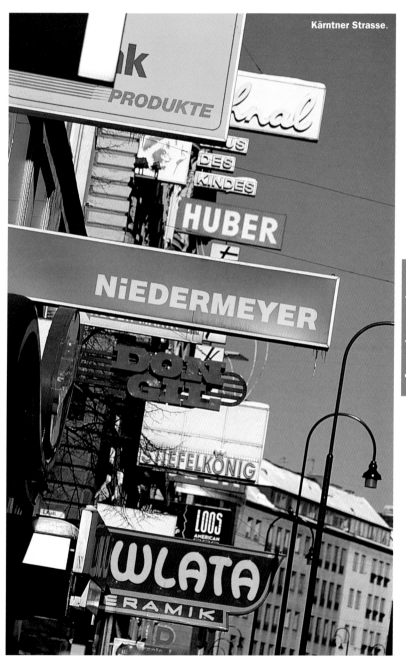

Kärntner Strasse.

Eat, Drink, Shop

Be a Good Girl – an unusual mix of hairdresser's and boutique. *See p134.*

to food mixers). There's also a two-storey Zara, an excellent Merkur supermarket (in the basement) and direct access to the U3 Neubaugasse station.

Ringstrassen Gallerien
1, Kärntner Ring 11-13. U1, U2, U4 Karlsplatz/ tram 1, 2, D, J/bus 3a. **Open** 7.30am-10pm Mon-Sat. **Credit** varies. **Map** p242 E8.
A huge shopping and office complex on three floors. Shops are mostly fashion outlets, with the best Billa supermarket in town in the basement and a number of cafés and bars. Expensive and a bit soulless.

Steffl
1, Kärntner Strasse 19 (514 31-0). U1, U3 Stephansplatz. **Open** 9.30am-7pm Mon-Fri; 9.30am-5pm Sat. **Credit** AmEx, DC, MC, V. **Map** p243 E7.
A chic department store with cosmetics and bags on the ground floor, designer clothes for men and women and an Amadeus books and stationery store. The basement is taken up with an outlet of the Don Gil chain, which sells French Connection, Diesel and other young fashion labels. On the top floor is the Skybar, a classy bar with some great views of Vienna.

Antiques

Austrians have a fondness for the old and antiquated and a corresponding reluctance to throw it away. Throughout the city you will see many junk shops (*Altwaren*), upmarket antique shops (*Antiquitäten*) and stamp, coin and postcard emporia. In the 1st district the streets around the Dorotheum (*see p54*) are dotted with

purveyors of antique furniture and fine art. Those with an interest in Jugendstil should check out the 7th district around Siebensterngasse. The streets around Josefstädter Strasse in the 8th have a good mix of antiques and *Altwaren*.

Es Brennt... Lichterloh
6, Gumpendorfer Strasse 15-17 (586 0520/ www.lichterloh.com). U4 Kettenbrückengasse/ bus 57a. **Open** 11am-6.30pm Mon-Fri; 11am-4pm Sat. **Credit** AmEx, DC, MC, V. **Map** p242 D8.
Es Brennt... Lichterloh has two sections: on one side of its big new store are spacious, high-ceilinged rooms full of offbeat design from the 1950s to the 1970s, including a basement with some wild rugs, and on the other a smaller room with art deco furniture and jewellery on display.
Branch: Glasfabrik 17, Lorenz-Mandel-Gasse 25 (494 3490).

Das Kunstwerk
4, Operngasse 20 (0650 230 9994/www.das kunstwerk.at). U1, U2, U4 Karlsplatz/bus 59a. **Open** 11am-6pm Mon-Fri; 10am-2pm Sat. **Credit** DC, MC, V. **Map** p242 E7.
Specialist in Murano and Lötz glass as well as art deco and art nouveau furniture and design up to 1980, including Thonet and Kohn. Das Kunstwerk also carries big names in Austrian design such as Otto Wagner and Adolf Loos. Wolfgang in this store and Harald in Laimgrubengasse, just off the Naschmarkt, are always delighted to show people round, and might make you an excellent Viennese coffee if you come at the right time.
Branch: 6, Laimgrubengasse 24 (0650 230 9999).

RaumInhalt
*4, Schleifmühlgasse 13 (409 9892/www.raumin
halt.com). U1, U2, U4 Karlsplatz.* **Open** noon-7pm
Mon-Fri; 10am-4pm Sat. **Credit** AmEx, DC, MC, V.
Map p242 E8.
One of the many great little shops offering modern
design from the 1950s to the 1980s. It specialises in
1950s Scandinavian design and the friendly staff are
always ready to help the uninitiated. Rauminhalt's
furniture and design also feature regularly in photo-
shoots and adverts.

Books & stationery

Amadeus
*6, Mariahilfer Strasse 99 (595 4550/www.amadeus
buch.co.at). U3 Neubaugasse.* **Open** 9.30am-7pm
Mon-Fri; 9.30am-5pm Sat. **Credit** AmEx, DC, MC, V.
Map p238 C8.
A four-storey emporium selling everything from stationery and art supplies to world music and videos,
with a big selection of English and other language
books, as well as a massive range of foreign magazines and newspapers. There's a pleasant café on the
first floor with a view of the shoppers thronging
Mariahilfer Strasse.
Branches: 3, Landstrasse Hauptstrasse 2a-2b
(Wien Mitte) (718 93 53); **Sun & holidays**, 21,
Ignaz-Köck Strasse 1/Shopping Center Nord
(271 66 41).

Babette's
*4, Schleifmühlgasse 17 (585 5165/www.babettes.at).
U1, U2, U4 Karlsplatz.* **Open** 10am-7pm Mon-Fri;
10am-5pm Sat. **Credit** MC, V. **Map** p239 E8.
Babette's has recipe books from all over the world
(a large number of them in English), as well as a cosy
little café at the back, where you can sit and enjoy
the dish of the day or a speciality coffee while watching more dishes being prepared and cakes being
baked. The staff also sell a huge range of herbs and
spices and organise cookery courses.

British Bookshop
*1, Weihburggasse 24-6 (512 1945/www.
britishbookshop.at). U3 Stubentor/tram 1, 2.*
Open 9.30am-6.30pm Mon-Fri; 9.30am-5pm Sat.
Credit AmEx, DC, MC, V. **Map** p243 F7.
English-language shop associated with Blackwell's,
with stacks of novels, history and Viennesia. It's also
the best EFL shop – teachers ply their trade on the
noticeboard at the back. Bargains can be found in
the summer when stock is sold off.
Branch: 6, Mariahilfer Strasse 4 (522 6730).

Comic-Treff Steiner
6, Barnabitengasse 12 (586 7627). U3 Neubaugasse.
Open 9.30am-6.30pm Mon-Fri; 9.30am-5pm Sat.
No credit cards. **Map** p238 C8.
The best comic emporium in Vienna, run by helpful,
clued-up English speakers. It has a decent line in
quirky American productions, and is good on
peripheral items, from the Simpsons and manga
merchandising to Hello Kitty.

Freytag & Berndt
*1, Kohlmarkt 9 (533 8685/www.freytagberndt.at).
U3 Herrengasse.* **Open** 9am-7pm Mon-Fri; 9am-5pm
Sat. **Credit** AmEx, DC, MC, V. **Map** p242 E6.
If maps are your bag, don't miss the chance to visit
this fine store located in Max Fabiani's Jugendstil
Artariahaus. Serious ramblers should call by to get
the excellent maps of the Wienerwald. There is also
a large selection of travel and cookery books.

Shakespeare & Co
1, Sterngasse 2 (535 5053). U1, U4 Schwedenplatz.
Open 9am-7pm Mon-Sat. **Credit** AmEx, DC, MC,
V. **Map** p243 E6.
This tiny shop is Vienna's most reliable for literature and academic titles in English. Shakespeare is
great on contemporary and classic literature, with
an eclectic selection of fine arts and music, sociolo-
gy and Vienna-related themes on shelves that reach
to the ceiling. The atmosphere is sedate, the decor
enhanced by photos of some of the luminaries who
have given readings on the premises.

Stationery
Basic stationery can be obtained cheaply at any
branch of **Libro** (which also sells English books).

Huber & Lerner
*1, Weihburggasse 4 (533 5075/www.huber-
lerner.at). U1, U3 Stephansplatz.* **Open** 9.30am-6pm
Mon-Fri; 10am-5pm Sat. **Credit** AmEx, DC, MC, V.
Map p243 E7.
H&L sells a vast range of fine handmade paper,
cards and stationery gifts. High-class and expensive,
but staff are friendly.

Theyer & Hardtmuth
*1, Kärntner Strasse 9 (512 3678-0/www.theyer-
hardtmuth.at). U1, U3 Stephansplatz.* **Open**
9.30am-6pm Mon-Fri; 10am-5pm Sat. **Credit** AmEx,
DC, MC, V. **Map** p243 E7.
The best address for top-of-the-range fountain pens,
diaries, organisers and handmade paper.

Cameras & computers

Cameras

Photobörse
*8, Lerchenfelder Strasse 62-64 (961 0964/www.photo
boerse.at). Tram 46.* **Open** 9am-6pm Mon-Fri; 9am-
1pm Sat. **Credit** AmEx, DC, MC, V. **Map** p238 B7/C7.
Vast selection of new and second-hand cameras as
well as trade-in possibilities.

Computers

Der Computer Doktor
18, Gentzgasse 9 (470 7005). U6 Volksoper. **Open**
9.30am-noon, 2.30-6pm Mon-Fri. **No credit cards**.
Map p234 C4.

The good doctor will repair your PC, Notebook or flatscreen monitor, but call in advance to book a slot. You can also phone the technical hotline on 0900 56 0201 during the same opening hours, but beware high call charges.

McShark Multimedia

5, Schönbrunner Strasse 71 (545 5251/www.mc shark.at). U4 Pilgramgasse. **Open** 10am-6pm Mon-Fri; 11am-1pm Sat. **Credit** MC. **Map** p238 C10.
The place to call for Apple queries.

Children

Giesswein

1, Ringstrassengalerie, Kärntner Ring 5-7 (512 4597). U1, U2, U4 Karlsplatz/tram 1, 2, D, J. **Open** 10am-7pm Mon-Fri; 10am-5pm Sat. **Credit** AmEx, DC, MC, V. **Map** p243 E8.
Dealers in very cute and wearable versions of traditional trachten clothes for children.

Hennes & Mauritz

6, Mariahilfer Strasse 53 (585 8550/www.hm.at). U3 Neubaugasse/bus 13a. **Open** 9.30am-7pm Mon-Fri; 9.30am-5pm Sat. **Credit** DC, MC, V. **Map** p242 C8.
Good for cheap and cheerful kids' clothes.

Kindergalerie Sonnenschein

7, Neubaugasse 62/1 (524 1766). U3 Neubaugasse. **Open** 10am-6.30pm Mon-Fri; 10am-5pm Sat. **Credit** V. **Map** p238 C8.
Stuffed toys, puppets and cushions for babies and children of all ages, and some lovely wooden toys.

Pachisi

1, Ringstrassengalerie (top floor), Kärntner Ring 9-13 (512 7150). U1, U2, U4 Karlsplatz/tram 1, 2, D, J. **Open** 10am-7pm Mon-Fri; 10am-5pm Sat. **Credit** AmEx, DC, MC, V. **Map** p243 E8.
The place to find the kind of things you don't see in a normal toy shop. It specialises in wooden toys and sells everything from trains to toadstools and a Noah's ark. Pachisi also has huge cuddly animals and lots of beautiful, small gift ideas.

Popolino

6, Barnabitengasse 3 (581 32 00/www.popolini.com). U3 Neubaugasse/bus 13a. **Open** 10am-6pm Mon-Fri; 10am-5pm Sat. **Credit** MC, V. **Map** p242 C8.
Apart from its ecological nappy system, Popolino specialises in beautiful colourful clothes in natural fabrics for babies and small children. Baby accessories are also a forte, including silk blankets, sleeping bags, so-called Pucksacks (snug bags for babies) and wooden toys.

Spielzeugschachtel

1, Rauhensteingasse 5 (512 44 94). U1 Stephansplatz. **Open** 9.30am-6.30pm Mon-Fri; 9.30am-5pm Sat. **Credit** AmEx, DC, MC, V. **Map** p243 E7.
A toy shop for demanding parents. You'll not find much plastic here, but a wide range of creative and educational toys for children of all ages.

Health & beauty

Cosmetics

Bipa

1, Kärntner Strasse 1 (512 2210/www.bipa.at). U1, U3 Stephansplatz. **Open** 8am-7pm Mon-Fri; 8am-5pm Sat. **No credit cards. Map** p243 E7.
Bipa, Billa's cosmetics and cleaning products outlet, is present in every shopping street and the best place to stock up on essentials. It also has cheap photo developing. Rival DM is very similar (you'll find it throughout Vienna; a central branch is at 1, Rotenturmstrasse 12; 512 39 60).
Branches: throughout the city.

Douglas

1, Kärntner Strasse 26 (512 9244/www.douglas.de) U1, U3 Stephansplatz. **Open** 9am-7pm Mon-Fri; 9am-5pm Sat **Credit** AmEx, DC, MC, V. **Map** p243 E7.
A wide range of perfumes, gifts and top-of-the-range cosmetics can be found at Douglas.
Branches: throughout the city.

Karin Van Vliet

1, Köllnerhofgasse 4 (513 1155/www.makeup-studio.com). U1, U4 Schwedenplatz. **Open** 10am-6pm Mon-Fri; 11am-5pm Sat. **Credit** DC, MC, V. **Map** p243 F6.
A beautiful frontage behind which lies own-brand non-animal-tested products. Treat yourself to a make-up session (€37) or a one-hour course (€100).

Nanadebary

1, Bauernmarkt 9 (533 1111/www.nana debary.com). U1, U3 Stephansplatz. **Open** 10am-6pm Mon-Fri; 10am-5pm Sat. **Credit** DC, MC, V. **Map** p242 E6.
Colourful, trendy own-brand make-up and perfumes in a minimalist display, as well as cool bags and little tops, are what you get here.

Hairdressers

Be a Good Girl

7, Westbahnstrasse 5a (524 4728-11/www.beagood girl.com). Tram 49. **Open** 10am-7pm Mon-Fri; 10am-5pm Sat. **Credit** AmEx, DC, MC, V. **Map** p238 B8.
Have your hair cut by friendly staff in a relaxed atmosphere. Be a Good Girl is also a shop selling wacky clothes and designer rings.

GmbHaar

7, Kirchengasse 39 (523 3763/www.gmbhaar.at). Bus 48a. **Open** 11am-9pm Mon-Fri. **No credit cards. Map** p242 C8.
Reini and the rest of the staff are Toni & Guy-trained and have been tending to Vienna's clubbers for over 15 years. Cuts take place in a trendy wood-panelled salon to trip-hop beats. GmbHaar also organises events; see the website.
Branch: 4, Margaretenstrasse 20 (585 6644).

The totally groovy – and very friendly – **Black Market**. *See p142.*

London Underground

8, Josefstädter Strasse 29 (407 1607). Tram J. **Open** 1-6pm Mon; 9am-6pm Tue, Wed; 9am-6pm Thur, Fri; 8am-1pm Sat. **No credit cards. Map** p238 B6.
Run by the talkative expatriate Brit Kurt, this salon caters for all ages, and its English-speaking staff are a godsend at moments of follicular anxiety. Excellent service includes a scalp massage.

Herbalists

Die Kräuterdrogerie

8, Kochgasse 34 (405 4522/www.kraeuter drogerie.at). Tram 43, 44/bus 13a. **Open** 8.30am-6pm Mon-Fri; 8.30am-1pm Sat. **Credit** AmEx, DC, MC, V. **Map** p234 C5.
Healing herbs and ether oils (Birgit is a trained pharmacist), as well as ayurvedic products. The food section gets regular deliveries of organic veg.

Opticians

Melitta Kleemann

1, Tuchlauben 12 (533 0098). U1, U3 Stephansplatz. **Open** 10am-6pm Mon-Fri; 10am-5pm Sat. **Credit** MC, V. **Map** p242 E6.
MK stocks lots of designer frames. Small repairs and adjustments are carried out free.
Branches: throughout the city.

Optiker Maurer (See Me)

8, Josefstädter Strasse 8 (405 0788). U2 Rathaus/ tram J. **Open** 9.30am-1 pm, 2-6pm Mon-Fri; 9am-12.30pm Sat. **Credit** AmEx, DC, MC, V. **Map** p238 C6.

An optician with a good mix of friendly service and reasonable prices. Top frames too.
Branch: 7, Siebensterngasse 40 (523 6494).

Design & household

Boudoir

9, Berggasse 14 (319 1079/www.boudoir.at). Tram D. **Open** 1-6pm Tue-Fri; 11am-3pm Sat. **Credit** AmEx, DC, MC, V. **Map** p242 D5.
Sheets and pillow cases decorated with winged phalli, subtitled 'The subconscious custom-made' are sold in this little boutique. Stock includes home furnishings, gifts such as chains of little pink willies, and frilly crotchless knickers. All this was dreamt up by Renate Christian, ex-pupil of Vivienne Westwood (and it shows).

Silenzio

1, Salzgries 2 (535 6750/www.silenzio.at). U1, U4 Schottenring/tram 1, 2. **Open** 10am-6pm Mon-Fri; 10am-5pm Sat. **Credit** AmEx, DC, MC, V. **Map** p243 E6.
One of the dozens of shops in unprepossessing back streets around the 1st district, selling everything from furniture and throws to candle holders, crockery and picture frames, some with a modern, minimalist look and some imitating 1960s and 1970s design.

Woka

1, Singerstrasse 16 (513 2912/www.woka.at). U1, U3 Stephansplatz. **Open** 10am-6pm Mon-Fri; 10am-1pm Sat. **Credit** AmEx, DC, MC, V. **Map** p243 E7.
Since 1978 Wolfgang Karolinsky and his firm Woka have been making superb reproductions of lamps

Pachisi sells wooden toys (for parents) and cuddly toys (for children). *See p134.*

and light fittings designed by members of the Wiener Werkstätte set, as well as by Adolf Loos. By acquiring many of the original tools, moulds and presses, Woka's lamps are as close to the real thing as you are likely to get.

Carpets

Metternich's adage that the Orient begins in Vienna remains true. The abundance of carpet and rug stores run by Iranians, Turks and Afghans is one prime indicator.

Adil Besim
1, Graben 30 (533 0910). U1, U3 Stephansplatz. **Open** 9.30am-6pm Mon-Fri; 10am-5pm Sat. **Credit** AmEx, DC, MC, V. **Map** p242 E6.
The most reputable address in the city and more a gallery than a shop. Sumptuous Persian carpets, some in gigantic sizes, at prices to match.

Kalash
1, Freyung 3 (0222 533 7027). U2 Schottentor/tram 1, 2, D. **Open** 10am-6pm Mon-Fri; 10am-1pm Sat. **Credit** AmEx, DC, MC, V. **Map** p242 E6.
Located just inside the Palais Harrach, Kalash is more a museum exhibition than a shop, with its superb display of antique brass and bronze figures and jewellery from Afghanistan, Bangladesh, Pakistan and Nepal.

Teppich-Galerie
8, Kochgasse 26 (403 6622). Tram 43, 44. **Open** 10am-6pm Mon-Fri; 10am-1pm Sat. **No credit cards. Map** p234 C5.

Typical carpet store, stocked to the ceiling with rugs and offcuts. Persian is the thing here and there are bargains to be had.

Erotic

Sex shops are present throughout the city; we list a couple of the more imaginative.

Condomi
6, Otto-Bauer-Gasse, 24 (581 2060/www.condomi. com). U3 Zieglergasse. **Open** noon-6.30pm Mon; 10am-2pm, 3-6.30pm Tue-Thur; 10am-6.30pm Fri; 10am-4pm Sat. **Credit** AmEx, DC, MC, V. **Map** p238 C9.
Condoms are the shop's forte – over 250 varieties in all, as well as lots of joke or gift articles from furry handcuffs and mugs to massage oils and body paint. There is a room at the back where the shop's display of vibrators is chained to a wall.

Tiberius
7, Lindengasse 2 (522 0474/www.tiberius.at). U3, U6 Westbahnhof. **Open** 3-6.30pm Mon-Fri; 10am-3pm Sat. **Credit** AmEx, DC, MC, V. **Map** p238 B8.
Vienna's foremost address for leather, rubber and S&M articles, with a huge selection of accessories.

Fashion

Vienna has come a long way from the fashion black hole it once was. European chains are mushrooming in the main shopping areas, from Mango, Zara and H&M to surf- and skatewear emporiums such as Rag. A foible seen in few other European countries is the fondness for traditional peasant garb, or *Trachten*. Even in Vienna you can see lots of people wearing traditional round-collared woollen jackets, and even a few in lederhosen or dirndl pinafores (*see* **Loden-Plankl** *below*). As designers go, apart from Helmut Lang, no other Austrians have really made it on the international scene.

Helmut Lang

1, Seilergasse 6 (513 2588/www.helmutlang.com). U1, U3 Stephansplatz. **Open** 10am-6.30pm Mon-Fri; 10am-5pm Sat. **Credit** AmEx, DC, MC, V. **Map** p242 E7.

He may be a long-time exile in New York, but Helmut Lang's flagship shop in Vienna still features low-key, classy clothes for men and women.

Loden-Plankl

1, Michaelerplatz 6 (533 8032/www.loden-plankl.at). U3 Herrengasse. **Open** 9am-6pm Mon-Fri; 10am-5pm Sat. **Credit** AmEx, DC, MC, V. **Map** p242 E7.

Loden-Plankl's store next to the Hofburg has been purveying fine woollen and traditional clothes since 1831. The whole family can be decked out in peasant hats, lederhosen and frilly pinafores, but note that the Von Trapp look does not come cheap.

Modus Vivendi

6, Schadekgasse 4 (587 2823/www.modus-vivendi.at). U3 Neubaugasse. **Open** 10am-1pm, 2-7pm Mon-Fri; noon-4pm Sat. **Credit** DC, MC, V. **Map** p238 C8.

Gorgeous knitwear for men and women, both off-the-peg and made-to-measure.

Pur

4, Operngasse 34 (585 1280). U1, U2, U4 Karlsplatz. **Open** 2-7pm Mon-Fri; 11am-5pm Sat. **Credit** V. **Map** p242 E8.

Angela Schwarzinger's simple, classy clothes in natural fabrics add a stylish twist to smart and casual fashion for men and women.

Rag

1, Sterngasse 4 (533 1961/www.rag.co.at). U1, U4 Schwedenplatz. **Open** 11am-6pm Mon-Fri; 10am-5pm Sat. **Credit** AmEx, DC, MC, V. **Map** p243 E6.

Where Vienna's youth comes for their arse-around-the-knees trousers and other surf 'n' skate wear, with lots of Quiksilver, Carhartt and Billabong stuff. A good place to pick up flyers.
Branch: 6, Mariahilfer Strasse 20 (523 67 97).

Designer discounts

Chegini Check-Out

1, Kohlmarkt 4 (courtyard) (535 6091). U3 Herrengasse. **Open** 2-6.15pm Mon; 10am-6.15pm Tue-Fri; 10am-5pm Sat. **Credit** AmEx, DC, MC, V. **Map** p242 E6.

A snooty designer boutique with two branches in the 1st. It's worth trawling through the stock, however, and this branch offers discounts on some labels.
Branches: 1, Plankengasse 4 (512 2231); 1, Kohlmarkt 7 (533 2058).

Pan

6, Mariahilfer Strasse 77 (in Generali Center) (585 3352). U3 Neubaugasse. **Open** 10am-7pm Mon-Fri; 10am-5pm Sat. **Credit** AmEx, DC, MC, V. **Map** p238 C8.

Prada, Lacroix, DKNY and many other designer fashions from last year and this year at half price.

Stiefelkönig Outlet (Markenschuh-Diskont)

4, Rilkeplatz 3 (505 6104). Tram 62, 65. **Open** 9am-6pm Mon-Fri; 9am-12.30pm Sat; 9am-5pm 1st Sat in mth. **Credit** AmEx, DC, MC, V. **Map** p239 E8.

Stiefelkönig Outlet is a pretty chaotic-looking place, but it offers hefty discounts on the likes of Hugo Boss, DKNY and Bruno Magli.

Lingerie

Palmers

1, Kärntner Strasse 53-55 (512 5772/www.palmers-shop.at). U1, U3 Stephansplatz. **Open** 9am-6.30pm Mon-Fri; 9am-5pm Sat. **Credit** AmEx, DC, MC, V. **Map** p243 E7.

Palmers, Austria's number one undies manufacturer and retailer, runs one of the most high-profile billboard advertising campaigns in the country and its images of scantily clad models are everywhere. Everything from thermals to basques is carried.
Branches: throughout the city.

Rositta

1, Kärntner Strasse 17 (512 4604/www.rositta.at). U1, U3 Stephansplatz. **Open** 9.30am-6pm Mon-Fri; 9.30am-5pm Sat. **Credit** AmEx, DC, MC, V. **Map** p243 E7.

Vienna is full of little designer lingerie boutiques, and Rositta is one of the nicest, selling nighties and slips as well as bras and knickers. The staff are a bit starchy, but it's worth it for the La Perla undies.

Wolford

1, Gonzagagasse 11 (535 99000). U2, U4 Schottenring. **Open** 9am-6pm Mon-Fri. **Credit** MC, V. **Map** p235 E5.

Its tights and stockings have a worldwide reputation, but Wolford also carries a range of underwear and some tops, dresses and skirts.
Branches: throughout the city.

Shoes

Humanic

1, Kärntner Strasse 1 (513 8922/www.humanic.at). U1, U3 Stephansplatz. **Open** 9.30am-7pm Mon-Fri; 9.30am-5pm Sat. **Credit** AmEx, DC, MC, V. **Map** pp243 E7.

Eat, Drink, Shop

The flagship store of Austria's leading shoe chain. Stocks a wide range of international brands. **Branches**: throughout the city.

Ludwig Reiter

1, Mölkersteig 1 (533 420 422/www.ludwig-reiter.com). U2 Schottentor. **Open** 10am-6.30pm Mon-Fri; 10am-5pm Sat. **Credit** AmEx, DC, MC, V. **Map** p242 D6.
Vienna is full of bespoke shoemakers but Ludwig Reiter has made an international name for himself, especially in the US. His superb trainers (based on regulation Austrian army issue) are a fine example of understated modernity.
Branches: 1, Führichgasse 6 (512 6146); 4, Wiedner Hauptstrasse 41 (505 2858).

Shu!

7, Neubaugasse 34 (523 1449/fax 523 1490). U3 Neubaugasse/bus 13a. **Open** 10am-6.30pm Mon-Fri; 10am-5pm Sat. **Credit** AmEx, DC, MC, V. **Map** p238 C8.
Austrian women go all misty-eyed when they talk about this shop, which has Patrick Cox, Camper and other trendy labels laid out in a spacious, airy store.

Vintage

For a range of trendy second-hand shops in a small area, look no further than Neubaugasse in the 7th district (U3 Neubaugasse), where these stores are doing a roaring trade next door to ethnic and alternative outlets.

EWA

6, Schadekgasse 3 (586 1245/www.kalimero.at.tt). U3 Neubaugasse/bus 13a. **Open** 10am-7pm Mon-Fri; 10am-5pm Sat. **No credit cards**. **Map** p238 C8.
An underground labyrinth of second-hand treasures and unworn vintage clothes, from shirts and dresses to leather and suede jackets, as well as plenty of real fur, which Austrians are still happy to wear. The friendly owners also make clothes (which they will alter on the spot if they don't quite fit), and organise fashion shows.

Flo Nostalgische Mode

4, Schleifmühlgasse 15a (586 0773). U1, U2, U4 Karlsplatz/bus 59a. **Open** 10am-6.30pm Mon-Fri. **Credit** MC, V. **Map** p239 E8.
Ingrid Raab has been selling vintage clothes in Vienna for 25 years and claims she introduced the expression to Austria. As well as one-off sales, she regularly kits out actors in television, film and stage shows in clothes from 1880 to 1980.

Polyklamott

6, Hofmühlgasse 6 (969 0337/www.polyklamott.at). U4 Pilgramgasse/bus 13a, 14a. **Open** 11am-7.30pm Mon-Fri; 11am-5pm Sat. **Credit** AmEx, DC, MC, V. **Map** p234 B4.
Lots of 1970s clothes neatly laid out in a trendy, laid-back atmosphere, as well as a smattering of random vintage items.

Flowers

Vienna has excellent florists. Seasonal specialities such as sunflowers, sticky buds and berries inundate the stands. There are shops and outlets all over the city, some more inspiring than others, but all packed with brightly coloured plants and flowers. In the centre you can find stands on the south side of the Stephansdom and one half-way down Kärntner Strasse.

Blumenkraft

4, Schleifmühlgasse 4 (585 7727/www.blumenkraft.at). U1, U2, U4 Karlsplatz/bus 59a. **Open** 10am-7pm Mon-Fri; 9am-2pm Sat. **Credit** AmEx, DC, MC, V. **Map** p239 E8.
Blumenkraft's display looks more like a design concept than a florist. Christine Fink decorates homes and offices with her fantastic selection of plants, flowers and trees. It is worth a visit just to see the building, designed by prominent Austrian architects Eichinger oder Knechtl.

Lederleitner

1, Römische Markthalle im Börsegebäude, Schottenring 16 (532 0677/www.lederleitner.at). U4 Schottenring/tram D. **Open** 10am-8pm Mon-Fri; 9am-5pm Sat. **Credit** DC, MC, V. **Map** p242 E5.
A huge Roman-style emporium under the Börse, Vienna's stock exchange, where paths are lined with plants, flowers and seasonal decorations as well as cookery books from all over the world. It's a really light-filled, tranquil place that also houses a smart restaurant, Hansen.

Food & drink

Delicatessens

Grimm

1, Kurrentgasse 10 (533 13840/www.grimm.at). U1, U3 Stephansplatz. **Open** 7am-6.30pm Mon, Tue, Thur, Fri; 7am-2pm Wed; 7am-noon Sat. **Credit** AmEx, DC, V. **Map** p242 E6.
Bread is invariably excellent in Austria. A quite bewildering range of cereals, seeds and spices is employed in its manufacture. With quality running so high you'll do well in bakeries almost everywhere within Vienna, but centrally based Grimm is considered to be one of the best.

Haas & Haas

1, Haas Haus, Stephansplatz 4 (512 9770). U1, U3 Stephansplatz. **Open** 9am-6pm Mon-Fri; 9am-5pm Sat. **Credit** DC, MC, V. **Map** p242 E6.
A magnificent range of teas and coffees, as well as delicacies from all over the world. Dangerous tasting samples make it hard to leave without spending huge amounts of money. There's also a smart tea-room (*see p128*).

An absolute must for a Saturday morning, the **Naschmarkt**. *See p141.*

Keck's

1, Herrengasse 15 (533 6367). U3 Herrengasse.
Open *Sept-June* 10am-10pm Mon-Fri; 10am-4pm Sat.
July, Aug 10am-7.30pm Mon-Fri; 10am-4pm Sat.
Credit DC, MC, V. **Map** p242 E6.
A designer deli specialising in Austrian products, and organic food. In addition, there's a little café at the back of the shop. Keck's also organises wine-tasting evenings.

Organic produce & health food

Austria is the European Union leader in organic farming, and so-called 'bio' products can be found everywhere. Both of its leading supermarket chains carry their own organic label on everything from meat to milk to ready meals: Billa/Merkur's is called Ja! Natürlich and Spar's is Natur Pur.

Reformhaus Buchmüller

7, Neubaugasse 17-19 (523 7297). U3 Neubaugasse /bus 13a. **Open** 9am-6.30pm Mon-Fri; 9am-5pm Sat.
Credit DC, MC, V. **Map** p238 C8.
A small shop selling everything from organic veg and vegan products to health-conscious cosmetics and homeopathic remedies. There is a little cafe in the back selling freshly-squeezed fruit juices and cheap meals, but it gets pretty packed at lunchtimes.

Reformhaus Verde

8, Josefstädter Strasse 27 (405 1329). Tram J.
Open 9am-6.30pm Mon-Fri; 10am-1pm Sat.
Credit AmEx, DC, V. **Map** p238 B6.

Reformhaus Verde is a well-stocked health-food store with organic vegetables, bread and over 200 varieties of tea. English is spoken.

Willi Dungl

1, Schottengasse 9 (535 48990). U2 Schottentor/ tram 1, 2, D. **Open** 7.30am-7.30pm Mon-Thur; 7.30am-6pm Fri. **Credit** MC. **Map** p242 D6.
Willi Dungl, one of Austria's prime advocates of a healthy lifestyle, died suddenly of a heart attack in 2002, at the age of 65. His network of health clubs and stores are still going strong, though, and the Schottengasse store has a good range of vegetarian sausages and tofu burgers, as well as organic fruit and vegetables, and healthy teas. There's a fitness room in the basement and a café at the back of the shop.

Pâtisserie

Look out for the magic word *Konditorei* (pâtisserie) for the largest selection of cakes, but most bakers have the basic strudels and *Golatschen* (like Danish pastries).

Café Central Konditorei

1, Herrengasse 17 (533 3763 26/www.palais events.at). U3 Herrengasse. **Open** 8am-10pm Mon-Thur; 10am-10pm Fri; 10am-6pm Sat. **Credit** AmEx, DC, MC, V. **Map** p242 E6.
The pâtisserie division of the famous Café Central (*see p122*) is a rather stuffy, luxurious establishment. However, it's worth a visit for a taste of their divine chocolate truffles.

Eat, Drink, Shop

Late-night shopping

Vienna is getting a little better for shopping outside normal opening hours, but if you want to buy milk in the city centre after 6pm you can still pretty much forget it. One life-saver is the so-called **Shop 24**, a massive vending machine in the U-Bahn passage at Karlsplatz which dispenses everything from fresh bread to Mars bars and tampons, although you have to fight your way through the tramps. It's near the Wiedner Hauptstrasse exit. The **Billa** (*see p140*) supermarkets at two railway stations,

Wien Nord (U1 Praterstern) and Franz-Josefs-Bahnhof (tram 5, 33), are open on Sundays and bank holidays till 7.30pm, and the branch in the airport is open every day from 7.30am-10pm. The **Okay Reiseproviant** is open till 11pm every day in the stations Landstrasse, Westbahnhof and Südbahnhof. One central life-saver is **Drugstore Kaunitzgasse**, opposite the Apollo (bus 13a, 14a), in the 6th district, open till 11pm every day, with a bit of everything, including cigarettes at normal prices.

Demel

1, Kohlmarkt 14 (535 17170/www.demel.at). U3 Herrengasse/bus 2a, 3a. **Open** 10am-7pm daily. **Credit** AmEx, DC, MC, V. **Map** p242 E6.
The mother of all pastry shops, the Demel is an authentic k.u.k. establishment sporting an incredibly extravagant interior where you can choose from vast array of beautifully packaged cakes and chocolates. It's a little too popular with tourists for comfort, however. *See p122.*

Lehmann

1, Graben 12 (512 1815). U1, U3 Stephansplatz. **Open** 8.30am-7pm Mon-Sat. **Credit** V. **Map** p242 E6.
A genteel coffeehouse/restaurant in a prime spot on Graben. Lehmann stocks all the principal Viennese sweets and cakes, as well as serving light meals.

Supermarkets

Billa, which you can find on almost every block, is revamping its city centre stores by bringing delicatessen counters and a selection of wines to the fore, but its classification system still follows a logic all of its own. Merkur, the bigger version of Billa, can be found under Gerngross (*see p130*) in Mariahilfer Strasse and has a range of vegetarian foods and the excellent Ja! Natürlich organic range.

All the Julius Meinl shops apart from Meinl am Graben (*see below*) were taken over by Spar a while ago; the so-called **Spar Gourmet** branches are the best supermarkets locally (although those accustomed to supermarkets in England should not expect too much).

Billa Corso

1, Kärntner Ring 9-13, Ringstrassengallerien (512 6625). U1, U2, U4 Karlsplatz/tram 1, 2, D, J/bus 3a. **Open** 7.30am-7pm Mon-Fri; 7.30am-5pm Sat. **No credit cards**. **Map** p242 E8.
The Billa Corsa is the best thing about the Ringstrassengallerien. This branch has a huge delicatessen area offering fresh meat and fish (not some-

thing to be taken for granted in Austrian supermarkets), as well as a pretty extensive drinks selection. Most Billa supermarkets have a deli counter where you can at least buy good fresh sausage or cheese rolls.

Bobby's Foodstore

4, Schleifmühlgasse 8 (586 7534/www.bobbys.at). U1, U2, U4 Karlsplatz/bus 59a. **Open** 10am-6.30pm Mon-Fri, 10am-5pm Sat. **Credit** MC, V. **Map** p239 E8.
For homesick expats, Bobby's imports all the food you miss from England, the US and Australia, and the welcoming English-speaking staff will give you a taste of home.

Meinl am Graben

1, Kohlmarkt (532 3334/www.meinl.com). U3 Herrengasse/bus 2a, 3a. **Open** 8am-7.30pm Mon-Fri; 8.30am-5pm Sat. **Credit** AmEx, DC, MC, V. **Map** p242 E6.
Austria's answer to Fortnum & Mason (on a smaller scale), Julius Meinl am Graben sells excellent food from all over the world, from simple ready meals to exotic condiments as well as fresh meat, fish and an enticing range of cheeses. The green fig mustard is a must. A wine bar and a coffee shop on site are further attractions.

Wine

Wein & Co

6, Naschmarkt (585 7257/www.nas.weinco.at). U1, U2, U4 Karlsplatz. **Open** 10am-midnight Mon-Sat; 11am-midnight Sun. **Credit** AmEx, DC, MC, V. **Map** p242 E8.
Wein & Co, on a corner of the Naschmarkt opposite Secession, has cheekily circumvented Austria's restrictive retail legislation by opening wine bars and shops in one store, so you can buy wine here until midnight. As well as wines from all over the world and plenty of food treats, such as dried mushrooms and fresh pasta, there is a smart wine bar serving drinks and tasty meals.
Branch: 1, Jasomirgottstrasse 3-5 (535 0916).

Jeroboam

4, Schleifmühlgasse 1 (585 6773/www.jeroboam. at). U1, U2, U4 Karlsplatz/bus 59a. **Open** 10am-3pm Tue, Sat; 3-8pm Wed-Fri. **Credit** MC, V. **Map** p239 E8.

A specialist shop dealing exclusively in Sekt, Spumante and all things sparkling. Over 80 different types of champagne are stocked.

Unger und Klein

1, Gölsdorfgasse 2 (532 1323/www.ungerund klein.at). U2, U4 Schottenring. **Open** 2pm-midnight Mon-Fri; 5pm-midnight Sat. **Credit** MC, V. **Map** p243 E6.

A magnificent 'theatre of drinking' designed by Eichinger oder Knechtl in 1992. A wine bar and store, Unger und Klein is a favourite of media bods, but don't let that put you off. Wines by the glass or bottle change from day to day, and the shop also holds special food nights and other events.

Gifts

Kaufhaus Schiepek

1, Teinfaltstrasse 3 (533 1575). U2 Schottentor/ tram 1, 2, D. **Open** 10am-6pm Mon-Fri; 11am-5pm Sat. **Credit** (on purchases over €6) AmEx, DC, MC, V. **Map** p242 D6.

Brightly coloured jewellery, gorgeous little bags and purses, plus lots of cheap and cheerful kitsch.

Replicart

1, Babenbergerstrasse 5 (585 7205/www.replic art.at). U2 Babenbergerstrasse. **Open** 10am-7.30pm Mon-Fri; 10am-6pm Sat, Sun. **Credit** AmEx, DC, MC, V. **Map** p242 D7.

A plethora of arty souvenirs are available at this franchise of New York's Metropolitan Museum of Art. They are all tastefully displayed in a 19th-century shop premises, and there's the bonus of a small café at the back.

Shipping

1, Teinfaltstrasse 4 (533 1575). U2 Schottentor/ tram 1, 2, D. **Open** 1-6pm Tue-Fri; 11am-5pm Sat. **Credit** (on purchases over €10) DC, MC, V. **Map** p242 D6.

Opposite Schiepek (*see above*) and owned by the same people, Shipping has plates, bowls, ashtrays and much more, all in brightly coloured plastic. It also sells excellent sets of bowls for Japanese meals with chopsticks.

Jewellery

Galerie Slavik

1, Himmelpfortgasse 17 (513 4812/www.galerie-slavik.com). U1, U3 Stephansplatz. **Open** 10am-1pm, 2-6pm, Tue-Fri; 10am-5pm Sat. **Credit** AmEx, DC, MC, V. **Map** p243 E7.

More of a gallery than a shop, Galerie Slavik shows off the work of international jewellery designers and changes its exhibitions regularly. Prices range from

around €100 for young designers, all the way up to almost priceless. It's worth checking the website to see what's on show before you go.

Wiener Interieur

1, Dorotheergasse 14 (512 2898). U1, U3 Stephansplatz. **Open** 10am-6pm Mon-Fri; 10am-1pm Sat. **Credit** AmEx, DC, MC, V. **Map** p242 E7.

Dorotheergasse and environs are full of antique jewellers. This small establishment deals in art nouveau, art deco and 1950s costume jewellery.

Markets

Brunnenmarkt

16, Brunnengasse. U6 Josefstädter Strasse. **Open** 6am-6.30pm Mon-Fri; 6am-2pm Sat. **Map** p238 A6.

Not as spectacular a sight as the Naschmarkt (*see below*) and more limited in its range of wares, the Brunnenmarkt is nevertheless a bustling, colourful market with a distinctly Balkan/Turkish flavour. Stretched out along Brunnengasse are stalls and shops offering fruit and vegetables, halal meat, kitsch decorative stuff and sticky Turkish pâtisserie. If you're still hungry, head for Café Kent on Brunnengasse – Vienna's finest and cheapest kebab house (veggies catered for, and there's a garden).

Naschmarkt

4, Linke und Rechte Wienzeile. U1, U2, U4 Karlsplatz. **Open** 6am-6.30pm Mon-Fri; 6am-5pm Sat. **Map** p242 E6.

A visit to Vienna's premier open-air food market should be on everyone's itinerary. Located on a long esplanade covering the course of the Wien river, this superb market can satisfy the most demanding culinary requirements, as well as being an ideal spot to eat, drink and hang. Saturdays are busy. Approaching from Karlsplatz, the first section is taken up with fishmongers, pork butchers and the market's priciest and most exotic greengrocers. Other highlights here include a number of excellent juice bars and the famous Sauerkraut stall. Further along are several Chinese and Indian shops, and behind them runs a line of stalls selling excellent Thai, Japanese and Italian food. Then the market is bisected by Schleifmühlgasse, from where the stalls are of the more workaday fruit and veg variety, all at far more reasonable prices than on the first stretch. There are places selling great falafel and stuffed vine leaves to nibble on as you wander among the stalls. This last section opens out on to a broad tract where, on Saturdays, there's a thriving flea market (*see p142*).

Organic Market Freyung

1, Freyung. U2 Schottentor. **Open** 8am-7.30pm Fri, Sat. **Map** p242 E6.

This market sells exclusively organic products directly from the growers. Some stalls also sell non-edible wares – such as basketware, candles and wooden toys.

Eat, Drink, Shop

Flea markets

Flea market burrowers can have the time of their lives in Vienna. Bargaining is de rigueur.

Flea Market

5, Kettenbrückengasse. U4 Kettenbrückengasse. **Open** dawn-5pm Sat. **Map** p239 D8.
This market has something for everyone, with the bargain basement stalls located beside the U-Bahn and the more specialised dealers further towards the Linke Wienzeile. There are stands selling furs, leathers and Loden stuff, lamps and lighting fittings, tin toys and dolls, antique watches and jewellery and loads of crocks. Look out for the attractive pastel-coloured Austrian Lilienporzellan from the 1950s. The atmosphere is quite unlike the flea markets of most European cities. The babble of languages is extraordinary – Russians flogging icons and Soviet memorabilia, Romanian gypsies plying (possibly fake) Roman coins and figures, and others from the Balkans selling more or less anything.

Music

Vienna is not badly served for music emporia and new establishments are constantly opening. If classical music is your bag, note that shops in the 1st district, such as **EMI Austria** on Kärntner Strasse, have high prices. **Teuchtler Alt&Neu** (*see below*) has a reasonable selection of classical music.

Audio Center

1, Judenplatz 9 (533 6849). U1, U3 Stephansplatz. **Open** 10am-7pm Mon-Fri; 10am-5pm Sat. **Credit** AmEx, DC, MC, V. **Map** p243 E6.
An excellent jazz store offering both CDs and vinyl. It has a good selection of world music too, and is not afraid to stock crazier improv and crossover jazz stuff. Headphones are available for checking out the wares and there's plenty of knowledgeable advice and jazz flyers.

Black Market

1, Gonzagagasse 9 (533 761712/www.black market.at). U2, U4 Schottenring. **Open** 10am-7.30pm Mon-Fri; 10am-5pm Sat. **Credit** AmEx, DC, MC, V. **Map** p235 E5.
The best hip hop/funk/dance store in town, now totally spruced up. It's run by Alexander Hirschenhauser, one of the original movers behind the current Vienna scene, and celebrated London DJ Alan Brown runs their distribution. You can listen to CDs and vinyl on headphones and get switched-on tips from the knowledgeable and helpful staff. There's a café, and a small selection of Stüssy clothes too.

Rave Up

6, Hofmühlgasse 1 (596 9650/www.rave-up.at). U4 Pilgramgasse/bus 13a, 14a. **Open** 10am-6.30pm Mon-Fri; 10am-5pm Sat. **Credit** AmEx, DC, MC, V. **Map** p234 B4.

Popular with local DJs on the hunt for beats, reggae, electronica and hip hop. It's a good place to come to for flyers, and also has a fairly comprehensive selection of Viennese stuff from the most upfront labels like Mego, Klein, Cheap and Spray. Nice staff and headphones are further pluses.

Record Shack

5, Reinprechtsdorfer Strasse 60 (544 9587/ recordshack@chello.at). Bus 14a. **Open** 2-7pm Tue-Fri; noon-5pm Sat. **Credit** AmEx, DC, MC, V. **Map** p238 C10.
Lapsed architecture student Jörg has an encyclopedic knowledge of '60s and '70s soul and regularly thrills crowds all over the city DJing under the moniker Jörg Record Shack. After running a mail order service supplying soul and funk rarities, he has branched into retailing with a small store (where the original 19th-century features have been funked up with '70s accessories). Treat yourself to some classic northern soul, Hammond-driven funk and vintage reggae on vinyl and CD.

Record Store

4, Operngasse 28 (586 3312). U1, U2, U4 Karlsplatz. **Open** 1-6pm Mon-Fri. **No credit cards**. **Map** p242 E8.
The address for vinyl recidivists since it stocks nothing but second-hand singles and LPs from jazz to prog rock, with treasures from Julie London to Glen Medeiros, and from Broadway hits to rap. Vienna DJs Kruder & Dorfmeister are regulars.

Substance

7, Westbahn Strasse 16 (523 6757). U3 Neubaugasse/tram 49. **Open** 11am-7.30pm Mon-Fri; 11am-5pm Sat. **No credit cards**. **Map** p238 C8.
A new record store where the goods on sale clearly correspond to the personal taste of the owners. With little genre subdivision, the alphabetically arranged racks house everything from Beefheart to Boss Hog, with odd sections dedicated to Zorn and Mego. There's vinyl and CDs in equal measures, listening facilities, regular Friday performances and free coffee and cake.

Teuchtler Alt&Neu

6, Windmühlgasse 10 (586 2133). U2 Babenbergergasse. **Open** 1-6pm Mon-Fri; 10am-1pm Sat (10am-5pm 1st Sat in month). **Credit** AmEx, DC, MC, V. **Map** p242 D8.
A long-standing Aladdin's cave selling used and new CDs and vinyl. Jazz and classical are its strong points. Prices are the best in Vienna, but the categorising is slightly chaotic. Staff are approachable, but don't bother inquiring after that elusive disc as stock turnover is huge.

33:45

3, Krummgasse 1 (713 6904/www.recordstore.at). U3 Rochusmarkt. **Open** 2-7pm Mon-Fri; 11am-5pm Sat. **Credit** AmEx, DC, MC, V. **Map** p240 G8.
A specialised DJ shop with lots of vinyl. Good for flyers – staff know what's going on club-wise.

One of the exquisite window displays at **Demel**. *See p140.*

Ton um Ton

7, Lindengasse 32 (523 8236). U3 Neubaugasse.
Open 11am-5pm Mon-Thur; 11am-4pm Fri.
No credit cards. Map p238 C8.
The emphasis here is on 1960s and 1970s obscure
British rock and folk, American jingle-jangle and
European stuff you've never heard of. There's a
large selection of vinyl in the basement, often at
giveaway prices.

Services

Contracting services, especially repairs, can
prove expensive. Always ask for an estimate.

Key cutting

Mister Minit

1, Führichgasse 4 (512 4865). U1, U3 Stephansplatz.
Open 9.30am-6pm Mon-Fri. **No credit cards.**
Map p242 E7.
Key-cutting and shoe repairs. For service on a
Saturday until 1pm, visit the branch in Gerngross.
Branch: Gerngross 7, Mariahilfer Strasse 48
(524 5654).

Laundry & dry cleaning

Bendix Laundrette

*7, Siebensterngasse 52 (523 2553). Tram 49/bus
13a.* **Open** 8am-6pm Mon, Tue, Thur; 8am-4pm
Wed; 8am-1pm Fri. **No credit cards. Map** p242 C8.
Self-service or service washing – from €8 per item.

Hartmann

*1, Jasimirogottstrasse 6 (533 1584/www.textil
pflege-hartmann.at). U1, U3 Stephansplatz.*
Open 9am-6pm Mon-Fri. **Credit** AmEx, DC, MC,
V. **Map** p243 E6.
A reliable, centrally located dry cleaners that also
does wonders with leather and suede.
Branch: 6, Linke Wienzeile 164 (597 0208).

Sport & Fitness

Bicycles

Cycling is big business in Vienna. There are
lots of excellent new and second-hand shops
throughout the city.

Bike Attack

*2, Praterstrasse 29 (264 5381/www.bike-
attack.at). U1 Nestroyplatz.* **Open** 10am-6pm
Mon-Fri; 10am-4pm Sat. **Credit** DC, MC, V.
Map p243 G5.
The emphasis is on mountain bikes, but there are
also plenty of tourers and racers, in a striking
baroque room near the Prater.

Cooperative Fahrrad

*6, Gumpendorfer Strasse 111 (596 5256/
www.fahrrad.co.at). U6 Gumpendorfer Strasse.*
Open *Oct-Feb* 10am-1pm, 2-6pm Mon-Fri;
10am-1pm Sat. *May-Sept* 10am-1pm, 2-6pm Mon-
Wed; 10am-1pm, 2-7pm Thur, Fri; 10am-5pm Sat.
No credit cards. Map p238 B9.
Cycle co-operative complete with workshops.

Crystal balls

Swarovski handbags at the Oscars, and its crystal-cut glassware is in hot demand.

Swarovski has been making crystal goods ever since Daniel Swarovski invented a unique glass-cutting machine in Tyrol, in western Austria, in the 19th century, and the diamond-like stones have often found themselves in the limelight. Audrey Hepburn wore Swarovski in *Sabrina* and *My Fair Lady*, Grace Kelly wore it in *High Society*, and more recently the crystals graced the stars of *Elizabeth*, *Moulin Rouge* and *Die Another Day*. The company has lately branched out into (not unattractive) home design, ranging from cool

Swarovski, with its kitsch little crystal animals peeping cutely from behind enormous price tags, is enjoying a bizarre, if not entirely undeserved, foray into the world of fashion. Stars such as Madonna, Nicole Kidman and Victoria Beckham have been caught buying the Austrian firm's jewellery, Bond girl Michelle Yeoh and Rosanna Arquette sported

chopstick holders to trendy napkin rings. Swarovski's Vienna headquarters is at Kärntner Strasse 8, just south of Stephansdom, where miniatures and animals mingle with showy jewellery, and ornaments at prices ranging from reasonable to plain ridiculous. For more, check out the website on www.swarovski.com.

Mountaineering & rambling

Mörtz
6, Windmühlgasse 9 (587 5787). U2 Babenbergergasse. **Open** 8.30am-1pm, 2-6pm Mon-Fri; 8.30am-noon Sat. **No credit cards**. **Map** p242 D8.
Mortz specialises in footwear for mountaineering and rambling.

ÖTK – Alpinsport
1, Bäckerstrasse 16 (512 3844/www.touristen klub.at). U1, U3 Stephansplatz. **Open** 10.30am-5pm Mon; 9am-7pm Tue, Thur; 9am-5pm Wed; 9am-3pm Fri. **No credit cards**. **Map** p243 F6.
Everything you need for mountaineering plus advice on locations. Also runs climbing courses.

Football

Caledonia
8, Strozzigasse 31 (0699 1072 1318). Tram J. **Open** noon-6pm Wed, Thur; noon-7pm Fri; 10am-5pm Sat. **No credit cards**. **Map** p238 C6.

Othmar is a one-man industry, selling football kits for Austrian regional clubs and others world-wide, as well as all sorts of footie merchandise; folk, country and blues music, and gifts ranging from pub souvenirs to Austrian wines. And Strozzigasse is a little enclave for football fans, with Der Fan Shop Strobl opposite at Nos.18-22, selling everything to do with Rapid Vienna, while its next-door branch sells kit for the capital's rival team Austria Memphis.

Travel

Die Restplatzbörse
1, Kärntner Ring 18 (505 01 70-0). U1, U2, U4 Karlsplatz/tram 1, 2, J. **Open** 9am-7pm Mon-Fri; 9am-noon Sat. **Credit** DC, MC, V. **Map** p243 E8.
With branches all over Vienna, Die Restplatzbörse is the best place to pick up bargain last-minute deals and flight tickets. You can also book over the phone on 580 850 from 8am-8pm Monday to Friday and 9am-4pm Saturday and Sunday.
Branches: throughout the city.

Arts & Entertainment

Festivals & Events

A year in the life of Vienna.

There can be few capitals which celebrate and move with the seasons as Vienna does. Austria sees hot summers, wet autumns and snowy winters, and every season brings new activities, on top of an already exciting cultural calendar. Events, big concerts and unscheduled fairs and festivals go on all year round, so check out the newspapers when you get there or visit some of the websites listed on *p225*.

Spring

Easter Market
1, Freyung. U2 Schottentor. **Date** two weeks around Easter. **Map** p242 D6.
A traditional Easter market in the centre of Vienna. Stalls open daily from 8am to 8pm for a fortnight, and sell food, drink, Easter eggs and knick-knacks.

Osterklang
Information & tickets: 1, Stadiongasse 9 (42 717/ www.osterklang.at/tickets@osterklang.at). U2 Rathaus/tram J. **Date** Easter. **Map** p242 D6.
'The Sound of Easter' festival features contemplative works from baroque to late 20th century in the city's most prestigious venues. It is always opened by the Vienna Philharmonic.

Frühlingsfestival
Konzerthaus, 3, Lothringerstrasse 20 (242 002/ info 242 00 100/www.konzerthaus.at). U4 Stadtpark/ tram D. **Map** p243 F8.
Musikverein, 1, Bösendorferstrasse 12 (505 8190/info 505 1363/www.musikverein.at). U4 Stadtpark/tram D. **Map** p243 E8.
Date Mar/Apr-May.
This famous spring festival is held in the Konzerthaus in even years and in the Musikverein in odd years. There are concerts by the Vienna Philharmonic and other leading ensembles from across the world, playing the works of major composers, most of them Austrian.

International Music Festival
Konzerthaus, 3, Lothringerstrasse 20 (242 002/fax 242 00 110/info 242 00 100/www.konzerthaus.at). U4 Stadtpark/tram D. **Date** May-June. **Map** p243 E8.
In odd years, when it is not hosting the Spring Festival, the Konzerthaus runs the International Music Festival, with different themes each year.

Vienna City Marathon
(606 9510/www.vienna-marathon.com). **Date** May.
The marathon starts at 22, Wagramerstrasse, Reichsbrücke (the bridge before the UNO City) in the 22th district and ends at the central Heldenplatz (Heroes' Square). Early online registration will save you a few euros on the entry fee (€43-€50).

Soho in Ottakring
(524 0909/www.sohoinottakring.at). **Date** May-Jun.
This arts festival does its bit to revitalise the scruffy multiculti section of the 16th district beside the Gürtel ring-road, by installing exhibitions, gigs and films in the area's bars, restaurants and empty shops.

Wiener Festwochen
Main festival office: 6, Lehárgasse 11 (589 2222/info 0800 664 020 from late Apr/www.festwochen.at). U1, U2, U4 Karlsplatz/bus 57a. **Date** May-June. **Map** p242 E8.
The Vienna Festival is a fixture on the international music scene – a smörgåsbord of orchestras, theatre groups, and opera and dance companies converge on Vienna for six weeks of performance madness, featuring everything from classics to contemporary arts premières. In even years, the Musikverein shows Festwochen concerts, while in odd years the festival coincides with the Konzerthaus's International Music Festival (*see above*).

Summer

In July and August the city has two open-air cinemas – the **Freiluftkino Krieau** and **Kino unter Sternen**, *see p157*. For the out-of-town **Wiesen** and **Konfrontationen** music festivals, *see p181*. For the **Rainbow Parade** and **Wien ist andersrum**, *see p167*.

JazzFest Wien
8, Lammgasse 12/8 (712 4224/www.viennajazz.org). **Date** June-July. **Map** p242 C6.
Vienna's largest jazz festival featured names in jazz, soul and blues, playing at venues all over town. JazzFest also organises jazz music films and Sunday brunches. Tickets can be purchased from All Event Tickets (319 0606) and Kurier-Corner (587 5789).

Love Parade
www.loveparade.at. **Date** July.
Vienna's (rather wan) reply to Berlin's Love Parade has been relegated to the Danube/Prater area after a couple of years along the Ringstrasse.

ImPulsTanz
7, Museumstrasse 5/21 (info/tickets 523 5558/ www.impulstanz.com). U2 Volkstheater/bus 48a. **Date** July-Aug. **Map** p242 D7.
Staged around the city, the Vienna dance festival features everything from renowned classics to up-

Having a ball

An ancient tribal ritual is re-enacted every year in Vienna to the pulsating rhythms of Strauss. However old and steeped in tradition it may be, the ball season is an integral part of the city's social fabric. Each year there are over 300 balls from 11 November to late June.

Biggest, most expensive and most celebrated of these bashes is the **Opernball** (Opera Ball), held on the Thursday before Ash Wednesday at the Staatsoper. Also known as the *Künstlerball*, or artists' ball, this is the one that draws the stars. Entrance costs €215, renting a table for six people €900, and a private box €9,000. With around 5,000 people in attendance, chaos reigns on the floor. This is a snobfest, a 'see and be seen' extravaganza. Many believe the money raised goes to charity, but the over €2 million the ball generates goes into the Staatsoper's already heavily subsidised coffers, hence the demonstrations that take place outside every year in protest.

Other particularly traditional balls include the **Philharmonikerball** at the Musikverein, the posh **Technikerball** at the Hofburg (invitation only), and the **Kaiserball** (Emperor's Ball) in the Hofburg on New Year's Eve and attended by the crème de la crème. Less elite balls include the **Zuckerbäckerball** (Confectioners'

Ball), the **Jägerball** (Hunters' Ball, where revellers wear national costume rather than tail coats), and the **Bonbonball** (Candy Ball) at the Konzerthaus, when balloons filled with candies burst over the crowd at midnight.

There are also more socially conscious balls such as the gay and lesbian **Regenbogenball** (Rainbow Ball), the **Life Ball**, an event benefiting Aids charities (*see p167*), and the **Ball der Strassenzeitung Augustiner**, hosted by the *Augustiner* newspaper produced and sold by the homeless.

At traditional balls dress is formal, and the ticket price and the venue will give some indication of exactly how dressed up you need to be. Others tend to be much more laid-back. The **Mauerblümchenball** (Wallflower Ball) prides itself on a 'come as you are' dress code, suggesting beige and grey as best colours for 'blending in', while at the **Ball des Schlechten Geschmacks** (Bad Taste Ball), just about anything goes.

The dates of the individual balls vary from year to year. The City of Vienna puts out a brochure, *Wiener Ballkalendar*, with a complete listing of dates and locations. You can also call the city info number 52 550, or try the ball calendars at www.ball.at or www.wien.gv.at.

Christkindlmärkte

From mid-November *Christkindlmärkte* (Christmas markets) begin to appear in Vienna, usually selling arts and crafts, Christmas decorations, and more importantly, *Glühwein*, *Kartoffelpuffer* (hot potato patties with garlic) and roast chestnuts. These are a few of the best:

Altwiener Christkindlmarkt Freyung

Billed as an old-style Christmas market, this market at Freyung (U2 Schottentor/tram 1, 2, D) is largely devoted to Austrian arts, crafts and hand-made toys. If you're lucky enough to arrive at the right time you might see some traditional Austrian dancing.
Map p242 D6.

Karlsplatz

Karlsplatz (U1, U2, U4 Karlsplatz) has arty stalls and a small funfair along with pony rides, but its real trump card is little tables built around flaming metal barrels, that allow you to drink your punch without the rest of your body freezing.
Map p242 E8.

Rathausplatz

In the square in front of City Hall (U2 Rathausplatz/tram 1, 2, D, J), this is the biggest and most touristy of Vienna's Christmas markets. It has a few fairground rides for kids as well as loads of cake, toy and craft stalls, but it can get a bit too packed.
Map p242 D6.

Schönbrunn

In a romantic setting outside Schönbrunn palace (U4 Schönbrunn), this 'culture and Christmas' market looks a bit slick with professional matching signs above each stall, but it sells some excellent *Kartoffelpuffer* and has plenty for kids to do, including a treasure hunt among Christmas trees.

Spittelberg

In the tiny cobbled streets between Burggasse and Siebensterngasse in the 7th district (U3 Volkstheater/tram 49/Bus 48a), this is one of the loveliest Christmas markets, with great apple punch at a stand outside the Lux bar. It specialises in ethnic arts and crafts and *Bergkäse* (mountain cheese), and draws a young crowd.
Map p242 C7.

Weihnachtsdorf am Unicampus

This so-called 'Christmas Village' is on the Vienna University campus, the former general hospital (entrance at the corner of Alserstrasse and Spitalgasse in the 9th district, tram 5, 43, 44). A favourite among students, it features musicians and a crib with real animals.
Map p242 C5/p234 C5.

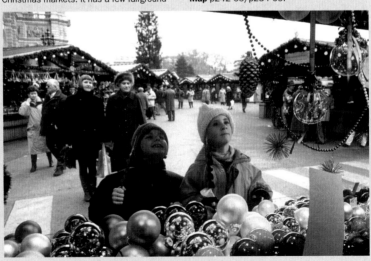

to-the-minute contemporary works. It attracts dance companies from all over the world. ImPulsTanz also includes a series of workshops on ballet, hip hop, children's dance and yoga, among others.

Klangbogen

1, Stadiongasse 9 (42 717/www.klangbogen.at). U2 Rathaus/tram D. **Date** July, Aug. **Map** p242 D6.
Just because the Philharmoniker goes off to Salzburg for the summer, it doesn't mean that Vienna rolls up its streets. Guest orchestras perform at the Musikverein, while opera and operetta take over the Theater an der Wien.

Rathausplatz Music Film Festival

1, Rathausplatz. U2 Rathaus/tram 1, 2, D, J. **Date** July, Aug. **Map** p242 D6.
Every evening at twilight, opera and classical music films are shown for free on a giant screen in the square in front of the city hall. Decent films and music bring culture buffs out in droves; food stands bring everyone else. Get there early for a seat.

Seefestspiele Mörbisch

Mörbisch am Neusiedlersee, Burgenland (02685 8181 July, Aug/02682 66210-0 rest of year/www.seefestspiele-moerbisch.at).
By car: A2 dir. Graz, to the A3 at Neusiedlersee exit, then Eisenstadt Süd to Mörbisch.
By bus: departs 6pm from Reisebüro Blaguss, Wiedner Hauptstrasse 15 (501 800).
Date July-Aug.
One of the hits of the summer season, this operetta festival is held on the shores of Neusiedler See (*see p207*). Director Harald Serafin combines high production values with operetta stars of yesterday and tomorrow, on this massive open-air stage. Book in advance and bring mosquito repellent.

Donauinselfest

22, Donauinsel. U1 Donauinsel, U6 Arbeiterstrandstrasse. **Date** Aug. **Map** p236 J3.
A massive party organised by the Social Democrats and one of the largest free events in Europe. The whole island is invaded for a weekend by a growing number of revellers (three million in 2002). Cheesy acts such as Zucchero top the bill; the rest of the festival is taken up with dreary rock and folk groups from the provinces, market stalls and food and beer stands. The nicest part of the festival is the Copa Kagrana, near Donauinsel U-Bahn station, where floating cocktail bars serve some mean Daiquiris.

Sequence

(961 8800/www.sequence.at). **Date** 10 days mid Aug.
The Sunshine crew's annual DJ fest enlivens Vienna's moribund month of August.

Autumn

Autumn brings grape harvests and *Sturm* (young half-fermented wine that tastes as sweet as lemonade, but with an unmeasured alcohol content), and delicious pumpkin and

Eierschwammerl (a type of mushroom) specialities in Austrian restaurants. In September, skaters and wheelchair athletes take to the streets for the **Vienna Inline Marathon** (www.inline-marathon.at).

Hallamasch

(548 4800/www.hallamasch.at). **Date** Sept.
This state-funded multi-cultural bun fight is still struggling to become a real crowd puller, and features numerous al fresco events such as craft markets and street parades.

Viennale

7, Siebensterngasse 2 (526 5947/www.viennale.at). U3 Neubaugasse or U3 Volkstheater. **Date** Oct. **Map** p242 D7.
Austria's biggest international film festival has been running since 1960 and features Austrian and international premières. *See p153.*

Wien Modern

Konzerthaus, 3, Lothringerstrasse 20 (242 002/ www.konzerthaus.at). U4 Stadtpark/tram D. **Date** Nov. **Map** p243 E8.
Founded by Claudio Abbado in 1988, the Modern Music Festival is devoted to post-1945 compositions and in recent years has run a dynamic programme.

Winter

Winter is arguably the loveliest time of year in Vienna, when snow blankets parks and cars, the **Christmas markets** appear (*see p148*), and the **ball season** starts (*see p147*). **Fasching**, the German-speaking world's version of Carnival, runs until Ash Wednesday.

New Year's Eve

www.wien-event.at
Vienna city centre is transformed into one giant party for *Silvester*. Children's events start at the Rathausplatz around 2pm, the streets of the old town are lined with food stalls and there are all manner of gigs and concerts taking place. The Prater hosts an enormous party called Soul City with DJs, bands and a snowboard contest (02236 49437-0). For the more sporty, there is a *Silvesterlauf*, a run around the 5.4km-long ring every New Year's Eve (www.lcc-wien.at).

Wiener Eistraum

1, Rathausplatz. **Date** Jan-Mar. **Map** p242 D6.
To beat the post-Christmas blues the Viennese don their ice skates outside City Hall, to the accompaniment of disco lighting and hackneyed tunes, including a fine selection of the awful German *Schlager*.

Vienna International Accordion Festival

(676 512 9104/www.akkordeonfestival.at). **Date** Feb-Mar.
A month-long squeezebox celebration held at various unusual venues throughout the city.

Arts & Entertainment

Children

Plenty to see, plenty to do.

Clay sculpting at the **Zoom Kindermuseum**, a must-see attraction for kids. *See p152.*

It is no longer true to say that the Viennese prefer their dogs to their children, but there is still something of a schizophrenic attitude towards youngsters. Anything that smacks of the innocence of childhood – mothers breast-feeding, toddlers singing, boys being helpful – is greeted with smiles. Other aspects, like boisterous behaviour, aggression and loud giggling, will receive hard stares and diatribes.

The good news is that both the government and the City are falling over themselves to provide incentives to produce children (including generous maternity benefits) and to give them things to do once they are around. Children's theatres, festivals and playgrounds have sprung up all over.

So where does that leave you with your kids? First, it means the basics for babies and toddlers are easy. You can wheel a buggy on to any bus (middle door) or U-Bahn. Trams are difficult (though the newer models are better), but the driver will get out and help if no one else does. Get on at the front and 'park' your buggy in the space provided. You can also breast-feed in any café or on a park bench.

There aren't many nappy-changing tables, but people don't mind you improvising. And the city is generally very safe.

WienXtra-kinderinfo

7, Museumsquartier, Museumsplatz 1 (4000-84 400/ www.kinderinfowien.at). **Open** 4-7pm Tue-Thur; 10am-5pm Fri-Sun. **Map** p242 D7.

Practically next door to the Zoom Kindermuseum (*see p152*) is WienXtra, providing information on what's going on in Vienna for children of all ages. It's a relaxed place with a large indoor play area where kids can scramble about while you gather information. You can change nappies here, too.

Activities

For activities such as ice-skating, swimming pools (outdoor and indoor) and the Oberlaa spa, *see pp187-192*. A day at one of the many open-air swimming pools around the city is recommended. Either visit a traditional municipal pool on the Old Danube (Gänsehäufl or Strandbad Alte Donau in Kagran) or head for the hills to the west of Vienna and enjoy one of the pools with a view or in the woods.

Attractions

The **Prater** is a must. Forget the Riesenrad (Big Wheel) for little ones – it's beautiful but boring. Walk straight past and up to the other end of the funfair, or take the Liliput Bahn steam train through the forest and back to the Hauptallee stop. Behind the Schweizerhaus beer garden, which is fine for kids, there's an array of rides for younger children. The best of them are straight out of the 1950s and earlier – including racing-car rides, a pony-carousel from the 19th century, and pony rides. For the less nostalgic, there's a Kinderparadies, where you pay once for all the rides and games you can take. The Prater used to be an imperial hunting ground and there is still plenty of forest left. You'll find a large number of playgrounds, from the fenced-in baby playground near the child-friendly and very pleasant Café Maierei Holzdorfer at Hauptallee 3, to the skateboard and mountain biking tracks nearly opposite, via the two big playgrounds and long slide on the dog-free Jesuitenwiese. At Prater 113 behind the Schweizerhaus, you can hire bikes by the day or hour – children's seats are thrown in free.

In the 1st district the Schmetterlinghaus (Butterfly House), in a palm house at the bottom of the Burggarten, is a playground for hundreds of huge, colourful tropical butterflies and a troop of dwarf quails. The atmosphere is weird – it's supposed to feel like a hot, steamy jungle, with gurgling streams, singing birds and luxuriant vegetation. The reality is a bit too plasticky, but it's worth suspending disbelief just to see the butterflies close up. The Burggarten itself is one of the few parks where lying on the grass is tolerated.

Also in the 1st, the Spanische Reitschule is great for children who want to see the dancing white Lipizzaner stallions, but going for an entire expensive performance is probably overdoing it. Tickets can be bought to see the horses train most mornings. Real fans can combine a visit with a trip to the **Lipizzaner Museum** across the road. *See p60.*

Go to the **Tiergarten** (zoo) at Schönbrunn (*see p91*) on a Sunday and you'll find lots of Viennese parents with kids in tow. It's the world's oldest zoo and some of the animals are still housed in the beautiful (but cramped) baroque buildings. The luckier ones (lions, bears and penguins, for instance) enjoy more modern quarters. The place is very relaxed, with a great playground for smaller kids, horse-rides, a wood full of wolves and a Tyrolean farmhouse with a range of organic food. Farm animals, elephants, monkeys and

hippos are also on display. Favourite slots include: washing the elephants (10am), feeding the seals (10.30am and 3.30pm), and feeding the wolves (11am).

Rathausplatz, the large square on the Ring outside the town hall, has become a year-round hive of activity, usually of interest to children. In January and February there's an outdoor ice-skating rink (no boot hire), plus food and trampolines. In summer an outdoor music and film festival takes place, with food from around the world. In December the whole park is turned into a magical Christmas market. The stalls are tacky, but the trees are beautifully decorated and there are pony rides and train rides around the park, plus a baking/modelling workshop for 3-16-year-olds inside the city hall. At other times of the year, circuses and concerts take place here. *See pp146-149.*

In midsummer, take a trip to the Donauinsel, the island separating the Old and the New Danube. The New Danube was built alongside the Old in the early 1980s to help prevent the river flooding. It has become a favourite destination for Vienna's nudists, youngsters and families (although the water quality isn't always great, so swimming isn't recommended for children). You can also head for the lively Sunken City (U1 Donauinsel) where you can rent roller-skates, in-line blades or bicycles, go boating, or eat and drink in a Costa del Sol style atmosphere.

Museums

The best of Vienna's museums offer wonderful guided tours for children – but only in German. The most enjoyable museums for English-speaking kids are those, like the Technisches Museum Wien (Technical Museum, Mariahilfer Strasse 212, 8999 86000) in the 15th, where doing and seeing take precedence over listening. This museum has lots of levers to pull and experiments to try, and for under-threes, there's a mini-museum with playful experiments, all watched over by a qualified child-minder. *See also p52* **Haus der Musik**.

The baroque Lobkowitz Palace houses the **Österreichisches Theatermuseum** (*see p60*) which has a small collection for children, accessible by a steep slide from the main museum. Here you can see magical stage sets and marionettes up close, and play in a mini-theatre. The **Puppen- und Spielzeugmuseum** (Doll and Toy Museum) has a huge private collection of antique dolls and toys – but you can't help wondering whether it's not more interesting for parents than for their children. The pick of the museum bunch for children, though, is the **Zoom Kindermuseum** (*see below*).

Zoom Kindermuseum

7, Museumsquartier, Museumsplatz 1 (522 6748/ www.kindermuseum.at). U2, U3 Volkstheater/tram 46, 49/bus 2a. **Open** 8.30-4pm daily. **Admission** €3.50 adults; €4 children; €12 family. **Credit** AmEx, DC, MC, V. **Map** p242 D7.

Perhaps a bit difficult for English-speaking tourists, but heaven for kids. Zoom has a great touchy-feely permanent exhibition on the theme of the sea, 'Ozean', for children aged up to six. There's also an 'Atelier' for 3-12-year-olds, exhibitions for 7-12-year-olds and labs ('Bildstudio' and 'Soundstudio') for 8-14-year-olds. You'll need to book in advance (a couple of days beforehand for weekends or public holidays) – participation is for a limited number and starts at specific times. Tours of the exhibition start at 8.30am, 10.30am, 1.30pm and 3.30pm on weekdays; 10am, noon, 2pm and 4pm at weekends. An hour in the ocean is at 9am, 10am, noon, 1pm, 2pm, 3pm and 4pm on weekdays, and hourly from 10am to 4pm at weekends and on public holidays. The Atelier has sessions at 2pm and 4pm on Fridays and Saturdays, and at 10am, noon, 2pm and 4pm on Sundays and public holidays. The two labs (Bildstudio and Soundstudio) are only open on Fridays, weekends and holidays, with sessions starting at 2pm and 4pm respectively.

Theatres

Märchenbühne Der Apfelbaum

7, Kirchengasse 41 (523 1729-20). U2, U3 Volkstheater then 10min walk/bus 48a. **Performances** phone to check. **Admission** €8. **No credit cards. Map** p238 C7.

For children learning German at school, it might be worth trying a puppet theatre performance of a well-known fairy tale. Märchenbühne Der Apfelbaum (the Fairy Tale Theatre) stages classics such as *Hansel and Gretel* and *Snow White*, for children aged from four years upwards.

Marionetten Theater Schloss Schönbrunn

13, Hofratstrakt, Schloss Schönbrunn (817 3247/ www.marionettentheater.at). U4 Schönbrunn. **Performances** phone to check. **Admission** €21-€28 adults; €15-€19 children. **Credit** DC, MC, V.

These exquisite puppet performances of *The Magic Flute, Aladdin,* or new stories such as *Sisi's Secrets* or *Magic Strauss* rely on music and costume rather than language to keep kids' attention. Most performances last about an hour – but beware, *The Magic Flute* is over two hours.

Original Praterkasperl

2, Prater Strasse des 1 Mai 118 (789 0301/ www.praterkasperl.at). U1 Praterstern then tram 21. **Map** p236 H5.

Kasperl is the Austrian equivalent of Punch and Judy. It's all in German of course, but children may enjoy the costumes and puppets.

Parks & playgrounds

In the centre of town, there are beautiful parks but few really good playgrounds. The best combination is the **Stadtpark** (*see p75*), which stretches from the Ring to the Hilton Hotel, across the Wien River. The playground (Hilton side) is large and fenced in, and good for smaller children. Nearby is a fountain designed for kids to splash around in. The more beautiful area of the park is on the Ring side, where there's a duck pond.

The Donaupark in the 22nd district is a huge park with lots of possibilities. At the main entrance it has Walkamals, large cuddly animals that wheel around with toddlers on their backs (€2 a go). A tiny train runs around the huge park. There's also table tennis, minigolf and huge chess and draught games; a mini-zoo, with a bird house and a petting zoo; and three playgrounds, with enormous slides and creative rides.

Also worth exploring with children is the **Lainzer Tiergarten** (*see p93*), a vast tract of countryside to the west of Hietzing, and of course, the Prater and Burggarten parks *(see p151).*

Babysitters

The best bet is to ask staff at your hotel if they can arrange babysitting. The only other service available is Babysittingagentur Peter Pan (616 9170), which, given three to four hours' notice, can provide English-speaking babysitters. For weekends, you must phone by Friday morning.

Eating out

This is no problem in summer – most restaurants have tables outside where the atmosphere is less smoky and more relaxed. But the best bet is to do what Viennese parents do on a hot evening and go to a *Heuriger* (wine tavern) in the hills. The worst of these are tourist traps, but the best are a grander version of a back-garden picnic, with benches and tables under the trees, and a self-service buffet. Some *Heurigen* feature a swing or slide; most have plenty of room to run around. Zawodsky on Reinischgasse in the 19th district and Rath on Liebhartstalstrasse in the 16th are two of the more popular for children.

If you really want to go local, try a *Wurstelstand* (sausage stand) – the best are behind the Opera and on Schwarzenbergplatz. Rosenberger on Maysedergasse in the 1st district has excellent self-service food on three floors. It isn't atmospheric, but it provides kids with crayons, balloons and cardboard crowns, has high-chairs and even a changing table.

Arts & Entertainment

Film

The tills are alive with *The Sound of Music* – and more.

Austria's film industry might not have the same worldwide reputation as its classical music, but actors such as Klaus-Maria Brandauer, Romy Schneider and Arnold Schwarzenegger have all enjoyed international success, while Austrian actress Hedy Lamarr made history in 1932 by appearing nude in *Ecstasy*. Many famous actors, directors and producers from Hollywood's golden age have Austrian backgrounds, among them Fred Astaire and Erich von Stroheim. Most began their careers in Germany but were forced to emigrate to the United States as the Nazis came to power. Recently, after years in decline, the country's film industry has seen something of a revival, attracting the attention of international audiences and critics. *See p154* **The austere Austrian**.

Two of the most enduring movies in film history were shot in Austria, of course – *The Third Man* and *The Sound of Music* – although Austrian audiences did not receive them well at the time. Now, however, *The Sound of Music* is often featured at sing-along screenings, particularly at gay festivals, while *The Third Man* is regularly shown at the Burgkino, and there is even a walking tour of its locations (*see p46*).

There are 44 cinemas and more than 100 screens in Vienna, some of which are Hollywood outlets and multiplexes, but plenty are art-house cinemas. On any given day in Vienna you will find not only Hollywood blockbusters but retrospectives and international films that have not found worldwide distribution. Many of the theatres showing mainstream Hollywood fare (such as the Haydn, the Burgkino and the Artis Kino-Treff) often screen films in English (without subtitles), whereas most art-house cinemas, such as the Gartenbaukino, the Votiv-Kino, the Stadtkino, and the Metro Kino have films in the original version with subtitles. Most cinemas have a bar as well as the usual refreshment counters, and sometimes a café.

LISTINGS & TICKETS
Films are listed in every newspaper, but for the most comprehensive overview of foreign-language movies try *Der Standard* (daily), which has an extra section for all films not dubbed into German. The most complete listings are in the weekly *Falter*, with an A-Z listing by film title. The small letters next to

The international film festival, the **Viennale**.

some films have the following meaning: OF is original version; OmU is original version with German subtitles; and OmenglU or OmeU is original version with English subtitles. Booking is advisable, as many of the city's cinemas are very small. Kino-Montag on Mondays means cheap seats in all cinemas.

FESTIVALS
In July and August most art-house cinemas drop their regular programming and screen classics and cult films during the **Sommer-Kino** season. Check out the flyers in cafés around the city for special listings, as well as the newspapers. In the summer Vienna also has two open-air cinemas, complete with food stalls – *see p157*. Vienna's international film festival – the **Viennale** – starts in mid October and lasts about two weeks. It premières films in Austria, showcases retrospectives and screens international feature, documentary and short films – an interesting mix of commercial and independent films by established directors and budding talents from around the world.

The austere Austrian

Two worldwide hits, *The Third Man* and *The Sound of Music*, have long overshadowed the homegrown product, so much so that for decades, when people did put 'Austria' and 'film-making' together in the same sentence, it was usually in much the same way that François Truffaut did with regard to the UK, when he politely suggested to Alfred Hitchcock that there was something incompatible about the words 'British' and 'cinema'.

But just as the *Nouvelle Vague* polemicist was conveniently forgetting about the achievements of Powell and Pressburger, Robert Hamer, Sandy Mackendrick, Thorold Dickinson and quite a few others, so those determined to downplay Austria's contribution to the filmic medium have neglected the likes of Fritz Lang, Erich von Stroheim, Josef von Sternberg, Fred Zinnemann, Edgar G Ulmer, Billy Wilder, Otto Preminger and Mr Vienna himself, Max Ophüls – a list that by any standards includes some of the greatest movie-makers of all time.

Admittedly, many of those masters emerged on to the international scene during cinema's first three or four decades (the post-war years were particularly unfruitful); true, too, that most of them came to artistic maturity in Hollywood, Berlin, Paris or elsewhere. But that's less to do with talent than with material resources. Moreover, one certainly might argue that many of the aforementioned continued to display, wherever they were working, a common sensibility: slightly detached, coolly ironic, non-judgmental, wary of facile sentimentality and reluctant to manipulate the audience's emotions by resorting to soothing clichés. Whether that adds up to a Viennese or Austrian approach to film-making is obviously a moot point; but it's intriguing that those qualities now appear to have been carried over into the films which during the last decade or so have suggested that Austrian film-making may be undergoing a revival of fortunes.

The undisputed leader of the new Austrian pack is Michael Haneke, who has actually been making features since 1989, when he turned from making television dramas and documentaries to direct the stunning *The 7th Continent*, an extraordinarily austere, unsentimental portrait of a bourgeois family's successful preparations for suicide, and the first film in a loose trilogy about the progressive 'emotional glaciation' of modern Austria. All Haneke's films have been seriously ambitious, challenging works, but it was only with 1997's controversial *Funny Games* that he really began to attract the attention of the international film-going public – albeit for all the wrong reasons. It was a deeply intelligent and wholly unexploitative study of how violence is presented, packaged, perceived and consumed as 'entertainment'; sadly, however, both its basic conceit and its aesthetic rigour were misunderstood, and Haneke gained a ludicrous reputation as a film-maker who specialised in sensationalist 'extreme cinema'. Happily, his next film, *Code Unknown* – a wonderfully perceptive account of modern life in all its interconnected complexities – persuaded those who saw it that transgression for transgression's sake was definitely not what Haneke was about, while the three Cannes prizes awarded to *The Piano Teacher* (pictured), a Bergmanesque study of twisted emotions centred on an amazing performance from Isabelle Huppert, helped to convince many remaining doubters that here was a film-maker of truly world-class status.

Although the festival holds no competition, FIPRESCI (the International Film Critics' Federation) awards a prize – 2002's winner was the Argentine *Tan de repente*, by Diego Lerman. Buy tickets in advance, as the festival is extremely popular (there were over 70,400 visitors in 2002).

Cinemas

Admiral
7, Burggasse 119 (523 3759). U6 Burggasse/ tram 5/bus 48a. **Tickets** €5.50. **No credit cards**. **Map** p238 B7.

An old, neighbourhood cinema with an Eastern Bloc façade but a cosy interior (from which you can hear passing traffic), with a long, thin screening room. Its programming features less commercial films – often original versions with subtitles.

Artis Kino-Treff
1, Schultergasse 5 (535 6570). U1, U3 Stephansplatz/bus 2a, 3a. **Tickets** €5.40 Mon-Wed; €8-€9.60 Thur-Sun. **No credit cards**. **Map** p243 E6.

An inner-city cinema that only shows (mainstream Hollywood) films in English. With six rooms it offers a large selection, but the screens are rather small (848 seats altogether, the biggest has 316).

Haneke's influence may perhaps be discerned in the first features of two young women who attended his lectures at the Viennese Film Academy. Valeska Grisebach's graduation film *Be My Star* is a beautifully perceptive account of adolescent love, at once tender and funny in its understanding of the temporarily bizarre mindset we all go through as teenagers, while Jessica Hausner's *Lovely Rita* takes a far darker view of the confusion and frustration felt by a girl caught awkwardly between childhood and womanhood. The chilly (but far from humourless) sense of alienation in Hausner's feature, and indeed in her acclaimed shorts *Flora* and *Interview*, runs parallel to the often grotesque focus on human idiocy, ugliness and cruelty that marks the highly stylised, even surreal documentaries of Ulrich Seidl, who himself found international success with his first feature, *Dog Days*. In all these movies, as in Haneke's, the personal is linked to the political, a tendency also to be found in the work of other young film-makers like Barbara Albert, Michael Sturminger and Andrea Maria Dusl. This may not exactly be a tidal wave of new Austrian talent, but it's certainly a very promising ripple, following currents that take it far from ferris wheels and nuns climbing mountains.

Bellaria

7, Museumstrasse 3 (523 7591). U2, U3 Volkstheater/tram 46, 49/bus 48a. **Tickets** €5.50; €4-€5.10 matinées. **No credit cards. Map** p242 D7.
As the original decoration (and the posters) show, time here seems to have stopped in the 1950s. The programming specialises in old German and Austrian light comedies from the 1930s to the 1960s, with some more recent films thrown in. If you're interested in *Heimat* films (kitschy Austrian-German genre featuring mountains and blondes in dirndls) or in Germany's golden film age, this cinema will appeal.

Breitenseer Lichtspiele

14, Breitenseerstrasse 21 (982 2173). U3 Hütteldorfer Strasse/tram 49, 10. **Tickets** €6.50. **No credit cards**.
Opened in 1909, and built within an art nouveau house, this is possibly the oldest operational cinema in the world. The 186 wooden seats haven't been changed in over 90 years and there is a private box for special guests. It normally screens English films with subtitles. Worth the detour.

Burgkino

1, Opernring 19 (587 8406/www.burgkino.at). U1, U2, U4 Karlsplatz/tram 1, 2, D, J/bus 57a. **Tickets** €6-€8. **No credit cards. Map** p242 E7.

De France, programmed by the film buffs at Votiv-Kino.

This centrally located, cosy cinema only shows original version films. Commercial films are shown in the bigger screening room (292 seats), whereas the smaller one (73 seats) concentrates on less mainstream or classic pictures, usually on Friday or Saturday nights. *The Third Man* has been shown here practically every weekend since 1980, and Stanley Kubrick's *Dr Strangelove* is another perennial favourite.

De France

1, Hessgasse 7 (317 5236). U2 Schottentor/ tram D, 1, 2. **Tickets** €5.50-€ 6.50. **No credit cards. Map** p242 D6.
Centrally located, this cinema recently reopened and now screens films in the original version with subtitles. Although the screens are rather small, the selection of films is varied and interesting and the seats are extremely comfortable.

Filmcasino

5, Margaretenstrasse 78 (587 9062/www.filmcasino.at). U4 Pilgramgasse/bus 13a, 14a. **Tickets** €5.50-€7.50. **No credit cards. Map** p239 D9.
It's worth a trip to see original version films amid well-preserved 1950s decor. The 254-seat auditorium is unusually spacious. The programming is centred on European films and also new Asian cinema, especially from Hong Kong. Documentaries are sometimes shown, although most are in German.

Filmhaus am Spittelberg

7, Spittelberggasse 3 (522 4816). U2, U3 Volkstheater/tram 49/bus 48a. Closed Aug.
Tickets €5.80-€6.50. **No credit cards.
Map** p242 C7.

This 100-seater art-house cinema in Spittelberg is surrounded by bars and restaurants. It is under the same ownership as the Stadtkino (*see p157*) and has similar programming of original version films.

Filmmuseum

1, Augustinerstrasse 1 (533 7054/ www.filmmuseum.at). U1, U2, U4 Karlsplatz/ tram 1, 2, D, J/bus 3a. **Tickets** €5 members; €9 non-members; €10.90 annual membership; €36 10-film card. **No credit cards. Map** p242 E7.
Located in the newly renovated and reopened Albertina (*see p60*), Filmmuseum was entirely left out of the renovation plans and continues to be as dingy and uncomfortable as ever. However, every film is in original version, and almost never subtitled. The programming includes exhaustive retrospectives of famous directors, Russian, German, Japanese and Iranian cinema, and all-time classics. Recent retrospectives have included Bollywood cinema and David Cronenberg.

Gartenbaukino

1, Parkring 12 (512 2354/www.gartenbaukino.at). U3 Stubentor, U4 Stadtpark/tram 1, 2. **Tickets** €6.50-€7. **No credit cards. Map** p243 F7.
Now under the ownership of Vienna's film festival Viennale (who saved it from becoming a multiplex), this art-house cinema screens current international films as well as classics in the original version – usually with subtitles – and often a dubbed version of the film in an afternoon screening. There's only one screen, but it also happens to be the largest one in town (seats 750). The original and beautiful 1960s-style foyer has an excellent bar and hosts club events as well as premières. Wheelchair accessible.

Haydn English Cinema

6, Mariahilfer Strasse 57 (587 2262/
www.haydnkino.at). U3 Neubaugasse/bus 13a, 14a.
Tickets €6.50-€7.50 Mon; €6.90-€10.50 Tue-Sun.
Credit AmEx, DC, MC, V. **Map** p238 C8.
Mainstream English-language fare (three screens).

Metro Kino

1, Johannesgasse 4 (512 1803/www.filmarchiv.at).
Tram 1, 2. **Tickets** €5-€7. **No credit cards.**
Map p243 F7.
This gorgeous belle epoque cinema has been run by
Film Archiv since September 2002, who use it for
features on great Austrian actors (for example, a
recent Oskar Werner retrospective) and thematic
shows (film-makers who perished in the camps).
Film Archiv has been around since 1955, has a stock
of over 60,000 films and is more concerned with the
history of Austrian film than Filmmuseum, the other
cinematheque. Their offices are in the Augarten
where, for the last two summers, they have held
screenings in a marquee (*see below*).

Schikaneder

4, Margaretenstrasse 24 (585 2867/
www.schikaneder.at). U1, U2, U4 Karlsplatz/bus 59a.
Tickets €6. **No credit cards. Map** p239 E8.
A hip, alternative cinema that puts on about ten
films a week, most of them in original version with
German subtitles. The programming ranges from
manga-inspired Japanese action to political cinema.
The screening room is small (80 seats). There's also
a modern bar, which hosts occasional poetry slams
and regular DJ spots. Notice the vitrine at the
entrance, the only clue that this was once a shop.

Stadtkino

3, Schwarzenbergplatz 7 (712 62 76). U1, U2, U4
Karlsplatz/tram 71, D. Closed Aug. **Tickets** €6.50;
€50 10-film card. **No credit cards. Map** p243 F7.
An art-house cinema showing original version films
in its 172-seat projection room. It's run by cinephiles
who publish informative, detailed brochures about
the films on show. There's also a varied selection of
some 1,000 videos (mainly documentaries and discussions) for viewing (€1.10 per person, per hour).

Votiv-Kino

9, Währinger Strasse 12 (317 3571/www.votivkino.at).
U2 Schottentor/tram 1, 2, 37, 38, 40, 41, 42, D.
Tickets €5.50-€8; €5.50 Mon. **No credit cards.**
Map p242 D5.
One of the best cinemas in the city, with a 1960s feel.
Votiv-Kino shows films in original version on its
three screens and programmes films for the
reopened De France (*see p156*). On Sundays there's
a Film-Breakfast: €9.50 buys breakfast and a film.

Open-air cinemas

Freiluftkino Krieau

2, Trabrennbahn Krieau (729 17 43/www.krieau.com).
Tram N. **Open** July, Aug from 9pm. **Tickets** €7.50.
No credit cards. Map p241 K6.

Set in the old Krieau racecourse in the Prater, and
screening a mixture of classic and contemporary
films. Note that films in English are the exception
rather than the rule.

Kino unter Sternen

2, Augarten-Park (tickets 350 4632/office 585
23 2425/www.kinountersternen.at). Tram 5.
Open mid July-Aug. **Tickets** €7.50.
No credit cards. Map p235 F4.
Six weeks of open-air cinema with classics in original version on a huge screen. Recent screening
themes have included blaxploitation cinema, as well
as horror double bills of Hollywood classics and
remakes. There are Indian, Greek and Austrian food-
stalls set up nearby. Look out for programme
booklets in cafés and cinemas; check the website for
the most updated schedule. Umbrellas are provided
in case of bad weather.

Video stores

Alphaville

4, Schleifmühlgasse 5 (585 1966). U1, U2, U4
Karlsplatz/tram 62, 65 Paulanergasse/bus 59a.
Open 10am-10pm Mon-Sat; 2-7pm Sun. **No credit**
cards. Map p239 E8.
Run by dedicated cinephiles, Alphaville offers close
to 9,500 foreign-language movies and TV series, on
DVD and video, including *The Sopranos*, *The
Fugitive*, and many more. DVD players can also be
rented here.

Bookshop Satyr Filmwelt

1, Marc-Aurel-Strasse 5 (535 5326). U1, U4
Schwedenplatz/tram 1, 2, 21, N/bus 2a. **Open** 10am-
7.30pm Mon-Fri; 9am-5pm Sat. **Credit** AmEx, DC,
MC, V. **Map** p243 E6.
On the same street as Pickwicks, this store specialises in film and stocks an excellent variety of
biographies, posters, scripts and approximately
8,000 English videos, DVDs and soundtracks.

British Council

1, Schenkenstrasse 4 (533 2616/www.britishcouncil.at).
Tram 1, 2, D. **Open** 11am-6pm Mon; 11am-5pm
Tue-Thur; 11am-1pm Fri. Closed Aug. **No credit**
cards. Map p242 D6.
Has a variety of videos at a weekly rental fee of
€4-€5. ID and police registration needed for membership (€25 for 2 months, €40 annual).

Pickwicks

1, Marc-Aurel-Strasse 10-12 (533 0182). U1, U4
Schwedenplatz/tram 1, 2, 21, N/bus 2a. **Open** 10am-
10pm Mon-Fri; 9am-10pm Sat; 2-8pm Sun. **No credit**
cards. Map p243 E6.
The largest English-language video/DVD rental
store in Vienna with over 9,500 movies, mainly
English, but also French, Italian and Spanish.
Quality leaves something to be desired, however.
Rental is €2.50 to €4.30 per night. At Pickwicks,
ID and police registration are needed to become a
member (€18 a year).

Arts & Entertainment

Galleries

With the advent of the Museumsquartier, Vienna's art world has become the scene of great flux, conflict and public interest.

Vienna's art scene is starting to have an impact on audiences outside the specialised art world. Projects in public spaces, party-like gallery openings and new fields of artistic endeavour have encouraged a broader spectrum of the populace to participate in the formerly exclusive 'art discourse'.

The opening of the **Museumsquartier** (*see p160* **Museumsquartier: labelling art**) has had a huge effect on Vienna's cultural map. Art is no longer confined to the 1st district. Galleries, shops and arty hangouts, as well as cultural institutions, now radiate out from the MQ, particularly in the 7th and 4th districts.

While public funding is declining, other sectors are slowly starting to recognise the profitable side-effects of artistic idealism. The Museumsquartier contains commercial enterprises; festivals such as Soho in **Ottakring** (*see p146*) are occupying empty shops in co-operation with the city developers and the Chamber of Commerce.

Not everyone is happy about this; those in opposition are forming alliances with like-minded players. Galleries have been clustering in the vicinity of the Museumsquartier, and holding openings on the same day as each other to gain more impact (and public attention). Museum chains, such as the subsidiaries of the MAK, Belvedere and the Kunsthistorisches Museum, are spicing up their spaces with flashy shows of contemporary artists. Sometimes it seems they're trying a little too hard. New spaces which have been developed recently include MAK's use of a flak tower as an **exhibition centre** (*see p79*), and the transformation of the currently traffic-plagued Karlsplatz into a *Kunstplatz* (art space). Here the new **Kunsthalle Project Space** (*see p81*) is running a scheme called 'Instructions for Actions' by 26 artists, both Austrian and international. Plaques exhort passers-by to perform various actions or thought processes as they walk through the area.

INFORMATION

The weekly *Falter* magazine provides the best overview of current exhibitions. Up-to-date information of increasing quality, unfortunately in German only, can also be found on the internet; *Artmagazine* (www.artmagazine.cc)

has listings as well as features, while *kunstnet* (www.kunstnet.at) focuses on the programmes of individual galleries. A database of contemporary artists, in English, can be found at www.basis-wien.at. The Esel-initiative (www.esel.at) promotes all forms of art and publishes a weekly overview of openings, performances and events on its website.

Look out too for a quarterly publication from the Austrian Society of Contemporary Art Galleries, and flyers promoting individual events, especially at the **Kunsthalle Café** (*see p184*), **Schikaneder** (*see p184*), **Futuregarden** (*see p184*), **Fluc** (*see p183*), **rhiz** (*see p186*) and **Das Möbel** (*see p185*).

Public galleries

See also **Albertina** (*p59*), **MAK** (*p75*), **Kunsthistorisches Museums (Palais Harrach)** (*p61*), **Secession** (*p81*), **Belvedere** (*p77*), **Leopold Museum** (*p73*) and **MUMOK** (*p73*).

Atelier Augarten

2, Scherzergasse 1a (www.atelier-augarten.at). *U1 Praterstern.* **Open** 10am-6pm Tue-Sun. **Admission** €4.50. **No credit cards. Map** p235 F4. Hidden in Augarten park, Atelier Augarten is run by the rather traditional Belvedere Galleries. Since the venue's reopening in 2001 its relaxed, contemporary shows have included Austrian post-1945 sculptures and an examination of the relationship between art and nature. The Atelier's primary focus, though, is on Austrian artists such as Hubert Schmalix, Lois Weinberger, Brigitte Kowanz and Peter Kogler. The building is beautiful, and incorporates a chic café, but its sculpture garden and the adjacent museum of Austrian sculptor Gustinus Ambrosi (1893-1975) are still in need of renovation.

Bawag Foundation

1, Tuchlauben 7a (532 2655/www.bawag-foundation.at). *U3 Herrengasse.* **Open** 10am-6pm daily. **Tours** 3pm Sat, Sun. **Admission** free. **Map** p242 E6.
This excellent inner-city exhibition space, financed by a bank, shows mainly international artists who work out of the limelight. As well as Tony Cragg's insightful sculpture outside, expect to see work by the likes of Hamish Fulton, Atelier van Lieshout, Lee Bull and Kutlug Ataman. Home-grown talent is also occasionally exhibited.

Art doesn't come any smarter than at the **Generali Foundation**.

Depot

7, Breite Gasse 3 (522 7613/www.depot.or.at).
U2, U3 Volkstheater. **Open** noon-7pm Mon-Fri.
Café noon-10pm Mon-Fri. **No credit cards.**
Map p242 D7.
Café and meeting place, the Depot is used by those who work in the arts world and others keen to chat about art, politics and society. A multimedia library is on hand to aid research. Moved from its original space in the Museumsquartier during the renovation, Depot couldn't afford to return, and set up camp instead at MQ's back door. Financially the place is in dire straits, but enthusiasm and idealism may win the day.

Futuregarden Art Club (Kunstbüro/Kunsthalle 8)

7, Schadekgasse 6-8 (585 2613/0699 01967 8488/www.kunstbuero.at). U3 Neubaugasse.
Open 3.30-7.30pm Mon-Fri; 11am-2pm Sat.
No credit cards. Map p238 C8.
Amer Abbas, owner of this popular multi-purpose arts space, has discovered and exhibited several national and international artists, including Gelatin, Marcin Maciejowski, Oliver Ressler and Pavel Braila. At the same time he has managed to maintain the Futuregarden's credentials as part of the independent art scene. The venue's bar has also hosted countless long nights crammed with Vienna's partying artistic types. Kunstbüro's third annexe in the same building, Kunsthalle 8, serves as an experimental space for young artists and up-and-coming curators. Go there during the week to check for flyers.

Generali Foundation

4, Wiedner Hauptstrasse 15 (504 9880/www.foundation.generali.at). U1, U2, U4 Karlsplatz. **Open** 11am-8pm Thur-Sun. **Admission** €6; €4.50 concessions. **Credit** MC, V. **Map** p242 E8.
Generali, a multinational insurance company, happens to run the smartest art space in town. The conversion of a former hat factory by architects Jabernegg/Palffy has provided an imposing space in which selected pieces from the company's exquisite collection are presented. Confronting conceptual art, media and performance from the 1950s and '60s from a contemporary viewpoint, director Sabine Breitwieser has applied a deft touch to political, feminist and economic issues. Expect to see artists like Valie Export, Adrian Piper, Hans Haacke, Mary Kelly, Martha Rosler and the ubiquitous Heimo Zobernig. There's also a media library, holding literature and rare videos.

KunstForum

1, Freyung 8 (537 330/www.kunstforum-wien.at). U3 Herrengasse. **Open** 10am-9pm daily.
Admission €8.70; €4.40-€7.30 concessions; €16 family ticket. **No credit cards. Map** p242 D6.
Already a pioneering force in late-night gallery opening, KunstForum then went on to blaze a trail by turning its museum shop into a money-spinner (look out especially for the charming children's catalogues of exhibitions). Work by the likes of Monet, Miró and Malewitsch has recently been exhibited here. A major retrospective on Italian Futurists is being shown until the end of June 2003, including over 200 items by Marinetti and his followers.

Arts & Entertainment

Museumsquartier: labelling art

MQ! 'Em-Kyu', 'Em-Coo', 'Moo-kwa'. Even the Viennese have yet to agree on the correct German pronunciation for the newest brand on the city's art scene – although it has been under discussion for the past 25 years. MQ (Museumsquartier) is one of the largest cultural complexes in the world, but you wouldn't guess this from its exterior: an early 19th-century structure (designed by Fischer von Erlach and completed by his son) that once contained the imperial stables. More exciting architectural proposals were blocked by local residents and conservative politicians in order to preserve the façade of Vienna's imperial glory.

Once inside there are ample opportunities to spend time and money without ever setting foot in a museum. You can browse the bookshops, pick up a Russian Lomo camera from its Viennese distributors, or simply have a bite to eat in one of the cafés or restaurants. It would be a pity, however, to come all this way and not set foot in the **Leopold Museum** or the **MUMOK** (Museum of Modern Art) – for both *see p73*.

The latter is currently endeavouring to establish taboo-breaking 'Viennese actionism' from the 1960s as the apogee of Austria's artistic history. Pop art sitting next to orgies depicted on canvas, made from materials including human deposits, gives new meaning to cross-overs between life and art. MUMOK's new director Edelbert Koeb is eager to overturn common preconceptions. The original architectural vision for the building, a dark shaft splitting the already claustrophobic edifice in two, has been modified by the installation of a walkable 'white cube' by artist Heimo Zobernig. This bridges the two sides thus gaining space for contemporary art shows (and, naturally, more paying visitors).

MUMOK shares a foyer with its neighbour and competitor, the **Kunsthalle Wien** (*see p160*). There's also a host of smaller, more specialised institutions hereabouts. The problem is finding them; even locals are still baffled by the layout. A proper guide has been promised but is long overdue. At least there's an information centre, to the right of the main entrance, which has plenty of flyers and details about events and exhibitions – so much information, in fact, that it sometimes loses track of what's currently happening.

Among the hidden gems is the **Architektur Zentrum Wien** (*see p73*), which occupies the right courtyard, by the original baroque arches of the grand stableyard. Under the arches you will also find the archives of the **basis wien** (www.basis-wien.at), which include documentary evidence of those small initiatives that had revitalised the area before it officially opened as MQ in 2001.

The most recent arrival is **Math Space** (http://math.space.or.at), which, in a backyard location, strives to reveal the importance of mathematics in everyday (and, of course, art). More adventures await both kids and grown-ups in the experimental grounds of the **ZOOM** children's museum (*see p152*).

Before vanishing into the venue of your choice, take a quick peek inside the 'theme malls' of **quartier21** (http://q21.mqw.at) directly behind the main façade. Opened in September 2002, this as yet undefined entity hovers between becoming a shopping mall, a cultural office space and an exhibition

Kunsthalle Wien

7, Museumsquartier, Museumsplatz 1 (infoline 52189-33/office 52189-1201/ www.kunsthallewien.at). U2 Museumsquartier. **Open** 10am-7pm Mon-Wed, Fri-Sun; 10am-10pm Thur. **No credit cards. Map** p242 D7.
For many years the Kunsthalle was the brightest star in Vienna's cultural constellation. For almost a decade it camped out in a big yellow container on Karlsplatz where its large retrospectives on figures such as Nan Goldin and Giacometti, and thematic shows featuring contemporary stars, earned it an international reputation. The old site now houses the Kunsthalle Project Space, a small venue where students work with established artists and the art

crowd sups cappuccinos. Despite securing a permanent location at the very heart of the Museumsquartier complex, the Kunsthalle appears to have drawn the short straw. Instead of getting proper sexy premises of its own like the neighbouring MUMOK, it was relegated to the bowels of the Winter Riding School, sharing an entrance with the performance halls. However, what it lacks in external visibility is more than compensated for by the shrill colours of the posters advertising its often ambitious thematic shows based around art history or popular culture. In addition to the Kunsthalle's two sizeable exhibition halls, director Gerald Matt places art throughout the MQ, separately promoting these external activities by billing them as the

MUMOK.

in fields ranging from the fine arts to internet activism and the production and sale of electronic music.

To Vienna's independent and publicly funded art scene, quartier21 embodies the enforced commercialisation of cultural practices; its heavily marketed events calendar creates stiff competition for them. MQ's director Wolfgang Waldner has also been criticised for his hierarchical management structure and his strict control over public spaces in the MQ and the activities held in them.

centre. For a restricted period various small initiatives – including non-profit idealists as well as commercially oriented cultural workers – are being allowed to rent space and promote their work using MQ's prestigious address. These temporary residents operate

At the beginning of the 21st century the Museumsquartier accommodates all kinds of cultural endeavours, but behind the tidy baroque façade the prestigious area itself has become a battlefield in the dispute over Vienna's cultural hegemony.

'project wall', 'video wall' or 'photo wall'. The strategy of campaigning for a broad selection of Austrian artists (Martin Arnold, Walter Niedermayr and Inge Morath, for instance) as well as showcasing big names from the international art circus – Vanessa Beecroft and Steve McQueen spring to mind – has been a success. A respectable two million visitors came during the first year.

Kunsthalle Project Space

4, Treitlstrasse 2 (512 189-33). U1, U2, U4 Karlsplatz/tram 1, 2, D, J. **Open** 1-7pm daily. **Admission** €2; €1 concessions. **No credit cards. Map** p242 E8.

While Prada-clad cultural power brokers discussed the feasibility of the MQ project, contemporary art

in Vienna squatted here for years in a yellow portakabin whose terrace bar soon became a favourite of the arty crowd. The Kunsthalle now has a permanent home (*see above*) and in its place sprang a less-is-more glass construction housing temporary installations and studio space for young artists. In its short life Project Space has played host to international names such as Santiago Sierra and resumed its function as a meeting point for the artistically inclined. Its café and terrace continue to be one of the places to hang on a summer's night, while soaking up the sounds of a varied DJ programme.

Kunsthaus Wien

3, Untere Weissgerberstrasse 13 (712 0491/www.kunsthauswien.com). Tram N, O.

Open 10am-7pm daily. **Admission** €8; €6 concessions. Half-price Mon. **Credit** AmEx, DC, MC, V. **Map** p240 H6.

Although designed by the late Friedensreich Hundertwasser, Kunsthaus Wien is not to be confused with the tourist-besieged Hundertwasser Haus that lies just around the corner. Here too you'll see plenty of spirals, slanted stairways and cave-like rooms with pillars and water fountains, along with undulating brick floors. Shows feature prominent photographers and other artists, perhaps including Lord Snowdon, Pierre & Gilles, David Lachapelle, Daniel Spoerri and the late Herb Ritts. The first two floors are devoted to the work of Hundertwasser, and you can experience his vision of harmony between man and nature in the leafy café.

Künstlerhaus

1, Karlsplatz 5 (587 9663/www.k-haus.at). U1, U2, U4 Karlsplatz/tram 1, 2, D, J. **Open** 10am-6pm Mon-Wed, Fri; 10am-9pm Thur. **Admission** €7; €2-€4.50 concessions; €13.50 family card. **No credit cards. Map** p242 E8.

This institution is the public face of the Kunstverein (Society of Artists). Recent exhibitions have looked at themes as varied as electronic items, designers' strategies and megalomania in the architecture of the future. Displays of Kunstverein members' work are shown on the second floor.

Sammlung Essel

An der Donau Au, 1 3400 Klosterneuburg (02243 37050/www.sammlung-essl.at). S4 from Spittelau to Weidling-Klosterneuburg/U4 Heiligenstadt then bus 239. **Open** 10am-7pm Tue, Thur-Sun; 10am-9pm Wed. **Admission** €6; €4.50 concessions. Free 7-9pm Wed. **No credit cards.**

To present and store their vast private collection of the Who's Who of post-1945 art, Agnes and Karl-Heinz Essl decided to build their own museum on the outskirts of Vienna. To quash accusations of quantity being chosen over quality, the art-loving DIY barons have recently been hiring internationally renowned curators. A visit here is also an excuse for a pleasant walk along the Danube, and a good view of Klosterneuburg monastery – a copy of El Escorial outside Madrid.

WUK

9, Währinger Strasse 59 (401 2110/www.wuk.at). U6 Währinger Strasse/tram 40, 41, 42. **Open** times vary; phone to check. **No credit cards. Map** p234 C4.

This long-established cooperatively run 'open house' is well worth a visit. WUK's programmes run the gamut from political activism to swanky night-time events attracting the city's glitterati. Institutions found within its perimeter include the art space Kunsthalle Exnergasse (www.kunsthalle.wuk.at), and the reputable Fotogalerie Wien (www.fotogalerie-wien.at), which features young photographers and interdisciplinary projects. Other spaces and ateliers are rentable and exhibit work of variable quality.

Private galleries

1st district

Galerie Charim

1, Dorotheergasse 12 (512 0915/www.charimgalerie.at). U1, U3 Stephansplatz. **Open** 11am-6pm Tue-Fri; 11am-2pm Sat. **No credit cards. Map** p242 E7.

Myriam Charim's range of art spans from the young Documenta participant and film-maker Edgar Honetschläger to 1980s paintings by Erwin Bohatsch and Hubert Scheibl. Her collection also includes old and new works by Austrian veteran Valie Export, and work by international artists such as Milica Tomic from Serbia.

Galerie Ernst Hilger

1, Dorotheergasse 5 (512 5315/www.hilger.at). Tram 1, 2. **Open** 10am-6pm Tue-Fri; 10am-4pm Sat. **No credit cards. Map** p242 E7.

Already occupying three floors in the original building, Hilger has set up an 'artlab' across the street to try out young artists from central Europe. He focuses on art that 'won't need a plug', selling canvases, objects and editions from Warhol to Hrdlicka and Picasso; from sexy Mel Ramos up to his latest discovery, joyful Sebastian Weissenbacher.

Galerie Grita Insam

1, Kölnerhofgasse 6 (512 5330/www.kunstnet.at/insam). U1, U3 Stephansplatz, U4 Schwedenplatz. **Open** 11am-6pm Tue-Sat. **No credit cards. Map** p243 F6.

As well as works by meta-curator Peter Weibel and architect-visionary Zaha Hadid, Grita Insam represents such artists as Medical Hermeneutics and Art & Language, complemented by a new generation of local talent such as Manfred Erjautz, Karl Heinz Klopf and Peter Sandbichler.

Galerie Hohenlohe & Kalb

1, Bäckerstrasse 3 (512 9720/www.hohenlohe-kalb.at). U4 Schwedenplatz. **Open** 11am-6pm Mon-Fri; by arrangement Sat, Sun. **No credit cards. Map** p243 F6.

This gallery was taken over in 1999 by Theresa Hohenlohe, who aims to establish younger Austrian artists such as Martha Jungwirth, Barbara Holub and Simon Wachsmuth.

Galerie HS Steinek

1, Himmelpfortgasse (512 8759/www.galerie.steinek.at). U1, U3 Stephansplatz. **Open** noon-6pm Tue-Fri; 11am-2pm Sat. **No credit cards. Map** p243 E7.

The facial projections of Tony Oursler and humorous nudes by Secession head Matthias Herrmann are the real highlights here. The Steineks also represent veterans of canvas such as Adolf Frohner, Franz Ringel and Hermann Nitsch, as well as conceptual painting by the infamous Viennese poster-activists Deutschbauer & Spring. The firm's

Christine König, the king of galleries. *See p164.*

second space, the Halle Steinek in the 9th district, features younger artists and such projects as the personal photographic diary of *Der Standard* art critic Thomas Trenkler.

Galerie Krinzinger

1, Seilerstätte 16 (513 30 06/www.galerie-krinzinger.at). U1, U3 Stephansplatz. **Open** noon-6pm Tue-Fri; 11am-4pm Sat. **No credit cards.** **Map** p242 E7.

For 30 years Ursula Krinzinger's gallery has shown established Austrian avant-garde artists (Hermann Nitsch, Arnulf Rainer, Peter Schwarzkogler); 'new painting' (Christian Ludwig Attersee, Hubert Schmalix, Siegfried Anzinger) and the internationally acclaimed (Jonathan Meese, Paul McCarthy). A new space in 7th district's Schottenfeldgasse 45 will exhibit more work from younger artists.

Galerie Krobath & Wimmer

1, Eschenbachgasse 9 (585 7470/www.krobathwimmer.at). U2 Museumsquartier. **Open** 1-6pm Tue-Fri; 11am-3pm Sat. **No credit cards.** **Map** p242 D8.

Having moved from a small art-shop-cum-gallery to a location in the well-positioned Palais Eschenbach, Krobath & Wimmer continues to help local names such as Octavian Trauttmansdorff, Ugo Rondinone, Florian Pumhösl, Maria Hahnenkamp and Dorit Margreiter to enter the big league, where the gallery's more established artists (Herbert Brandl, Franz Graf, Otto Zitko) already roam.

Galerie Martin Janda-Raum aktueller Kunst

1, Eschenbachgasse 11 (585 7371/www.raumaktuellerkunst.at). U1, U2, U4 Karlsplatz. **Open** 1-6pm Tue-Fri; 11am-3pm Sat. **No credit cards.** **Map** p242 D8.

Whether it's Jun Yang reflecting upon his cultural heritage, Gregor Zivic overseeing the artistic transformation of his own apartment or Christine and Irene Hohenbüchler thinking about shelters for Kosovo, Martin Janda encourages art that reflects its social, political, economical and cultural milieu.

Galerie Meyer Kainer

1, Eschenbachgasse 9 (585 7277/www.meyer kainer.at). U2 Museumsquartier. **Open** 1-6pm Tue-Fri; 11am-3pm Sat. **No credit cards.** **Map** p242 D8.

From the Vanessa Beecroft preview in the Kunsthalle, Austrian Heimo Zobernig getting his first solo show in the MUMOK (*see p73*) or the riotous boy band Gelatin at the Venice Biennale, expect Christian Meyer and Renate Kainer (former partners of Georg Kargl) to have fingers in the pie. A star-spangled programme includes Franz West, Liam Gillick, Marcin Maciejowski and Raymond Pettibon.

Galerie Nächst St Stephan Rosemarie Schwarzwälder

1, Grünangergasse 1 (512 1266/www.schwarzwaelder.at). U1, U3 Stephansplatz. **Open** 11am-6pm Mon-Fri; 11am-4pm Sat. **No credit cards.** **Map** p243 F7.

An attractive, well-lit Gründerzeit apartment, which lies on the site of the first commercial gallery in Vienna. Opened in 1923 by Otto Kallir and then reopened in 1954 by the Catholic preacher Monsignore Otto Mauer, it became notorious as a post-war meeting place for the avant-garde movements that sparked Viennese actionism in the 1960s. The new owner, Rosemarie Schwarzwälder, turned it into a serious space devoted to contemporary abstract painting (and photography) with works by Herbert Brandl, Rainer Ganahl, Jakob Gasteiger and Ernst Caramelle.

Hoffmann & Senn

1, Dominikanerbastei 19 (535 9930). U1, U3 Stephansplatz. **Open** 11am-6pm Tue-Fri; 11am-3pm Sat. **No credit cards. Map** p243 E6.

Gabriele Senn introduced Hamburg Collective Isotrop and Cosima von Bonin to Vienna, and Martin Gostner, Hans Weigand, as well as younger generations of artists, to the world.

4th district

Christine König

4, Schleifmühlgasse 1a (585 7474/www.kunstnet.at/koenig or www.artsacts.net/koenig). U1, U2, U4 Karlsplatz/bus 59a. **Open** 1pm-midnight Tue; 1-7pm Wed-Fri; 11am-3pm Sat. **No credit cards. Map** p239 D8.

Christine König lives up to her regal name and has become one of the mainstays of Vienna's gallery world. Her Saturday 'Lunch Lectures' encourage discussions with current protagonists from the art world, while her gallery programme promotes local heroes (GRAM), the established (Gerhard Rühm) and the internationally acclaimed (Kara Walker, Werner Büttner, Leon Golub). Look out for permanent fixture Johanna Kandl.

Georg Kargl

4, Schleifmuhlgasse 5 (585 4199/www.kunstnet.at/kunst-wien/index_g.html). Tram 62, 65/bus 59a. **Open** 1-7pm Tue, Wed, Fri; 1-8pm Thur; 11am-3pm Sat. **No credit cards. Map** p239 D8.

At first glance it looks like a smart shopfront, but the basement space is deceptively vast. Kargl is probably the star among the gallery owners in town, both as a personality and for his work at the now-defunct Galerie Metropol. This gallery was the first to open in the area and provided the incentive for neighbouring showrooms Gabriele Senn, Christine König and Kerstin Engholm, as well as the student outlet 'Art ATOM' and all the fashionable flower stores, cafés and so on. Kargl exhibits seriously saleable art by Gerwald Rockenschaub, Mark Dion, Muntean/Rosenblum and Elke Krystufek.

Kerstin Engholm Galerie

4, Schleifmühlgasse 3 (585 7337/www.kerstinengholm.com). Tram 62, 65/bus 59a Schleifmühlgasse. **Open** 1-7pm Tue-Fri; 11am-3pm Sat. **No credit cards. Map** p239 D8.

Kerstin Engholm shows young, conceptually challenging artists from all walks of media. Names to watch out for here at the moment include Lois Renner, Angela Bulluck, Constanze Ruhm and Hans Schabus.

7th district

Galerie Hubert Winter

7, Breitegasse 17 (524 0976/www.galeriewinter.at). U3 Volkstheater. **Open** 11am-7pm Tue-Fri; 11am-2pm Sat. **No credit cards. Map** p242 D7.

For 30 years Hubert Winter has been introducing to Austria international artists such as Weiner, Lüthi, Steinbach and Matta-Clark. He has also exhibited the Austrian generation (including Peter Weibel, Robert Adrian X, Brigitte Kowanz and Franz Graf), accompanying them to stardom – or at least to a job at the Academy of Fine Arts. Currently a new, younger generation is being featured: such as Ingo Nussbaumer.

Galerie Knoll

7, Esterházygasse 29 (587 50 52/www.kunstnet.at/knoll/index.html). U3 Neubaugasse, U4 Pilrimgasse. **Open** 2-6.30pm Tue-Fri; 11am-2pm Sat. **No credit cards. Map** p238 C8.

Hans Knoll, who also chairs the powerful Society of Contemporary Art Galleries, has been doing pioneer work in building links between central and eastern Europe. His gallery is due to relocate in summer 2003, but the office will remain here.

mezzanin

7, Karl-Schweighofer-Gasse 12 (526 4356/www.mezzaningallery.com). U2 Museumsquartier. **Open** noon-6pm Tue-Fri; 11am-2pm Sat. **No credit cards. Map** p242 D8.

Young art-lovers used to mob the openings at Karin Handlbauer's former location, in a private apartment. Her new premises open straight to the street, right at the back door of the MQ. Handlbauer continues to catapult her young national and international protégés (like Russian-Austrian video-artist Anna Jermolaewa) into the spotlight.

Westlicht

7, Westbahnstrasse 40 (522 6636/www.westlicht.at). Tram 49. **Open** 2-7pm Tue, Wed, Fri; 2-9pm Thur; 11am-7pm Sat, Sun. **Credit** AmEx, DC, MC, V. **Map** p238 B8.

Westlicht is Vienna's leading independent photography forum, and dedicates its gallery space to the work of 26 young Austrian photographers. While the effects of technological advances in photography are evident in much of the work, the use of traditional techniques such as tinting is also common, suggesting an interface between photography and painting. A visit to Westlicht is highly recommended for all fans of photography, not just for the excellent photographic exhibitions, but also for the permanent display of historic cameras, with the emphasis on rare Leicas.

Gay & Lesbian

A safe, if not a scintillating scene.

Café Willendorf. *See p166.*

The formation of a coalition government which included the right-wing Freedom Party under the leadership of Jörg Haider a couple of years ago had many people threatening to leave the country, but recent events, which saw the party publicly eviscerate itself, have led to a much more optimistic attitude among Austria's gays and lesbians, who in any case are determined to have a thoroughly good time whatever the government.

And things do change in Austria, if a little slowly. The much hated Article 209, for example, which set the age of consent for gay men at 18 and 14 for everyone else, has been repealed as unconstitutional. Vienna's options for gay-friendly restaurants, clubs, saunas and bars have also improved over the last decade.

In any case Vienna remains a relatively safe city for gays and lesbians with gay-bashing almost unheard of and events like the **Life Ball** and the **Rainbow Parade** becoming important dates in both the gay and straight calendar. The first port of call for gay visitors to the city is usually the **Rosa Lila Villa** (*see p166*); the nerve centre of gay activism in Vienna.

Cafés & bars

See also **Motto** (*p110*) and **Orlando** (*p112*).

Café Berg/Löwenherz Bookshop

9, Berggasse 8 (café 319 5720/bookshop 317 2982-1/ www.loewenherz.at). Tram 37, 38, 40, 41, 42. **Open** *Café 10am-1am daily. Bookshop 10am-7pm Mon-Fri; 10am-5pm Sat.* **Credit** (bookshop) V. **Map** p242 D5.
This cool and stylish café and bookstore sits on the same street as Freud's former residence and practice. Opened by Leo Kellerman in 1993, its friendly staff serve great breakfast and brunch combinations as well as cheap lunch specials and evening meals. A well-stocked gay bookstore adjoins the café and carries magazines and videos as well as books.

Café Savoy

6, Linke Wienzeile 36 (586 7348). U4 Kettenbrückengasse. **Open** *5pm-2am Mon-Fri; 9am-2am Sat.* **No credit cards.** **Map** p239 D8.
A classic old café with a rather camped-up interior – plenty of chandeliers and feathers. Stop by on Saturdays on the way to or from the Naschmarkt when the clientele is mixed and the atmosphere very lively, if a little smoky. At other times the clientele is made up of men of all ages.

Café Willendorf/Rosa Lila Villa

6, Linke Wienzeile 102 (587 1789). U4 Pilgramgasse.
Open 6pm-2am daily. **No credit cards. Map**
p238 C9.

This prominent pink and purple building is one of
the most popular places in Vienna for gays and lesbians. Owned and run by Andreas Pilz and Michael
Rehrl since 1991, it houses a bar and restaurant with
a pretty, ivy-covered courtyard (open during summer) and has a reasonably priced menu (until midnight) offering everything from snacks to full meals,
local beer to imported wines. Discussion groups and
counselling services for all age groups take place in
the Villa and are listed in *Extra* (see p167).

Chamäleon

*6, Stiegengasse 8 (585 1180/www.chamaeleon
bar.com). U4 Kettenbrückengasse.* **Open** 7pm-2am
Mon-Thur, Sun; 7pm-4am Fri, Sat. **No credit cards.**
Map p239 D8.

The hottest American-style gay bar in Vienna with
good cocktails and a nice atmosphere. It gets very
crowded at weekends.

Eagle

6, Blümelgasse 1 (587 2661/www.eagle-vienna.com).
Bus 57a. **Open** 9pm-4am daily. **No credit cards.**
Map p238 C8.

You'll need to buzz to get into this popular late-night
men-only bar with videos, an active darkroom with
individual cabins, and a small selection of toys and
videos for sale.

Frauen Café

*8, Lange Gasse 11 (406 3754). U2 Lerchenfelder
Strasse.* **Open** 7pm-2am Tue-Sat. **No credit cards.**
Map p242 C7.

A small, cosy lesbian bar with reasonably priced
drinks and friendly service. There's a disco three
times a year for girls that want to have fun.

Lo:sch

*15, Fünfhausgasse 1 (895 9979). U6 Gumpendorfer
Strasse.* **Open** 10pm-2am Fri, Sat. **No credit cards.**
Map p238 A9.

A strict dress code applies at this men-only leather
and fetish bar. Not for the faint hearted.

Mango Bar

6, Laimgrubengasse 3 (587 44 48/www.mangobar.at).
U4 Kettenbrückengasse/bus 57a. **Open** 9pm-4am
daily. **Credit** AmEx, DC, MC, V. **Map** p242 D8.

This cruisy and crowded bar for gay men has a
door buzzer and spyhole entrance system. The staff
are very friendly and the place is always lively, particularly on Saturdays. Mango Bar's clientele is
generally young.

Nightshift

*6, Corneliusgasse 8 (586 23 37). U3 Neubaugasse/
bus 13a,14a.* **Open** 10pm-4am Mon-Thur, Sun;
10pm-5am Fri, Sat. **No credit cards. Map** p238 C9.

This is the place for those who failed to pick up in
the Eagle (it's just around the corner), with videos
and a lively darkroom with individual cabins.

The totally fabulous **Life Ball**. *See p167.*

Santo Spirito

*1, Kumpfgasse 7 (512 9998). U1, U3 Stephansplatz/
tram 1, 2.* **Open** 6pm-2am Mon-Thur; 6pm-3am Fri;
11am-3am Sat; 10am-2am Sun. **Credit** AmEx, DC,
MC, V. **Map** p243 F7.

This bar and restaurant (serving Mediterranean and
Austrian cuisine) is popular among artists and musicians (gay and straight) and is known and loved for
its classical music – played loud.

Stiefelknecht

5, Wimmergasse 20 (545 2301). Tram 62, 65.
Open from 10pm daily. **No credit cards.**
Map p239 D10.

A serious leather bar with slings, swings, and so on.
Don't even think about coming in unless you're
dressed for the occasion.

Clubs

Heaven in U4

*12, Schönbrunner Strasse 222 (815 8307/
www.u4club.at). U4 Meidling Hauptstrasse.*
Open 10pm-5am daily. **Credit** AmEx, DC, MC, V.
Map p238 B10.

U4 hosts a mixed gay and lesbian disco – Heaven –
every Thursday night with three bars, two dancefloors and a darkroom. This is very popular with
younger scene gays and lesbians. For more information on U4, *see p186.*

Why Not?

1, Tiefer Graben 22 (535 1158/www.why-not.at).
U1, U3 Stephansplatz. **Open** 9pm-3am Wed, Thur;
11pm-4am Fri-Sun. *Upstairs bar* 10pm-4am Thur;
10pm-5am Fri, Sat. **Credit** AmEx, DC, MC, V.
Map p242 E6.

A popular bar-disco in the centre of town. Generally
younger guys go here, but dykes are also welcome,
except on Wednesdays, which is men only. The
quieter upstairs bar has a lounge area, a darkroom
and is open from Thursday to Saturday.

Cruising areas

Cruising and loitering outside public lavatories
and in park areas is mostly safe and police
seem to turn a blind eye to such activities.
The Rathauspark – on the left-hand side as
you face the Rathaus, past the fountain – is
the most popular turf in spring and summer.
Just plonk yourself on a park bench or go for
a wander and you'll see and hear the paths and
bushes come to life. Summer is also the best
time to check out the Donauinsel (the Danube
Island) a man-made island in the middle of the
river in front of the United Nations complex.
Swimming, cycling, volleyball, in-line skating
and serious cruising are all on the cards.

Throughout the year, though, a number of
U-Bahn passages are well visited from noon to
early evening. The Babenberger Passage on the
U2 line (at Burgring), the Albertina passage
crossing the ring that connects the Staatsoper
to Café Aida (where there's a peculiar mixture
of old Viennese, tourists, and gay men on the
prowl) and the front of the Staatsoper itself, are
all well known cruising grounds. The Venediger
Au near the big wheel at Prater and the Schweizer
Garten next to Südbahnhof are less popular and,
because of other mixed trade, fairly risky.

Events

Life Ball

9, Porzellangasse 32/3 (595 5600/www.lifeball.org).
This AIDS fund-raising event has established itself
as a glamorous event; expect to see celebrity guests
such as Elton John. The annual ball usually takes
place in the Rathaus at the end of May or beginning
or June and tickets tend to disappear within an hour
of going on sale. The website is worth a look.

Rainbow Parade

319 4472-33/www.pride.at. **Date** late June.
Vienna's wild and wonderful celebration of
Christopher Street Day.

> ▶ For gay help and information contacts,
> *see p217.*

Wien ist andersrum

1, Casanova Revue Theater, Dorotheergasse 6-8
(www.andersrum.at). *U1, U3 Stephansplatz.* **Date**
June. **Map** p243 E7.

Vienna's principal gay song and stage event has
abandoned the circus tent for the more shrill surroundings of the Casanova Revue Theater. Which
just happens to be one of the city's oldest bars and
scene of Joseph Cotten's late-night detective work in
The Third Man.

Media

Extra

The most established of Vienna's gay publications,
this free monthly magazine has a calendar of events,
classified ads, columns, bar listings and a more
political leaning than its competitors. It's available
at theVilla and most other gay venues.

Vienna Gay Guide

www.gayguide.at
A city map for gay tourists, indicating hotels, restaurants, bars, clubs, saunas, shops and cruising areas
around town. Available in most venues.

Saunas

Kaiserbründl

1, Weihburggasse 18-20 (513 3293/www.gaysauna.at).
U1, U3 Stephansplatz/tram 1, 2. **Open** 2pm-midnight
Mon-Thur; 2pm Fri-midnight Sun. **Admission** (per
day, incl locker) €15; €9 after 9pm Mon-Thur &
concessions. **No credit cards.** **Map** p243 E7.

These Moorish-style men's baths were built in 1870
and constitute Vienna's biggest sauna. The painter
Stefan Riedl (a young, gay artist who supervised the
restoration of the baths) more recently took on the
task of adding wall paintings alongside the hand-
finished mosaics from Istanbul. You'll find relaxation rooms, cabins, a darkroom, a Finnish sauna,
massage, a solarium and a new bar area. The baths
aren't as popular as they once were, but certainly
worth a visit. Mostly older guys nowadays.

Sport Sauna

8, Lange Gasse 10 (406 7156/www.sportsauna.at).
U2 Lerchenfelder Strasse. **Open** 3pm-1am daily.
Admission €12; €7 concessions. **No credit cards.**
Map p242 C7.

Popular sauna for the younger crowd, complete with
steam bath, bar, videos, cabins and fitness equipment.

Sex shops

For a selection of leather, rubber and S&M gear,
see p137 **Tiberius.**

Man for Man

5, Hamburgerstrasse 8 (585 2064/wal.wal@chello.at).
U4 Pilgramgasse. **Open** 11am-11pm Mon-Sat.
Credit AmEx, DC, MC, V. **Map** p239 D9.
Lube, condoms, gay magazines and videos.

Arts & Entertainment

Music: Classical & Opera

A musical city without equal, Vienna has been the crucible of the European classical repertoire for more than two centuries.

Vienna's musical heritage is evident at every turn, but although the city may seem stuck in the past, appearances can deceive. Granted, the old outnumbers the new by about ten to one if we're talking classical music venues – and 'new' is usually encased within an old and comfortable shell – yet there is evidence not only of renovation, but innovation.

One of the newest and most exciting additions is the **Haus der Musik** (*see p52*). It combines everything under one roof: history, contemporary hands-on learning, and a look to the future to boot. Another recent addition is the Museumsquartier, which provides two new halls in a city already bursting with them. The Konzerthaus, one of the old guard, was lately given a face-lift; its renovation included the building of a new hall in the basement with a sleek modern look.

But though the bricks and mortar may be impressive and beautiful, chances are you'll have come to Vienna to experience the music. It is here in abundance. For orchestral concerts look first to the Wiener Philharmoniker or Wiener Symphoniker. If you're interested in early and baroque music, try the Concentus Musicus conducted by Nikolaus Harnoncourt. High-calibre chamber ensembles such as the Alban Berg Quartet also call Vienna their home. There is, too, a small but well-established musical comedy scene (*see p174*).

This is not to say, however, that every performance is a gem. The downside to the historical awe accorded Vienna and its music is a certain complacency that sets in occasionally, a feeling of 'we are because we have always been'. This can also manifest itself in other ways: from a lacklustre performance 'good enough for the punters', to a feeling emanating from cloakroom staff that 'you should be grateful just for the experience'. Then again, perhaps we should.

Tickets & information

Information on programmes is also available from tourist offices (*see p46*), in listings magazines such as *Falter* and on information columns scattered all over the city. Tickets can be bought in advance from the outlets listed below. At some major venues, tickets and prices are divided into five categories; in descending order of expense, these are: G (gala), P (première), A, B, and C. Vienna also hosts festivals with classical music and opera throughout the year (*see p146*). For the Music Mile Vienna walking tour, *see p46*.

Österreichischer Bundestheaterkassen

1, Hanuschgasse 3 (514 44 7880/7881/7882/credit card bookings 513 1513/www.bundestheater.at). U1, U2, U4 Karlsplatz/tram 1, 2, D, J. **Open** 8am-6pm Mon-Fri; 9am-noon Sat, Sun, public holidays and all Sats in Advent. **Credit** AmEx, DC, JCB, MC, V. **Map** p242 E7.

The State Theatre Booking Office has tickets to the Akademietheater, Schauspielhaus, Staatsoper, Volksoper and Burgtheater. Tickets for the Staatsoper and Volksoper go on sale one month before the date of performance and can be booked by telephone with a credit card one day after the advanced sale begins. The credit lines are open 10am-9pm daily and English is spoken. You can also order tickets online, at any time.

Wiener Staatsoper

1, Hanuschgasse 3 (www.wiener-staatsoper.at). U1, U2, U4 Karlsplatz/tram 1, 2, D, J. **Credit** AmEx, DC, JCB, MC, V. **Map** p242 E7.

Last-minute tickets can be bought at the main ticket office here, and from the information office in the arcades at the Staatsoper, from 9am one day before the performance, at a standard price of €30, depending on availability. Get there early as the queue forms quickly and tickets go fast. For a recorded message in German on last minute ticket availability, phone 514 44 2950.

Wien-Ticket

6, Linke Wienzeile 6 (58 885). U1, U2, U4 Karlsplatz (exit Secession). **Open** 9am-9pm daily. **Credit** AmEx, DC, MC, V. **Map** p242 D8.

This office has tickets for the Theater an der Wien, Raimund Theater and Etablissement Ronacher, each of which also has its own box office open 10am-1pm and 2-6pm Mon-Fri. Last minute tickets are available at the theatres for €11, one hour before curtain.

Arts & Entertainment

Main venues

Orchestral, opera & operetta

Kammeroper

*1, Fleischmarkt 24 (box office 513 0100-77/
513 6072/www.wienerkammeroper.at). U1, U4
Schwedenplatz/tram 1, 2.* **Open** *Box office* noon-
6pm Mon-Fri; 4-7.30pm Sat (on performance days).
Tickets €14-€40. **Credit** AmEx, DC, MC, V.
Map p243 F6.

Ruled with an iron hand from its inception in 1953
by founder Hans Gabor, the Kammeroper, dedicated to smaller-scale opera productions, floundered a
bit after his death in 1994, but seems to have picked
up since his widow, Isabella Gabor, and Holger
Bleck took over the reins in 2000. The accent is now
on performing works that are neither included in the
repertoire of the bigger houses, nor likely to be produced by the independent companies. The highly
successful summer season, which was at one time
held amid the mock-Roman ruins in the park of
Schönbrunn Palace, continues indoors at the
Schlosstheater Schönbrunn. (The ruins have been
declared a historic site and can no longer be used;
interested parties are working on developing a Park
Theatre in the grounds.)

The permanent home of the Kammeroper is a tiny
Jugendstil theatre on the Fleischmarkt. The small
space brings the action up close and personal.
Besides the Kammeroper itself, Gabor also institut-
ed the Belvedere International Singing Competition,
held every summer, usually in July.

Konzerthaus

*3, Lothringerstrasse 20 (box office 242 002/infoline
242 00-100/www.konzerthaus.at). U4 Stadtpark/
tram D.* **Open** *Box office* 9am-7.45pm Mon-Fri;
9am-1pm Sat. **Tickets** €10-€104. **Credit** AmEx,
DC, JCB, MC, V. **Map** p243 F8.

A massive and much needed renovation was completed on the Konzerthaus in 2000, returning the
Grosser Saal, Mozartsaal and Schubertsaal to their
previous glory and adding another hall on the lower
level. Rather mundanely named the New Hall, this
has been put to good use continuing the
Konzerthaus tradition of promoting new music. The
Konzerthaus also features three further rooms, the
Schönbergsaal, the Alban Berg Saal and the
Wotruba Salon as well as a very fine restaurant run
by top Austrian chef Joachim Gradwohl. As for the
music, the Wiener Symphoniker and Concentus
Musicus both play here, but its offerings are not all
classical. Not as stuffy as the Musikverein, the
Konzerthaus sometimes marches to a different
drummer – even one with a definite rock rhythm.

Musikverein

*1, Bösendorferstrasse 12 (505 8190/www.musik
verein.at). U1, U2, U4 Karlsplatz/tram 1, 2, D, J.*
Open *Box office* 9am-7.30pm Mon-Fri; 9am-5pm Sat.
Tickets €16-€85; *standing room* €5-€7. **Credit**
AmEx, DC, JCB, MC, V. **Map** p242 E8.

Staatsoper. *See p170.*

Wien-Ticket Pavillon

U1, U2, U4 Karlsplatz/tram 1, 2, D, J. **Open**
10am-7pm daily. **Credit** AmEx, DC, MC, V.
Map p242 E8.

This booth is located right next door to the
Staatsoper. Wien-Ticket Pavillon supplies tickets for
all venues.

Arts & Entertainment

You'll wait a long time to see a woman playing in the **Wiener Philharmoniker**. *See p173.*

If you've ever joined the millions worldwide who watch the New Year's Day concert of the Vienna Philharmonic on TV, you've already seen its unofficial main home, the lavishly opulent Musikverein. The magnificent main hall of this building is more than just a pretty face, though: it's also an acoustical miracle. The ceiling above its 1,750 seats isn't joined to the walls, but hangs freely to allow for better vibration; there is also an entire room underneath that polished wooden floor for the same reason. The smaller 660-seat Brahmssaal is no less ornate, and is used for chamber concerts and recitals. Tickets to a Saturday afternoon or Sunday morning Vienna Philharmonic concert are among the hottest in town; as for the 1 January event, you must have your written request for the next year in by 2 January. Like the Staatsoper, the Musikverein offers standing room tickets, but here you can buy them at the normal box office up to three weeks in advance. The best buy is a seat in the last few rows of the parterre. These are raised, adding a panoramic view to that incredible sound.

Radiokulturhaus

4, Argentinierstrasse 30a (box office 501 70/377/ café 503 74 04). U1 Taubstummengasse. **Open** *Box office* 2-7pm Mon-Fri; 90min before performance Sat, Sun. *Café* 9am-1am Mon-Fri; 9am-5pm Sat (until 1am on performance days). **Tickets** *Backstage tour* €6 adult, €4 child. **Credit** AmEx, DC, MC, V. **Map** p239 E9.

A three-part complex housing the Grosser Sendesaal, home of the Vienna Radio Symphony Orchestra, the Radio Café and the Klangtheater Ganzohr ('all ears'). The last of these offers tours of the Funkhaus, which is the radio arm of the Austrian Broadcasting System (ORF). The tours last 90 minutes and include a visit to the Erlebnis Studio (Experience Studio) where visitors can play reporter and take the tape home with them, as well as look behind the scenes at one of the ORF radio stations. Tours are available in English for groups of at least ten, but must be booked in advance. The Grosser Sendesaal hosts everything from classical, jazz and New Age music to cabaret, exhibitions and spoken theatre. The Radio Café, open every day, is poorly designed and has neither old-world charm nor modern flair, but offers an eclectic mix of evening entertainment in a casual atmosphere.

Schlosstheater Schönbrunn

13, Schloss Schönbrunn/Schönbrunner Schlossstrasse (894 6690-51). U4 Schönbrunn. **Open** *Box office* from 1hr before performance. **Tickets** €18-€48, *standing room* €7. **No credit cards**.

Opened in 1749 to entertain the court of Maria Theresia, this is the oldest working theatre in Vienna, and the closest you'll come to the inside of a gilded music box. It's used in summer for performances by the Kammeroper. During the regular autumn-spring season it's rented out to a variety of ensembles and interested parties, including the nearby Hochschule für Musik und Darstellende Kunst (University for Music and the Performing Arts).

Staatsoper

1, Opernring 2 (51 444/2960/2959/www.wiener-staatsoper.at). U1, U2, U4 Karlsplatz/tram 1, 2, D, J. **Open** *Box office* from 1hr before performance.

Tickets *Gala performances (G)* €18-€251; *premières (P)* €11-€220; *(A)* €10-€178; *(B)* €9-€157; *(C)* €5-€91; *standing room* €2-€3.50. **Credit** AmEx, DC, JCB, MC, V. **Map** p242 F7.

The State Opera House, or Staatsoper, was built in 1861-9 according to plans by the architects August Siccardsburg and Eduard van der Nüll. The neo-Renaissance-style structure initially met with ferocious criticism from the local public, who called it the 'sunken crate' and the 'stone turtle'. Siccardsburg never designed again and died of a weakened heart; Van der Nüll, not to be outdone, killed himself. Neither lived to see the opera house officially opened, on 25 May 1869, with a performance of *Don Giovanni*. However, the citizenry eventually took the building to its heart, to the extent that after 1945, when the Staatsoper had been almost completely destroyed, the Viennese painstakingly reconstructed it. During the reconstruction, the Staatsoper company took up residence in the Theater an der Wien, where the legendary Vienna Mozart Ensemble came into being.

Many men have overseen this pinnacle of musical and operatic achievement over the years – great conductors such as Richard Strauss, Karl Böhm, Clemens Krauss and Herbert von Karajan. It was, however, Gustav Mahler, director from 1897 to 1907, who left the most significant mark on the Staatsoper, and simultaneously changed opera itself in ways that are now taken for granted. Dimming the audience lighting during the performance, shortening intermissions to 15-20 minutes, and seating late arrivals only after the prologue or first intermission were all radical innovations brought in by Mahler.

The first innovation of this millennium occurred on 1 September, 2001, when the Staatsoper unveiled its new seat-back subtitle system. The Viennese accepted this change with surprisingly little resistance, and have even been heard to admit to following along with the German text when the opera is being sung in that language. At present there is a choice of German and English titles, regardless of the language being sung. The fact the small screens can be switched off if preferred was a definite aid to their acceptance.

The Staatsoper has one of the largest opera repertoires in the world (some 70 different productions each year), achieved thanks to a combination of a long season (1 Sept-30 June) and a rotation system that calls for a different opera every day of the week. Although this occasionally plays havoc with the quality of the performances, it does enable visitors to see many different works in a short period of time and keeps native opera lovers busy checking out the latest cast changes. The Wiener Philharmoniker, under the stage name 'Das Orchester der Wiener Staatsoper', plays in the pit.

Good seats at the Staatsoper go quickly. Often the only way to get a ticket is by buying one from the touts. Try for one of the 567 bargain standing-room places. You can normally only get them from one hour before curtain, at the window marked *Stehplätze*; queues can be long. The view from the standing-room area at the back of the stalls is excellent, but it's worth the exhausting climb to the gallery for the best sights and sounds in the house.

Tours of the Staatsoper building are provided almost daily – for exact times, check the website or phone. Tours are available in seven languages (English, French, German, Italian, Japanese, Russian, and Spanish) and last about 40-45 minutes; tickets cost €4.50 (children €1.50).

Volksoper

9, Währingerstrasse 78 (51 444-30/www.volksoper.at). U6 Währingerstrasse-Volksoper/tram 40, 41, 42/ bus 40a. **Open** *Box office* 8am-6pm Mon-Fri; 9am-noon Sat, Sun. **Tickets** €17-€65; *standing room* €1.50-€2.* **Credit** AmEx, DC, JCB, MC, V. **Map** p234 C4.

The traditional role of the Volksoper (literally 'people's opera') has been as Vienna's flagship operetta house and it offers over 100 performances in that genre every year. Added to this are musicals, modern dance, and concerts by the Volksoper orchestra, as well as some operas. It has come to specialise in modern settings of traditional operas, as well as interesting works from all eras that the Staatsoper for some reason can't or won't do. The Volksoper ensemble seems to have more rehearsal time and fewer 'stars for the evening' than its much grander colleague across the city, which tends to add to (rather than subtract from) the final result. The house has a functional exterior and a stark, plain, almost astringent interior design, somewhat relieved by the red plush decor. The acoustics are also a little dry, especially at the sides. Don't even think of sitting in the back row of a box: you'll hear little and see nothing. The Volksoper is, though, more affordable than the Staatsoper and tickets are easier to obtain. The standard is generally high, even if the occasional evening disappoints. The 72 standing-room tickets (balcony or stalls) are a bargain.

Other venues

Arnold Schönberg Center

3, Palais Fanto, Zaunergasse 1-3 (712 1888-50/ www.schoenberg.at). Tram D. **Open** 10am-5pm Mon-Fri. **Tickets** *Exhibitions* €3-€5; *concerts* €13-€20. **Credit** DC, MC, V. **Map** p243 F8.

Opened in April 1998, the non-profit Schönberg Center encompasses an archive, a library, a concert hall, an exhibition hall and seminar rooms. Its mission is to promote interest in and knowledge of Schönberg and the Viennese school of the early 20th century, and related contemporary music. The 200-seat hall is used for a plethora of events; performances often include a free pre-lecture or discussion.

Bösendorfersaal

4, Graf Starhemberggasse 14 (504 6651). Tram 62, 65. **Open** *Box office* 8.30am-4.30pm concert days only. **Tickets** free or €12-€20. **Credit** DC, MC, V. **Map** p239 E9.

A permanent exhibition of pianos gives you something to look at in the intermission at this small concert venue. The room has nice acoustics, but poorly placed columns and a low ceiling make for unfortunate sight lines. Various small-scale recitals take place here, by performers from students to professionals. All have one thing in common: great pianos.

Herbert von Karajan Centrum

1, Kärntner Ring 4 (50 600-100/shop 50 600-200/ www.karajan.org). U1, U2, U4 Karlsplatz/tram 1, 2, D, J. **Open** 9am-5pm Mon-Fri; *shop* 10am-6pm Mon-Fri. **Credit** AmEx, DC, JCB, MC, V. **Map** p242 E8.
This centre contains an ultra-modern shop fitted with two high-tech research modules and helpful archivists. The complex also boasts a concert hall, built by Emperor Franz Josef for his mistress Katharina Schratt (it is part of the connecting Palais Königswarte, a protected national monument). Various events are held there, from recitals and chamber concerts to discussions and book readings. A standard donation/contribution of €3.50 is requested. The mix of state-of-the-art technology and old-world beauty is a fitting tribute to the man who, to this day, is responsible for two-thirds of all classical CDs sold by Deutsche Grammophon.

Jugendstiltheater

14, Baumgartner Höhe 1 (911 2492-93/tickets through Klangbogen 427 17/www.jugendstil theater.co.at). Bus 48a. **Open** Box office from 1hr before performance. **Tickets** €15-€35, €10 students. **Credit** AmEx, DC, MC, V.
Located in the grounds of the city psychiatric hospital, this Otto Wagner-designed masterpiece never seems to get the attention it deserves; badly needed renovations are left undone year after year. Most of Vienna's independent opera companies still use the venue, but its lack of amenities and the distance from the city centre mean that most of the audience consists of doting relatives of the performers.

Museumsquartier

7, Museumsplatz 1 (523 5881/www.mqw.at). See p72 for more details. **Map** p242 D7.
This major, fairly recent addition to Viennese culture is largely devoted to the visual arts, but it does incorporate two halls that are sometimes used for operas, classical concerts and musical theatre: the stirringly named Hall E and the smaller, no less winningly dubbed Hall G. Hall E is a modern space with state-of-the-art acoustics, and a variable audience capacity (from 377 to 1800). Hall G can be found on the lower level. With up to 380 seats and the same excellent acoustics, it is perfect for chamber works and song recitals. The Wiener Festwochen is just one of the many groups to perform here.

Odeon

2, Taborstrasse 10 (216 5127/www.odeon-theater.at). U1, U4 Schwedenplatz/tram N, 21. **Open** Box office 10am-6pm Mon-Fri. **Tickets** €15-€40. **No credit cards**. **Map** p243 F6.
Used for a variety of performances and events, from classical concerts to raves, the Odeon is little more than an empty shell of a building, waiting for proper

seating and a stage. Performances by the Neue Oper Wien, among others, take place here. It's not plush, but it does the trick.

Ensembles & associations

Alban Berg Quartet

1, Lothringerstrasse 20 (in the Konzerthaus building) (24 200-0). **Map** p243 F8.
In a city saturated with music of all kinds, an Alban Berg Quartet concert is still an event not to be missed. Günter Pichler, Gerhard Schulz, Thomas Kakuska and Valentin Erben have presented the string quartet repertoire, old and new, with an unsurpassed combination of intelligence and intuition, technical perfection and artistic freedom since the early 1970s, and are still going strong.

Concentus Musicus Wien

1, Lothringerstrasse 20 (in the Konzerthaus building) (24 200-0). **Map** p243 F8.
One of the world's premier ensembles for *Altemusik*, early to baroque music from the 13th to the 18th centuries. It's impossible to separate the Concentus Musicus from its founder and musical guru, Nikolaus Harnoncourt. Together, the man and the group have succeeded in making once-dusty and apparently boring baroque music come alive again, on original instruments.

Jeunesses Musicales Austria

1, Lothringerstrasse 20 (in the Konzerthaus building) (5056356/www.jeunesse.at). U4 Stadtpark/tram D. **Map** p243 F8.
1, Bösendorfer Strasse 12 (in the Musikverein building) (710 3616). U1, U2, U4 Karlsplatz/tram 1, 2, D, J. **Map** p243 E8.
Open 9am-7.30pm Mon-Fri. **Tickets** €7-€35 over-26s; €7-€15 under-26s. **Credit** DC, MC, V.
Going strong for over 50 years, the Jeunesses organises over 600 concerts and events throughout Austria every year. Its initial aim was simply to provide music for young people, but its concert programmes, presented in Vienna at the Musikverein or the Konzerthaus, are of such exceptional quality that music lovers of all ages vie for tickets which sell out quickly. Well worth a try.

Klangforum Wien

7, Kirchengasse 1a (521 67-0/www.klangforum.at).
This 'soloist ensemble' came together in 1985 as a democratic forum, promoting equal rights between interpreters, conductors and composers. It follows a 'working-together' style not usually found in the hierarchical musical world. The genre is contemporary music, ranging from classical modern to works of up-and-coming young composers, and including experimental jazz and free improvisation. The ensemble performs over 80 concerts internationally each season, as well as an annual thematic concert series at the Konzerthaus. In 2001, the Klangforum Wien was nominated for a Royal Philharmonic Society Award for its performances in Britain.

Radio Symphonieorchester Wien

4, Argentinier Strasse 30a, Radiokulturhaus (5017 0377/www.kultur.orf.at/radiokulturhaus).

The Vienna Radio Symphony Orchestra welcomed Bertrand de Billy as its conductor-in-chief on 1 September 2002, just as budget cuts within the Austrian Broadcasting Corporation threatened its existence. As the time of writing, the future remains far from certain. A penchant for the new, the unknown or the almost forgotten is the RSO's forte and, at the same time, perhaps, what keeps the orchestra from making a bigger name for itself. The RSO has performed the Vienna premières of works by the crème de la crème of contemporary composers such as Henze, Krenek, Ligeti, Penderecki, Rihm, Cerha and Martin. As with most radio orchestras, a high level of musicianship, combined with a 'this is being taped' awareness, makes for excellent performances. With luck you'll still be able to find the RSO on its home turf in the Radiokulturhaus or in the Musikverein or Konzerthaus.

Wiener Philharmoniker

Musikverein, 1, Bösendorfer Strasse 12 (505 6525).

The 140-member Vienna Philharmonic Orchestra has financed and managed itself since 1908 (it was founded in 1842). This is important, as it allows the orchestra the freedom to make decisions unmolested by pesky details such as fashionable ideas of equality: it gave up approximately €180,000 in state subsidies in order to retain its right to run things as it sees fit, including remaining virtually an all-boys club. (This cut in the budget was hardly in a main artery as that amount of money barely subsidised a single Philharmonic concert with choir.) The only woman admitted to the hallowed circle, a harpist, has since retired; another created headlines after being spotted in the viola section at the 2003 New Year's Concert, but has not yet been made an official member. In any case, the distinctive sound and impeccable musicianship of this world-class ensemble needs no adjustment. As well as presenting a full season of concerts every year between September and mid-June at the Musikverein, including the traditional New Year's Day Concert, the Philharmonic performs each summer at the Salzburg Festival, tours widely, and is the house orchestra of the Staatsoper, under the alternative title of Orchester der Wiener Staatsoper.

Wiener Sängerknaben (Vienna Boys' Choir)

2, Obere Augartenstrasse 1 (216 3942/www.wsk.at).

Undoubtedly one of Vienna's most valuable exports, these little cherubs in blue and white sailor suits are the darlings of Austria. The boys' musicianship and general professionalism are at an indisputably high level, but at times they seem a bit jaded – more red-eyed than rosy-cheeked. It's scarcely any wonder, with their schedule. They have a regular gig at the **Burgkapelle** (9.15am every Sunday and religious holiday during the school year).

Wiener Symphoniker

6, Lehargasse 11 (589 7951/ www.wiener-symphoniker.at).

Known as Vienna's 'second' orchestra, the Wiener Symphoniker might be internationally in the shadow of the Philharmoniker, but has a long and impressive history and presents some 200 concerts a year, mostly in the Konzerthaus and the Musikverein. It also tours extensively and serves as the festival and opera orchestra for the summer Bregenz Festival.

Wiener Tschuschenkapelle

6, Gumpendorferstrasse 77/22a (596 1213/0699/ 123 788 71/www.tschuschenkapelle.at).

'Tschuschen' was originally a derogatory term used by Viennese to describe people from the Balkans, which was expanded in true Viennese fashion to include just about anyone from an eastern country. The five-member Wiener Tschuschenkapelle turns this idea on its head with a mix of oriental, Slavic, gypsy, classical and Viennese music that celebrates multiculturalism. It performs at a variety of venues.

Independent opera companies

None of the *Freigruppen* or independent companies has a permanent home; they perform at various venues including the Odeon, Semper Depot, Jugendstiltheater, Museumsquartier and the New Hall in the Konzerthaus. Some of the groups can be hard to get in touch with. Here are the two most prominent and easily accessible.

NetZZeit

www.netzzeit.at. Tickets through the Konzerthaus (242 002/www.konzerthaus.at).

NetZZeit (Network Time) has dedicated itself to promoting and presenting contemporary works, especially those with an interdisciplinary approach. One of its attempts to include the audience in proceedings was entitled *Rauschkonzert* ('inebriation concert') and involved the audience drinking their 'after show drinks' before the performance, leading the tipsy public to feel more free to join in.

Neue Oper Wien

Ticket Infoline 427 17/www.neueoperwien.at.

Of the four main ensembles in Vienna, New Opera Vienna is the most successful in terms of number and size of productions per year. This is perhaps due to its penchant for co-productions with more established, traditional groups. Tickets are sold through Klangbogen Wien or Wien-Ticket.

Musical theatres

Etablissement Ronacher

1, Seilerstätte 9 (5141 1207/www.wien-ticket.at). Tram 1, 2. **Open** *Box office* from 1hr before performance. **Tickets** €20-€100. **Credit** AmEx, DC, MC, V. **Map** p243 E7.

Josephine Baker was among the attractions here, in the days when this was Vienna's most glamorous theatre. After a brief stint as a restaurant, the Ronacher became a stand-in for the Burgtheater when that building was destroyed in World War II. Now part of the Vereinigte Bühnen Wien, it was given a much needed face-lift, and is currently being rented out to other groups for a variety of (mostly musical) events.

Metropol Theater

17, Hernalser Hauptstrasse 55/Geblergasse 50 (4077 7407/www.wiener-metropol.at). U6 Alser Strasse/ tram 43. **Open** *Box office 10am-8pm Mon-Sat and concert days.* **Tickets** €12-€35. **Credit** DC, MC, V. **Map** p234 B5.
Various styles of entertainment are offered here, with one common trait: good value for money. A typical month might include gigs by New Age guru Gandalf, a gala featuring stars from the hit shows in town, evenings of Viennese cabaret and star-quality drag artistes on tour from Paris. On the musical side, the Metropol has begun producing original works as well as offering German translations of Broadway shows.

Raimund Theater

6, Wallgasse 18-20 (59 977/www.musicalvienna.at). U6 Gumpendorfer Strasse. **Open** *Box office 10am-1pm, 2-6pm daily.* **Tickets** €10-€95. **Credit** AmEx, DC, MC, V. **Map** p238 B9.
The Raimund opened in 1893 as a theatre for the middle classes in what was then an outer suburb of Vienna. Only spoken drama was presented until 1908, when director Wilhelm Karczag introduced opera and operetta. The Raimund had its heyday between 1948 and 1978, under the direction of Rudolf Marik. In 1987 it merged with **Etablissement Ronacher** and **Theater an der Wien** to form the Vereinigte Bühnen Wien or 'United Stages of Vienna', and has had a very successful comeback as a musical-comedy theatre. The Vereinigte Bühnen Wien has premièred the German-language versions of *Cats*, *The Phantom of the Opera*, *Kiss of the Spider Woman* and *Beauty and the Beast*. A new production of *Barbarella* is due to be staged in 2004.

Theater an der Wien

6, Linke Wienzeile 6 (58 830/tickets 5883 0265/ www.musicalvienna.at). U1, U2, U4 Karlsplatz. **Open** *10am-7pm daily; box office 10am-1pm, 2-6pm daily.* **Tickets** €23-€95. **Credit** AmEx, DC, MC, V. **Map** p242 D8.
This 1,200-seat treasure is most famous for hosting the premières of Beethoven's *Fidelio* (1805), Strauss Jr's *Die Fledermaus* (1874) and *Wiener Blut* (1899). Beethoven actually lived here during preparations for the presentation of his only opera. Since its opening in June 1801 the theatre has also seen many performances of the *Magic Flute* (if not the première of that piece, as is often claimed). Today it is part of the Vereinigte Bühnen Wien company, which uses it mainly as a venue for large-scale musicals. Beginning with *Freudiana* in 1990, the company has occasionally presented its own productions (*see above* **Raimund**

Theater). A further two works, *Elisabeth* and *Mozart*, have seen productions abroad. The Staatsoper will take over Theater an der Wien in 2006, using it for performances suitable to the smaller space. Until then, the Festwochen and Klangbogen festivals continue to take over the theatre from May to September with a range of opera and operetta productions. The rest of the time, the musical is master of the house.

Sacred music

A visit to Sunday Mass is a fine way to combine architectural, musical and possibly spiritual sightseeing. As well as the Burgkapelle, in the 1st district, the Augustinerkirche, Karlskirche, Minoritenkirche, Michaelerkirche and Stephansdom are all worth a visit.

Burgkapelle

1, Hofburg (533 9927/www.bmbwk.gv.at/kultur). U3 Herrengasse/tram 1, 2, D, J. **Open** *Box office 11am-1pm, 3-5pm Fri.* **Tickets** €5-€29. **No credit cards.** **Map** p242 E8.
The Wiener Sängerknaben (Vienna Boys' Choir) performs here every Sunday and on religious holidays at 9.15am except during the summer, between 10 July and mid-September. Tickets must be booked in advance.

Traditional Vienna

If you're looking for the definitive performance of *Eine Kleine Nachtmusik*, don't bother with these shows. Nevertheless, they provide a good opportunity to enjoy some nice tunes in beautiful surroundings. Their standard varies, but those listed below are the most popular.

Deutschordenskloster 'Sala Terrena'

1, Singerstrasse 7 (911 9077/www.mozarthaus.at). U1, U3 Stephansplatz. **Open** *Box office 10am-9pm Thur, Sat, Sun.* **Performances** *7.30pm Thur, Sun; 5pm Sat.* **Tickets** €21-€35; €21 students. **Credit** MC, V. **Map** p243 E7.
Mozart concerts are performed here year-round. The artistes wear concert dress rather than period costumes, but this newly renovated 50-seat jewel (part of the church and cloister of the Order of the Teutonic Knights) needs no other decoration.

Hofburg: Festsaal, Zeremoniensaal & Redoutensaal

1, Heldenplatz (Festsaal & Zeremoniensaal); Josefsplatz (Redoutensaal) (536 450/www.hofburg orchester.at). U3 Herrengasse. **Performances** *May-Oct 8.30-10pm Tue, Thur, Sat.* **Tickets** €42. **Credit** MC, V. **Map** p242 D7.
Artistes from the Staatsoper and Volksoper perform in the historic rooms of the Habsburgs' imperial palace. It offers by far the highest level of this sort of thing available. There are two box offices (one for

The delightful chocolate box interior of **Schlosstheater Schönbrunn**. *See p170.*

each platz), which open one hour before each concert. It's best to book by phone, but as none of the halls has numbered seating, arrive early to get a good spot.

Konzerthaus/Musikverein

Konzerthaus (see p169); Musikverein (see p169) (www.mozart.co.at). **Performances** *May-Oct* 8.15pm Mon, Wed, Fri, Sat. **Tickets** €35-€55 (A, B, C), €72 (Superior), €200 (VIP). **Credit** (website only) AmEx, DC, JCB, MC, V.

The venues are top notch and so is the music. Even better, the Wiener Mozart Orchester performances follow the style of the 'Musical Academies' popular at the end of the 18th century. Only the most favoured movements of symphonies or parts of concertos are played, alternating with operatic arias and duets. Tickets can be bought off season on the website, in season from costumed ticket sellers around town.

Orangerie in Schloss Schönbrunn

13, Schönbrunner Schlossstrasse (812 500 40/ www.imagevienna.com). U4 Schönbrunn. **Open** *Box office* 9am-7pm daily. **Performances** 8.30pm daily except 24 Dec. **Tickets** €36, €43, €50. **Credit** AmEx, DC, JCB, MC, V.

A small professional group performs every day at 8.30pm in the Orangery at Schönbrunn. The setting is magnificent, and the concerts offer a full evening's

entertainment of Mozart and Strauss, with a pair of dancers, soprano and baritone in period costume, accompanied by the Schönbrunner Schlossorchester.

Palais Palffy

1, Josefsplatz 6 (726 4475/www.imperial-concerts. netway.at). U3 Herrengasse. **Open** *Box office* 9am-10pm daily. **Tickets** €35-€48. **Credit** AmEx, DC, JCB, MC, V. **Map** p242 E7.

Imperial concerts are staged in baroque and Biedermeier costumes in the tiny Figarosaal and the slightly larger Beethovensaal. Standards, if not exceptional, are good and the musicians enjoy themselves immensely, which is quite infectious.

Wiener Kursalon

1, Johannesgasse 33 (512 5790/www.strauss-konzerte.at). **Performances** *22 Mar-31 Oct* 8.30pm daily; *1 Nov-28 Feb* 7.30pm daily. **Tickets** €32-€49. **Credit** AmEx, DC, JCB, MC, V. **Map** p242 E7.

Built in Italian Renaissance style, the Wiener Kursalon once hosted the famous promenade concerts of the Strauss dynasty. The Salon Orchestra 'Alt Wien' (Old Vienna) performs an all-Strauss programme, including ballet and operetta, daily from 22 March to 28 February. The Kursalon building itself is worth a look; while you're at it, visit the Mozart statue nearby on the edge of the Stadtpark.

Music: Rock, Roots & Jazz

Boomtime for all forms of popular music, with electronica centre stage.

The early 21st century sees a Vienna with a thriving music scene supported by a variety of new clubs and established (or re-established) popular venues. Over the last decade, bands, venues and music labels have boomed for a variety of reasons. Municipal authorities, led by populist Mayor Michael Häupl, have loosened up and actually welcomed a club scene which generates diversity, tax revenue, economic growth and, often, votes on election day. On at least two occasions, local officials were able to help clubs relocate from their original locations in heavily residential neighbourhoods to vastly improved premises where excessive sound levels were not a problem: the **Chelsea**, for example, was relocated several years ago to four arches beneath the U6 train line, while **Flex** relocated from the Meidling neighbourhood in the 12th district to a disused part of a tube tunnel sandwiched between the Ringstrasse and the Danube Canal.

Austria was more culturally isolated in the post-war era than other western European nations, wedged tightly along the fortified borders of the former Soviet bloc. Its entry into the European Union in the mid-1990s, combined with the fall of communism in central and eastern Europe, brought an influx of new people, including musicians, DJs and other artists. Another sea change has taken place with technology; the techno and electronic music movements have found willing adherents in Vienna, a trend which has only grown over the last decade as it has become cheaper and easier to create, record and perform.

JAZZ

Jazz has been a part of Vienna's musical landscape since the early days of the last century, and has influenced a young generation of classically trained musicians, including the late pianist Friedrich Gulda, and Michael Mantler, best known for his musical collaboration with ex-wife Carla Bley. Another member of Bley's band is sax and flautist Wolfgang Puschnig; he also worked with with Linda Sharrock, Jamaaladeen Tacuma and Kip

Hanrahan. NY-based Austrian Wolfgang Muthspiel, a fêted jazz guitarist, is another who plays regularly in Vienna.

The most famous Austrian jazz musician, however, remains Joe Zawinul, who left Vienna for the United States in the late 1950s, where he worked with Dinah Washington and Cannonball Adderly before teaming up with Miles Davis in the mid 1960s. He then went on to co-found the seminal jazz-rock group Weather Report, and since then has led the Zawinul Syndicate. Though based in the US, Zawinul is a frequent visitor to his home city where he occasionally performs (usually during the city's summer jazz festival), or hobnobs with his boyhood friend and current President of Austria, Thomas Klestil.

Jazzland has been a fixture on the international music circuit for more than 30 years, and the Vienna jazz scene has been vastly enriched recently with the opening of the new **Porgy & Bess** club. The **Konzerthaus**, traditionally a classical music palace, has recently added a jazz series to its season which has featured the likes of Cassandra Wilson, Dee Dee Bridgewater and Lalo Shifrin.

THE SCENE

Younger DJs have also been inspired by the international success of Kruder & Dorfmeister or the chameleon-like duo Pulsinger & Tunakan, whose Cheap Records label releases some of the city's most eclectic music. Dzhian & Kamien of Couch Records produce an ethno-tinged downbeat that has surfaced on a million chill-out albums and the Vienna Scientists, a loose collective around DJ-producer Jürgen Drimal, garnered a big deal with Sony on the tide of the K&D explosion. The latter's G-Stone label has also released credible albums by Viennese artists such as DJ DSL, Walkner & Möstl and Stereotyp, as well as their own solo projects – Kruder's Peace Orchestra and Dorfmeister's Tosca, whose third album *Dehli 9* appeared in early 2003.

By blending the electronic ethos with compellingly unconventional musicianship, the Sofa Surfers have produced some great albums on their Klein Records label. A broad range of

Arts & Entertainment

WUK – a funky, community-based arts complex. *See p180.*

bands ranging from the Incognito-esque funk of Count Basic to the confrontational noise of Fetish 69 or Heinz and Garish's intelligent pop to hip-hoppers such as Aphrodelics and the Waxolutionists are examples of Vienna's thriving music scene.

Vienna's uncompromising electronic label Mego releases music by local boys such as Pita, Fennesz and Farmers Manual as well as international names like Jim O'Rourke and Merzbow. Touring the world's experimental festivals circuit, they rack up more air miles than the average multinational exec but can be occasionally spotted in Vienna at **rhiz** (*see p186*).

WHAT'S GOING ON
Austria has a high percentage of internet users, and most clubs have useful websites, although handbills and posters still form mini-collages around the city. The best overall local source to find out what is going on remains the weekly newspaper *Falter*, which also features a charts page in which six music distributors and shops provide their top ten lists from the previous week; it's a good gauge of what people in Vienna are listening to. *See also p182* **Nightlife**.

Venues

Arena
3, Baumgasse 80 (info 798 85 95/bar 798 33 39/ www.arena.co.at). U3 Erdberg. **Open** *Summer* 2pm-2am daily. *Winter* 4pm-2am daily. **Concerts** free-€30. **No credit cards. Map** p240 J9.
A former slaughterhouse scheduled for demolition when it was occupied in the late 1970s by local students in a rare outburst of Austrian civil disobedience. It's favoured by the techno and neo-punk crowds, although recent attractions have included Asian Dub Foundation and Moby.

B72
8, Hernalser Gürtel Stadtbahnbögen 72 (409 2128/ www.b72.at). U6 Alser Strasse/tram 43. **Open** 8pm-4am daily. **Admission** €3-€5. **Concerts** €5-€10. **No credit cards. Map** p238 B6.
One of the new clubs which has popped up in the arches beneath the U6, B72 – which stands for *Bogen* (arch) 72 – primarily features DJs spinning alternative and reggae. Bands play about twice a week. The interior is trendy-industrial.

Café Carina
8, Josefstädter Strasse 84 (406 4322). U6 Josefstädter Strasse/tram J, 33. **Open** 5pm-2am daily. **Credit** AmEx, DC, MC, V. **Map** p238 B6.

Arts & Entertainment

Flex.

A friendly, scruffy little bar-café located under the U6 arches of the Josefstädt U6 station. There is a small kitchen serving snacks and soups, and a cheap pool table; occasionally jazz, folk and country acts play.

Café Concerto
16, Lerchenfelder Gürtel 53 (406 4795/ www.cafeconcerto.at). U6 Josefstädter Strasse/ tram 5, 33, J. **Open** 4pm-late Tue-Sat. **Admission** €5-€12. **No credit cards.** **Map** p238 B7.

A popular after-hours joint. There are gigs most nights (from 9pm) ranging from jazz, Celtic, and klezmer to folk and light rock. Staff are friendly, but the venue (in the basement) is more conducive to socialising than actually listening to music.

Chelsea
8, Lerchenfelder Gürtel U-Bahnbögen 29-31 (407 9309/www.chelsea.co.at). U6 Thalia Strasse/tram 5, 46. **Open** 6pm-4am Mon-Sat; 4pm-3am Sun. **Admission** €8-€11. **No credit cards.** **Map** p238 B7.

The hottest place on the Gürtel. Located in the arches beneath the U6, the recently expanded and refurbished Chelsea is a major venue for alternative rock, dance and techno. DJs usually spin on the nights when there are no performances, and three bars guarantee that no one goes thirsty. The action usually begins around 9pm.

Davis
21, Kürschnergasse 9 (258 4554/www.davis.at). U1 Kagran, then tram 25. **Open** 6pm-3am Tue-Sat; 6pm-1am Sun. **Admission** €10. **No credit cards.**

Not to be confused with Miles Smiles, the other Vienna club named after the late trumpeter. A cavernous club, located in and surrounded by high-rise municipal housing, it's difficult to reach by public transport; best to take a taxi. Interesting local acts include Karl Hodina, who proves the accordion can be a jazz instrument, and the very talented but underrated guitarist Karl Ratzer, who spent years in the States and cut his chops playing with the likes of Chet Baker and Eddie 'Lockjaw' Davis. There are gigs most weekends, from around 9pm.

EKH
10, Wielandgasse 2-4 (no phone). U1 Keplerplatz/ tram 6. **Open** 8pm-late Tue-Sat. **Admission** €5-€12. **No credit cards.**

The Ernst Kirchweger Haus (named for a man who died in an altercation with police) is an anarchic squatted property belonging to the Austrian Communist Party, who couldn't bring themselves to evict the intruders. The music featured is hardcore punk and as loud as it gets. Not for daytrippers or the faint of heart.

Flex
1, Donaukanal (access from Augartenbrücke) (533 7525/www.flex.at). U2, U4 Schottenring. **Open** 8pm-4am daily. **Admission** €5-€20. **No credit cards.** **Map** p243 E5.

Flex has one of the best sound systems around and uses it to maximum effect for both events and DJ nights. The club is divided into a narrow bar at the front and a performance area and bar at the back. Depending on the night, the musical menu includes techno, punk, garage, house, ska and hardcore rock.

Flex has become a major venue since relocating from its humble beginnings in Meidling. The crowd tends to be on the young side.

Galerie-Café

7, Lerchenfelder Strasse 9-11 (523 4232). U2 Lerchenfelder Strasse. **Open** 1pm-2am Mon-Fri. **No credit cards. Map** p242 C7.

A very homely place located in a half-cellar behind a bookshop. A variety of blues, funk and jazz musicians are featured, in an intimate atmosphere. The regular audience here tends to be enthusiastically loyal to the performers and to the friendly owner, Poldi Grossbard, who is also a font of information about the local music and art scenes. The walls of Galerie-Café feature regularly changing exhibitions of work by local artists, much of it quite interesting and reasonably priced.

Gasometer/BA Halle

11, Guglgasse 12 (tickets 96 096/www.g-town.at). U3 Gasometer. **Admission** from €10. **Credit** MC, V. **Map** p241 K10.

Located in one of four huge brick cylindrical gasometers recently redeveloped into a housing/shopping/entertainment complex. This long overdue medium-sized venue (with a capacity of 3,000) has recently featured Paul Weller, David Gray and Goran Bregovic. There is also the occasional rave or club night with DJs.

Jazzland

1, Franz-Josefs-Kai 29 (533 2575/www.jazzland.at). U1, U4 Schwedenplatz/tram 1, 2. **Open** 7pm-2am Mon-Sat. **Admission** varies. **No credit cards. Map** p243 F6.

A local institution. Along the bare-brick walls hang pictures of jazz musicians who have performed at the club over the last 30 years or so, from local talent to international performers. The jazz on offer ranges from dixieland to boogie, gospel and neo-swing, and there is also a rising star series which features younger talent (and once featured Diana Krall). Food, some of it vegetarian, is available, along with expensive drinks. Weekends nights can be crowded, so it is best to arrive early; concerts start at 9pm.

Konzerthaus

3, Lothringerstrasse 20 (box office 242 002/ infoline 242 00-100/www.konzerthaus.at). U4 Stadtpark/tram D. **Open** *Box office* 9am-7.45pm Mon-Fri; 9am-1pm Sat. **Tickets** €10-€104. **Credit** AmEx, DC, MC, V. **Map** p243 F8.

A pillar of the classical music establishment, the Konzerthaus nevertheless hosts an annual jazz series running from October to May. The 2002/2003 season featured Charlie Haden, Jim Hall, veteran Viennese jazz pianist Fritz Pauer, Toots Thielemans, New York based Austrian guitarist Wolfgang Muthspiel, and Wynton Marsalis with the Lincoln Center Jazz Orchestra. More challenging stuff from Vienna's electronica brigade also surfaces during festivals.

Metropol

17, Hernalser Hauptstrasse 55 (tickets 407 77 407/ www.wiener-metropol.at). U6 Alserstrasse/tram 43. **Open** 8pm-midnight Mon-Sat. **Admission** €12-€35. **Credit** AmEx, DC, MC, V. **Map** p234 B5.

This venue was originally a music hall and theatre which catered to the workers who lived in the district (Hernals) at the turn of the last century. It remains an attractive venue with plenty of tables and a very long bar, but the musical fare is all over the shop. Recent offerings have included Bill Haley's Original Comets, the Dubliners, an evening of Greek folk songs, outtakes from popular musicals, and an Elvis impersonator, along with the occasional surprise, such as a wonderful Jill Scott concert.

Miles Smiles

8, Lange Gasse 51 (405 9517). U2 Rathaus/ tram J. **Open** 8pm-2am Mon-Thur, Sun; 8pm-4am Fri, Sat. **Admission** varies. **No credit cards. Map** p242 C6.

Performers make only sporadic appearances here outside festivals such as JazzFestWien *(see p146)*, but an excellent and eclectic music collection makes for a good atmosphere regardless. Food is available at the bar.

Nachtasyl

6, Stumpergasse 53 (596 9977). U3 Zieglergasse. **Open** 8pm-4am daily. **Admission** €5-€12. **No credit cards. Map** p238 B9.

A slightly dingy cellar with a conspiratorial vibe, once a meeting place for Czechs and other refugees from communism. Even Vaclav Havel showed up once. The 'Night Asylum' now provides refuge for a younger generation with both DJ sets and eclectic acts. L-shaped, with walls covered in posters and handbills, the place provides a friendly ambience, good pub grub, and decent prices. Upstairs there is a daytime café.

Nashville

5, Siebenbrunnengasse 5a (966 7549/www.nash ville.at). Bus 12a. **Open** 6pm-2am Mon-Sat. **No credit cards. Map** p238 C10.

Off the beaten track in the blue-collar Margareten district, just down the street from the local headquarters of the Hell's Angels. But don't be alarmed: the music (from around 8pm) is mostly country, but also occasionally features blues and Celtic folk. Expect to meet many regulars and die-hard country and western fans.

Planet Music

20, Adalbert-Stifter-Strasse 73 (332 4641/ www.planet.tt). Tram N. **Open** varies. **No credit cards. Map** p235 E2.

Planet Music is located in a slightly scruffy part of the city, in a blocky, unappealing building dating back to the 1970s. It features third-rate local bands and numerous international has-beens – recently T-Rex and Big Brother & the Holding Company have both performed here, minus Marc Bolan and Janis Joplin, naturally.

Arts & Entertainment

Porgy & Bess

1, Riemergasse 11 (512 88 11/www.porgy.at). U3 Stubentor. **Open** 7.30pm-late daily. **Credit** MC, V. **Map** p243 F7.

A seedy porno cinema prior to being renovated, this is the place to hear modern and non-traditional jazz, attracting rave reviews at home and internationally. Recent international guests have included David S Ware, Tomasz Stanko, the VAO, Louis Sclavis, Leena Conquest and Lee Konitz. On Wednesdays there are jam sessions from 9pm, and DJs take to the stage at midnight at weekends. The Friday-night thinking person's house club 'Besides' (free if you've been to the concert before) features many big names. A dimly lit, plush yet relaxed outfit.

Radiokulturhaus/Radio Café

4, Argentinierstrasse 30a (box office 501 70 377/ café 503 74 04). U1 Taubstummengasse. **Open** *Box office* 2-7pm Mon-Fri; 90min before performance Sat, Sun. *Café* 9am-1am Mon-Fri; 9am-5pm Sat (until 1am on performance days). **Admission** varies. **Credit** AmEx, DC, MC, V. **Map** p239 E9.

Two venues located alongside each other in the ORF Funkhaus, the headquarters of the Austrian Broadcasting Company. One is used for larger events, the other for readings and smaller musical performances. A variety of events are held inside during cooler months, while there is an outdoor stage for summer events. Music runs from classical and jazz to world music.

Reigen

14, Hadikgasse 62 (894 0094/www.reigen.at). U4 Hietzing. **Open** 6pm-4am on concert days. **Admission** €10-€20. **No credit cards**.

Reigen features primarily jazz and world music, with a strong emphasis on Latin American performers. Recent gigs have featured guitarist Mike Stern, jazz bassist Kyle Eastwood (Clint's son), and Allegre Correa, an oft-recorded Brazilian guitarist and long-time Vienna resident.

Sargfabrik

14, Goldschlagstrasse 169 (9889 8111/ www.sargfabrik.at). U4 Hietzing/tram 52 Diesterweggasse. **Open** noon-3pm, 6pm-2am daily. **Admission** up to €30. **No credit cards**.

Named after the coffin factory which once stood here, which has been redeveloped as a much-praised housing co-operative. The café-restaurant here has an eclectic music policy, with an emphasis on small jazz ensembles and sounds from all over the world. Recent performers at Sargfabrik have included pianist Uri Caine, guitarist and bandleader Marc Ribot, Bulgaria's Ivo Papasov and local Roma violinist Mose Sisic and his group, the Modern Gypsies. Cabaret, performance art and events for children also feature.

Spark7.com

2, Südportalstrasse, Messegelände Halle 1 (1726 5665). U1 Praterstern. **Map** p240 J6.

A barn-like venue featuring big name acts but cursed with less-than-perfect acoustics. Massive Attack and Placebo both played here in spring 2003. Open on concert days only.

Stadthalle

15, Vogelweidplatz 14 (98 100-0/www.wiener stadthalle.at). U6 Burggasse. **Map** p238 A7.

A huge hall which can seat up to 10,000 fans, and is used only for big-draw events. Stadthalle also hosts occasional weekend record fairs (check the website). Open on concert days only.

Szene Wien

11, Hauffgasse 26 (749 3341/www.szenewien.com). Tram 71, U3 Enkplatz. **Admission** €25. **No credit cards**.

A medium-sized, laid-back venue with a bar and reasonable eats, staffed by a friendly young crew. A wide variety of interesting local and international jazz, world, rock and blues musicians. Recent gigs at Szene Wien have included reclusive guitarist Peter Green, 'Queen of the Macedonian Gypsies' Esma Redzepova, Calexico and the Navajo punk band Blackfire.

Tunnel

8, Florianigasse 39 (405 3465). Bus 13a. **Admission** free-€5. **No credit cards**. **Map** p238 B6.

A student café which features jazz and rock in the cellar, and inexpensive food and drink. What is lacked in talent at Tunnel is often made up for in sheer enthusiasm.

Vorstadt

16, Herbststrasse 37 (493 1788/www.vorstadt.at). U6 Burggasse. **Open** 11am-2pm Mon-Sat; 10am-midnight Sun. **No credit cards**. **Map** p238 A7.

A *Beisl*-style attraction beyond the Gürtel, an oasis in the still rather grim west end of the 16th district. Vorstadt has a highly eccentric musical programme featuring everything from string quartets to Balkan bands and singalong sessions. The odd big name such as Czech violinist/vocalist Iva Bittova or Roma singer Mona Sisic occasionally surface. Food is above-average Beisl fare and the shady courtyard a joy in summer. Well worth the long trek from the U-Bahn.

WUK

9, Währinger Strasse 59 (401 2110/www.wuk.at). U6 Währinger Strasse/tram 40, 41, 42. **Open** varies. **No credit cards**. **Map** p234 C4.

WUK stands for Werk und Kultur, or work and culture, which pretty much sums up what goes on in this large brick complex. There are workshops for courses, a gallery, kindergarten, bike repair shop, and studio space for artists. There is also a bar and a café as well as an interior courtyard to hang out in during the warmer months. In addition to theatre, dance and performance art, the large hall features DJ nights with both local and international turntable artists and musicians, usually at weekends. A funky and alternative atmosphere.

Arts & Entertainment

Porgy & Bess, a major player on the jazz scene. *See p180*.

Zu-ga-be

4, Schwarzenbergplatz 10 (no phone). Tram D.
Open 6pm-2am Tue-Sat. **Admission** €5-€15.
No credit cards. Map p243 E8.

Formerly known as Papas Tapas, Zu-ga-be shares a corner with a club called the Atrium. Good local bands (and others) play most nights; the sounds are mainly blues, but jazz, funk, and R&B get a look in too. Recurring guests include British blues singer Dana Gillespie, who has a strong following in Vienna, and tenor sax man Big Jay McNeeley. Decent food is marred by sometimes surly service. The place gets very smoky and crowded at weekends.

Festivals

For the **JazzFest Wien**, held every year from mid June to early July, and the **Wiesen** festival, *see p146* and *p181*.

The small town of **Waidhofen an der Thaya** in the Waldviertel region of Lower Austria (about a 90-minute drive north from Vienna) puts on a raucous international music festival at the end of June every year. It often seems more like a party than a festival and features folk, world, jazz and blues from near and far. For information, check out the website: www.int.musikfestwaidhofen/thaya.at.

Konfrontationen

Jazzgalerie Nickelsdorf, Untere-Hauptstrasse 13, 2425 Nickelsdorf (43 2146 235/www.konfront ationen.at). Train from Vienna Südbahnhof to Nickelsdorf Untere-Hauptstrasse. **Dates** late July.

The Nickelsdorf improvisation festival is three days of sonic madness, held in a *gasthaus* on the Hungarian border. Featuring the cream of contemporary avant-jazzers, this is one of Europe's major out-there events. 2002 featured Peter Brötzmann's Die Like A Dog quartet, British improvisors John Butcher and John Edwards and Viennese electronic dudes Fennesz and Pita. The intimate atmosphere (barely 200 people can squeeze in) of a country courtyard bedecked in vines is an ideal backdrop for experiencing some of the most challenging music around. Note that ticket prices are hefty.

Wiesen

(02626 81648-0/fax 02626 81648-29/ www.wiesen.at). Train to Südbahnhof, change at Wiener Neustadt on to regional line headed for Mattersburg-Sopron. Get off at station Wiesen-Sigless, then 15min walk to the grounds (shuttle service available).
Dates various throughout the year.

If the weather's fine, a trip out to Wiesen to catch some good sounds in well-equipped, yet utterly rural surroundings cannot be recommended too highly. Wiesen was initially a three-day Jazzfest, which throughout the 1980s attracted the very best performers. Today, in addition to the jazz, there are also a number of other weekends dedicated to pop, rock and reggae, as well as one-off concert dates throughout the year. Facilities have been improved too, and – a further plus – the stage area is now covered by a giant dome to pre-empt the unpredictable Austrian summer.

Nightlife

A laid-back, unthreatening scene, with relaxed licensing laws – bring it on.

Beyond the 1st district, Vienna's nightlife action is focused on three main areas. Just beyond the Ringstrasse lies Karlsplatz and the Naschmarkt, with bars and clubs such as **Schikander** and **Café U**. From here you're a step away from Mariahilfer Strasse, bisecting the 6th and 7th districts. On either side of this shopping concourse sit everything from cocktails bars and gay bars to several of the city's most fashionable lounges such as **Bar Italia**, **Café Leopold** and the **Ra'mien Bar**. The third major node is conveniently concentrated along the busy Gürtel ring road, in the arches beneath the U6 U-Bahn line between the stations Thalia Strasse and Josefstädter Strasse.

Megaclubs are scarce in Vienna as the locals are just not prepared to put up with the queues, the crush and the prices. However, the attraction of clubs – or *clubbings*, as they're known here – has been growing steadily since Kruder & Dorfmeister, Pulsinger & Tunakan, Waldeck and other spinners put Vienna on the remix map. The cradle of what is known here as 'underground music' is **Flex**. Promoters Sunshine Club are currently working on a new location in the Babenberger Passage, a subway beneath the Ringstrasse, opposite the Burggarten. Due to open in autumn 2003, it will probably herald the return of big name DJs to Vienna (see www.sunshine.at).

To find out what's on, check the listings weeklies *City* and *Falter* or look out for flyers. The night bus service is fairly comprehensive; it will take you home from 12.45am (when the U-Bahn stops) until 5am.

1st District

American Bar (Loos Bar)

1, Kärntner Strasse 10 (512 3283). U1, U3 Stephansplatz. **Credit** (over €20) AmEx, DC, MC, V. **Map** p243 E7.
Locals refer to it as the 'Loos Bar' after the architect Adolf Loos who designed the place in 1908. A jewel of Modernist interior design, it's now run by Marianne Kohn, grande dame of the bar scene. Cocktails are pricey but delicious.

Café Alt Wien

1, Bäckerstrasse 9 (512 5222). U1, U3 Stephansplatz. **Open** *May* 10am-2pm Mon-Thur, Sun; 10am-4am Fri, Sat. *June-Sept* 11am-4am daily. **No credit cards. Map** p243 F6.

A good café during the day, but also a fine drinking establishment after dark, with nicotine-stained ceilings, poster-covered walls and a general air of Paris circa 1968. The clientele is a mixture of students and elderly bohemians. It can get crowded.

Club Habana

1, Mahlerstrasse 11 (513 2075). U1, U2, U4 Karlsplatz/tram 1, 2, D, J/bus 3a. **Open** 8pm-4am Mon-Thur, Sun; 8pm-6am Fri, Sat. **Credit** AmEx, DC, MC, V. **Map** p243 E7.
One for serious Latin American fans, with rum and rhythms energising a devoted crowd.

Flex

1, Donaukanal (access from Augartenbrücke) (533 7525). U2, U4 Schottenring. **Open** *Bar* Oct-Apr 8pm-4am daily. May-Sept 6pm-4am daily. *Club* 10pm-4am Mon, Tue; 11pm-4am Fri-Sun. **No credit cards. Map** p243 E5.
If you only make it to one club in Vienna, aim for Flex. From humble beginnings in the suburbs when it ran a sound system, it soon became a forum for the city's best talents and a magnet for international acts and DJs. The Monday night Dub Club and Tuesday's blend of tech-house and electro are two of the most popular fixtures; Saturdays see the monthly Kruder & Dorfmeister G-Stone sessions. *See also p178.*

Kleines Café

1, Franziskanerplatz 3 (no phone). U1, U3 Stephansplatz. **Open** 10am-2am Mon-Fri; 1pm-2am Sat, Sun. **No credit cards. Map** p243 E7.
As the name suggests, the place is tiny, though architect Hermann Czech's design makes great use of mirrors. Customers, and indeed staff, are an eccentric mix of arty-intellectual, proto-bohemian types.

Onyx

1, Stephansplatz 12 (Haas-Haus, 6th Floor) (535 3969). U1, U3 Stephansplatz. **Open** 10am-2am daily. **Credit** V. **Map** p243 E7.
Politicos, celebs and captains of industry meet here for an evening drink to see and be seen. In the day the close-up view of the Stephansdom is the attraction.

Planter's Club

1, Zelinkagasse 4 (533 33 93). U2, U4 Schottenring/tram 1, 2. **Open** 5pm-3am daily. **Credit** AmEx, DC, MC, V. **Map** p242 E5.
While the front of this smart bar looks like an old library, the back has an air of a British colonial-style club. Connoisseurs say the Planter's has the best bar crew in town and a superb choice of drinks; check out the vintage rums. There is a small dancefloor where you can shuffle to predominantly Latin sounds as well as DJ Samir's rare grooves.

Roxy. *See p184.*

Volksgarten

1, Burgring 1 (532 4241). U2, U3 Volkstheater/tram 1, 2, D, J. **Open** 8pm-5am daily. **Admission** €5-€12.50. **Credit** AmEx, DC, MC, V. **Map** p243 D7.
Vienna's best-loved party complex has a magnificent location. A recent renovation has given the dancefloor a hi-tech look but the curved salon overlooking the garden retains its gorgeous 1950s fittings. Equipped with a decent sound system, the Volksgarten's crowd-pleasing menu of dance genres attracts all-comers. Drinks are expensive.

Volksgarten Pavilion

1, Burgring (532 0907). U2, U3 Volkstheater. **Open** *Mar-May, Oct* 10pm-2am daily. *June-Sept* 11am-4am daily. **No credit cards**. **Map** p242 D7.
This beautiful 1950s folly is a delight on a summer evening. At night you can enjoy floodlit boules along with a fine view of the illuminated Neue Burg to a selection of laid-back tunes. Admission is usually free, but entrance is charged for the oversubscribed Techno Café on Tuesday nights.

Bermuda Dreieck

This once hip area (the 'Bermuda Triangle') has since been deserted by the cooler DJs, although there are still some nice bars and places to eat.

First Floor

1, Seitenstettengasse 5 (533 7866). U1, U4 Schwedenplatz. **Open** 7pm-4am Mon-Sat, 7pm-3am Sun. **Credit** AmEx, DC, MC, V. **Map** p243 F6.
Designed by the fêted Eichinger oder Knechtl team, who incorporated original fittings from the 1930s Mounier Bar. The setting is attractive and dimly lit, and the staff are great.

Ma Pitom

1, Seitenstettengasse 5 (535 4313). U1, U4 Schwedenplatz. **Open** 5pm-3am Mon-Thur, Sun; 5pm-4am Fri, Sat. **No credit cards**. **Map** p243 F6.
Ma Pitom attracts a fairly mixed crowd and is usually packed at weekends. There is a splendid terrace and the place is open 365 days a year.

Roter Engel

1, Rabensteig 5 (535 4105). U1, U4 Schwedenplatz. **Open** 6pm-2am Mon-Wed, Sun; 6pm-4am Thur-Sat. **No credit cards**. **Map** p243 F6.
Designed by Coop Himmelb(l)au, this place caused a bit of a sensation at first. Now it's just another bar that's packed at the weekends. It's more enjoyable in summer when you can sit outdoors.

2nd District

Bricks

2, Taborstrasse 38 (216 3701). Tram N. **Open** 8pm-4am daily. **No credit cards**. **Map** p235 F4.
This small, dimly lit basement bar has been a late-night stalwart for years. In need of a technical and aesthetic overhaul, Bricks has good vibes and a kaleidoscopic musical programme. DJ Elk's Wednesday night '60s Forever session is popular.

Fluc

2, Praterstern (next to the cyclist subway) (0699 1925 5637/www.fluc.at). U1 Praterstern/tram 5, 21. **Open** 8pm-4am daily. **No credit cards**. **Map** p236 G5.
Fluc showcases the skills of local electromeisters such as Bernhard Fleischmann. No-holds-barred experimentation is the focus, but the atmosphere is totally chilled and the amateurish set-up (beer crates for chairs) charming.

Kafé Shabu

2, Rotensterngasse 8/Glockengasse (0664 460 2441). U1 Schwedenplatz, then tram 21, N. **Open** 9pm-2am Tue-Sat. **Credit** AmEx, DC, MC, V. **Map** p243 F6.
The itinerant Kafé Shabu appears to have settled in this former taxi drivers' hangout. Run by the owners of Schöne Perle (*see p108*), Shabu serves the local cognoscenti a selection of absinthe from around Europe. Check out the tiny 'Japanese room'.

Krieau

2, Südportalstrasse Verlängerung/Trabrennverein (720 0175). U1 Praterstern, then tram 21/U3 Schlachthausgasse, then bus 83a, 84a. **Open** varies; phone for details. **No credit cards**. **Map** p240 J6.

Arts & Entertainment

A section of Vienna's trap-racing circuit in the Prater becomes a popular club venue during the summer months. Open-air club nights feature anything from drum 'n' bass to DJ Samir's rare groove sessions. Get a taxi here, as it's a hassle by public transport.

4th District

Café Anzengruber
4, Schleifmühlgasse 19 (5878 2979). U1, U2, U4 Karlsplatz/bus 59a. **Open** 11am-2am Mon-Sat. **No credit cards. Map** p239 E8.
A favourite with the art crowd from the Schleifmühlgasse galleries. Dusty, charming art covers the walls and the atmosphere is pleasantly old-world; the food is also good. Perfect for afternoon intimacies and more boisterous entertainment later.

Club U
4, Künstlerhauspassage (505 9904/www.club-u.at). U1, U2, U4 Karlsplatz. **Open** 10pm-2am Thur, Sun; 10pm-4am Fri, Sat. **No credit cards. Map** p242 E8.
Located in one of Otto Wagner's railway pavilions, Club U is a coffee house by day and improvised danceteria when the sun goes down. Its semi-subterranean setting means that the glasses rattle on the marble tabletops when the U-Bahn goes by.

Freihaus
4, Margaretenstrasse 11/Schleifmühlgasse 7 (587 1665). U1, U2, U4 Karlsplatz/bus 59a. **Open** 11am-2am Mon-Fri; 5pm-2am Sat. **Credit** AmEx, DC, MC, V. **Map** p239 E8.
A large early-evening hangout primarily for boozers, although the food's not bad. The art crowd like it, maybe because it has curious vending machines selling second-hand English books from Shakespeare & Co (*see p133*).

Kunsthalle Café
4, Treitlstrasse 2 (586 9864). U1, U2, U4 Karlsplatz. **Open** 9am-2am daily. **No credit cards. Map** p242 E8.
A favourite of Vienna's bohos. Occupying considerably more space than the gallery itself, the bar comes into its own in summer when you can chill on the wooden-decking terrace to accomplished DJs.

Roxy
4, Operngasse 24/Faulmanngasse (961 8800). U1, U2, U4 Karlsplatz/tram 1, 2, D, J/bus 59a. **Open** 11pm-late Wed-Sat. **Admission** €5-€10. **No credit cards. Map** p242 E8.
This central late-nighter, with a plush interior, defective soundsystem and tiny dancefloor is often packed to the seams when various Vienna Scientists, Sofa Surfers and guests from abroad come to do the honours on the decks. Run by the Sunshine crew, it may well be abandoned when their new club opens in autumn 2003.

Schikaneder
4, Margaretenstrasse 22-4 (585 5888). U1, U2, U4 Karlsplatz/bus 59a. **Open** 8am-2am daily. **No credit cards. Map** p239 E8.

In late 1999 the foyer of the Schikaneder Kino (a small rep cinema) was extended to form an attractive DJ bar. Seats are sometimes removed from the cinema so that larger-scale events can be held. The regulars are a young arty set, and the Schikaneder is one of the motors behind the Naschmarkt neighbourhood's recent renaissance.

6th District

Aux Gazelles
6, Mariahilfer Strasse 1b (Rahlgasse 5) (585 6645/ www.auxgazelles.at). U2 Museumsquartier. **Open** 10am-2am Mon-Thur; 10am-4am Fri, Sat; 10am-9pm Sun. **Credit** DC, MC, V. **Map** p242 D8.
This gargantuan Moroccan fantasy (*see p112*) has a beautiful club-bar with plushly upholstered modern furnishings and a gorgeous illuminated tableau of lionesses. Musically, it's the preserve of DJs such as Cay Taylan from Vienna's Couch Records, who deal in an accessible blend of ethno-cool.

Bar Italia Lounge
6, Mariahilfer Strasse 19-21 (585 2838/www.bar italia.net). U3 Neubaugasse/bus 13a. **Open** 6.30pm-2am daily. **Credit** MC, V. **Map** p238 C8.
Beneath the cool Bar Italia (*see p126*) you'll find the even icier Bar Italia Lounge, currently one of Vienna's most happening designer boozers. Professional service includes fine cocktails, and there's an intimate atmosphere. The crowd ranges from suits to slackers and good DJs provide a lounge/downbeat soundtrack every day of the week.

Futuregarden Bar & Art Club
6, Schadekgassen 6 (585 2613). U3 Neubaugasse. **Open** 9pm-2am Tue-Sat. **No credit cards. Map** p258 C8.
An improvised hangout in the shadow of the Esterházy Park flak tower, Futuregarden blends minimal decoration, exhibitions by young artists and regular DJ nights. Relaxed, cheap and cheerful.

Jenseits
6, Nelkengasse 3 (587 1233). U3 Neubaugasse/bus 13a. **Open** 9pm-4am Mon-Sat. **No credit cards. Map** p238 C8.
The period chintz and velvet interior appears to confirm the legend that Jenseits ('the beyond') was once a brothel. It remains a wonderfully retro environment for a couple of drinks and the odd waltz round the tiny dancefloor. The music is an always appealing blend of vintage soul and funk, lounge sounds and *chansons*. Come early to avoid the late crush.

Titanic
6, Theobaldgasse 11 (587 4758/www.titanicbar.at). U2, U3 Volkstheater/bus 57a. **Open** 10pm-4am Mon-Thur; 10pm-5am Fri, Sat. **Credit** AmEx, DC, MC, V. **Map** p242 D8.
Longstanding disco-bar Titanic reinvented itself as a slightly more salubrious Latino joint. The ground floor looks pretty swish with its restaurant (pan-American cuisine), cigar lounge and cocktail bar, but

Late-night eats

Café Drechsler

*6, Linke Wienzeile 22 (587 8580). U1,
U2, U4 Karlsplatz, U4 Kettenbrückengasse/
bus 59a.* **Open** 3am-8pm Mon-Fri;
3am-6pm Sat. **No credit cards**.
Map p242 D8.

Sunrise on the Naschmarkt is best viewed
from this old coffee house, a renowned
asylum for insomniacs, Naschmarkt stall-
holders, tramps and ball-goers. The food
is good and very cheap. Like Salz & Pfeffer
(*see below*), this place is also frequented
by party people.

Gräfin vom Naschmarkt

*4, Linke Wienzeile 14 (586 3389).
U4 Kettenbrückengasse.* **Open** 4am-
2am daily. **Credit** AmEx, DC, MC, V.
Map p239 D8.

The Gräfin's kitsch interior is inhabited by
some of the city's strangest fauna. A good
place for a reconstructive goulash after a
night on the town.

Goodman

*4, Rechte Wienzeile 23 (967 44 15). U4
Kettenbrückengasse.* **Open** from 4am Mon-
Sat. **No credit cards**. **Map** p239 D8.

Eating until 8am, dancing until 10am to
anything from German crooners Schlager to
commercial hip hop and reggae, depending
on the DJ. After your meal, watch your step
on the steep descent to the club in the cellar,
home to assorted creatures of the night.

Salz & Pfeffer

*4, Joanelligasse 8 (586 6660). U4
Kettenbrückengasse/bus 57a.* **Open** 6pm-
8am Mon-Thur, Sun; 6pm-9am Fri, Sat. **Credit**
(over €26) AmEx, DC, MC, V. **Map** p239 D8.

Where post-clubbers head for food or further
refreshment. The restaurant at the back,
beyond the bar, has a large selection of good-
value Viennese dishes and is famous for its
spare ribs. You might want to close your eyes
to the kitsch decor, but the mixed clientele
and the open fire make it cosy in winter.

downstairs is still a bit dingy. Two dancefloors offer
Latin, funk, groove and hip hop to a largely South
American crowd.

7th District

Blue Box

*7, Richtergasse 8 (523 2682/www.bluebox.at). U3
Neubaugasse/bus 13a.* **Open** 6pm-2am Mon; 10am-
2am Tue-Thur, Sun; 10am-4am Fri, Sat. **Credit** MC,
V. **Map** p238 C8.

The Blue Box has been around for years, and is one
of the most popular bars in the city. There are DJs
every night, playing everything from electronica to
swing. However, the place is starting to look tatty
and late at night the thick clouds of smoke and sometimes relentless music are minuses.

Café Leopold

*7, Museumplatz 1 (523 6732/www.cafeleopold.at).
U2 Museumsquartier.* **Open** 10am-2am Mon-Fri, Sun;
10am-4am Sat. **Credit** DC, MC, V. **Map** p242 D7.

Built into the Leopold Museum, Café Leopold is the
most kicking venue in the complex. Once the museum
visitors have left, it mutates into a bar featuring reliable DJs. For visual entertainment, choose between
the video wall showing experimental films or the
panoramic window at the back.

Europa

*7, Zollergasse 8 (526 3383/www.hinterzimmer.at).
U3 Neubaugasse/bus 13a.* **Open** 9am-4am daily.
Credit (over €20) MC, V. **Map** p238 C8.

Attracts a young, clubby crowd day and night. This
is one of the few places in town where you can eat,
drink and chill out until the early morning. Behind
the steel door lies the Hinterzimmer, a backroom
club hosting regular DJ nights like Sunny Side Up,
with fm4 DJ John Megill. The look is minimalist.

Das Möbel

7, Burggasse 10 (524 9497). U2, U3 Volkstheater.
Open noon-1am Mon-Fri; 10am-1am Sat, Sun.
No credit cards. **Map** p242 D7.

Furniture is the thing here. All the pieces in the café
are the work of local designers and are for sale.
Inhabited by a groovy crowd, Das Möbel is good for
a few drinks, but food is not its finest attribute.

Pulse

*7, Schottenfeldgasse 3 (523 6020/www.pulse.co.at). U3
Zieglergasse, U6 Westbahnhof.* **Open** 7pm-2am Mon-
Fri; 8pm-2am Sat. **No credit cards**. **Map** p238 B7.

If you like a drink with a variety of beats booming
out at top volume, Pulse is a good choice. It has a
youngish crowd, good drinks and a cool, minimal
interior. A snack menu is served until 1am.

Shebeen

*7, Lerchenfelder Strasse 45 (524 7900/www.shebeen.at).
Tram 46/bus 13a.* **Open** 5pm-2am Mon; 5pm-4am
Tue-Fri; 2pm-4am Sat; 10am-2am Sun. **No credit
cards**. **Map** p238 B7.

One of Vienna's numerous pubs, heaving with
Anglophone expats and locals. Big screen footie and
draught Guinness and Kilkenny are the draws.

Arts & Entertainment

Shultz

7, Siebensterngasse 31 (522 9120). U3 Neubaugasse.
Open 9am-2am Mon-Thur; 9am-3am Fri, Sat; 5pm-
2am Sun. **Credit** AmEx, DC, MC, V. **Map** p238 C8.
A spacious '60s-style bar in a splendid Jugendstil
building, Shultz is one of the rare breed of designer
bars in Vienna. Cocktails are the mainstay. Music is
a pleasing blend of cool funk and nu-beats.

Subzero

*7, Siebensterngasse 27 (0676 544 1804/www.sub
zero.at). U3 Neubaugasse/tram 49.* **Open** 9pm-4am
Wed; 10pm-5am Fri, Sat. **Admission** €3-€8.
No credit cards. Map p238 C8.
Popular underground club with a young crowd; it's
a little claustrophobic, but good fun (witness
Playstation, ancient Pac-Man consoles and an amazing foot massage machine). Two small dancefloors
see house, techno, ragga and drum 'n' bass sessions.

Wirr

7, Burggasse 70 (929 4050/www.wirr.at). Bus 48a.
Open 6pm-2am Mon-Thur; 6pm-4am Fri, Sat; 10am-
2am Sun. **Admission** free Mon-Thur, Sun; €4-€5
Fri, Sat. **Credit** MC, V. **Map** p238 B7.
This bar-club has become the extended front room
of the alternative crowd, one that's full of mismatched sofas and thrift shop tat. The rather airless
downstairs dancehall features some of Vienna's best
nights – for example, the vintage reggae sessions.
Check the website for details.

8th District

Loop

*8, Lerchenfelder Gürtel, Stadtbahnbögen 26-7 (402
4195/www.loop.co.at). U6 Lerchenfelder Strasse/tram
46.* **Open** 7pm-2am Mon-Thur, Sun; 7pm-4am Fri,
Sat. **No credit cards. Map** p238 B7.
A fairly chilled out, attitude-free place with a relaxed
musical policy. Here you can eat, chat or rent a
boardgame in comfortable comfort.

rhiz

*8, Lerchenfelder Gürtel, Stadtbahnbögen 37-8 (409
2505/www.rhiz.org). U6 Josefstädter Strasse/tram J.*
Open 6pm-4am Mon-Sat; 6pm-2am Sun. **Admission**
free-€7. **No credit cards. Map** p238 B6.
rhiz is all plate glass, bare brickwork and visible
ducts and wiring. Fêted as the temple of Viennese
electronica, the challenging musical programme,
curated by Pita and other Mego fellas, may disturb
the uninitiated. It's not all white noise, though, and
you might hear jazz and even Johnny Cash. In summer it's all a lot less earnest, and the terrace is packed.

9th District

For **WUK**, *see p180.*

Café Stein

*9, Währinger Strasse 6-8/Kolingasse 1 (310 9515/
319 7241/www.cafe-stein.com). U2 Schottentor/
tram 1, 2, 40, 41, 42, D.* **Open** 7am-1am Mon-Sat;

9am-1am Sun. *Stein's Diner* 7pm-2am Mon-Sat.
No credit cards. Map p242 D5.
Students frequent Stein, located beside various university faculties, throughout the day. At night they
are joined by media trash and models. The food is
generally excellent, though drinks are a little
expensive and staff can be a bit humourless. Stein's
Diner boasts a lot of red leather, low lights and
occasional DJs.

Lo Vienna

*9, Alserstrasse 63 (403 52 39/www.lovienna.com).
Tram 43, 44/bus 13a.* **Open** 6pm-2am Thur, Fri;
6pm-4am Sat. **No credit cards. Map** p234 B5.
What was once Vienna's most authentic British pub
has been transformed into a 1970s lounge bar, full
of quirky lighting effects and Verner Panton-style
plastic seating, which purports to be 'your home, living room and kitchen'. Late dining, good drinks and
proximity to the Gürtel area are bonuses.

Mute

*9, Liechtensteinstrasse 104 (403 5393). U6
Nussdorferstrasse/tram D.* **Open** 5pm-2am Mon-
Wed; 5pm-4am Thur-Sat. **No credit cards.**
Map p235 D3.
Another chapter in the winning formula of noodles,
cocktails and DJs. This sleek lounge bar has low
lighting, low seating and a high posing quotient.
Music-wise, Mute got off to a good start with vari-
ous Vienna Scientists providing an appropriately
jazzy soundtrack.

12th District

U4

*12, Schönbrünner Strasse 222 (815 8307/
www.u4club.at). U4 Meidlinger Hauptstrasse.*
Open 10pm-5am daily. **Credit** AmEx, DC, MC, V.
Map p238 B10.
A cornerstone of Viennese nightlife for over two
decades. Regulars go dewy-eyed remembering
past glories (club mythology talks of aftershow
gigs by Prince and Sade) – these days it's a more
humdrum existence of such regular club events as
the popular Heaven gay night (*see p166*). Doorman
Conny de Beauclair is a local institution after 20
years in the job.

18th District

Spark

*18, Währinger Gürtel 107 (968 57 02/www.spark.at).
U6 Währinger Strasse/tram 40, 41, 42.* **Open** 6pm-
4am Mon-Fri; 7pm-4am Sat. **No credit cards.**
Map p234 C4.
Another far-flung loungey affair, Spark is an excellent bar with fine sounds, great beer and a large
selection of absinthes. (The latter can be purchased
from Absentium, a small store next door.) Decked
out in threadbare 1970s furnishings with a magnificent circular bar, Spark's DJ line-up is consistently
one of Vienna's best. Worth the trek.

Sport & Fitness

A great city for outdoor activities.

Having the Alps running through the middle of the country, Austrians are major skiing and hiking enthusiasts and the Viennese share the passions of their country cousins. While moderate mountains and wooded nature are easily reachable by public transport – with *Lederhosen* optional – there are also plenty of good places in Vienna itself to walk, run, cycle or in-line skate.

Major stadia

Ernst-Happel-Stadion
2, Meiereistrasse 7 (728 0854). U1 Praterstern, then tram 21, bus 80a. **Map** *p241 K7.*
The 49,000-seat Prater stadium – its renaming honours the Austrian international player and coach who died in 1992 – is Vienna's largest and the main venue for international football, big domestic and European fixtures, as well as some concerts.

Stadthalle
15, Vogelweidplatz 14 (981 000/ www.stadthalle.com). U6 Burggasse/Stadthalle, U3 Schwegler Strasse/tram 6, 19, 18, 49/bus 48a. **Map** *p238 A7.*
The Stadthalle hosts sporting events as varied as ice hockey (including the World Championship) and ice skating, dance, acrobatics and indoor football, as well as concerts and other non-sports events. Tickets are available from event organisers, not from the stadium itself.

Spectator sports

Football

Football is not a sport for which Austria is renowned at present, although it was not always that way – the country played a major role in the development of the game between the two world wars. Austria will also have another turn in the limelight as joint host with Switzerland to the European Championship in 2008. Vienna's two Bundesliga teams, Austria Memphis and Rapid Vienna, have the heated rivalry of any teams sharing the same city. To stereotype: Austria's fans come from the bourgeoisie, Rapid's from the working class; Austria play a more technical, intellectual game, Rapid take a more traditional, fighting approach. Both teams have participated in European cup finals – Rapid twice, Austria

once. Thanks to the massive financial support of millionaire Frank Stronach for players and coaches (hence the German star coach Christoph Daum), Austria is now the stronger team. Sold-out games are a rarity in Vienna, so it's pretty easy to get tickets up to the last minute. The national team play at the Ernst-Happel-Stadion. For tickets (around €30) call the Austrian Football Federation (727 180).

Austria Memphis Franz-Horr-Stadion
10, Fischhofgasse 10-12 (688 01 50-301, tickets 710 4528/www.fk-austria.at). U1 Reumannplatz, then tram 67/bus 15a. **Tickets** €5-€21. **Credit** (internet sales only) DC, MC, V.
The stadium has a 10,500 capacity.

Rapid Vienna Gerhard-Hanappi-Stadion
14, Keisslergasse 6 (info 910 010/www.skrapid.at). U4 Hütteldorf. **Tickets** average €15. **Credit** AmEx, DC, MC, V.
Rapid are the biggest club in Austria and they play in a stadium named after their former player turned architect, Gerhard Hanappi, who designed it. The capacity is 19,600. Tickets are also available from branches of Bank Austria.

Horse racing
The Prater has both flat-racing and trotting tracks.

Wiener Galopp-Rennverein (Viennese Galloping Race Association)
2, Freudenau/Rennbahnstrasse 65 (728 95 17). U3 Schlachthausgasse, then bus 77a. **Open** *Mar-Nov* 1 weekend day (usually for afternoon racing) every other wk. **No credit cards.**
The track at Freudenau is one of Europe's oldest racetracks, and boasts splendid, more than 150-year-old stands.

Wiener Trabrenn-Verein (Viennese Trotting Association)
2, Nordportalstrasse 274 (728 00 46/ www.krieau.at). U3 Schlachthausgasse, then bus 83a, 84a; U1 Praterstern, then tram 21. **Open** 2pm most Sun. Closed July, Aug. **No credit cards.**
Map *p236 J5.*
The Krieau track has Europe's first steel and concrete construction grandstand, built in 1912 by a student of architect Otto Wagner. It's used in summer as an open-air cinema and club location.

Arts & Entertainment

Activities

Beaches

In the summer, the Viennese convert the banks of the Danube into a river beach. The Reichsbrücke has plenty of bars and restaurants, not to mention bike and skate rental. Take the U1 to Donauinsel; free swimming spots with grassy or concrete areas to lie out on are both north and south of the bridge on either side of the Neue Donau.

Topless sunbathing is generally acceptable, but head south for the nude spots (marked FKK on maps). The Alte Donau has paying beach clubs and is more family-oriented. The most popular is the Gänsehäufel (U1 Kaisermühlen-Vienna International Centre and then bus 90A, 91A or 92A to Schüttauplatz) with both swimming pools and beaches including a peaceful nudist area.

Angelibad
21, An der oberen Alten Donau (263 22 69). U6 Neue Donau.
A large swimming area on the Old Danube, and much loved by denizens of neighbouring working-class Floridsdorf. This means there are plenty of people about, but there's lots of parkland to escape them. Make an obligatory visit to the nearby quintessential Viennese Gasthaus Birner after a day in the sun (*see p120*).

Boating

The Alte Donau is more popular for sailing; pedal and other boats can also be rented there and on the Neue Donau.

Sailing School Hofbauer
22, An der oberen Alten Donau 191 (204 3435/ www.hofbauer.at). U1 Kagran. **Open** *Apr-Oct* 9am-9pm daily. **No credit cards. Map** p237 L1.
22, Corner of Arbeiterstrandbadstrasse and Wagramerstrasse. U1 Alte Donau. **Open** *Apr-Oct* 9am-11pm daily. **Rates** phone for details. **No credit cards. Map** p237 L2.
Sailing classes in English are available at the Kagran location of the Hofbauer Sailing School. Photo ID needed as deposit. All kinds of boats and windsurfers for hire.

Wolfgang Irzl Segel-und Surfschule
22, An der unteren Alten Donau 29/Florian Berndlgasse 33-34 (203 6743/www.irzl.at). U1 Alte Donau. **Open** *Mid Apr-Sept* 9am-8pm daily. **Rates** €11 per hr sailing boat; €6 per hr rowboat; €9 per hr pedal boat; €12 per hr motorboat; €9 per hr windsurfer; €6 per hr surfbike. **Map** p237 L2.
Offers both sailing and windsurfing classes, as well as all manner of craft for hire.

Bowling

Brunswick Bowling
2, Prater Hauptallee 124 (728 0709/www.us-play.com). Tram N. **Open** 10am-1am daily. **Rates** €3.70 per person. Shoe rental €1.70. **Credit** AmEx, DC, MC, V. **Map** p234 A4.
Also at 17, Schumanngasse 107 (486 4361). Both locations have 32 lanes; the Brunswick has Big Lebowski-inspired Thursday night club sessions with name DJs.

Chess

Playing chess was a popular pastime during the heyday of Vienna's cafés, and the city still has enough of a chess tradition to support the dozens of clubs that meet regularly in cafés today. **Café Museum** (*see p125*) is the best-known café for a pick-up chess game. There's almost always someone playing a match and games are often for money. You can also play at **Café Sperlhof** (2, Grosse Sperlgasse 41, 214 5864).

Chess clubs take place on Thursday evenings at **Café Wilhelmshof** (3, Erdbergerstrasse 27, 713 2701), with a kids' session from 5-6pm, and **Wiener Billardcenter** (4, Rechte Wienzeile 35; 587 1251). Newcomers are welcome and there is usually someone who speaks English.

For further information, contact **Wiener Schachverband**, Viennese Chess Federation (14, Penzingerstrasse 72, 897 21 080/ www.chess-vienna.at). It's open from 4-8pm on Monday and 4-7pm on Wednesday.

Climbing

Kletterwand am Flakturm
6, Esterházypark (585 47 48, info 513 8500 at the Alpenverein). U3 Neubaugasse/bus 13a, 14a, 57a. **Open** *Apr-Oct* 1pm-dusk daily. **Fee** about €10 for 1hr 30min. **No credit cards. Map** p238 C8.
Scale this imposing flak tower built by the Nazis during World War II. There are 25 climbing routes reaching up to 34m (111ft), with climbing difficulties ranging from 4 to 8. Inexperienced climbers can get instruction or a safety spotter, but should call first to make a reservation. For more about the flak towers, *see p82*.

Cycling

Generally flat and with more than 700km (435 miles) of bike paths in the city and its surroundings, Vienna is excellent for cyclists. In town, bike lanes are pretty safe and convenient – they are often on the pavement, so it's the pedestrians in Vienna who need to

The mighty **Ernst-Happel-Stadion** in the Prater. **See p187**.

watch out. Popular spots for cycling include the Prater, along the Donaukanal and around the Alte and Neue Donau and on the Donauinsel (*see p86 and p87*), with bike rental places in several spots near the river (*see also p188* **Beaches***.at*). The Prater has hectares of green space and wooded areas beyond the amusement park. The Hauptallee boulevard through the Prater is popular for cycling, skating, jogging and strolling. You can also circle the Ring on a bike path. Or, for a pleasant route out of town, follow the Danube heading west (*see p202*).

Bikes can be taken on the U-Bahn and local S-Bahn trains from 9am to 3pm and after 6.30pm Monday to Friday, after 9am on Saturday and all day Sunday and holidays. Bicycles must go in carriages marked with a bike symbol and require a half-price ticket. They can be taken on trains that are marked with a bicycle symbol on their timetable; outside Vienna's central transport Kernzone (Zone 100), which covers the entire city, bikes require a special ticket. Only folding bikes can be taken on trams and they are not allowed at all on buses.

Fahrradverleih Skaterverleih Copa Cagrana

22, near the Reichsbrücke bridge, close to the Schuhski-house, on the east side of the Neue Donau in the Copa Cagrana (263 5242/0664 345 8585/ www.fahrradverleih.at). U1 Donauinsel. **Open** *Mar, Oct* 9am-6pm. *Apr, Sept* 9am-8pm. *May-Aug* 9am-9pm. **Rates** from €4.80 per hr, €24 per day city bike; €7.40 per hour, €37 per day mountain bike; €6 per hr, €30 per day in-line skates. **No credit cards**. **Map** p236 J3.

Centrally located for Donauinsel and river route exploration. All sorts of bikes for hire, including tandems, rickshaws, and bikes for the handicapped that can be pedalled with the hands. One hour free with four-hour rental. Photo ID and deposit required.

Pedal Power Radverleih

2, Ausstellungsstrasse 3 (729 7234/ www.pedalpower.at). U1 Praterstern. **Open** *Apr-Oct* 8am-8pm daily. **Rates** *(24-gear bicycle)* from €5, €4 concessions per hr; €27, €21 concessions per day. **Credit** AmEx, DC, MC, V. **Map** p236 H5.

Bikes come with locks and a map, and staff will provide advice on routes. The store can drop off and pick up bikes from hotels. From 1 May-30 September, PP offers half-day bike tours of Vienna starting at 10am from the Prater (€23, €19 concessions).

Golf

There are about 15 clubs in and around Vienna.

Golf Club Schloss Schönborn

2013, Schönborn 4 (02267 2863). By train: S-Bahn to Göllersdorf station. By car: take the A22 towards Stockerau take the Obermallebarn exit. **Open** *Mar-Nov* 9am-6pm daily. *Dec-Feb* open in good weather only – phone to check. **Fee** €55 per person/game Mon-Fri; €70 weekends. **No credit cards**.

This club, about 40km (25 miles) north of Vienna, has 27 holes spread over the grounds of a baroque castle, which now holds the clubhouse. To play during the week, golfers must be members of another club. At weekends they also need a minimum handicap: 28 for men and 36 for women.

Golf Club Wien

2, Freudenau 65a (0222 728 9564/www.ecs.net). U3 Erdberg, then bus 77a. **Open** daylight hours daily. *Office* 8.30am-12.30pm, 2-6pm daily. **Fee** €60 per person/game. **No credit cards**.

The Vienna club is Austria's oldest, founded in 1901, although the current course was built after World War II on the site of former polo grounds. An 18-hole site, it cuts through the Freudenau horse racetrack. Non-members can play during the week, if they are members of another club and have a minimum 28 handicap. At weekends, visitors may only play as guests of members.

Health & fitness

Club Danube

3, Franzosengraben 2-4, (798 8400/ www.clubdanube.at). U3 Erdberg. **Fee** day membership €13.60. **Credit** DC, MC, V. **Map** p241 K10.

The club is in the same building as U3 Erdberg, so come out of the station and take the lift to the 7th floor. With over ten locations in Vienna and uncomplicated day membership (€13.60), Club Danube is one of the most accessible fitness clubs in Vienna. It offers a wide range of activities and facilities, including fitness classes, tennis, squash, badminton, volleyball, sauna, solarium, at reasonable prices.
Branches: throughout the city.

Wiener Eislaufverein. *See p191.*

Holmes Place Lifestyle Club

1, Wien Börseplatz, Wipplingerstrasse 30 (533 97 9090/www.holmesplace.at). U2 Schottentor. **Open** 6.30am-11.30pm Mon-Fri; 9am-10pm Sat-Sun. **Fee** phone for details. **Credit** AmEx, DC, MC, V. **Map** p242 E6.

One of the most luxurious health clubs in Vienna with all the usual facilities, including a swimming pool. If you are a member of Holmes Place in the UK or elsewhere you can get half-price day membership at both the two Vienna locations. Otherwise you need to know a member in Vienna and pay full price. **Branch:** 20, Wien Kaiserwasser, Wagramerstrasse 17-19 (263 89 89).

John Harris

1, Nibelungengasse 7 (587 3710/www.john harrisfitness.at). U1, U2, U4 Karlsplatz. **Open** 6.30am-11pm Mon-Fri; 9am-9pm Sat, Sun. **Fee** €25.50 one-day pass. **Credit** AmEx, DC, MC, V. **Map** p242 E8.

Facilities include weights, cardiovascular machines, aerobics and dance classes, solarium, massage, sauna, jacuzzi, t'ai chi classes and a swimming pool. If you belong to a club with IHRSA affiliation, the discounted pass is €15.

Manhattan Fitness & Squash

19, Heiligenstädter Lände 17 (368 7311-0/ www.manhattan.at). U4/U6 Spittelau/tram D. **Open** 7am-midnight Mon-Fri; 9am-10pm Sat, Sun. **Rates** one-day pass €22 (includes squash). **Credit** AmEx. **Map** p235 D1 .

A large club with 22 squash courts, as well as weights, sauna, steam room, pool, golf practice court, badminton court, restaurant, shop, aerobics and t'ai chi classes.

Wellness Park Oberlaa

10, Kurbadstrasse 16 (6800 99700/www.oberlaa.at). U1 Reumannplatz, then tram 76. **Open** *Racket sports* 8am-10pm Mon-Fri; 8am-9pm Sat, Sun. *Fitness centre* 7.30am-11pm Mon-Fri; 8am-9pm Sat, Sun. **Rates** *Racket sports* €26 per day. *Fitness centre* €16 day card. **Credit** DC.

This park has a fitness centre with weights and machines, aerobics and other classes, a sauna and massage rooms. It also has 13 indoor and five out-door tennis courts, as well as 14 squash courts and 15 badminton courts.

Hiking

Hiking is extremely popular among Austrians. For a touch of the woods and mountains, the **Wienerwald** (*see p200*) to the north-west of the city is a good place to explore. Equally, the area around the spa towns **Baden** and **Bad Vöslau** (*see p200*) to the south of the city (and worth a visit for themselves) is also great for day trips. Trails are pretty well marked and the free tourist office map is enough to orient you. For a detailed map of the

Wienerwald with hiking and bike routes, Freytag & Berndt publishes the *Wienerwald Wanderatlas* for €13.90.

Another place to try hiking is the Donau-Auen national park, created in 1996, which spreads east from the Danube near Vienna. To reach a 3km nature walk laid out in the park, take the U1 to Kagran, then bus 93a to the Danzergasse stop. Or try the Lainzer Tiergarten – former royal hunting grounds, open March to November. *See p93.*

If you fancy a good long walk without the hassle of getting there, you can also head for the 'green' Prater (U1 Praterstern or terminus of tram N). You can either walk straight up the Hauptallee and back or branch off into the woods on either side. The so-called Lusthaus, a quaint round former hunting pavilion, or the Altes Jägerhaus restaurant next to it at the end of the Hauptallee are good for a well-earned coffee and cake.

Ice-skating

Try these outdoor skating rinks to get a feeling of Vienna as a winter wonderland. Or, if you fancy something more close to nature and have your own skates, head out to the Old Danube for a skate on the river (U1 Alte Donau). From late January to early March an annual ice-skating rink opens in Rathausplatz (*see p69*). The Eistraum (Dream on Ice) festival (9am-11.30pm daily) has evening light shows and bands.

Wiener Eislaufverein

3, Lothringerstrasse 22 (713 6353). U4 Stadtpark. **Open** late Oct-early Mar 9am-8pm Mon, Sat, Sun; 9am-9pm Tue, Thur, Fri; 9am-10pm Wed. **Admission** €7; €2.50-€5 concessions; boot rental €5.50. **No credit cards. Map** p243 F8.

This open-air rink also has a Punsch bar.

In-line skating

The outdoor sites listed for cycling are popular with in-line skaters too, though it's also not uncommon in Vienna to see someone doing their grocery shopping on skates. There's a small ramp area for skaters in the Prater near the Riesenrad. There are other skate rental places near the Danube, including at the Floridsdorfer Brücke on the Donauinsel. *See also p189* **Fahrradverleih Skaterverleih Copa Cagrana.**

Skatelab

2, Engerthstrasse (214 9565/www.skatelab.at). U1 Vorgartenstrasse/bus 11a. **Open** *Nov-Apr* 2-9pm Tue-Fri; 10am-8pm Sat, Sun. **Admission** €6.75; €3.50-€5.30 concessions. **No credit cards. Map** p236 H4.

This indoor in-line-skating rink has a street course with obstacles, mini-ramps and videos for skaters who can't wait for good weather. It's popular with teenagers, although older folks do skate here too. You have to bring your own skates, but (free) skateboards are available.

Jogging

Jogging is a popular pastime in Vienna and the city has a safe enough feel that runners (in particular women) shouldn't feel afraid. For a pleasant run convenient to the centre, try the path along the Donaukanal. The most popular stretch is the Prater Hauptallee, but joggers also like the Augarten in the 2nd district and the grounds of the Belvedere in the 3rd district. For those that fancy a competitive race, there's the **Silversterlauf** on New Year's Eve (*see p149*) and the **Vienna Marathon** in May (*see p146*).

Skiing

Austrians claim that this is where modern alpine skiing developed and more than 60 per cent of the country is classified as 'alpine landscape'. Snow sports are hugely popular, with almost half the population practising either downhill, cross-country skiing or snowboarding. One-day package trips from Vienna are an easy way to sample this most Austrian of activities. Many travel agencies offer one-day bus trips to ski slopes from December to March – try Columbus Reisebüro (1, Lueger Ring 8, 534 110). Austrian Railways also offers an all-inclusive day trip. Dieters Schizug ('Dieter's ski train') runs at weekends and holidays from early December to early March. The €37 cost includes a round-trip train ride, transfers to the slopes and a one-day lift ticket at **Semmering** area sites. Check with travel agencies at Vienna train stations or phone 5800 34247. *See also p208.* Also during the ski season, look for the *Snow & Fun* brochure in train stations. It lists a few one-day ski trips to Lower Austria from Vienna, with train, transfer to the ski site and lift ticket packages available for €37 to €45.

Hohe Wand Wiese

14, Mauerbachstrasse 174 (979 1057). U4 Hütteldorf, then bus 249, 449. **Open** *Dec-Mar* 9am-9.30pm Mon-Fri; 9am-10pm Sat, Sun. **Fees** €6 10-ride lift ticket; €13 1-day pass; €9 half-day pass (from 1pm). **No credit cards**.
A good local skiing site. Hohe Wand Wiese has snow cannons ready once there's a deep enough natural base, but season opening may be delayed until there's sufficient snow.

Swimming

Vienna has a large number of indoor and outdoor pools and is one of the few capital cities in Europe where you can swim in the river in summer (*see p188* **Beaches**). Many of the older baths are worth a visit for touristic as well as sporting purposes.

Amalienbad

10, Reumannplatz 23 (607 4747). U1 Reumannplatz.
Amalienbad offers beautiful *Jugendstil* baths with solarium, massage, towel service, foot and cosmetic treatments and a restaurant, along with indoor pools. There are men's, women's and mixed sessions in the two large sauna rooms.

Krapfenwaldbad

19, Krapfenwaldgasse 65-73 (320 15 01). Bus 38a.
Vienna's poshest pool, in a magnificent setting high above Grinzing, with stupendous city views. Run by the council since 1923, K has period-piece wooden changing rooms, Mediterrenean pines and two pools. Bars, nude area and wooden loungers. Gets very crowded in summer.

Thermalbad Oberlaa

10, Kurbadstrasse 14 (6800 99600/www.oberlaa.at). U1 Reumannplatz, then tram 76.
This spa has five indoor and outdoor thermal pools, two children's pools, three whirlpools and men's, women's and mixed saunas, as well as services including a solarium and massage and herbal and eucalyptus rooms. The spa is part of a large complex; *see p191* **Wellness Park Oberlaa**.

Tennis

Vienna has dozens of tennis courts, more indoor than out. Look at the *Gelbe Seiten* (Yellow Pages) under *Tennishallen*. The city also hosts the CA (Creditanstalt Bank) Trophy tournament every October. *See also p191* **Wellness Park Oberlaa**.

Tennis Point Vienna

3, Corner of Baumgasse and Nottendorfergasse (799 9997/www.tennispoint.at). U3 Erdberg.
Open 7am-10pm daily. **Fees** €21-€30 per hr tennis; €8-€10 per 30min squash. **No credit cards**. **Map** p240 J9.
A complex with ten indoor tennis courts, six badminton courts and two squash courts.

Tennis Wien Leistungszentrum

2, Wehlistrasse 320 (726 2626-0/ www.tenniswien.at). U1 Praterstern then tram 21/bus 83a, 80b. **Open** 8am-10pm daily.
Rates €14.50-€26 per hr. **Credit** DC.
Run by the Viennese Tennis Federation. The centre has nine indoor and 11 outdoor courts; tennis classes are available. Phone for a reservation. There's also a restaurant, sauna and shop.

Theatre & Dance

State-funded yet often cutting-edge, the city's performing arts thrive.

The Volksoper ballet troupe performing at **TanzQuartierWien**. See p194.

The Viennese love and hate their theatre with a passion. Beyond their identification with a great theatre tradition, they in fact have a personal stake in it: a laudable proportion of the taxpayers' money subsidises the performing arts. The funding for both established institutions and fringe groups is unsurpassed in Europe. The result is a thriving theatre culture, and a large, sophisticated theatre-going audience of all ages. Regarded as much more than entertainment, theatre plays a vital role in social life and in debates on Austrian cultural politics. This is due, at least in part, to the fact that the heads of the state theatres are government appointees. Controversial directors, programming and productions are discussed as seriously as political scandals, and people take sides in the arguments regardless of whether they have actually ever been to the theatre in question or not. When the conservative People's Party formed a coalition government with Jörg Haider's Freedom Party in 2000, protesters piled into the plush seats of the **Burgtheater** and **Volkstheater** to hear local and international intellectuals hash out the issues in theatre-sponsored panel discussions. Today journalists are keeping a watchful eye on the present government, to ensure that fringe groups do not lose their funding.

The Viennese are on the whole disdainful of spectacle, so global blockbuster touring troupes are generally confined to peripheral venues. At the core of the scene is reliable, well-crafted theatre, ranging from classical to experimental. Young playwrights, directors and actors are fostered at venues as diverse as the great classical Burgtheater and the fringe **Rabenhof**, which offers the most provocative plays and productions in town. The **Schauspielhaus** regularly hosts new work from Eastern Europe, the Middle East, and elsewhere. The **TanzQuartierWien** is pursuing an experimental, interdisciplinary 'performance' programme, which renders formal distinctions between artistic genres superfluous.

For a special treat, check out the English Lover's late-night improvisations and theatre jams at **dietheater Künstlerhaus**, the **Ensembletheater** and the **Theater in der Drachengasse**. There is also a large enough audience in Vienna to have supported two English-language theatres, the **English Theatre** and **International Theater**, for many years.

Every month, the tourist information office puts out a calendar (*Program*) of cultural events. The English-language newspaper *Austria Today* also provides some listings. The most comprehensive listings and reviews are in the programme section of the weekly magazine *Falter*. Most of Vienna's theatres are closed in July and August. The **Wiener Festwochen** (*see p146*) runs from mid May through June, featuring an excellent, broad selection of premières and contemporary productions of new and classic works. The new festival series **forumfestwochen ff.** focuses on young directorial talent, primarily from Eastern Europe.

Dance

Contemporary dance has now found a base in Vienna. Located in the MuseumsQuartier, the multifunctional dance centre **TanzQuartierWien** (TQW) began its second season in September 2002. Director Sigrid Gareis runs a densely packed, rigorous programme of local and international experimental performance, theoretical discussions, interdisciplinary projects, and training for professional dancers. Under constant fire at home for its consistently experimental programming, the TQW is the object of great interest, admiration and envy abroad. The **Volksoper** ballet has been transformed into a first-rate modern ballet company and box-office draw by Liz King and her **TanzTheaterWien**. Extraordinarily, the new Volksoper director is axing them after June 2003. Look for them elsewhere in town as of September 2003. The talented dancers of the **Staatsoper** ballet are artistically underchallenged by choreography one would expect in a provincial theatre rather than a great opera house.

A very active fringe scene of local companies keeps dance on the programme of numerous smaller venues. **dietheater Künstlerhaus** hosts the fine **imagetanz** festival of small contemporary dance works every March and October. **ImPulsTanz** (mid July to mid August; *see p149*), a high-quality, broad-based international dance festival, provides the opportunity to view seminal works of contemporary dance, as well as the work of young choreographers from Johannesburg to Estonia and, of course, Austria. The festival also offers an extensive selection of workshops from beginner to professional levels in nearly every conceivable form of movement and dance, by top artists and trainers from all over the globe.

TanzQuartierWien (TQW)

7, Museumsplatz 1 (581 3591/evening box office 524 3321-1126/www.tqw.at). U2 Museumsquartier, U2,U3 Volkstheater/tram 1, 2, D, J, 49. **Box office** 10am-8pm Mon-Fri; 10am-7pm Sat; from 1hr before evening performance. **Tickets** €4-€17. **Credit** AmEx, DC, MC, V. **Map** p242 D7.

Vienna's first facility dedicated exclusively to dance. The ambitious local and international experimental performance programme usually runs from Thursday to Saturday, and changes nearly every week. Performances generally take place in Halle G, in the Kunsthalle building next to the lava-grey Museum Moderner Kunst. Dance workshops, theoretical discussions and symposiums are held in the TQW studio spaces near the Leopold Museum.

Theatre

Main venues

The **Burgtheater**, **Akademietheater** and **Kasino am Schwarzenbergplatz** are all under the Burgtheater's management. Tickets may be obtained at its ticket office, and through the **Österreichische Bundestheaterkassen** (*see p168*). On Tuesdays, many theatres charge half price for tickets.

Akademietheater

3, Lisztstrasse 1 (info 51444-4140/tickets 51444-4740). U4 Stadtpark/tram D, 71. **Box office** 8am-6pm Mon-Fri; 9am-noon Sat, Sun; from 1hr before evening performance. **Tickets** €7-€44. **Credit** AmEx, DC, MC, V. **Map** p243 F8.

The 500-seat Akademie was taken over in 1922 by the Burgtheater, at the request of the actors, for staging chamber works. Visitors to the city often overlook the Akademietheater in favour of the more famous Burgtheater, but the Viennese themselves appreciate the opportunity to see the actors in a more intimate atmosphere.

Burgtheater

1, Dr-Karl-Lueger-Ring 2 (info 51444-4145/tickets 51444-4440/www.burgtheater.at). U2, U3 Volkstheater or U2 Schottentor/tram 1, 2, D. **Box office** 8am-6pm Mon-Fri; 9am-noon Sat, Sun; from 1hr before evening performance. **Tickets** €7-€44. **Credit** AmEx, DC, MC, V. **Map** p242 D6.

The Burgtheater has upheld its status as the standard-bearer of classical theatre in the German-speaking world since it opened its doors in 1888. Like many Ringstrasse edifices, the building itself was blighted by functional defects and had to be remodelled shortly after completion to improve its appalling acoustics and poor visibility. A joke at the time claimed that 'In Parliament you can't hear anything, in the Rathaus you can't see anything and in the Burgtheater you can neither see nor hear anything'. Today the theatre is a fabulous historical monument, but what happens on stage is usually

The **Volkstheater**, a cornerstone of establishment drama. *See p196*.

anything but antiquated. The Burgtheater's outstanding ensemble is a magnet for such innovative directors as Martin Kusej and Andrea Breth, whose profound reconsiderations of classic works make for compelling theatre. There are no regular performances in July and August, but guided tours are available all year round. The Burgtheater seats 1,175 with standing room for 85.

English Theatre

8, Josefsgasse 12 (402 12 60-0/www.english theatre.at), U2 Lerchenfelderstrasse. **Box office** 10am-7.30pm Mon-Fri. *Non-performance days* 10am-5pm Sat. *Performance days* 5-7.30pm Sat. **Tickets** €13.50-€35.50. **Credit** MC, V. **Map** p238 C7.

Founded in 1963, the English Theatre has built a reputation for quality performances among the Anglophile and expat communities that it doesn't always live up to – especially when producing its own work. It hosts visiting groups from the UK and the US and has attracted the varied likes of Anthony Quinn, Larry Hagman and Leslie Nielsen to its boards. *The Red Hot Devil Battery Sign* by Tennessee Williams and Edward Albee's *Three Tall Women* had their Austrian premieres here.

International Theatre

9, Porzellangasse 8 (319 6272/www.international theatre.at). Tram D. **Box office** 11am-3pm Mon-Fri. *Performance days* 6-7.30pm. **Tickets** €20-€22; €11 concessions. **Credit** MC, V. **Map** p235 D4.

A youthful, gung-ho expat company that will celebrate its 30th anniversary in 2004.

Kasino am Schwarzenbergplatz

3, Schwarzenbergplatz 1 (51444-4830). U4 Stadtpark/tram D, 71. **Box office** 8am-6pm Mon-Fri; 9am-noon Sat, Sun; from 1hr before evening performance. **Tickets** varies. **No credit cards.** **Map** p243 F8.

Many a young directorial talent has launched a career in this most gorgeous of small theatre spaces in Vienna. The Kasino was originally the residence of Franz Josef's brother, Archduke Ludwig Viktor. With seating for a maximum of 200, it has been used by the Burgtheater since the 1970s for up-close experimental work.

Rabenhof

3, Rabengasse 3 (712 82 82/www.rabenhof.at). U3 Kardinal Nagl Platz/bus 74a. **Box office** 3-6pm Wed-Fri. *Performance nights* until 8pm. **Tickets** €16-€22. **Credit** MC, V. **Map** p240 H9.

This theatre, which reopened rather tumultously under the direction of Karl Welunschek in January 2001, has earned a reputation for refreshingly unpredictable work which teeters titillatingly between intellectualism and trash. For truly tilted takes on morbidness and other Viennese obsessions, this is the place to go.

Schauspielhaus

9, Porzellangasse 19 (317 0101/www.schaus pielhaus.at). U4 Rossauer Lände/tram D. **Box office** 3pm to 1st performance Mon-Fri; from 5pm Sat, Sun. **Tickets** €20; €10 concessions. **Credit** AmEx, DC, MC, V. **Map** p235 D4.

Under the energetic new direction of Airan Berg and Barrie Kosky, this theatre puts on original

The **Burgtheater**. *See p194.*

wider public than the Burgtheater. The theatre has added plays in translation to its repertoire; for example, *Master Class*, starring the divine Andrea Eckert. The Volkstheater's director Emmy Werner is the first female director of a mainstream Viennese theatre.

Smaller venues

For details of the Odeon, *see p172.*

dietheater Konzerthaus
3, Lothringerstrasse 20 (tickets 587 0504/office 587 8774/www.dietheater.at). U4 Stadtpark/tram D. **Box office** 4.30-7pm Mon-Sat; from 1hr before evening performance. **Tickets** €13; €10 concessions. **No credit cards. Map** p243 F8.
Housed in what was once a restaurant in the cellar of the original Konzerthaus, this 50-seat space shares only a front door with the rest of the Konzerthaus.

dietheater Künstlerhaus
1, Karlsplatz 5 (tickets 587 0504/www.dietheater.at). U1, U2, U4 Karlsplatz/tram 1, 2, D, J. **Box office** 4.30-7pm Mon-Sat; from 1hr before evening performance. **Tickets** €14.50; €11.50 concessions. **No credit cards. Map** p243 E8.
Two stages, dietheater Konzerthaus and dietheater Künstlerhaus, joined forces under the umbrella label dietheater Wien, to provide a performance forum for young local and international artists and small companies across the spectrum of the performing arts.

Ensembletheater
1, Petersplatz 1(office 535 3200/evenings 533 2039/ www.ensembletheater.at). U1, U3 Stephansplatz. **Box office** 10am-6pm Mon-Fri; from 1hr before evening performance. **Advance ticket sales** 1, Marc-Aurel-Strasse 3-6. **Tickets** €9-€18. **Credit** DC, M, V. **Map** p243 E6.
Cellar arches lend charm – not to mention a bar area where drinks are served until 1am. The accent is on 20th-century works with a political bent; lots of Brecht, plus German-language versions of Pinter and O'Neill.

Gruppe 80
6, Gumpendorferstrasse 67 (586 5222/ office@gruppe80.at). U2 Volkstheater/bus 13a. **Box office** 10am-6pm Mon-Fri. *Performance nights* 7-9pm. **Tickets** €8-€12. **Credit** V. **Map** p238 C8.
Founded in 1980, Gruppe 80 has established itself as one of Vienna's leading female theatres, and as a particularly receptive partner for contemporary Austrian playwrights premiering new work.

Theater in der Drachengasse
1, Drachengasse 2/Fleischmarkt 22 (tickets 513 1444/www.drachengasse.at). U1, U4 Schwedenplatz. **Box office** 3.30-7pm Tue-Sat. **Tickets** €7.50-€15. **Credit** V. **Map** p243 F6.
A tiny space that presents avant-garde chamber works in various languages. Look for the itinerant English Lovers improvisation group playing every second Friday night at the bar.

productions tackling difficult social and political themes, as well as fresh renderings of classics (such as an all-female *Macbeth*). Young authors and discussions of a wide variety of theatre-related issues, are promoted in the Writers' Laboratory and through regularly scheduled readings. Enjoy pre- and post-play conversation in the congenial S-bar.

Theater Akzent
4, Theresianumgasse 18 (501 65 3306/www.akzent.at). Tram D. **Box office** main office (Argentinierstrasse 37) 8am-6pm Mon-Fri; from 1hr before evening performance. **Tickets** varies. **Credit** AmEx, DC, MC, V. **Map** p239 F9.
Performances at the Akzent include everything from drag revues to children's theatre. The quality of the productions and price of the tickets vary, as the stage is rented by different groups.

Theater in der Josefstädt
8, Josefstädter Strasse 26 (42 700/ www.josefstadt.org). U2 Rathaus/tram J. **Box office** 10am to 1st performance Mon-Fri; 1pm to 1st performance Sat, Sun. **Tickets** €4-€50. **Credit** AmEx, DC, MC, V. **Map** p238 C6.
Built in 1788 and remodelled in neo-classical style by Josef Kornhäusel in 1922, the theatre is one of the oldest and best loved in Vienna. The first-time visitor will be impressed by the sight of the ornate chandeliers rising as the lights go down. The Theater in der Josefstädt reached its apotheosis between the wars under Max Reinhardt's direction, before he fled to Hollywood. Today its productions are generally more traditional than those of the Burgtheater.

Volkstheater
7, Neustiftgasse 1 (info 523 35 01-0, tickets 524 7263/7264/info@volkstheater.at). U2 Volkstheater/ tram 49/bus 48a. **Box office** 10am to performance Mon-Sat. **Tickets** €7.50-€38. **Credit** AmEx, DC, MC, V. **Map** p242 D7.
A founding principle of the Volkstheater, built in 1889, was to present German dramatic literature to a

Trips Out of Town

Getting Started

Stunning scenery – only an hour away.

Vienna is located within an hour of breath-taking countryside: vineyards, the Danube, the Alps, the Vienna Woods, forests, and marshlands. Those with a yen for the east can explore Slovakia, Slovenia, Hungary and the Czech Republic – all no more than two hours' drive away.

The Austrian Tourist Board is so organised that even Austrians use it. Staff book hotels that often include extras such as a ski pass or wine tasting. The main office for the places below is the **Lower Austria Tourist Information** in Vienna, where phones are usually answered promptly, correct information is provided and English spoken. The website also yields useful travel material. For detailed information about areas or tours, phone the regional offices below.

Lower Austria South Alpine Region/Semmering

Passhöhe, Semmering (02664 20 025). **Open** 8am-noon, 1-4pm Mon-Fri.

Lower Austria Tourist Information

1, Walfischgasse 6 (513 8022-0/www.tiscover.com). U1, U2, U4 Karlsplatz/tram 1, 2, D, J. **Open** 9am-6pm Mon-Fri.

Thermal Baths Region Wienerwald

Kurdirektion, Baden by Vienna (02252 45 030/ www.wienerwald.info). **Open** 10am-10pm daily.

Tourist Region Vienna Woods

Hauptplatz 11, Purkersdorf (0223 1621 7612/ tourismusregion.wienerwald@netway.at). **Open** 9am-5pm Mon-Fri.

Wachau-Nibelungengau Tourist Information

Undstrasse 6, Krems (02732 85620). **Open** 9am-6pm Mon-Fri; 10am-noon, 1-7pm Sat.

By boat

It's easy to travel by boat to Bratislava, Budapest and the Wachau in summer – vessels leave from Reichsbrücke on the Danube canal. Children aged 10-15 travel half price, under-10s free. Bicycles are allowed, but passengers should state their intention to bring them when booking a ticket. It takes longer to travel against the current (north), so cyclists often take the boat one way, and pedal back.

DDSG Blue Danube

Booking and information: 1, Friedrichstrasse 7 (58 880-0/fax 5888 0440/www.ddsg-blue-danube-at). U1, U2, U4 Karlsplatz. **Open** 9am-6pm Mon-Fri.
Boats to Bratislava: *19-30 Apr* leaves 9am, returns 5pm Wed-Sun; *3 May-2 Sept* leaves 9.30am, returns 5.45pm Wed-Sun; *6 Sept-29 Oct* leaves 9am, returns 4pm Wed-Sun. **Journey times** *outwards* 1hr 30mins; *return* 1hr 45mins. **Tickets** *One way* €21, €10.50 6-15s; *return* €32, €16 6-15s.
Boats to Budapest: *Apr-Oct* leaves 9am, returns 9am daily; *1 May-28 July* leaves 8am, returns 8am daily; *29 July-3 Sept* leaves 8am, 1pm, returns 8am, 1pm daily. **Journey times** *Outwards* 5.5hrs; *return* 6hrs 20mins. **Tickets** *One way* €75, €37.50 6-15s; *return* €99, €44.50 6-15s.
The Wachau: *11 May-28 Sept* leaves Vienna Reichsbrücke 8.45am, arrives Krems 1.55pm, Dürnstein 2.30pm; leaves Dürnstein 4.30pm, Krems 4.50pm, arrives Vienna 8.45pm, Sun. **Tickets** *One way* €16.50, €8.25 10-15s; *return* €22, €11 10-15s; free under-10s.

By bike

Vienna's excellent bike paths are well marked along most roads of the inner city. If you want to cycle out of town, it's best to hit the Danube Bike Trail and either head south towards Budapest, or, even better, north towards Klosterneuburg and the Wachau. For more information, *see p200*. For bike hire firms within Vienna, *see p189*.

By train

Fast, reliable Austrian Railways is the main public transport system for travelling outside Vienna. There are four types of train: *Schnellzüge* are the fast trains with few stops, *Eilzug* trains are slightly more ponderous, and the *Intercity* and *Eurocity* only travel between major conurbations. Only the Schnellzug, IC and EC take reservations. For short trips from Vienna, most trains leave every hour, so it's possible simply to arrive at the station and take the next service. There are three train stations in Vienna: the Franz-Josefs-Bahnhof (for trains travelling north), Westbahnhof (west) and Südbahnhof (south and east). It's usually, but not always, fairly logical which train station to choose based on the direction you want to travel. However, as train schedules change frequently, check the times first with the ÖBB

Trips Out of Town

information service (*see below*). Staff are easy to get hold of and speak English. You can buy a ticket either on the train or in the station. It's almost always cheaper to buy a train ticket in conjunction with other public transport, so if you arrive by U-Bahn, tram or bus, show your ticket to the conductor.

ÖBB Austrian Railways

(Information 05 1717; booking 05 17001).
To Baden bei Wien: From Südbahnhof, *first train* 4.38am, *last train* 00.37pm; trains leave every 30min at peak times, with fewer trains in the evenings. **Journey time** 30mins. **Tickets** €3 one way in conjunction with a used public transport ticket, otherwise €4.50.

To Klosterneuberg: From Franz-Josefs-Bahnhof, *first train* 5.03am, *last train* 23.38pm; trains leave every 30min Mon-Fri, hourly Sat, Sun. **Journey time** 15mins. **Tickets** €1.50 one way (one public transport ticket) in conjunction with a used public transport ticket, otherwise €3.

To Krems (for Wachau): From Franz-Josefs-Bahnhof, *first train* 5am, *last train* 7pm; trains leave hourly. **Journey time** 1hr 10mins. **Tickets** €10.20 one way.

To Melk: From Westbahnhof, *first train* 5.07am, *last train* 11.40pm; direct trains leave every 2hrs. You can also travel to St Pölten and change; trains leave on the hour. **Journey time** 1hr 10mins. **Tickets** €12.90 one way.

To Schneeberg (Puchberg am Schneeberg) (spring, summer, autumn only): From Südbahnhof, *first train* 5.38am, *last train* 8.57pm; trains leave every 2hrs. Change trains in Wiener Neustadt for Puchberg. **Journey time** 1hr 30mins. In winter the Wiener Neustadt to Puchberg section is closed. There are special steam trains that leave for Puchberg up the Schneeberg mountain. Check with the Lower Austria Tourist Information (*see p198*) or any train station for times, and book, as it fills up fast. **Tickets** €22 return.

To Semmering: From Südbahnhof, *first train* 4.38am, *last train* 10.45pm; trains leave hourly. **Journey time** *Schnellzug* 1hr 15mins; *Eilzug* 2hrs. As the journey is particularly beautiful, take the slower train (sit on the left-hand side of the train for the best views). **Tickets** €14 one way.

By bus

The Austrian railway infrastructure, especially out of Vienna, is so good that most people opt for the train when not using their car. Buses are mainly used by Vienna's eastern European residents when travelling back to their homelands. As Austria's eastern borders form a gateway to the entire European Union, border control for buses tends to be time consuming.

Eurolines Austria

3, Invalidenstrasse 5 (712 0453/www.eurolines.at). *U3 Erdberg, Erdbergstrasse/bus 74a.* **Open** for reservations 6.30am-8.30pm Mon-Fri; noon-4.30pm Sat, Sun. **Credit** AmEx, DC, MC, V.
To Bratislava: *first bus* 8am, *last bus* 10pm; 7 times daily. **Journey time** 1hr 30mins. **Tickets** *One way* €10.90, €9.90 under-26s; *return* €19.60, €17.40 under-26s.
To Budapest: 7am, 11am, 5pm, 7pm Mon-Fri, Sun; 7am, 11am, 3pm, 5pm, 7pm Sat. **Journey time** 3hrs 45mins. **Tickets** *One way* €28; *return* €39.

Postbus

Information 71 101/www.postbus.at
In winter months there is a bus service that operates to some ski areas near Vienna. Phone Postbus information for details.

By car

The Austrian motorways are mostly four lanes and fast. Until recently they were also free. Heavy traffic from eastern Europe has taken its toll on the roads, so now a *Pickerl* road tax sticker is required for all cars using the motorways. Valid for one month or one year, the sticker can be bought at the borders and at most Trafik shops. Fines can be heavy if drivers are caught without a Pickerl.

Getting out of Vienna is easy: just follow the Ringstrasse to find all roads and signposts you need. The A2 takes you south to Graz; the S6, a well-posted motorway, goes to Semmering. The Rax turn-off is at Gloggnitz, follow route 27 to Reichenau and Payerbach. For Schneeberg, leave the A2 at Weiner Neustadt, following route 26 to Puchberg.

The A4 is a new motorway all the way to Budapest, follow signs to Schwechat airport. Bratislava is also beyond the airport off the A4 on route 7.

To Mikulov in the Czech Republic: follow the A7 north along the Danube canal in the direction of Brno; Mikulov is around 10 kilometres (six miles) across the border.

To the Wachau: take the A1 to Melk, then drive down either side of the Danube to Krems, returning along route 3 over Stockerau and Klosterneuburg.

Trips Out of Town

The Vienna Woods

Discover the verdant bronchioles of the city's green lungs.

The Vienna Woods, or Wienerwald, inspired Schubert, Beethoven, Mozart, Strauss and Schönberg, and still make Viennese hearts sing. Few cities have the luxury of such a large area of protected natural reserves at such close hand. The Woods cover an enormous area of forests, hills and wilderness – 1,250 square kilometres (483 square miles) in all – and encircle the northern, western and southern three-quarters of the city. Many parts of the Wienerwald can be reached by public transport in half an hour from the city centre.

The Wienerwald owes its existence to a 19th-century Austrian conservationist, Josef Schöffel, who launched a campaign in the *Wiener Tagblatt* newspaper to prevent the cutting down of the Woods to finance the government's heavy war losses against the Prussians. After two years, the outraged citizens put an end to the project. A century later, the Viennese are still congratulating themselves on their foresight.

Today many Viennese live in the small villages scattered throughout the Wienerwald. Touring the Woods is an easy way to experience 'rustic' life without wandering far from Vienna. If you've only an hour or two to spare, take a short taxi or bus ride along Höhenstrasse (the Vienna High Road), an old cobblestone road that winds between the mountains of Kahlenberg and Leopoldsberg before continuing on to Klosterneuburg. Here, **Nierscher** (Hauptstrasse 190, 02243 339 33) is a large *Heuriger* with good food and gorgeous gardens – a treat for kids.

The 483-metre (1,585-foot) summit of Kahlenberg affords a magnificent view of Vienna. Meander along to Cobenzl or to Leopoldsberg to drink coffee and enjoy the scenery from the lovely tree-shaded terrace just behind the castle (*see also p98*). But in order to appreciate the Wienerwald fully, you'll need an entire day.

MOUNTAIN BIKING

A new mountain biking trail network within the Vienna Woods was inaugurated in June 1999. More than 40 cycle paths, all well-signposted, cover more than 900 kilometres (560 miles) of the Woods. There are 80 restaurants along the way. Mountain bikes and city bikes can be hired from most train stations, and some hotels and restaurants: information is available from a tourist information centre. For bike trail maps, visit www.mtbwienerwald.at or contact **Wienerwald** tourist office (*see p198*).

Baden & Bad Vöslau

Paddling in hot thermal pools is a popular diversion. Baden (meaning 'baths') is where generations of Habsburgs used to come to take the waters. With its Biedermeier architecture, grandiose baths, spa park, quirky museums, theatre and casino, Baden still has a faded, turn-of-the-century charm. In summer, operettas are staged at the theatre. **Hotel Schloss Weikersdorf** (Schlossgasse 9-11, 02252 483 010, www.hotelschlossweikersdorf.at) is a castle-like hotel with all mod cons, including a swimming pool. The spa complex in Bad Vöslau is worth visiting just to ogle the architecture.

Baden is 25 kilometres (16 miles) south of Vienna, Bad Vöslau only a few kilometres beyond Baden. Both can be easily reached by car, train, or bus (leaving from the Staatsoper on the hour). Baden makes an excellent starting point to tour the southern and western Vienna Woods. There are many hotels in both towns, so it may be worth staying overnight to enjoy the hot thermal waters one day, and tour the southern Vienna Woods on the second. Restaurants around here tend to be a bit pompous, so it may be worth the drive to **s'Gwölb** in Ebreichsdorf (Rathausplatz 2, 02254 72947); it's 14 kilometres from Baden but has some of the best cooking on Vienna's southern edge.

Gumpoldskirchen, a whimsically named community just a few miles outside Baden, is the most popular wine-growing village south of Vienna. Obviously, the main reason for stopping here is a visit to a *Heuriger* to try some of the world-famous Gumpoldskirchner vintages. Wienerstrasse and Neustiftgasse are packed with them, but it's worth the walk to **Veigl Hütte** (Beethoven-Wanderweg 40, 0699 1706 2026) for great views of the vineyards and Vienna.

Tourist information

Bad Vöslau Information

Schlossplatz (02252 70743/www.badvoeslau.at). **Open** 9am-12.30pm, 2-4.30pm Mon-Fri; 9am-noon Sat. English spoken.

Tourist Board Baden

Brusattiplatz 3 (02252 22600/www.baden.at). **Open** *1 May-30 Sept* 9am-6pm Mon-Sat; 10am-1pm Sun. *1 Oct-30 Apr* 9am-5pm Mon-Fri. English spoken.

Heiligenkreuz & Mayerling

Driving from Baden to Heiligenkreuz will take you through the Helenental, the valley of St Helena, one of the most beautiful valleys in the Woods. Napoleon thought it so gorgeous he wanted to end his days here. The Helenental is more wild and woolly than the civilised rolling hills of the northern Wienerwald. On either side of the road you'll see steep rock faces, thick forests with overhanging branches and rushing rivers. Napoleon, of course, ended his days in a different St Helena.

Mayerling is famed for a tragic suicide pact immortalised in a 1935 film of the same name. Once the hunting lodge of Crown Prince Rudolf, Mayerling became a household word after the mysterious double suicide in 1889 of the heir to the throne Rudolf and his 17-year-old mistress, Baroness Maria Vetsera. Emperor Franz Josef converted the hunting lodge into a convent of atonement of the Carmelite nuns, so there's not much to see, but it's still popular with tourists.

A few miles from Mayerling lies **Heiligenkreuz Abbey** (Stift Heiligenkreuz, 2532 Heiligenkreuz 1, 02258 8703-0, www.stift-heiligenkreuz.at). It's a romantic Cistercian abbey that blends elements of the Romanesque, Gothic and baroque periods. Set within the wilderness of the southern Vienna Woods, it feels peaceful and isolated. The complex houses a number of treasures. The basilica, begun in 1135, is the oldest example of ribbed vaulting in Austria; the chapter-house, a Babenberg burial place, contains Austria's oldest ducal tomb. The tragic Maria Vetsera is buried here. There's a decent restaurant in the complex; otherwise try **Hanner** in Alland (Mayerling 1, 02258 237841), in the hotel of the same name. There's a wonderful garden and good, if pricey, international cuisine.

Tourist information

Heiligenkreuz Tourist Office

Heiligenkreuz 15 (02258 8720/www.heiligenkreuz.at). **Open** 8am-4pm Mon-Fri. No English spoken.

Mödling

About 20 minutes from Vienna by S-Bahn, Mödling is an idyll in the woods. Its poise and elegance have seduced nobility and artists since the Babenberg reign. Beethoven, Schubert, Wagner and Strauss all found their muse here. Other luminaries such as musician Hugo Wolf and painters Egon Schiele and Gustav Klimt called this spa town home.

Mödling is the starting point for 85 kilometres (53 miles) of marked hiking trails that lead to the ruins of the Babenbergs' castle, the Romanesque Liechtenstein Castle and the neo-classical Enzersdorf Palace (both in nearby Enzersdorf). Mödling's pool, **Stadtbad** (Badstrasse 25, 02236 22335) is the only art nouveau pool in Lower Austria and has an enormous outdoor pool, an indoor pool, a sauna and two kids' pools. A good spot to eat is **Babenbergerhof** (Meiereigasse 12, 02236 233 02).

In the neighbouring village of Hinterbrühl is the **Seegrotte** (Grutschg 2, 02236 263 64), Europe's largest underground lake. In 1912, this former mineral mine was flooded with 20m litres of water. In World War II, the Nazis pumped the grotto dry and assembled the fuselage of the world's first jet fighter. Boat tours run from here.

Tourist Information

Mödling Tourist Information

K Elisabethstrasse 2 (43 2236 26727/ www.moedling.at). **Open** 9am-5pm Mon-Fri.

Baden. See p200.

The Danube Valley

The river's environs are fertile grounds for exploration, dining and wining – just go with the flow.

The Danube winds through an ever-changing landscape. To the east, it carves through the narrow Wachau, lined with terraced vineyards and hills crowned by fortresses and ruins. In turn, this spectacular riverscape gives way to the broader Danube basins of Krems and Tulln.

The peaceful flow of the Danube contrasts with the river's violent past. Control of these waters – forming, as they did, a corridor between east and west – was hotly contested. The landscape is punctuated by castles and fortified monasteries (550 in Lower Austria alone). Today, as well as the area's historical importance, you'll discover some of life's great pleasures – fine wines, top restaurants, superb views. It's not surprising people flock here.

If time is short, just explore the exquisite Wachau section of the river 80 kilometres (50 miles) north-west of Vienna: that stretch of 35 kilometres (22 miles) between the towns of Melk and Krems. The district begins as the Danube turns north past **Stift Melk** abbey. The river then flows into a magical landscape of rolling hills, monasteries, cloisters and castles set among manicured vineyards. Along the banks are cycle and hiking paths, sightseeing boats, beaches for swimming, as well as restaurants and wineries. In spring, when the apricot trees blossom, the Wachau looks achingly beautiful. Later in the year, the heavenly Marillenknödeln (apricot dumplings) are a delicious reason to head for a local restaurant (*see p203*).

The Wachau is accessible and well organised for tourists. You can reach both Melk and Krems by train in just over an hour from Vienna; in three hours by boat. A day trip is easily possible, but to make the most of the countryside stop a night or two. There are many small hotels and restaurants with rooms.

One of the most enjoyable ways to experience the Danube Valley is by bike. The Danube Bike Path runs for 1,300 kilometres (808 miles) by the river from Donaueschingen in Germany to Budapest. The path (quite flat) runs through 258 kilometres (160 miles) of Lower Austria. There are many *Heurigen* on the way. Bikes can be hauled on the trains and boats going up and down the Wachau. Wanderkarte – good maps of the region – are provided free by Lower Austria Tourist Information (*see p198*); ask them about bicycle hire too.

DDSG Blue Danube Boat Trips

Information (58 880-0).
From Krems *5 Apr-11 Oct* 10.15am, 1pm, 3.45pm daily. **From Melk** *28 Apr-28 Sept* 11am, 1.50pm, 4.15pm daily (stopping at Spitz, Dürnstein).
Tickets *Krems-Melk* €15.50 one way; €20.50 return. *Melk-Spitz/Spitz-Krems* €9 one way; €12 return.

Tulln

Tulln an der Donau lies on the southern shore of the Danube making it a popular destination for cyclists along the river trails. The town is just 30 kilometres (19 miles) upstream from Vienna, yet has a lively cultural life all its own. Formerly a Roman camp called 'Comagena', Tulln trumpets itself as the 'Birthplace of Austria', and was, in effect, the country's first capital. But since the reigning families left for Vienna, the city's significance has diminished. Stacks of information can be found at the local tourist office which is in easy walking distance of the train station, 'Tulln Stadt'.

When at the tourist office, you need simply to pivot on your heels to view the magnificent 18th-century Minoritenkirche. Formerly a convent, it has been painstakingly restored. Don't miss the Neue Turm (the tower on the south-east corner) and the excessively rococo Kirchenraum (chapel). Stroll along the Danube pedestrian walk and look for the quirky granite Donaubrunnen, the significance of which remains one of the town's mysteries. A few steps further, at Donaulände 28, is the Egon Schiele Museum. This establishment's excellent collection – exhibited in the former jail where painter Schiele was imprisoned for corrupting minors with erotic nude portraits of pubescent girls – documents the life of this infamous 'Son of Tulln'. Yet Tulln's most cherished landmark is the 1,700-year-old Römerturm, a watch-tower built by the Roman Emperor Diocletian for the town's security.

The village blossoms in summer, shuttling tourists around in a 'hop-on hop-off' train. Stay until dusk and get tickets to one of the many open-air concerts performed on a moored barge. To eat, try **Zur Rossmühle** (Hauptplatz 12-13, 02272 624 1133).

Tourist information

Tulln Stadt Tourist Office
Minoritenplatz 2 (02272 658 36). **Open** *May-Oct* 9am-noon, 2-8pm Mon-Fri. *Nov-Apr* noon-6pm Sat, Sun.

Krems

The historical centre of Krems is more than 1,000 years old and forms the eastern border to the Wachau. The town is made up of restored, clean, delightful pastel buildings and cobbled streets. Krems is also a vinicultural centre; at the Weinkolleg Kloster Und (wine college), visitors can attend wine seminars and tastings. Six kilometres (3.7 miles) south of Krems is its monastery, **Stift Göttweig** (3511 Furth bei Göttweig, 02732 855 81-231, www.stiftgottweig.at), founded in 1083. This baroque complex was designed by Johann Hildebrandt. A restaurant in the grounds has fabulous views.

If you've an itch for more modern creations, stroll Krems' 'Art Mile' which runs parallel to the Danube from Kloster Und into the historical centre via Steiner Landstrasse, finishing at the Göttlicher Gallery. Along its course are three cultural institutions: the Lower Austrian Independent House of Literature (Unabhängiges Literaturhaus NÖ), the architecture network ORTE and Artothek Niederösterreich. Also on the Art Mile is the Caricature Museum,

Karikaturmuseum (Kunstmeile Krems, Steiner Landstrasse 3a, 2732 90 80 20, www.karikaturmuseum.at). For food, try **m.kunst.genuss** in the Kunsthalle, the Hofbauer Museum restaurant or the Salzstadl. There are lots of *Heurigen* in Krems-Stein – it's 10 kilometres from Krems and home to the famous winemakers of the same name. **Heurigenhof Bründlmayer** (Langenlois, Walterstrasse 14, 02734 2833) offers a creative take on *Heurigen* grub, a cosy interior and a gorgeous garden. Two which have stupendous views of the Danube are **Hambock Erich** (Kellergasse 31, 02732 84568) and **Kogel Hexe** (Kogelweg 45, 02732 85356). The first has excellent food and the other more simple fare.

Tourist information

Austropa Travel Office
Krems Undstrasse 6 (02732 82676). **Open** *May-Oct* 8.30am-6.30pm Mon-Fri; 10am-noon, 1-6pm Sat; 10am-noon, 1-4pm Sun. *Nov-Apr* 8.30am-5pm Mon-Fri.

Dürnstein

In 1192, Austrian Archduke Leopold V caused a sensation when he took Richard the Lionheart prisoner while the latter was returning from the Crusades. Richard was accused of insulting Leopold and locked in the Fortress of the Künrings in Dürnstein; many believed the King of England to be dead. Legend has it that

Rural gourmandising

Austrian gastronauts drive to this region simply to eat and drink. The mild climate is renowned for viniculture, so when Emperor Joseph II's 1784 decree permitted producers to serve their own wines, the Wachau, with its myriad vineyards, flourished. White wines like Grüner Veltliner, Riesling and Burgund are a speciality.

Weingut Jamek is a lovely vineyard and restaurant on the northern bank of the Danube in Joching. Indulging in Wachau delicacies, plus a glass of Jamek's own Grüner Veltliner while sitting on the terrace overlooking the river, is heavenly. Wines can also be sampled at Weinkolleg Kloster Und in Krems, Kellerschlössl of the Freie Weingärtner in Dürnstein, Winzer Krems in Krems and the WG Dinstlgut in Loiben.

One of Austria's best restaurants is in Mautern, on the south side of the Danube. Here top chef Lisl Wagner-Bacher presides

over **Bacher**. Lisl's sister Gerda Schickh runs a less formal restaurant with rooms, **Schickh**, in Klein-Wien below Göttweig Abbey.

Bacher Hotel & Restaurant
Südtiroler Platz 2, Mautern (02732 82937/www.landhaus-bacher.at). **Open** 11.30am-2pm, 6.30-9pm Wed-Sun. **Credit** DC, V.

Schickh
Arastrasse 2, Klein-Wien (02736 7218/ www.schickh.at). **Open** 11.30am-2.30pm, 6-9.30pm Mon, Tue, Fri; 11.30 am-9.30pm Sat, Sun. **Credit** MC, V.

Weingut Jamek
Joching 45, Weissenkirchen (02715 2235/ www.jamekweingut.at). **Open** 11.30am-4pm Mon-Thur; 11.30am-11pm Fri, Sat. **Credit** DC, MC, V.

Trips Out of Town

The interior of **Stift Melk**, the magnificent Benedictine monastry.

Richard's faithful minstrel Blondel took off, lute in hand, to find his master. Playing his master's favourite tune under the windows of Dürnstein Castle, Blondel was answered by Richard's voice. Richard was released upon payment of a large ransom, that went towards the building of Wiener Neustadt. The ruins of Künringerburg, the King's forced residence, stand on a hill over the village and offer great views of the Danube. The Chorherrenstift, part of a 15th-century Augustinian monastery, has been restored and can be visited between April and October.

For restaurants, try **Wachauerstuben** (Unterloiben 24, 02732 85950).

Tourist information

Dürnstein Town Hall
Dürnstein 25, 3601 (0271 1219/www.duernstein.at).
Open 8.30am-noon, 1.30-4pm Mon-Fri.
Tourist information is available within the town hall.

Spitz

Surrounded by vineyards, orchards and ancient ruins, Spitz an der Donau embodies the spirit of the Wachau. Its land and climate enable high-quality wines to be made. In a good year this town of 2,000 residents produces 56,000 litres (12,320 gallons) of 'liquid gold'. Carolingian monks lived around Spitz in the Middle Ages; several churches bear witness to the fact. The late-Gothic Stadtpfarrkirche, on Kirschenplatz, is notable; statues of the 12 Apostles encircle the organ that faces a magnificent baroque altar. *Heurigen* include

Weingut Rondellenhof (Radlbach 7, 02713 2612) and **Weingut-Gastezimmer-Buschenschank** (Radlbach 11, 02713 2208); the latter has rooms. A history of rowing and sailing on the river can be seen in Schifffahrtsmuseum im Schloss Erlahof (02713 22 46).

Tourist information

Tourist Office
Hauptstrasse 8 (02713 2363). **Open** 2-4pm Mon-Fri.

Melk

Melk cowers in the shadow of its abbey, **Stift Melk** (02752 555 232, www.stiftmelk.at), perched on a cliff over the Danube. The abbey is huge – 17,500sq m (188,370sq ft) in area. Its side façade is an incredible 1,115m (3,695ft) long. Once the residence of the Babenberg family, it has been a Benedictine monastery since 1089 (and remains so). Master builder Jakob Prandtauer built the abbey in its present form in the 18th century. The marble hall and the library, with their high, tiered ceilings, are astonishing. If you're in need of refreshment, close by is the simple but homely **Stadt Melk** (Hauptplatz 1, 02752 524 75). Five kilometres (three miles) outside Melk lies the magnificent castle **Schloss Schallaburg** (Loosdorf, 43 2754 6317, www.schallaburg.at). It's a compendium of architectural styles: Romanesque, Gothic, Renaissance and Mannerist. Even the floor, a mosaic of 1600 pieces, is a riot of antics depicting mythological figures, creatures and gods. The Schloss is now an exhibition centre.

Burgenland

A mecca for music fans, bird-watchers – and lovers of the astonishing Austrian countryside.

To the east of Vienna there is a clear border to the habitats of many plants and animals found in eastern Europe and Asia. This is particularly evident around the **Neusiedler See** (Neusiedler Lake), only 45 minutes from Vienna by car, rail or bus. In the same way that the landscape, flora and fauna flow into one another in this region, many cultures meet here – primarily Austrian and Hungarian. Until 1921 the Burgenland region belonged to the Hungarian part of the Danube monarchy. In addition there are Slovakian influences from the north; the Neusiedler See is visible from the towers of Bratislava Castle. Croatians who settled 500 years ago in Burgenland contribute southern Slavonic elements. The smallest ethnic group in Burgenland are the Roma, as cruelly persecuted by the Nazis as were the Jews.

Eisenstadt

Traces of this old multiculturalism can be found in the provincial capital, Eisenstadt. The town's most famous resident, Josef Haydn, lived here for 31 years. Though he died in Vienna, his tomb is in Eisenstadt's baroque **Bergkirche** (Haydnplatz 1, 2682 62638). Haydn's headless

body was buried here in 1932, followed by the head itself – stolen by fans 150 years earlier – in 1952.

Standing above the town is **Schloss Esterházy** (Esterházy Platz, 02682 719 3000, www.schloss-esterhazy.at) the palace of the powerful Hungarian family. The palace, still owned by the Esterházys, dates from the 14th century and houses Haydnsaal (Haydn Hall). It was here that Haydn conducted the court orchestra for nearly 30 years. His symphonies are performed every September at the palace during the International Haydn Festival (02682 618 660, www.haydn.festival.at).

Close to the palace is the old Jewish ghetto. The **Jüdisches Museum** (Unterbergstrasse 6, 02682 65145, www.ojm.at) tells of the history (and extermination) of the Jews in Burgenland.

Eisenstadt has few hotels. **Gasthof Familie Ohr** (Ruster Strasse 51, 02682 624 60, www.hotelohr.at) is a three-star hotel; **Hotel Burgenland** (Franz-Schubert-Platz 1, 02682 696) is a four-star establishment, with an indoor swimming pool and sauna. Otherwise, the regional tourist office can help visitors find rooms in the town or a place to stay around the Neusiedler See.

The Sopron shop stop

Sopron is in the north-west of Hungary, sitting in a little Magyar nodule that extrudes into Austria. It managed to escape devastation by both Mongols and Turks and retains a medieval feel. Austrians flood here to go shopping on the cheap.

The Várkerület, which encircles the Old Town, bustles with tiny shops selling cigarettes and booze, salamis and household gadgets. Nearly every business doubles as a money-changer.

Step away from all this into the Old Town. Here, the medieval-patterned streets are relaxed and traffic-free. Medieval dwellings rub gables with Gothic churches and baroque monuments. Commerce continues, but quietly, in discreet boutiques and jewellery shops.

The Firewatch Tower, symbol of Sopron, sums up the town's history and offers a view that takes it all in. The Tower was built on Roman foundations, with a 12th-century base, a 16th-century column and balcony, a 17th-century spire, and a 'Fidelity Gate' installed in 1922 to mark the town's decision to remain part of Hungary following the Treaty of Trianon. From the top you can see the streets and walls of the Old Town and vine-covered hills beyond.

Though there's plenty to look at in the daytime – the old houses and museums around Fötér and the medieval synagogue at Új utca 22 are interesting, for example – it's at night, after the trippers have gone, when the town of Sopron is at its most intriguing and atmospheric.

Nearby is Raiding, the village where Franz Liszt was born in 1811. A small museum in **Franz-Liszt-Geburt-Haus** (02619 722 0), his birthplace, displays photos and documents as well as his childhood church organ.

Tourist information

Burgenland Tourismus
Schloss Esterházy, Eisenstadt (02682 633 8416/ www.burgenland.info).
Some English spoken.

Oslip to Burg Forchtenstein

Oslip

Leaving Eisenstadt in the direction of the Neusiedler See, travellers are often charmed by Oslip. Home to a Croatian-speaking community, it is picturesque and villagey. During summer, many people sit on benches in front of their doors selling fruit and vegetables, wine and spirits. On the edge of the village lies the **Cselley Mühle** (Cselly-Mühle Kultur,

The hills are alive

If you've children who have watched *The Sound of Music* so many times they know all the lyrics, maybe it's time to skip the movie and take to the very hills where once countless von Trapps roamed freely.

The Austrian countryside can be a great budget destination – and one attuned to families – if you stay at a *Bauernhof* ('farmhouse'). These family farms have grown into sophisticated tourist operations, yet the housing still has an attractive down-on-the-farm feel. At about €300 a week, it's an affordable and unique way to get to know the Austrian countryside.

The landscape can be breathtaking – from lowland vineyards to Alpine pastures. Children can get hands-on experience of the farm animals too. Most *Bauernhöfe* specialise in such seasonal activities as skiing, hiking and horse-riding. They usually cater for all child-care needs: from cribs to children's cutlery. Farm-fresh food and activities such as petting zoos and music evenings are added incentives. Where else could you find both 'bright copper kettles and warm woollen mittens?'

Visit www.farmholidays.com for a listing of the network of 3,400 family-run farms.

Aktionszentrum Sachsenweg, 02684 2209, www.cselley-muehle.at), a mill that provides a romantic setting for high-quality concerts. You can eat quite well in the gardens and cave-like interiors here.

Nearby is the quarry of St Margareten. In the Middle Ages, the quarry supplied stone for Vienna's Stephansdom. Over the centuries a huge crater landscape has taken shape. Since 1959 this has provided a setting for one of the most important sculptors' symposia. Artists from around the world meet in summer to exchange information, teach – and leave the works they've produced standing here.

Rust

A few kilometres further on, roosting high above the lake, is Rust, one of the smallest towns in Austria. Its Renaissance and baroque houses have been almost completely preserved. Hidden behind the mighty yard doors are beautiful inner courtyards where regional wines are offered for tasting and sale. For great Pannonian cooking, try **Rusterhof** (Rathausplatz 18, 02685 6416). There are also lots of great *Heurigen* in town serving lake specialities such as goose liver and smoked eel.

Rust's most famous citizens are the white storks who nest on the village chimneys. They start arriving in late March, rear their young, then fly off in August. It's considered good luck to have a nesting stork on your house, but should the stork fail to return, disaster is said to strike. A good vantage point is from the tower of the Fischerkirche, the oldest church in Rust.

Mörbisch & Burg Forchtenstein

Neighbouring Rust and just a couple of kilometres short of the Hungarian border, is the tiny colony of Mörbisch. The village's strong Hungarian tradition is apparent in its typical Magyar-style dwellings. Whitewashed houses with brightly coloured doors, and dried corn dangling from the shutters add a painterly quality to this romantic spot. The village has a lakeside beach and a popular operetta festival the Mörbisch Seefestspiele (every July/August; tickets can be bought on the website – www.see festpiele-moerbisch.at). South of Mörbisch cyclists can cross into Hungary but there's no road for cars.

To the west of Mörbisch lies **Burg Forchtenstein** (02626 81212, www.forch tenstein.at). On the eastern slope of the Rosaliengebirge hills, the castle overlooks the Hungarian plains from a position so invincible the Turks failed to seize it during their invasions of 1529 and 1683. Built in the

Vineyards near **Eisenstadt**.
See p205.

14th century by the Counts of Mattersdorf it was acquired by the Esterházy family in 1622. They gradually expanded the castle, turning it into an armoury that now houses the largest weapons collection in central Europe. The best way to reach the castle is by car.

Tourist information

Mörbisch tourist office

Hauptstrasse 23, Mörbisch am See (2685 8430/2685 8856). **Open** 8am-4pm Mon-Thur; 8am-1pm Fri.

Neusiedler See

This, the westernmost lake of the Eurasian salt steppe region, contains water almost as salty as the Mediterranean, but where the salt comes from is a mystery. The lake has a unique micro-climate: long, hot summers (ideal for swimming, sailing or exploring the mostly flat shores on a bicycle) and long cold winters when the lake, only 1.8 metres (6 feet) at its deepest, freezes into Europe's largest skating rink. The 230-square-kilometre (89-square-mile) body of water is surrounded by a belt of reeds, sometimes up to 400 metres (1,313 feet) wide, making it an ideal habitat for a variety of rare or endangered plants and animals. The lake is important for birds; about 300 species breed or rest here on their migratory flights.

There are daily guided tours during the summer. These start from the **National Park Centre** (Hauswiese, 02175 3442) in Illmitz – also a starting point for bike tours around the lake. Three restaurants on the lake's shores highlight the quality of food in this region. **The Taubenkobel** (Dovecote) in Schützen (Hauptstrasse 33, 02684 2297, www.tauben kobel.at) is one of Austria's best restaurants. Maître Walter Eselböck uses ingredients almost exclusively from the region in dishes such as cold pea soup with avocado and mint; and wels (a freshwater fish of the catfish family) with veal brawn, cabbage and white asparagus.

In Podersdorf on the eastern shore (the most popular tourist destination on the lake), there's a small restaurant called **Zur Dankbarkeit** (Hauptstrasse 39, 02177 2223, www.dank barkeit.at). 'To Gratitude' is run by the Lentsch family, which has created a menu from the forgotten treasures of Jewish cooking. In Weiden, on the lake's northern shore, the Weissberger family tends the **Blaue Gans** (Am Seepark, 02167 7510, www.blaue-gans.at). The Blue Goose marks the eastern limit of haute cuisine from Alsace. A four-course meal in its garden on the lake-shore is a blissful way to end a day. There's one native species, however, that alfresco diners could well do without; at 9pm mosquitoes emerge from the reeds.

Trips Out of Town

Southern Alpine Region

For peak enjoyment grab some skis or hiking boots and head for Vienna's local mountain range.

Many people envisage Alpine scenery when they think of Austria, but in fact the Alps peter out before they hit Vienna. That's why the Alpine region, only 90 kilometres (60 miles) outside the city, is so special to the Viennese. It is their little mountain range close to home, the last Alpine hiccup before the land flattens as it heads toward the Hungarian steppes. A sunny day on the mountainside will transform the sedate Viennese into friendly nature buffs. Dressed in Lederhosen, and often sporting ski poles, they will tramp the mountain trails for hours.

The most popular mountains close to Vienna are Rax, Schneeberg and Semmering – all within an hour's drive of the city. Semmering is the favourite port-of-call with day-and weekend-trippers from Vienna, and has its own railway. Semmering also has the Panhans Grand Hotel and many faded fairy-tale villas.

Rax, Schneeberg and Semmering are all easy mountains to *wandern* – the relaxed Austrian version of mountain hiking. All three have trains, gondolas or ski lifts working year-round that will take you a fair way up the mountain-side. Adventurous hikers and climbers can follow well-marked trails covering the three mountains. For winter skiing, Semmering is well equipped for day-trippers. Schneeberg and Rax also have their own cross-country slopes.

This mountain region is a favourite with retired people, which means plenty of skiing, walking, good hotels and cultural attractions within walking distance of each other. Travelling further afield to Rax or Schneeberg, taking in Reichenau and Semmering on the way back to Vienna, is easiest by car.

SKIING

In winter, people descend on sedate Semmering for downhill and cross-country skiing at one of two ski areas. Hirschenkogel, 1,318 metres high (4,326 feet), is within walking distance of all Semmering's hotels and has both artificial snow and a floodlit ski-piste. There's also a gentle children's slope; toboggans can be hired from the ski rental shop. In Spital am Semmering, 10 kilometres (6 miles) further on, is the less crowded Stuhleck which has 20 kilometres (12 miles) of pistes and its own floodlit run (open 6-9pm Mon-Sat). Information on cross-country ski routes can be obtained from the tourist office.

Semmering-Hirschenkogel

Semmering (02664 8038/snowline 02664 2575/ www.semmering.hirschenkogel.at). **Open** *pistes* 8.30am-4pm Mon-Fri; 8am-4pm Sat, Sun. **Cost** *Day card* €25, €15 children; *from 11am* €22.50, €13.50 children; *half day* €20, €12 children; *day pass for all 3 local ski regions* €27.50.

Facilities include an eight-person gondola, a double ski lift, a T-bar and a help lift on the Panhans side.

Semmering

Until 1854 Semmering was an undisturbed mountain pass. Then Carl Ritter von Ghegas' Semmering Railway succeeded in connecting this Alpine wilderness to Vienna. Never before had it been so easy to reach the mountains (nowadays, direct trains leave every 2 hours from Südbahnhof). The first railway to become one of UNESCO's World Heritage Sites, it is admired as a feat of engineering and for its functional beauty. The train meanders along a series of 31 viaducts and tunnels amid beautiful Alpine scenery.

Over the next 20 years, Semmering, with its mild weather and its stunning views of the mountains Schneeberg and Rax, gained in popularity. In 1882, the first villas were built on the edge of the mountain, and in 1889, the first Hotel Panhans, with 44 rooms, was opened. By 1900 Panhans had become a massive Grand Hotel. Today **Panhans Grand Hotel** (Hochstrasse 32, 02664 8181) is a four-star hotel with 113 rooms, a swimming pool and sauna. Rooms in the modern wing, individually styled from cosy country to art nouveau, are the most expensive. Those in the original hotel are vast with huge balconies, but some can be tatty.

Semmering was *the* place to go, right up to World War II. The Panhans guest book from 1900 to 1938 reads like a roll-call of high society. Emperor Franz Josef, Austro-Hungarian aristocracy, writers, artists, actors and intellectuals from Europe and America all lived it up here (there's even a photograph of Josephine Baker riding a sled outside the hotel).

Requisitioned by the Nazis during World War II, Panhans became popular with Erwin Rommel and Field Marshal Göring. After the war, Semmering never regained its place in society, and the hotel closed in 1969.

Schneeberg – Vienna's very own mountain.

However, in 1994 Panhans was reopened, refurbished to something approaching its former glory. With the reopening, Semmering has blossomed. Thousands of well-marked walks start from both the Panhans and the **Panorama Wagner** (Hochstrasse 267, 02664 25120) hotels. Smaller than the Panhans, the Wagner has wonderful views, Swedish-designed rooms, a top restaurant and that Austrian rarity – a no-smoking policy.

For the best views, take the **Sonnwendstein** chair lift (02663 8525/www.tiscover.com/schottwien) at Maria Schutz. Maps are free from hotels and the **Tourismusregion Süd-alpin**. Semmering is also the best area close to Vienna for skiing.

Tourist information

Tourismusregion Süd-alpin
Passhöhe 248, 2680 Semmering (02664 2539-1/www.tiscover.com/noe-sued). **Open** 8am-4pm Mon-Fri. The English-speaking staff at this regional tourist office can advise on daily excursions and will also provide maps.

Mount Rax

Mount Rax (2,007 metres/6,587 feet) is a great place to experience the Alps without having to travel too far from Vienna. The Rax is well-signposted and has an unusually large, 34-kilometre (21-mile) plateau dotted with eight mountain huts, all with superb views, so there's always somewhere to stop to eat or drink.

You can get most of the way up Rax with little effort. Following the signs to the Rax-Seilbahn in Hirschwang, you reach the Rax Gondola (Reichenau-Hirschwant, 02666 52497/53821, www.raxseilbahn.at) which transports you 1,017 metres (3,338 feet) in eight minutes. In 30 minutes you reach the **Ottohaus** (1,644 metres/ 5,395 feet) for refreshment. For a more vigorous hike, drive beyond the Rax Gondola to Prainer Gscheid, where you can park and take the trail for a few hours towards Karl Ludwighaus (1,804 metres/5,920 feet), then up to the top of Rax.

Tourist information

Reichenau/Rax Tourism Office
Hauptstrasse 63, 2651 Reichenau/Rax (02666 528 65/fax 02666 542 66/www.reichenau.at). **Open** 9am-noon, 2-4pm Mon-Fri.

Schneeberg

Schneeberg is Vienna's 'local' mountain and at 2,075 metres (6,810 feet) is the highest peak in Lower Austria. It stands just outside Wiener Neustadt on the A2 motorway south. As a result, Schneeberg tends to be more crowded than Rax. A railway line compounds its popularity; a steam engine and a train called the Salamander (02636 366120, www.schnee bergbahn.at) leave from the town of Puchberg am Schneeberg to carry visitors 9.5 kilometres (6 miles) to Hochschneeberg, near the summit. Trains operate late Apr-early Nov; full ascents take 55 minutes.

Directory

Features

Directory

Getting Around

Arriving & leaving

By air

Flughafen Wien-Schwechat

General flight information 7007 22233/www.viennaairport.com.
Vienna's international airport lies south-east of the city on the Ostautobahn (direction Budapest) and is the international airport for both Vienna and Bratislava. The above phone number is the central infoline, from which you'll be connected to departures, arrivals and so on.

TO AND FROM THE AIRPORT

Getting to and from the airport by public transport is easy – it's a 20-minute ride by bus or train from the centre of town. The airport shuttle buses operate two routes: to/from the **City Air Terminal** (Wien Mitte) near the Vienna Hilton, and from Vienna's **Westbahnhof**, via Südbahnhof (it takes 35 minutes from Westbahnhof). The fare is €5.80 one way, €10.90 return per passenger, including luggage (children up to 6 free, 6-15 years €2.90 one way, €5.40 return). Pay the bus driver as you board or get the ticket at the automat machine. Buses run about every half hour. By train, the **Schnellbahn 7** leaves from Wien Nord, via Wien Mitte, costing €3 one way. For more information phone (05 17 17). If you choose to take a taxi, use an airport taxi rather than a standard taxi as it will charge a cheaper flat rate. Most Viennese use **C+K Airport Service** (444 44), which charges a flat rate of €22, one way. Upon arrival in the airport, go to its stand directly to the left of the exit hall; drivers are usually immediately available. Limousines and a selection of large and small vans are available from **Airport Service Mazur** (7007 36422), but need to be reserved in advance.

Vienna Airport Lines (Airport Shuttle Bus)

Airport office 93 000-2300. **Open** 9am-5pm daily. **Credit cards** only at the automat machines.

Airlines

Aeroflot 512 1501/fax 512 1501-78
Alitalia airport office 7007 32643/reservations, town office 505 1707/www.alitalia.com
Austrian Airlines reservations 05 17 89/www.aua.com
British Airways town office 50 660/reservations 7956 7567/www.britishairways.at
Delta Airlines reservations 7956 7023/www.delta.com
KLM reservations 0900 359556/www.klm.com
Lauda Air (Austrian Airlines Group) reservations 05 17 89/www.laudaair.at
Lufthansa reservations 0810 1025 8080/www.lufthansa.at
Swissair reservations 0810 810 840/ www.swiss.com
Tyrolean Airways (Austrian Airlines Group) 05 17 89/www.tyrolean.at

By rail

Trains are used for most domestic travel within Austria, and travelling on them is a very pleasant experience. Timetables can be picked up from the information office at any train station.

There are all sorts of special services available, such as a pick-up for customers with confirmed reservations, where a reserved taxi or hotel representative meets you at the train station or accommodation (usually free); or the Haus zu Haus luggage service, which picks up and delivers your bags (up to three bags, maximum 25kg per bag), charging €12.30 for one bag, €16.70 for two, €21 for three. It is especially useful for skiers not wanting to lug their equipment around.

If travelling west towards Salzburg or Tirol, try to take a 'Panorama' compartment, a first-class car with huge windows that are just perfect for viewing the fabulous scenery.

There are three main train stations: **Westbahnhof** for trains to the west, to locations such as Salzburg, Frankfurt, London and Paris; **Südbahnhof** for trains to Bratislava, Budapest, Prague, Venice and Rome; and **Franz-Josefs-Bahnhof** for north-western Austria

and Prague. For all reservations and information call the numbers below.

ÖBB

Austrian Railways 24hr information 05 17 17. **Booking office open** *Westbahnhof* 4.45am-10.45pm Mon-Sat; 5.25am-10.45pm Sun. *Südbahnhof* 5.30am-10.45pm daily. *Wien Mitte* 5.45am-9.30pm daily. *Franz-Josefs-Bahnhof* 6.40am-7.15pm daily. *Wien Nord* 6am-6.30pm daily.

By bus

The central bus station, Wien Mitte, closed in 2001. All buses arriving or leaving the city now stop at different stations all over Vienna.

Infocenter postal & railroad buses

711-01. **Open** 7am-8pm Mon-Fri.

Public transport

Vienna has excellent public transport and is an easy city to get around. A public transport day ticket can be used on any of the trams, buses or U-Bahn lines that zig-zag and encircle the city centre. Forget taking a car into the 1st district as parking spaces are rare and garages are expensive.

Sooner or later, whether by foot, bus, train or tram, you end up at the Ringstrasse, a broad road encircling the 1st district. Trams circle the Ringstrasse and can serve as a hop-on, hop-off city tour.

Public transport is safe, reliable, fast, and goes almost everywhere. The **Eastern Region Transportation Association (VOR)** is a network of eight zones covering a huge area that includes Vienna and surrounding towns. The central zone is known as the Kernzone (zone 100). There are trams, buses and five U-Bahn metro lines that run until midnight, with nightline bus services running overnight. Maps of Vienna's transport system, as well as timetables can be bought at any U-Bahn station.

Fares & tickets

Tickets can be bought at any U-Bahn station, at the tobacconist's shop as well as the many little Tabak newsstands sprinkled all over Vienna. Most U-Bahn stations have automat machines that sell tickets and dispense change. If you don't speak German, buy your tickets from a person rather than a machine, as they can help you choose the ticket and explain how to validate it. A ticket needs to be validated upon starting a journey. You can use as many forms of transport as you want with one ticket, as long as it is within one hour of its validation. The validation machines are relatively small and inconspicuous boxes at the entrance of each U-Bahn station, and within all buses and trams. Take the ticket and slide it into the mouth of the blue box (until you hear the punching sound and a bell), which will imprint the card with the time and relevant travel information.

It is an honour system, but guards do wander on and off the buses, trams and U-Bahn. A fine costs €62, and take note that the dumb-tourist routine doesn't work. The important thing to remember is that once you validate your ticket, keep it with you in case you get checked.

If you are going to be in Vienna for more than a day, public transport costs can be reduced by purchasing either monthly (€45), weekly (€12.50), three-day ('72 hours Vienna' ticket, lasting 72 hours from when it is validated – €12) or daily ('Vienna Shopping Card' 8am-8pm – €4; '24 hours Vienna' ticket, lasting 24 hours from when it is validated – €5) cards on the U-Bahn, buses and tram.

Tickets come in either a multi-strip or single form. The strip tickets (Streifenkarten) are valid for four trips (€6; one punch per journey) or eight days (one punch per day, valid until 1pm the day after – €24). Strip tickets can be used by groups, with one punch per person.

Another option is the Vienna Card (€16.90) is valid for 72 hours and also entitles you to discounts at museums, galleries and restaurants. Single public transport tickets from a newsstand or at the U-Bahn station cost €1.50 for adults. They are valid for one hour. Tickets purchased on the trams and in buses are more expensive and cost €2 for adults. You must have the correct change.

Children up to the age of six can travel free all year round, and children up to the age of 15 can travel free on Sundays, public holidays and Austrian school holidays. Otherwise they can travel with half-price tickets, which can be purchased on the tram (€1), in the bus (€1) or at the automat machines (80¢) at the U-Bahn station.

All senior citizens (women over 60, men over 65, not only Austrians) can travel with a two-journeys half-price

ticket (€2; one punch per journey). They must travel with ID proving their age.

For short distances on public transport, buy a half-price strip ticket called a Kurzstrecken-fahrschein (€3), which will allow you four trips: two to three stops on the tram or two stops on buses and U-Bahns. All transport tickets or cards are valid for nightlines.

Transport Information Offices

Vorverkaufsstellen der Wiener Linien

General information (7909/105/ www.wienerlinien.at). **Open** *phone enquiries* 6am-10pm Mon-Fri; 8.30am-4.30pm Sat, Sun.
There are offices located at selected U-Bahn stations across the city. Those at U-Bahn stations Stephansplatz, Karlsplatz and Westbahnhof are open 6.30am-6.30pm Mon-Fri; 8.30am-4pm Sat, Sun. Those at Landstrasse (Wien Mitte), and Volkstheater are open 6.30am-6.30pm Mon-Fri. All accept credit cards (AmEx, DC, MC, V) and provide information plus tickets for the bus, tram and U-Bahn networks.

U-Bahn

The U-Bahn is reliable, quick and comfortable. Routes are self-explanatory, and you'll find pamphlets in English available in most information offices in the U-Bahns. Routes on maps are colour-coded (U1 is red, U2 is purple, U3 is orange, U4 is green and U6 is brown) with all station signs in the same colours. Doors don't automatically open on the U-Bahn, so pull the handle sharply or press the lighted button. The peculiar statue of a red-haired person with an elephant trunk standing at the entrance of some U-Bahn stations is meant to remind passengers to throw their cigarettes away before entering (most people ignore it).

Local trains

The S-Bahn and Lokalbahn are the local and fast railways that run in Vienna and further afield. The Badner Bahn connects Vienna and the town of Baden (*see p200*).

If you are taking an S-Bahn within Vienna, you probably don't have to purchase another ticket, but if you travel outside zone 100, you'll need to buy an additional ticket according to how many zones you are travelling in. You can find this out by looking at the bull's eye zone map posted in all stations.

For lost property offices *see p219*.

Trams

Vienna has a great system of trams, or Strassenbahnen, that will take you everywhere within the city and its outskirts. All tram stops are clearly marked, with timetables. Every stop is announced by name, with corresponding connecting lines. Tram line numbers or letters stand alone, for example 2, J, D.

Buses

Buses go to all the places that trams can't. Their stops look just like the tram stops and also have maps and timetables clearly displayed. Bus lines are identified by numbers ending with an 'a' or by three-digit numbers, for example 13a, 149, 234.

Bus information

Details about timetables and fares are provided by Transport Information Offices, *see above*.

Useful bus, tram & U-Bahn routes

Tram 1 circles the 1st district clockwise along the Ringstrasse, and tram 2 circles it anti-clockwise. Hop on either tram and ride it in a full circle for probably the easiest and cheapest way to view some of Vienna's most beautiful buildings.

The only public transport possible within the 1st district is provided by bus lines 1a, 2a and 3a. The stops are clearly marked and have maps posted on them. The routes zig-zag through the 1st district, but as everywhere is within walking distance, you can't go too far wrong.

The U-Bahn line U2 runs along the Ringstrasse, and the U1 and U3 lines stop at Stephansdom.

Nightline

Vienna rolls up its pavements at midnight but safe, reliable Nightline buses run from 12.30am to 5am on the half hour on 22 routes. All transport tickets or cards are valid for nightlines.

Vienna's taxis are reliable and not too expensive. Most taxi drivers can speak a smattering of English. You can't hail them on the street, but will find them at clearly marked taxi ranks. Phoning for a taxi often takes less than three minutes' waiting time. A small tip or 'rounding off' of the fee is expected. There's a basic rate on weekdays (€2-€4 when phoning it) plus a per-kilometre charge and a small transport fee. On Sundays, public holidays and at night (1-6am) both the basic fare and per-kilometre rate go up. There's also a waiting charge. Few taxis take credit cards.

Taxi phone numbers
31 300/40 100/60 160/81 400.

Driving

Like everything else in Austria, driving is highly regulated and relatively safe. You are required by law to carry all documents and driving licences on you in case you are stopped. Austrians are aggressive drivers, but not as bad as their German neighbours. Speed limits are 50-50km per hour (18-31mph) in residential areas, 100km per hour (62mph) on country roads and 130km per hour (80mph) on motorways. Spot checks are common in Austria, and so is the breath test.

Breakdown services

Austria has two 24-hour major breakdown services. The service is free for members; however, non-members can call on their services and pay by cash or credit card. Funds can be reimbursed at a later stage if you have motor insurance that covers you for Austria.

ARBÖ
15, Mariahilfer Strasse 180 (24hr emergency hotline 123/ 24hr information hotline 891 217/ office 891 210/fax 8912 1236/ www.arboe.at). Tram 52, 58. **Credit** AmEx, DC, MC, V. **Map** p242 D8.

ÖAMTC
1, Schubertring 1-3 (24hr hotline 120/office 711 990/fax 711 99-1320/www.oeamtc.at). Tram 1, 2, D, J. **Open** 9am-6pm Mon-Fri; 9am-noon Sat. **Credit** DC, MC, V. **Map** p243 F7.
A fee of €130 (at night) or €95 (daytime) will be charged on top of other costs if you use this service as a non-member. The cost of towing a car within Vienna is €144.

Fuel stations

All international petrol stations take credit cards, but the local stations may not. Those listed below are open 24 hours a day.

Aral
10, Triester Strasse 68 (667 6173) 19, Heiligenstädterstrasse 46-48 (368 2380). **Map** p235 D1.

BP
3, Erdberger Lände 28-30 (715 4826). **Map** p240 G7.
13, Hietzinger Kai 133 (877 1451).

Mobil
1, Morzinplatz 1 (Franz-Josefs-Kai/ Schwedenplatz) (533 7398). **Map** p243 F6.

Shell
22, Wagramerstrasse 14 (263 3691). **Map** p237 K2-K3.

Parking

Parking in most areas of the 1st district is a nightmare and the police are quick to ticket and tow, which can cost anything from €21 to €165 – so avoid it wherever possible.
Districts 1-9 and 20 have blue zones (*Kurzparkzonen*), where you purchase parking vouchers at newsstands. In the 1st district you can park for up to 90 minutes, 9am-7pm Mon-Fri, and Saturday as marked. In other districts you can park for up to two hours, 9am-8pm Mon-Fri, and Saturday as marked. Look for designated parking spaces marked with blue lines. Vouchers come in 30-, 60- and 90-minute increments. Cross off the appropriate date, time and hour to the closest 15 minutes, and display it on your windshield. In the 1st or 7th district it might be simpler to use a parking garage, marked with a blue P.
On the Ringstrasse, parking garages, plus the number of parking spaces available, are marked in lit-up signs on the road. Remember to pay for the ticket at the automat machines that are placed at the entrances before you get into the car.

Vehicle hire

Renting a car is a fairly standard procedure in Austria, but do specify if you plan to drive into eastern Europe as there are numerous car thefts and you need to ensure adequate insurance.

Autoverleih Flott
6, Mollardgasse 44 (597 3402/ fax 596 7429/www.flott.at). U4 Margaretengürtel. **Open** 7am-6pm Mon-Fri; 7am-noon Sat. **Credit** AmEx, DC, MC, V. **Map** p238 C10.

Avis
1, Opernring 3-5 (town office 587 6241/fax 587 4900/24hr reservation hotline 0800 0800 8757/ www.avis.at). U1, U2, U4 Karlsplatz/tram 1, 2, J, D. **Open** 7am-6pm Mon-Fri; 8am-2pm Sat; 8am-1pm Sun. **Credit** AmEx, DC, MC, V. **Map** p242 E7.

Europcar
3, Erdbergstrasse 202 (town office 799 6176/fax 796 4295/airport 7007 33316/fax 7007 33716/ www.europcar.at). U3 Erdbergstrasse. **Open** *Town office* 7am-7pm Mon-Fri; 8am-2pm Sat; 8am-1pm Sun. *Airport* 7.30am-11pm Mon-Fri; 8am-7pm Sat; 8am-11pm Sun. **Credit** AmEx, DC, MC, V. **Map** p240 J8.

Hertz
1, Kärntner Ring 17 (512 8677/fax 512 5034/www.hertz.at). U1, U2, U4 Karlsplatz/tram 1, 2, D, J. **Open** 7.30am-6pm Mon-Fri; 9am-3pm Sat, Sun. **Credit** AmEx, DC, MC, V. **Map** p243 E8.

Cycling

Vienna is a great city for cyclists, as long as you avoid main roads and tram lines. The 7km (4-mile) bike path around the Ringstrasse is a lovely way to tour the city without getting lost. The Danube also has bike paths to south Hundertwasser Haus and to the Prater, which is filled with bike paths, children and dogs. (*See also p200*). A booklet called *Radwege* shows Vienna's cycle routes and is available at book stores. For bike rental *see p189*.

Walking

Vienna is a very walkable city. In the 1st district, with its pedestrian zones and narrow one-way streets, walking is the best way to get around. Jaywalking is frowned upon by locals, and could even result in a fine if the police feel so inclined. For all their orderliness, Austrians become aggressive, Lauda-like drivers when they get behind the wheel, so be careful when crossing the street – zebra crossings are often ignored.
The Vienna Tourist Board cooperates with a company called **Wiener Spaziergänge** (walks in Vienna), that organises walking tours named 'Vienna walks and talks'. A monthly multi-language brochure about these tours exploring themes such as baroque or *Biedermeier* Vienna can be found at the Vienna Tourist Office (*see below*). No need to book in advance, just show up at the designated meeting point mentioned in the brochure. Tours last about 90 minutes.

Wien Tourismus
Vienna Tourist Information
1, Albertinaplatz 1 (town office 211 14/hotel reservations & information 24 555). U1, U2, U4 Karlsplatz/ tram 1, 2, D, J. **Open** 9am-7pm daily. **Map** p242 E7.

Resources A-Z

Addresses

House and building numbers, and door numbers, follow the street name (for instance, Alserbachstrasse 54/9). Numbers are even on one side of the street and odd on the other. *Strasse* (street) is often abbreviated *Str*. Smaller streets (usually all side streets off a bigger street) are called *Gasse* (Webgasse, for example). All district numbers are preceded by a 1 or a 10 and followed by 0 . For the purposes of this guide, we've dispensed with the postcode system and listed district numbers on their own at the start of the address (thus Wittgenstein-Haus is at 3, Parkgasse 18 in the third district).

Age restrictions

The legal age for drinking and smoking is 16 and for driving 18. The age of consent for heterosexual sex is 14, for homosexual 16.

Business

Conventions & conferences

Hofburg Congress Centre & Redoutensaele Vienna
1, Heldenplatz (5873 6660/ www.hofburg.at). Tram 1, 2, D, J. **Map** p242 D7.

Reeds Exhibitions Messe Wien/ Congress Centre
2, Messestrasse, Tor 1 (7272 0208/ fax 7272 0195). U1 Praterstern. **Map** p242 D7.

World Trade Centre Convention Centre
Hotel AstronVienna Airport (70 15 10/www.astron-hotel.com).

Couriers

DHL
3, Steingasse 6-8 (71 181). Tram 71. **Open** 8am-7.45pm Mon-Fri; 8am-12.30pm Sat. **Credit** AmEx, DC, MC, V. **Map** p240 H9.

Mail Boxes Etc
3, Landstrasse Hauptstrasse 99-101 (512 4515/www.at.mbe.com). U3 Rochusgasse. **Open** 9am-7pm Mon-Fri; 9am-2pm Sat. **Credit** AmEx, DC, MC, V. **Map** p240 G8.

UPS
Express Counter, 1, Kärntnerring 14 (office 503 75 440/service hotline 0810 00 66 30/www.ups.com). U2 Oper/tram 1, 2, D, J. **Open** 10am-8pm Mon-Fri. **Credit** AmEx, MC, V. **Map** p243 E8.

Office hire & secretarial services

Regus Business Centres
1, Schottenring 16 (53 712-0/ www.regus.com). U2 Schottentor/ tram 1, 2, D. **Map** p242 D6.
1, Parkring 10 (516 33-0). Tram 1, 2. **Map** p243 F7.
6, Mariahilfer Strasse 123 (59 999-0). U3 Neubaugasse. **Map** p238 C8.
Regus Twin Tower, 11, Wienerberg Strasse 11 (99 460). U6 Philadelphia Brücke, then Twin Tower Shuttle Bus.
All **Open** 8am-5pm Mon-Fri. **Credit** AmEx, DC, MC, V.
Regus provides office space to rent, plus all kind of related business services (secretary, phone, fax machines and so on).

Translators & interpreters

UNIVERSITAS – Österreichischer Übersetzer – und Dolmetscherverband
Austrian Association of Translators and Interpreters
19, Gymnasiumstrasse 50 (368 60 60/www.universitas.org). U6 Nussdorfer Strasse. **Map** p234 C3.
The Association will provide all the necessary information regarding translating or interpreting services and connect you with the most suitable translator or interpreter.

Useful organisations

Amerika Haus Information Resource Center (AHIRC)
8, Schmidgasse 14 (405 3033/ www.usembassy.at/en/embassy/ arc.htm). U2 Rathaus. **Open** by appointment only. **Map** p242 C6.

For serious researchers only. The AHIRC provides current information on US government and public policy, economic and social issues.

British Trade Council
1, Laurenzerberggasse 2 (533 1594). U1, U4 Schwedenplatz/tram 1, 2. **Open** by appointment. **Map** p243 F6.
A directory of British companies in Austria is kept here.

US Chamber of Commerce
9, Porzellangasse 35 (319 5751/ www.amcham.or.at). Tram D. **Open** 9am-noon Mon-Fri. **Map** p235 D4.

US List
fax 310 51 51/office@amcham.or.at.
A directory of US firms, subsidiaries, affiliates and licensees in Austria is available for members for €30 and non-members for €40. It can be ordered directly by fax or email.

Webster University Library
22, Berchtoldgasse 1 (2699 29320). U1 Vienna International Centre/tram 90, 91/bus 92a. **Open** 10am-8.30pm Mon-Thur; 10am-6pm Fri; 2-6pm Sat. **Map** p237 L4.
A reference only library focusing on management, international relations, computer science and psychology and arts.

Women's Career Network (WCN)
19, Sieveringer Strasse 22a/1 (966 29 25/www.wcnvienna.org). U4 Heiligenstadt, then bus 39a. **Open** 10am-3pm Mon, Tue, Thur, Fri; 1-6pm Wed.
Affiliated with the American Women's Association, this network acts as a resource and support network for women seeking to develop their careers in Austria. It offers bi-monthly meetings, a newsletter and members' directory.

Consumer

If you have questions about your rights as a consumer, contact the organisation below:

Consumer Information Association (VKI)
6, Mariahilfer Strasse 81 (58 877-0/www.konsument.at). U3 Neubaugasse. **Open** 9am-6pm Mon-Fri. **Map** p238 C8.

Directory

Customs

Austria is part of the EU, so provided you purchased them in another EU state, you can bring limitless goods into the country as long as they are for personal use. Guidelines are given as follows: 800 cigarettes, 400 cigarillos, 200 cigars, 1kg tobacco; 10 litres spirits, 20 litres of fortified wine (such as port or sherry); 90 litres wine (or 60 litres sparkling wine) and 110 litres of beer. You are also allowed to take out of Austria these quantities of goods, provided you are entering another EU state.

When entering from a non-EU country or when purchasing in duty-free shops within the EU you can bring: 200 cigarettes or 100 cigarillos or 50 cigars or 250g tobacco; 2 litres wine and 1 litre spirits; or 2 litres spirits or 2 litres champagne; and 50g perfume and 250ml eau de toilette, and 500g coffee and 100g tea.

Items subject to import and/or export control include: controlled drugs, weapons, indecent material, certain plants, meat, meat products and products of animal origin; such as hides, skin, eggs, milk and dairy products (however, 1 kg per person of fully cooked meat/meat products, in cans or hermetically sealed containers is permitted).

VAT refunds can be claimed by travellers with destinations in non-EU countries. You can get the necessary forms from stores where you bought the items. Allow an extra 15 minutes at the airport to queue and process your refund.

Disabled

In general, Vienna is a relatively easy city to get around; however, the public transport system is not geared towards people with disabilities. Trams and buses don't have wheelchair lifts, although most U-Bahn stations do.

Several organisations are able to provide specific advice. The train service publishes a magazine especially for disabled travellers, *Behindertenführer der ÖBB*. You can also pick up a guide for handicapped people, available in English, from Vienna tourist information offices. On their website, www.wien.info, go to 'special programmes' ('Vienna for visitors with disabilities') and you'll find all kinds of information about hotels, sightseeing, restaurants, theatres, cinemas and so on.

Bizeps
5238 92123/www.bizeps.or.at.
Open 10am-4pm Mon-Thur.
A multilingual support group run by and for people with disabilities.

Fahrtendienst Gschwindl
810 4001. **Open** 6am-6.30pm Mon-Thur; 6am-6pm Fri.
Taxis equipped to transport wheelchairs, with a flat-rate charge of €28 to destinations within Vienna.

Information on the U-Bahn for the blind
7909 41300. **Open** 8am-3pm Mon-Fri.

Drugs

Although no drugs, either soft or hard, are allowed in Austria, the possession of marijuana seeds is not illegal. On the other hand, prescription drugs such as sleeping pills, sedatives and Prozac are considered illegal in large quantities. If you bring any of these drugs into Austria, you should take your prescription with you to avoid the risk of their being confiscated.

For the past decade or more, the Austrian drugs authorities have been fighting a problem of dealers pushing hard drugs and many of them operate under police surveillance, concentrated in places such as at the Kettenbrückengasse U4 station, the tunnels leading to Karlsplatz and certain stations on the U6 U-Bahn.

Vienna's strong social system means there is a network of social workers, doctors and psychologists working to help addicts. Three-quarters of the city's 7,000 or so addicts are in drug therapy, and strict rent control means that most drug users aren't homeless.

Drugs laws are complicated, but basically if you are caught with a small amount of soft drugs you will receive a slap-on-the-wrist type caution, or *Anzeige*, from the police, but probably nothing more. Punishment varies, but can include obligatory therapy. If you are Austrian, you stand to lose your driver's licence. The new government looks likely to introduce more draconian measures to deal with any perceived drug problems, judging from the announcements made in its election campaign.

Drogenberatungstelle
6, Esterhazygasse 18 (24hr hotline 586 0438-0). Bus 13a, 14a. **Open** 4-8.30pm Mon; 2-8.30pm Tue-Sun. Advice and help for drug addiction. **Map** p238 C9.

Websites
More information about consulting services can be found at www.drogen.at and www.drogenhilfe.at. Both homepages are in German.

Electricity

The current used in Austria is 220v, which works fine with British 240v appliances. If you have US 110v gadgets, it's best to bring the appropriate transformers. Plugs have two pins, so bring an adaptor.

Embassies & consulates

Australian Embassy
4, Mattiellistrasse 2-4 (506 74/ www.australian-embassy. at). U2, U3 Karlsplatz. **Open** 8.30am-1pm, 1.40-4.30pm Mon-Fri. **Map** p243 E8.

British Consulate
3, Jaurèsgasse 10 (716 13-5151). Tram 71. **Open** 9.15am-noon, 2-4pm Mon-Fri. **Map** p239 F8. British passport holders only in the afternoon.

British Embassy
3, Jaurèsgasse 12 (716 13-5151/ www.britishembassy.at). Tram 71. **Map** p239 F8.

Canadian Embassy
1, Laurenzerberggasse 2 (5313 83000/www.kanada.at). U3 Schwedenplatz/tram 1, 2. **Open** Consular section 8.30am-12.30pm, 1.30-3.30pm Mon-Fri. **Map** p243 F6.

Irish Embassy
1, Rotenturmstrasse 16-18 (715 42 46). U1, U4 Schedenplatz. **Open** 9.30-11.30am, 1.30-4pm Mon-Fri. **Map** p243 F6.

South African Embassy
19, Sandgasse 33 (3206 4930/www. southafrican-embassy.at). U6 Nuss-dorf. **Open** 8.30am-noon Mon-Fri.

US Consulate
1, Gartenbaupromenade 2 (31 339-2351/3005/consularvienna@ stategov). U3 Stubentor/tram 1, 2. **Open** Visas 8.30-11am Mon, Tue, Thur, Fri. *Phone enquiries* 2.30-4.30pm Mon-Fri. **Map** p243 F7.

US Embassy
9, Boltzmanngasse 16 (31 339/ www.usembassy.at). Bus 40a. **Open** 8.30am-5pm Mon-Fri. **Map** p235 D4.

Emergencies

Beware: *Ambulanz* means emergency room or outpatient clinic, and *Rettung* means ambulance. *See also* **Health**.

Ambulance
Rettung (144).

Fire

Feuerwehr (122).

Police

Polizei (133).

Vienna Medical Association Service Department for Foreign Patients

1, Weihburggasse 10/12 (5150 1213/24hr hotline 513 95 95/ www.aekw.at). U1, U3 Stephansplatz. **Open** 8am-4pm Mon-Wed; 8am-6pm Thur, Fri. **Map** p243 E7.

Gay & lesbian

For information about HIV/AIDS, see below.

Hosi

2, Novaragasse 40 (216 6604/ www.hosiwien.at). Tram N, 21. **Open** 5-10pm Tue-Thur. *Phone service* 6-8pm Tue; 7-9pm Wed, Thur. **Map** p243 G5.
A political meeting point for those interested in fighting discrimination. Regular events include: open house (5-10pm Tue); lesbian group (7pm Wed); coming out groups (from 6pm Thur); and occasional dance nights for women (7pm Fri).

HUK

Homosexuals and the Church
1, PO Box 513 (983 3403/huk-wien@gay.at).
This Christian group meets every Tuesday at 7.30pm in the chapel of the Albert Schweizer Haus (9, Schwarzspanierstrasse 13) or at 8pm in the Villa (see p166).

Rosa Lila Tip

6, Linke Wienzeile 102 (Gays 585 343/schwulenberatung@ villa.at/Lesbians 586 8150/ lesbenberatung@villa.at). U4 Pilgramgasse. **Open** 5-8pm Mon-Fri. **Map** p238 C9.
Counselling, discussion groups and advice for gays (5-8pm Mon-Thur) and lesbians (5-8pm Mon-Fri).

Health

Most doctors in the Austrian Health Service (*Krankenkasse*) speak English. Hospital care is divided between general care (*allgemeine Klasse*) or Special (*Sonderklasse*), which is like the BUPA private health scheme in the UK. Treatment is available for citizens of all countries that have special treaties with the Austrian Krankenkasse – in effect most European states. Britain has a reciprocal arrangement with Austria so that emergency hospital

treatment is free when you show a British passport. Technically, seeing doctors, dentists or getting treatment at outpatient departments is also free. However, receiving free medical treatment can involve much bureaucracy, so it's best to take out full health insurance. Few hospitals will accept credit cards.
If you fall ill in Vienna, take a completed E111 form to the Wiener Gebietskrankenkasse, where it will be exchanged for a blue *Kranken-schein* (medical certificate), which you can present to the doctor, or to the hospital in an emergency.

Wiener Gebietskrankenkasse

10, Wienerbergstrasse 15-19 (601 22-0/www.gkkwien.at). U6 Meidling/bus 7A, 10A, 15A. **Open** 8am-2pm Mon-Thur; 8am-1pm Fri. Non-Austrians with an E111 form should go to room 56.

Accident & emergency

There are many accident hospitals (*Unfallspitäler*) listed under hospitals (*Krankenhäuser*) in the white pages of the phone book. The following hospitals accept emergencies 24 hours a day, seven days a week.

Allgemeines Krankenhaus (AKH)

9, Währinger Gürtel 18-20 (40 400-0/www.akh-wien.ac.at). U6 Michelbeuern. **Map** p234 B5.
The largest hospital in Europe, the AKH is affiliated with the University of Vienna. It is probably your best option if you are in central Vienna.

Lorenz Böhler Unfall Krankenhaus

20, Donaueschingerstrasse 13 (33 110/www.ukhboehler.at). U6 Dresdnerstrasse. **Map** p235 F2.

Saint Anna Kinderspital

9, Kinderspitalgasse 6 (401 700). U6 Alser Strasse/tram 43, 44. **Map** p234 B5.
This friendly, hectic children's hospital has doctors on hand 24 hours a day to check out high fevers, rashes or worse.

AIDS

AIDS-Hilfe Wien

6, Mariahilfer Gürtel 4 (599 370/ wien@aidshilfe.or.at). U6 Gumpendorfer Strasse/tram 6, 18. **Open** 4-8pm Mon, Wed; 9am-noon Thur; 2-5pm Fri. **Map** p238 B9.
For tests, results and counselling.

Complementary medicine

The organisations below can suggest specialist practitioners.

Austrian Scientific Council in Acupuncture

4, Schwindgasse 3/9 (505 8594). U1 Taubstummengasse. **Map** p239 E8.

Austrian Society of Homeopathic Medicine

7, Mariahilfer Strasse 110 (526 7575/www.kaiserkrone.at). U3 Neubaugasse. **Open** 8am-6pm Mon-Fri; 8am-noon Sat. **Map** p238 C8.
A list of doctors practising in homeopathy is available from this English-speaking group.

International Academy for Alternative & Complementary Medicine

SMZ Baumgartner Höhe, 14, Sanatoriumstrasse 2 (688 75 07/ www.gamed.or.at). Bus 47A, 48A. Information and seminars for doctors.

Internationale Apotheke

1, Kärntner Ring 17 (512 2825). U1, U2, U4 Karlsplatz/tram 1, 2, D, J. **Open** 8am-6pm Mon-Fri; 8am-noon Sat. **Credit** AmEx, DC, MC, V. **Map** p243 E8.
Specialists in all types of homeopathic medicine.

Vienna School of Osteopathy

13, Frimbergergasse 6-8 (879 38 36/ www.wso.at). U4 Braunschweiggasse.

Contraception & abortion

Outpatient Clinic for Pregnancy Help

1, Fleischmarkt 26 (512 9631). U1, U4 Schwedenplatz/tram 1, 2. **Open** 8am-5pm Mon-Fri; 9am-1pm Sat. **Map** p243 F6.
Pregnancy tests, birth-control advice and confidential abortion counselling. English spoken.

Dentists

Austrians have good dental care, but only some costs are covered by the state system. Many Austrians skip across the border to Hungary, where they can usually get the same treatment for a third of the cost.

Directory

On-duty dentists

512 2078. **Open** 8am-1am Mon-Fri;
9am-6pm Sat, Sun.
A recording giving names and phone
numbers of dentists on emergency
call. See also 'Emergency Services'
(*Notdienst*) in the newspapers.

University Dental Clinic

*9, Währinger Strasse 25a (outpatient
4277-67000/dental prosthesis 4277-
67072/67082). U2 Schottentor, then
tram 37, 38, 40, 41, 42.* **No credit
cards. Map** p242 D5.
The university emergency dental
clinic is open Mon-Fri, but only for a
few hours. Phone to confirm times.

Doctors

If you need an English-speaking
doctor, phone 513 95 95 (24-hour
hotline, daily). The British Embassy
(716130) can also provide you with
a list of English-speaking doctors.
Take your E111 or private insurance
documents with you.

Hospitals

There's a number of private clinics
and hospitals in the city, but the
largest and most comprehensive
hospital is the Vienna General
Hospital (AKH) in the 9th district
(*see p217*).

Opticians

See p135.

Pharmacies

Pharmacies (*Apotheken*), signposted
with a cursive 'A', are found in all
districts of Vienna and are normally
open 8am-noon, 2-6pm Mon-Fri; 8am-
noon Saturdays, although many in
the 1st district are open longer.
    Many over-the-counter drugs
can also be found in local Bipa or
Douglas stores (*see p134*).
Pharmacies take turns in opening
24 hours, and all hang up a sign
giving the address of the nearest
chemist's to remain open.

Medicine Delivery Service

Medikamentenzustelldienst
(89 144).
For €18.53 (free in districts 21 and
22) this 24-hour service will pick up
and deliver medicines from
pharmacies.

Pharmacy Information

Apotheken-Bereitschaftsdienst
(1550).

A recording in German lists the
pharmacies that are open after
normal business hours and at
weekends.

Helplines

Alcoholics Anonymous

*3, Barthgasse 7 (English speakers
317 8876/0664/German speakers
799 5999/www.anonyme/
alkoholiker.at). U3 Schlachthofgasse.*
Open 6-9pm daily. **Map** p240 J9.
A number of English-speaking
groups meet regularly, two evenings
and two days a week.

Befriender's Crisis Intervention

713 3374. **Open** 9.30am-1pm,
6.30-10pm daily.
Psychiatric help/suicide hotline
answered by English speakers.

Viennese Children & Youth Protection

**Wiener Kinder- und
Jugendanwaltschaft**
*9, Sobieskigasse 31 (1708 85905).
U6 Nussdorferstrasse/tram 37.* **Open**
9am-5pm Mon-Fri. **Map** p234 C3.
English spoken.

Women's Emergency Centre

Frauen Notruf der Staft Wien
(71 719).
If you have been raped, phone this
number and an English speaker will
provide help.

ID

There is no law obliging citizens to
carry means of identification.
However, if the police want to check
it and you don't have it with you,
they may insist on accompanying
you to wherever you've left it.

Internet

For such a traditional city, Vienna is
surprisingly up to date when it
comes to e-commerce and the
internet. Post Telekom has just
launched an ADSL service,
throughout Austria. Internet access
for tourists, however, is limited to
the venues listed below. The AOL
access number from Vienna is
(585 8483), EUnet is (899 330) and
Compuserve is (0049-180 570 40 70).
    For free internet access, head for
one of the three branches of
Amadeus (*see p133*) or Big Net, a
chain of cafés throughout the city –
the largest branch is at Mariahilfer
Strasse 27 (205 06/www.bignet.at).
Café Stein (*see p186*) has four

terminals, but sets you back a
whopping €4 per half hour. Much
cheaper are Das Möbel (*see p185*)
and rhiz (*see p186*) at €3.60 per hour,
but there's only one terminal in each.
    If you find yourself in the main
hall of Flex (*see p182*) – and can hear
yourself think – you could try and
bag one of its two free terminals.
Einstein at Rathausplatz 4 also has
internet access. Café Nanubar at
Schleifmühlgasse 11 (587 2987) has
three terminals (€4 per hour).

Left luggage

At the airport, left luggage is in
the entrance hall across from the
rental cars and costs €2.70 per day,
depending on the size of luggage.
All credit cards are accepted.
    In the larger train stations in
Vienna, there are no longer any left
luggage offices, but you are able to
leave your luggage in a locker (€2).

Legal help

If you run into legal trouble, contact
your insurers or your national
consulate (*see p216*).

Libraries

American International School Secondary Library

*19, Salmannsdorfer Strasse 47
(4013 2220/www.ais.at). U4
Heiligenstadt.* **Open** 8am-4pm
Mon-Fri.
A good selection of American
magazines, newspapers and journals
is available. Books may be borrowed
for up to two weeks. Closed during
school holidays.

Austrian National Library

*1, Josefsplatz 1 (53 410/
www.onb.ac.at). Bus 2a, 3a.* **Open**
9am-9pm Mon-Fri; 9am-12.45pm Sat.
Map p242 E7.
Browse the catalogue, select what
you want, pick the books up the
next day to take to the reading
room. There's a varied choice of
English titles.

British Council Library

*1, Schenkenstrasse 4 (5332 61682/
www.britishcouncil.at). Tram 1, 2, D.*
Open 11am-6pm Mon; 11am-5pm
Tue; 11am-5pm Wed, Thur; 11am-
1pm Fri. **Map** p242 D6.
Over 21,000 volumes of literature
from all English-speaking
Commonwealth countries are kept
here. Films can be rented too, for a
fee. The library is open to the public,

but membership is required (annual €40, two months €25). Proof of identity is required for registration.

Städtische Büchereien

7, Urban-Loritz Platz 2 (4000-84 500/www.buechereien.at). U6 Stadthalle/tram 6, 18. **Open** 11am-7pm Mon-Fri; 10am-2pm Sat. **Map** p238 B8.

Vienna's public libraries have an excellent collection of books, tapes, CDs and records, with around 20,000 non-German works. For the nearest branch phone the main library above.

Lost property

If you've left something behind on public transport, there's a good chance you will get it back again. To trace possessions left on a tram or bus, phone the General Information Office (790 943-500); on a train phone Südbahnhof (5800 22 222). Each bus and tram has a station where found articles are taken. After one week, everything is removed to the central police lost and found office. Go in person, with plenty of patience.

Central Lost & Found

Zentrales Fundamt
9, Wasagasse 22 (313 4492-11). Bus 40a. **Open** 8am-noon Mon-Fri. **Map** p242 D5.

Media

Press

International newspapers and magazines are widely available from kiosks, street sellers and tobacco stores all over Vienna. The one English-language newspaper published in Vienna, *Austria Today*, a weekly, contains some solid news coverage (especially of UN and embassy matters), but has rather incomplete entertainment listings.

An extraordinary number of titles on sale in Austria belong to the ever-expanding News Group. Led by the enterprising Fellner Brothers, its publications tend to resemble buy-by-post catalogues.

Augustin

Big Issue-style monthly magazine sold and partly produced by homeless people. *Augustin* carries features, listings and fiction.

Bazar

www.bazar.at
A classified ads paper that comes out on Tuesdays, Thursdays and Saturdays. Weekly editions covering housing and cars are also published. It carries quite a number of porn ads and photos.

City

www.city2003.at
A cheaper version of *Der Falter*, minus the politics, and with more frivolous listings. Good for basic what's-on information.

Der Falter

www.falter.at
The darling of Vienna's younger, left/progressive intellectuals, *Der Falter* comes out on Wednesdays and offers the best listings information in town, focusing on nightlife, music, film, theatre, exhibitions and restaurants. It has a socially committed agenda and is one of Austria's few practitioners of investigative journalism, fearlessly denouncing institutional racism, police brutality and political incompetence. *Falter* also publishes an excellent quarterly guide to shopping and services, *Best of Vienna* and has a useful website.

Format

www.news.at/format
This News Group-owned news weekly is easy to mistake for *Profil* (*see below*) but apart from the design, *Format*'s content is far inferior.

Kurier

www.kurier.at
Also owned by the Media Print group, *Kurier* is the petit bourgeoise version of the '*Krone*' (*see below*), with more serious political content and fewer offensive columnists.

Neue Kronen Zeitung

www.krone.at
Proportionally the best read newspaper in the world, selling almost 900,000 a day to a population of eight million. The power of this detestable populist rag is overwhelming; its editor and minority shareholder Hans Dichand is Austria's great unelected opinion maker. His reactionary columnists turn out a stomach-turning brew of tinpot patriotism, sentimental animal protectionism and topless models.

News

www.news.at
Aggressive reporting and a high nipple count are the two hallmarks of the Fellners' best-selling news weekly. Yet among the tiresome lists of the 50 richest/best-dressed Austrians, there are some serious articles and plenty of Haider baiting.

Die Presse

www.diepresse.at
Serious and extremely conservative, Die Presse is the successor to the venerable *Neue Freie Presse* of imperial times. The paper contains plenty of analysis and background information, particularly financial.

Profil

www.profil.at
Another News Group title, *Profil* is Austria's most serious weekly,

containing highly critical yet well-founded political coverage. Keen to unearth scandal and with above-average foreign news.

Der Standard

www.derstandard.at
A *Guardian*-style paper covering politics, business, arts and culture. It is immediately recognisable by its salmon-pink colour.

Radio

The liberalisation of the broadcasting laws in 1997 spawned dozens of private radio stations, none of which have seriously challenged the hegemony of state broadcasting.

The state-run ÖRF's station, **Österreich 1** (92.0 FM, 87.8 FM) offers a blend of classical, jazz and opera music, including live concerts and other cultural programmes. **Radio Wien** (89.9 and 95.3 FM), one of ÖRF's regional stations, has pop, news, weather and traffic. **Ö3** (99.9 FM) is a slick commercial station.

Despite becoming a tad more mainstream, ÖRF-run **FM4** is still the best option for indie/dance music, broadcasting 24 hours daily (on 103.4 FM), in English from 1am to 2pm, with English-language news on the hour from 6am to 7pm.

Radio Austria International (6,155kHz, 5,945kHz, 13,730kHz) is ÖRF's short-wave station designed by the government to be the 'voice of Austria' abroad. It has news and information and an English, Spanish and Russian service.

Probably the best bet for more diverse programming is **Radio Orange** (94 FM), which features soul, hip hop, jazz and African music.

Television

Since the 2001 Private TV Law created a framework for the terrestrial commercial TV, only one licence has so far been granted. **ATV** is a grim collage of re-runs, bad movies and *The Lugners*, an Osbournes-inspired chronicle of a society building contractor, best known for bringing Fergie and Pam An to the Opera Ball. Austrian TV therefore consists of two state-run national channels, **ÖRF1** and **ÖRF2** (www.orf.at). Other channels are only available via cable or satellite.

ÖRF1 has the more popular schedule, with sports coverage, movies at night, and US serials in the afternoon. ÖRF2 tends towards more cultural programming, including opera, music, plays and document-aries – as well as awful talk shows and nightmarish Alpine folk singing.

Telekabel is Vienna's only cable television provider and offers various

Directory

packages including foreign stations, principally German. Channels in English include CNN, BET (Black Entertainment Television), BBC World, BBC Prime, Eurosport and MTV (90 per cent in German). It also provides internet and phone services.

Money

From January 2002, Austria jettisoned its Schillings and its unit of currency became the euro, usually abbreviated as €. One euro is made up of 100 cents. There are seven banknotes – €5 (grey), €10 (red), €20 (blue), €50 (orange), €100 (green), €200 (yellow-brown), and €500 (purple) – and eight coins – 1 cent, 2 cents, 5 cents, 10 cents, 20 cents, 50 cents, €1 and €2.

ATMs

Bankomat machines are dotted throughout Vienna and have a lit sign with two horizontal green and blue stripes. Most take credit and Eurocheque cards, and many offer the service in different languages. *Bestätigung*, the green button, means 'confirm'. None of the machines gives receipts. There are also a few automatic currency-converting machines, stating 'Change/Cambio' with instructions in English, that will accept foreign banknotes.

Banks

The best place to exchange money is in a bank, as it will give you a better rate. You'll also save money by exchanging a larger sum in one go, as there is often a minimum commission charge. Eurocheques are acceptable at many restaurants, shops and hotels as long as you present a valid Eurocheque card.

Most banks open 8am-12.30pm and 1.30-3pm during the week, extended to 5.30pm on Thursdays. A few banks, such as the main Creditanstalt bank on Schottengasse and the Die Erste Bank on Graben 21, do not close for lunch. Some banks, generally at railway stations and airports, stay open longer.

Bank opening times are set to change and soon more branches might stay open during lunch hours.

Bureaux de change

City Air Terminal
U3, U4, Schnellbahn Wien Mitte. **Open** 8am-12.30pm, 2-6.30pm daily.

Opera/Karlsplatz
U1, U2, U3, U4/tram 1, 2, D, J. **Open** 8am-7pm daily.

Schwechat Airport Shuttle
Open 6.30am-11pm daily.

Südbahnhof
Tram D. **Open** 6.30am-10pm daily.

Westbahnhof U3
Tram 5, 6. **Open** 7am-10pm daily.

Credit cards

Compared to western Europe, Budapest and Prague, Vienna is not a credit-card friendly town. Many of the smaller hotels and restaurants do not take credit cards, and retail credit card percentages are very high compared to the rest of Europe.

American Express
1, Kärntnerstrasse 21-23 (515 110). U1, U3 Stephansplatz. **Open** 9am-5pm Mon-Thur; 9am-4pm Fri. **Map** p243 E7.
Holders of the card can use the company's facilities here, including the cash advance service.

Lost/stolen cards

If you lose your credit card, or it has been stolen, phone one of the emergency numbers listed below. All lines are open 24 hours daily.
American Express 0800 900 940
Diners Club 501 350
Master Card 0800 218 235
Visa 711 11 770

Tax

Non-EU citizens can claim back Austrian value-added tax (*Mehrwertsteuer* or MwSt) on goods purchased in the country. Ask to be issued with a Tax-Free shopping Cheque (or U34 formular) for the amount of the refund and present this, together with the receipt, at the refund office at the airport.

Opening hours

Shops tend to open at 8.30am or 9am and close at 6pm. Many smaller shops, especially outside the 1st district, still close for lunch. Some larger shops, especially in the centre, are now open on Saturdays until 5pm. All stores in Vienna close on Sunday and public holidays. For after-hours shopping *see p140*.

Police stations

The emergency number for the police is 133. The police are generally straightforward, speak English and are polite – as long as you do what they say. There are police stations located in central Vienna at: 1, Am Hof 3 (313 47 2118); and 3, Juchgasse 3 (717 800).

Central Police HQ
1, Schottenring 7-9 (313 100). U2 Schottentor. **Map** p242 D5.

Vocabulary

High German (*Hochdeutsch*) is the official language, but Austrians speak German with a softer, more lilting accent filled with their own particular colloquialisms. The Viennese speak *Wienerisch*, a twangy and curious dialect of German littered with Czech, Hungarian and Yiddish words and distorted vowel sounds. Sometimes it can seem that the odd shopkeeper finds it easier to speak English than high German.

Austrians greet each other not with the German *Guten Tag* ('good day') but with *Grüss Gott* ('greetings to God'). It is considered bad form not to greet someone in a lift or in a shop when you meet eyes, so when in doubt a 'Grüss Gott' will never go amiss. Ingratiate yourself to the Viennese by greeting them with a hearty '*Servus*' and seeing them off with '*Baba*' (stress on the first 'ba').

The Würstelstand is the ideal location to hear dialect first-hand.

Order a Bratwurst (in Vienna the subtleties of the German indefinite article are conveniently reduced to a simple Anglo-Saxon 'a') and you will be asked '*Schoaf od'r sues*', referring to the type of mustard you require: hot or sweet. If you're not happy with your sausage, you could always complain with a provocative '*Dis is a Schaas*' (it's crap).

The following is a basic survival vocabulary:

Closed – *Geschlossen/Gesperrt*
Danger – *Gefahr*
Entrance – *Eingang*
Info – *Auskunft*
No vacancies – *Besetzt*
Out of order – *Ausser Betrieb*
Please/you're welcome – *Bitte*
Pull – *Ziehen*
Push – *Drücken*
Signature – *Unterschrift*
Thank you – *Danke, Danke Schön*
Exit – *Ausgang*
WC – *Toiletten, WC*
Working – *In Betrieb*

Directory

Postal services

The postal service is efficient and easy to use. Every post office has a window marked *Fremdsprache* (Foreign Language) although most workers speak English anyway. Postboxes are bright yellow little boxes sporting a two-ended horn, often mounted on buildings. An orange stripe denotes that the box will be emptied at weekends.

To post a letter within Austria or Europe priority class will cost 51¢. Worldwide airmail costs €1.09. To have the receiver sign for a letter will cost €2.54. There are also next-day and two-day services available. To send a package inland costs €3.27 for 2kg; to send the same package in the EU will cost €10.17. For more information call the Post Office 24-hour hotline (08100 10100).

All post offices offer express mail and faxing services. Look in the telephone directory's white pages under *Post- und Telegraphen verwaltung* for locations of post offices and their opening times. The following post offices have extended opening hours.

Franz-Josefs-Bahnhof
9, Althanstrasse 10. Tram D. **Open** 6am-10pm daily. **Map** p235 D3.
Main Post Office
1, Fleischmarkt 19 (0800 100 100). U1, U4 Schwedenplatz/tram 1, 2. **Open** 24 hours daily. **Map** p243 F6.
Post Office Information
(51 551-0). **Open** 8am-5pm Mon-Fri.
Südbahnhof
10, Wiedner Gürtel 1b. Tram D. **Open** 7am-10pm daily. **Map** p239 F10.
Westbahnhof
15, Europaplatz. Westbahnhof U3. **Open** 6am-11pm daily. **Map** p238 B8.

Poste restante

Poste restante facilities are available at any post office, but only the main post office (*see above*) has a 24-hour service. Letters should be addressed to the recipient 'Postlagernd, Postamt' – along with the address of the particular post office. They can be collected from the counter marked *Postlagernde Sendungen*. Take your passport.

Public holidays

New Year's Day (1 Jan); Epiphany (6 Jan); Easter Monday; Labour Day (1 May); Ascension Day (6th Thurs after Easter); Whit Monday (6th Mon after Easter); Corpus Christi (2nd Thurs after Whitsun); Assumption Day (15 Aug); Austrian Public Holiday (26 Oct); All Saints' Day (1 Nov); Immaculate Conception (8 Dec); Christmas Day (25 Dec); St Stephen's Day (26 Dec).

Religion

Because of Vienna's musical importance, many people attend church simply to appreciate the fantastic musical repertoire. Look out particularly for details of Sunday Mass at the **Augustinerkirche**, **Minoritenkirche, Karlskirche, Stephansdom** and **Michaeler kirche**. The acclaimed Vienna Boys' Choir can be heard during Mass at the Burgkapelle every Sunday and religious holidays at 9.15am except from July to mid-September, but to hear the choir you must pay both a concert fee and have a bag thrust under your nose for donations. If you can't arrange tickets in the chapel ground, don't bother with the balconies – you'll be crammed into an uncomfortable room without a view and will have to watch the whole thing on a television monitor.

Anglican

Christ Church
3, Salesianergasse 24 (714 89 00). U4 Stadtpark/tram 71. **Map** p243 F7. Members of Viennese choirs are often invited as guest singers.

Protestant

Church of Jesus Christ & Latter Day Saints
19, Silbergasse 1 (367 5647). Tram 38/bus 10a.
International Baptist Church
12, Rotenmühlgasse 63 (817 41 63). U6 Philadelphiabrücke, then bus 9A.
United Methodist Church
15, Sechshauser Strasse 56 (604 53 47). Bus 57a. **Map** p238 A10.

Roman Catholic

St Augustin
1, Augustinerstrasse 3 (533 7099). U1, U2, Karlsplatz. **Map** p242 E7.
St Stephan's Cathedral
1, Stephansplatz 3 (51522 3553). U1, U3 Stephansplatz. **Map** p243 E6.
Votivkirche
9, Rooseveltplatz 8 (4085 05014). U2 Schottentor. **Map** p242 D5.

Jewish

City Synagogue
1, Seitenstettengasse 2 (531 040). U4 Schwedenplatz. **Map** p243 F6. In order to be admitted, you must show your passport.

Safety & security

Vienna is one of the safest cities in Europe. Many people, including women, don't think twice about walking alone in most districts even at night. Public transport is generally safe day and night. The opening up of the borders with eastern Europe, however, has begun to have an effect. An increasing amount of pick-pocketing and petty crime is occurring in tourist locations, so it is wise to take precautions, especially in crowded areas such as the Naschmarkt. There are very few places to steer clear of in Vienna – Karlsplatz station is notorious as a drugs centre; the Prater at night is known for pickpockets.

Smoking

Austrians are among the heaviest smokers in western Europe. Smoking is banned on public transport (but many people ignore this, especially in U-Bahn stations) but tolerated just about everywhere else.

Study

Language classes

Berlitz
Main office: 1, Graben 13 (512 82860). U1, U3 Stephansplatz/ bus 1a. **Map** p242 E6.
6, Mariahilfer Strasse 27 (586 5693). U2 Babenbergerstrasse. **Map** p242 D8.
1, Rotenturmstrasse 1-3 (535 6120). U1, U3 Stephansplatz/ bus 1a. **Map** p243 E6.
10, Troststrasse 50 (604 3911). U1 Reumannplatz, then bus 66a, 67a. All **Open** 8am-8pm Mon-Fri. **No credit cards**.
Individual, intensive and evening courses in German.

Cultura Wien
1, Bauernmarkt 18 (533 2493). U4 Schwedenplatz/bus 1a, 3a. **Open** 9am-6pm Mon-Fri. **No credit cards**. **Map** p243 E6. Offers intensive four-hour classes taught daily, and evening classes two days a week in courses lasting four and eight weeks. Good summer programme for younger students.

Inlingua Sprachschule
1, Neuer Markt 1 (512 2225). U1, U3 Stephansplatz/tram 1, 2, D, J. **Open** 9am-6pm Mon-Fri. **No credit cards**. **Map** p242 E7. Four hours a day intensive courses are run in sessions lasting two weeks or longer. Inlingua also offers twice a

week evening courses in business German. Classes are limited to four to eight students.

Talk Partners

1, Fischersteige 10/16 (535 9695).
U4 Schwedenplatz/tram 1, 2.
Open 8.30am-4.30pm Mon-Thur; 8.30am-2.30pm Fri. **No credit cards. Map** p243 E6.
Programmes at Talk Partners are individually designed by the students, who choose content, time, place, duration and intensity of course.

University of Vienna

1, Ebendorferstrasse 10/4 (405 1254). U2 Schottentor/tram 1, 2, D. **Open** 9am-5pm Mon-Wed, Fri; 9am-5.30pm Thur. **No credit cards. Map** p242 D6.
Cheap nine- or 12-week courses in German for foreigners.

Universities

Club International Universitaire (CIU)

1, Schottengasse 1/Mezzanine (533 6533/www.ciu.at). U2 Schottentor/tram 1, 2, D. **Open** 9am-8pm Mon-Fri. **Map** p243 D6.
Lectures, debates, social events, courses and trips are organised by this focal point of international student activity in Vienna.

Institute of European Studies

1, Johannesgasse 7 (512 2601). U1, U3 Stephansplatz/tram 1, 2. **Open** 9am-5pm Mon-Fri. **Map** p243 E7.
The Institute offers a semester or academic year abroad for college juniors and seniors. Most classes are taught in English. Subjects include

East-West studies, humanities, German and international business. About 100 students are enrolled.

International Christian University

3, Rennweg 1 (718 5068-13).
Tram 71. **Map** p239 F10.
A small American university offering undergraduate and graduate degrees and certificates in marketing, management, accounting, economics, computers, English and German.

Open University

1, Fischersteige 10 (533 2390). U1, U4 Schwedenplatz. **Map** p243 E6.
A complete English curriculum is offered in the humanities and social sciences, as well as a selection of Masters degrees and postgraduate programmes in management and business studies.

Webster University

22, Berchtoldgasse 1 (269 9293).
U1 Vienna International Centre/ tram 90, 91/bus 92a. **Map** p237 L4.
A fully accredited American university recognised in Austria with BA, MA and MBA programmes in English. Subjects include international relations, management, computer science and psychology.

Telephones

Until a few years ago, Post und Telekom Austria, the state communications monopoly, had some of the most expensive tariffs in Europe. Deregulation in the late 1990s was a godsend. Now there are plentiful public telephones sprinkled through the city. However, if you are staying in a hotel you might want to follow an Austrian custom and use the local post office, where the tariffs

are much cheaper, to make any long-distance call. Every post office has a phone cabin for telephone calls. Go to the post office counter and say you want to make a call and you'll be directed to a numbered cabin. Pay at the counter after you have finished. Business telephone hours are 8am-6pm Mon-Fri; cheaper rates are charged at evenings and weekends.

Directory Enquiries

Austria, EU countries, neighbouring countries from Austria (11 811/11 88 77). World (0900 11 88 77). Conference calls (0820 100 100). Mobile phones (0800 664 664). Telegrams (0800 100 190).

Telekom Information

0800 100 100. **Open** 7am-6pm Mon-Fri; at other times phone 11 811.
Information about the wide range of telephone tariffs in Austria.

Making a call

To make an international call, dial 00, then the country code, city code and telephone number. A few country codes are: Australia 61, Germany 49, Hungary 36, India 91, Ireland 353, Japan 81, New Zealand 64, South Africa 27, UK 44, USA/ Canada 1.

All telephone numbers in Austria have prefixes, which are usually printed in parentheses. To make a call to Vienna from elsewhere in Austria, dial 01 and then the number. To phone Vienna from abroad, dial 00 43, followed by 1 and then the number. To dial an Austrian mobile phone from abroad (usually 0676, 0699 or 0664 numbers) dial 00 43, then the number without the 0.

Don't be concerned if the telephone number you want to call has only four digits. Many general city numbers, such as the train station or post office, only have four digits. Austrian telephones have direct-dial extensions that are often placed at the end of the telephone number, preceded by a hyphen.

Public telephones

Newly designed smart glass public telephone booths are popping up all over Vienna. A few cents (minimum 20 cents) are enough for a quick local call, but have a few extra on hand if you need them.
Information operator *11 811.*

Mobile telephones

A mobile telephone is called a *Handy*, a nifty English word that Austrians

Climate by month

	Average min °C/°F	Average max °C/°F	Average temp °C/°F
Jan	2/36	-2/28	0/32
Feb	4/39	-1/30	1/33
Mar	9/49	2/35	6/42
Apr	15/59	5/41	9/49
May	19/67	9/49	15/59
June	22/72	13/55	18/64
July	25/77	15/59	20/68
Aug	25/77	15/59	20/68
Sept	20/68	12/53	16/61
Oct	14/57	7/45	11/51
Nov	7/44	2/35	4/40
Dec	4/39	-1/30	1/34

are disappointed to learn isn't used in Britain. As there is plenty of competition, you can get your mobile phone free and just pay for your calls plus your monthly line rental.

Max.mobil
3, Kelsenstrasse 5-7 (0676 2000). Tram 18. **Map** p240 G10-H10.

Mobilkom
0800 664 300.

One
21, Brünner Strasse 52 (277 28-3040/service team, price information 0800 7777 99).

Telekom Information
1, Fleischmarkt 19 (535 3801). U1, U4 Schwedenplatz/tram 1, 2. **Open** 8am-6pm Mon-Fri. **Map** p243 F6. 3, Erdberger Lände 36-48 (715 2512). U3 Rochusgasse. **Open** 8am-5pm Mon-Fri. **Map** p240 H7.

Time

Austria is on Central European Time, which means it is an hour ahead of Britain. Like Britain, Austria puts its clocks forward an hour on the last Sunday of March, and puts them back an hour on the last Sunday of October.

Tipping

There are no fixed rules about tipping, but in a restaurant it is customary either to give a ten per cent tip or to round up the bill. Announce the total sum to the waiting staff as they take your money – they will normally pocket the tip and then return your change.

Taxi drivers normally receive an extra ten per cent over the metered fare, and €1 per bag is normal for porters and bellhops. Tipping is common in Austria, so an extra €1 or €2 for workers, hairdressers or any services will never hurt.

Toilets

There are 330 public toilets in Vienna marked by a large WC sign. Some are open 24 hours a day, others vary but are generally open from 9am to 7pm daily. Public toilets with attendants cost 50¢, but at least are clean. The WC on the Graben was designed by Adolf Loos and is worth a visit to admire the art nouveau decor. Other usefully located WCs are in the Opernpassage and Rathauspark. U-Bahn stations have toilets, but not all are open all the time.

Tourist information

City Hall Information
(Rathaus) 1, Friedrich-Schmidt-Platz 1 (52 550-0). U2 Rathaus/tram 1, 2,

D. **Open** 8am-6pm Mon-Fri; 8am-4pm Sat, Sun. **Map** p242 D6. Although not a tourist office, the City Hall does provide a number of maps and brochures in English. Phone for details of opera performances, ticket sales and museum hours.

Vienna Tourist Board
1, Albertinaplatz 1 (513 88 92). U1, U2, U4 Karlsplatz/tram 1, 2, D, J. **Open** 9am-7pm daily. **Map** p242 E7. 2, Obere Augartenstrasse 40 (211 140). Tram 31. **Open** 8am-4pm Mon-Fri. **Map** p235 F4.

Youth Information Vienna
1, Babenbergerstrasse 1 (1799). U2, U3 Volkstheater. **Open** noon-7pm Mon-Fri; noon-7pm Sat. **Map** p242 D7.

Visas & immigration

Citizens of other EU countries have the right to enter Austria and remain for an indefinite period of time. However, anyone staying in Austria in a private house or apartment for more than 60 days is technically required to register with the Magistratisches Bezirksamt, although this is not enforced (see below Residence permits).

Officials at Austria's road and train borders with eastern Europe tend to be particularly fierce if you are holding a passport from an eastern European state.

A visa is not required for US citizens for up to three-month periods; at the end of a six-month stay you must leave the country if you do not have a residence permit.

Residence permits

If you are planning on staying in Austria for more than 60 days, you'll need to register yourself with the Magistratisches Bezirksamt (of your district) to obtain a Meldezettel – a confirmation of where you live. Meldezettels are requested for everything from renting a flat to applying for a library card. Buy the forms at any newsstand and locate the Magistratisches Bezirksamt in your area (in the phone book under Magistratisches Bezirksamt). File the form 8am-3.30pm Mon-Wed, Fri; 8am-5.30pm Thur. Bring your passport with you.

If you don't want to disclose what may seem like private information under the 'Religion' section, make sure to write 'ORB' ('not admitting religion'). Otherwise, you'll be automatically registered as having

a religion and will get calls demanding tithes from, say, the Evangelical church, if you are registered as Protestant. Religion is taken very seriously in Austria, so shrugging off the call won't work. The religious orders have the right to a percentage of your salary unless you are registered as ORB.

If you change address, you'll need to de-register yourself at your current Magistratisches Bezirksamt and re-register yourself in the new one.

When to go

Vienna has a rather mild continental climate, hot in summer and cold in winter. Wind can often make the temperature seem lower than it really is. During the winter the city sometimes ices over. During summer rain is frequent. The best time to go is May-June and September-October. See also p222 **Climate by month**.

Women

For the **Women's Career Network (WCN)**, see p215. See also p218 **Helplines** and p217 **Health**.

American Women's Association (AWA)
1, Mahlerstrasse 3/7 (966 29 25). U1, U4 Karlsplatz/tram 1, 2. **Open** 10am-3pm Mon, Tue, Thur, Fri; 1-6pm Wed. **Map** p243 E7. A non-profit organisation to help American women and other English-speaking women living in Vienna.

Working in Vienna

Citizens of the European Economic Area are exempt from the bureaucratic requirements of obtaining work permits. If you're not a citizen of the EEA, then gaining a permit is a hassle, as Austrians are already struggling to manage the large number of eastern Europeans entering the country (legally and otherwise). You will need a work permit (Arbeitsgenehmigung) unless you are specifically exempt according to the law governing the employment of foreigners (Ausländerbe-schäftigung-sgesetz).

If you marry an Austrian, life becomes easier. However, in order to work you must have a residence permit (Aufenhalts-bewilligung) and a written confirmation from the regional Labour Office (Arbeigs-marktservice) which certifies your work permit exemption. Look in the phone book 'white pages' under 'Arbeitsmarktservice' to find the closest office to you.

Further Reference

Ilse Barea *Vienna*
Readable historical account of
the city from the Baroque era
to World War I by a Viennese
émigrée.

Thomas Bernhard
Cutting Timber
Vituperative novel portraying
contemporary Viennese artistic
and literary circles. Bernhard
at his trademark maniacal and
misanthropic best (he was even
sued by one of the characters).

Bill Bryson *Neither Here
Nor There*
Includes a flippant but often
perspicacious account of his
Vienna sojourn as a teenage
backpacker in Europe.

Elias Canetti *Auto-da-Fé*
Perhaps the best-known work
of fiction by the Nobel Prize
winner. A misanthropic
sinologist living in Vienna at
the turn of the century finds
his life disintegrating after he
falls for the machinations of
the coarse, scheming cleaning
woman he marries.

Elias Canetti *The Tongue
Set Free*
The author spent his formative
school days in Vienna in the
years leading up to World
War II. Fond memories of the
Tunnel of Fun at the Prater,
and a family friend who spoke
of Bahr and Schnitzler and
was 'Viennese if for no other
reason than because she
always knew, without great
effort, what was happening
in the world of the intellect.'

George Clare *Last Waltz
in Vienna*
Moving account of ominous
pre-Anchluss years seen
through the eyes of a young
middle-class Jew who managed
to escape to Britain.

Lilian Faschinger
Magdalena the Sinner
A leather-clad woman on a
motorbike kidnaps a priest
and ties him to a tree in order

to confess her sins. Enjoyable
and blasphemous antidote to
Viennese Catholicism.

Françoise Giroud *Alma
Mahler: Or the Art of
Being Loved*
Racy defence of Alma's
talents, scathing on Gustav
Mahler's attempts to stifle
her musical career.

Patrick Leigh Fermor
A Time of Gifts
Contains a lengthy amusing
chapter on the Vienna stage
of his walk from London to
Constantinople in 1933-4.

Peter Handke *The
Goalkeeper's Fear of the Penalty*
Austria's most celebrated
contemporary novelist. His
work does not include anything
specifically about Vienna.

Brigitte Hamann
Hitler's Vienna
Grim, fascinating and essential
reading about pre-war Vienna
in an appalling translation.

Ingrid Helsing *Almaas
Vienna; a guide to recent
architecture*
Pocket-sized, opinionated and
well illustrated.

John Irving *Setting Free
the Bears*
High jinks in Schönbrunn –
the story concerns a plot to
liberate all the animals from
Vienna Zoo.

Louis James *The Xenophobes
Guide to the Austrians*
A quirky look at Austrians.

**Allan Janik and Stephen
Toulmin** *Wittgenstein's
Vienna*
Guidebook to Vienna tracing
the aesthetic and literary
background to Wittgenstein's
life. Rendered in clogged prose
and plagued with typos.

Elfriede Jelinek *The Piano
Teacher* Recently filmed by
Michael Hanneke, it catches
the stifling atmosphere of
1950s Vienna. Numerous
other works by one of
Austria's most critical spirits
are available in English.

William M Johnson *The
Austrian mind: An Intellectual
and Social History 1848-1938*
Dry but thorough American
work conveniently subdivided.

**John Lehmann and
Richard Bassett** *Vienna,
A Travellers' Companion*
Eye-witness accounts, letters,
stories of Vienna.

Claudio Magris *Danube*
Brief but to the point on Vienna,
packed with literary landmarks
and coffee house visits.

Jan Morris *50 Years of
Europe: An Album*
Several illuminating pieces on
Vienna show her barely
disguised contempt for the city.

Franz Maier-Bruck *Das
Grosse Sacher Kochbuch*
A great collection of Austrian
recipes and grand cuisine.

Robert Musil *The Man
Without Qualities*
Impressive in size and
reputation: the kind of book
you really should read, but
never quite get round to (you
could just read chapter 15, for
its account of the intellectual
revolution). Set in the years
leading up to the outbreak of
World War I.

Frederick Morton *A
Nervous Splendour: Vienna
1888-89* and *Thunder at
Twilight: Vienna 1913-14*
Engrossing dramatised
accounts of end of Habsburg
Vienna. The first centres on the
Mayerling affair and the latter
on events prior to World War I.

Hella Pick *Guilty Victim*
Semi-personal account of
modern Austria by a Jewish
exile form Vienna and former
Guardian foreign editor.

Christoph Ransmayr
The Dog King
An absurd, beautifully written
tale about the horrors of war,
set in a fictional Alpine town.

Joseph Roth *The String
of Pearls*
The Shah of Persia visits
Vienna, demands the services

of a countess, and gets a look-alike whore instead. Lots of melancholic doomed characters and scenes in coffeehouses.

Joseph Roth *Radetzky March* and *The Emperor's Tomb*
Roth's finest novels chronicle the decline of the Empire. Splendid new translations by Michael Hofmann.

Arthur Schnitzler
Dream Story
Keep your eyes wide shut while reading and try to forget Tom and Nicole as Fridolin and Albertine.

Carl Schorske *Fin de Siècle Vienna*
Seven scholarly studies.

Paul Strathern *Wittgenstein in 90 Minutes*
Summary of Wittgenstein's life and philosophy ('if people did not sometimes do silly things, nothing intelligent would ever get done').

Georg Trakl *Selected Poems*
For serious and professional melancholics.

Stefan Zweig *The World of Yesterday*
Fascinating explanation of the key role the Jews played in the artistic development of Vienna.

Stefan Zweig *The Royal Game*
The influence of Freud and the early psychoanalysts is impossible to miss.

Music

An arbitrary selection of modern music to put you in the mood for a visit to Vienna. The more obscure items are available via mail order from Mego's online distribution service at www.mdos.at or from local shops such as Rave Up or Substance (*see p142*) .

Attwenger *Sun* Latest release by John Peel's favourite Upper Austrian folk punks.

Bernhardt Fleischmann
Pop Loops for Breakfast
Clicky-poppy micro techno.

Café Drechsler *Café Drechsler* Groovy stuff played with real instruments.

DJ DSL *#1* Aka Stefan Biedermann, Austria's undisputed old skool turntable *meister* mashes up Kool Keith with Yellowman.

Dzhian & Kamien *Freaks & Icons* Balkan-tinged downbeat slips down easily at Café del Mar.

Fennesz *Endless Summer*
Vienna's laptop romantic just gets better and better.

Fetish 69 *Antibody* Hard-core confrontation.

I-Wolf *Soul Strata*
Triumphant collage of post-rock, broken beats and sweet soul vocals.

Kruder & Dorfmeister
K&D Sessions Essential listening. Annie Nightingale described it as the *Hotel California* of the 1990s.

Louie Austen *Consequences*
Resident crooner at Vienna's Intercontinental given the electronic once-over by Cheap's Mario Neugebauer.

Peace Orchestra *Peace Orchestra* Hugely inventive Kruder solo project.

Pita *Get Out* Full-on noise attack from Mego mastermind Peter Rehberg.

Pungent Stench *Been Caught Buttering* Tautological Viennese death metal with big Australian following.

Radian *rec.extern* Heavy bass and electro crackle 'n' pop. Now in the Tortoise stable.

Sluts & Strings & 909
Carerra One of Pulsinger & Tunakan's early recordings also available in remixes by Si Begg, Peter Kruder and others.

Sofa Surfers *Encounters*
Dark 'n' dubbed-up head music with the likes of Junior Delgado and Mark Stewart in tow.

Tosca *Suzuki* Gorgeous, slippery downbeat from Dorfmeister and school chum Rupert Huber.

Trio Exclusiv *Trio Exclusiv*
First album by four-piece jazzy, funk/electronic surfniks. Best performers in Vienna.

VA *Fried Kutz* Sabotage Records' hip hop primer with

Texta, Waxolutionists, DJ DSL and lesser members of the 'hood.

Various artists *Vienna Scientists Vols 1-3* Good intro to the city's downbeat delights.

Waldeck Sumptuous
Balance of the Force This take on 'Aquarius' is this triphopping ex-copyright lawyer's best-known work. Variously remixed by Thievery Corporation and Rockers Hi-Fi.

Wolfgang Muthspiel *Real Book Stories* Currently Vienna's leading jazzman in the company of Brian Blade and Marc Johnson.

Websites

www.wien.gv.at A list of events in Vienna and general info on Austria.

www.info.wien/at The Vienna Tourist Information site: coverage of tourist events and other info about the city.

www.tiscover.com Features on sports, leisure activities (including live cams at ski resorts) and holidays.

www.austria.org An Austrian press and information service based in Washington, DC.

www.mqw.at Full details of events at the city's new arts complex.

www.virtualvienna.com
An amusingly amateurish site run by Vienna's large expat community.

www.falter.at The site of Vienna's best listings paper. In German.

www.wienguide.at An exhaustive guide to walking tours in the city.

www.austriatoday.at By the weekly English-language newspaper of the same name.

www.viennahype.at An official tourist info site aimed at young visitors, designed by the Lomographic Society.

www.magwien.gv.at/english/
A site run by the City Council with excellent newsy and anecdotal pieces, as well as listings.

Directory

Index

Index

Index

Maps

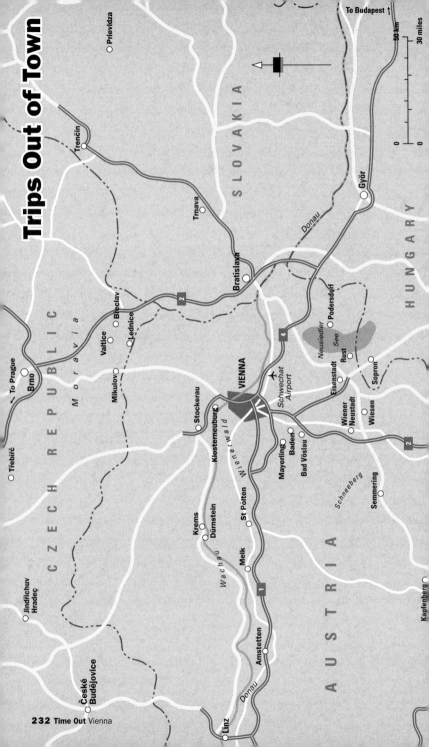

Trips Out of Town

To Budapest ↑

50 km

30 miles

SLOVAKIA

HUNGARY

CZECH REPUBLIC

AUSTRIA

Prievidza

Trenčín

Trnava

Bratislava

Donau

Győr

Břeclav

Lednice

Valtice

Mikulov

To Prague

Brno

Třebíč

M o r a v i a

Stockerau

Klosterneuburg

VIENNA

Schwechat Airport

2

4

2

Neusiedler See

Podersdorf

Rust

Eisenstadt

Sopron

Wiener Neustadt

Wiesen

Mayerling

Baden

Bad Vöslau

Schneeberg

Semmering

Krems

Dürnstein

St Pölten

Melk

Wachau

1

Amstetten

Donau

Linz

Jindřichův Hradec

České Budějovice

Kapfenberg

Wienerwald

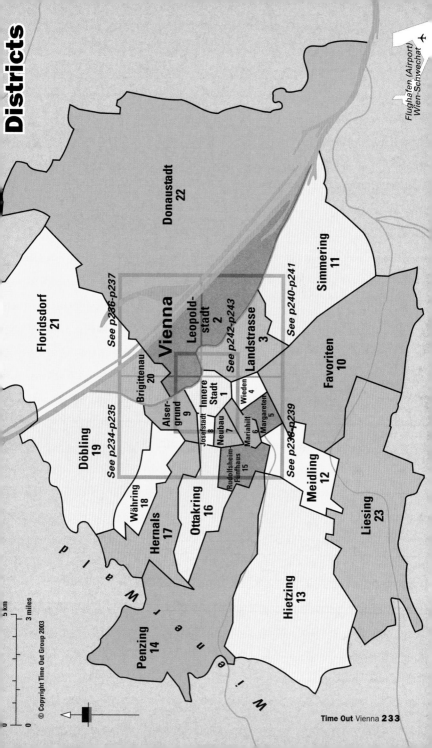

Districts

Flughafen (Airport)
Wien-Schwechat

Donaustadt 22

Floridsdorf 21

Simmering 11

See p236-p237

Vienna

Leopold-stadt 2

Landstrasse 3

See p242-p243

See p240-p241

Brigittenau 20

Innere Stadt 1

Alser-grund 9

Wieden 4

Favoriten 10

See p234-p235

Döbling 19

Josefstadt 8

Neubau 7

Mariahilf 6

Margareten 5

See p238-p239

Rudolfsheim-Fünfhaus 15

Währing 18

Ottakring 16

Meidling 12

Hernals 17

Liesing 23

Penzing 14

Hietzing 13

5 km

3 miles

© Copyright Time Out Group 2003

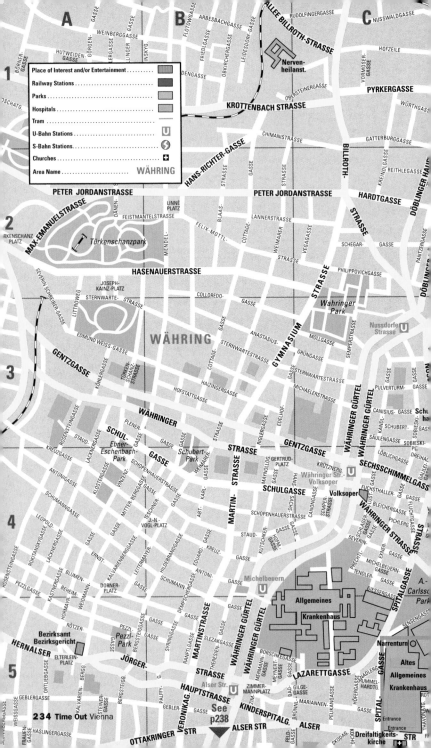

See p238

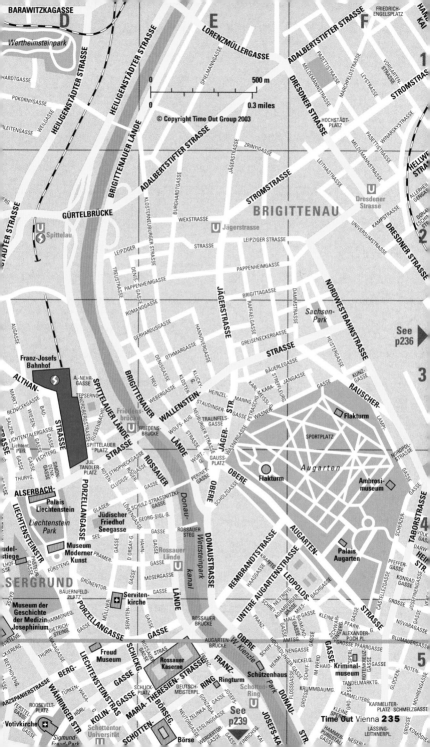

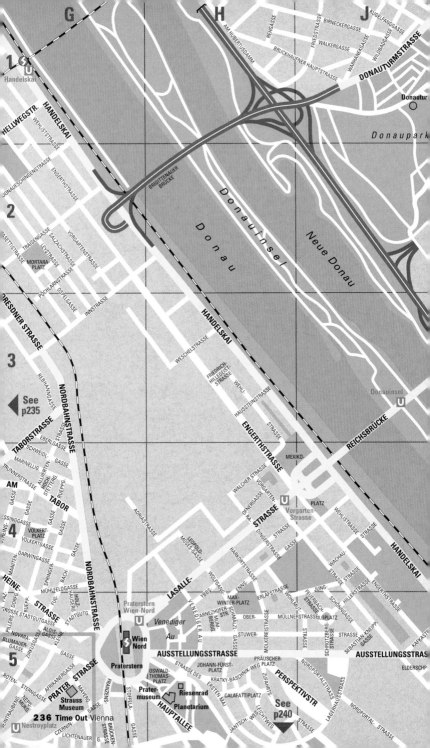

1
U
Handelskai

HELLWEGSTR.
HANDELSKAI
WEHLISTRASSE

ENGERTHSTRASSE

JONAUESCHINGENSTRASSE

TRAISENGASSE
SALZACHSTRASSE
LEYSTRASSE
VORGARTENSTRASSE

CASETTISTRASSE
MORTARA
PLATZ
PÖCHLARNSTRASSE
OSTFELGASSE
INNSTRASSE

2

DRESDNER STRASSE

HANDELSKAI

WECHSELSTRASSE

FRIEDRICH-
HILLEGEIST-
STRASSE
WEHLI-
HAUSSTEINSTRASSE
STRASSE

3

See
p235

ENGERTHSTRASSE

REICHSBRÜCKE

Donauinsel
U

Donau

Donauinsel

Neue Donau

AM HUBERTUSDAMM

REHGASSE
FRIEDLSTRASSE
BIRNECKERGASSE
KUGELFANGGASSE

WALKERGASSE
WARHANERGASSE
WILDBADGASSE

BRUCKHAUFNER HAUPTSTRASSE

DONAUTURMSTRASSE

Donauturm
O

Donaupark

BRIGITTENAUER
BRÜCKE

REBHANNGASSE

NORDBAHNSTRASSE

TABORSTRASSE
EBERLGASSE
SCHWEIDL-
GASSE
MARINELLIG-
ALLIIERTEN-
HOCH-
RUEPPG.

TRUNNERSTRASSE

AM
TABOR
GASSE

MEXIKO-

WALCHER STRASSE
VORGARTEN-
OFNERGASSE
RA.
STRASSE

PLATZ
U
Vorgarten-
Strasse

WEHLISTRASSE
STRASSE

4
VOLKERT-
PLATZ
VOLKERTGASSE

GASSE
GASSE
GASSE
SPRINGER-
BACH-
FUG-
HOLZ-
STADTGUTG.
MÜHLFELDGASSE

MANITEN-
DARWINGASSE

ADRIASTRASSE

LEOPOLD-
MUSEE-GASSE

HARKORTSTRASSE

DINGERSTRASSE
GASSE

WACHAU

HANDELSKAI

HEINE

STRASSE
DUERR.
GROSSE STADTGUTGASSE
STADTGUTG.

PILLERS-
NOVARA-
BLUMAUER-
GASSE
KLEINE
ALOIS-
GASSE

GASSE

Praterstern
Wien-Nord
U

Venediger

Au

Wien
Nord

Praterstern

LASALLE-

VENEDIGER AU
ARNEZHOFER STR.
YBBS-
WOLFGANG-
SCHMALZ-
MAX-
WINTER-PLATZ
ENNS-
BERGE-

OBER-
STUWER-
GASSE

MÖLKEREISTRASSE

ERLAFSTRASSE
WOHLAU.

JUNG-

FEUERBACH-
STRASSE
SCHÖNNGASSE

SCHROTZBERG-
STRASSE
STRASSE
SEBASTIAN-KNEIPP-
GASSE

KAFKAST.

5
ROTEN-
STERNGASSE
NEPO
MUK
HANG

AFRIKANERGASSE

PRATER STRASSE
MAYERG.

FRANZENS-
STOFFELA

Strauss
Museum

Prater-
museum
Riesenrad

Planetarium

OSWALD-
THOMAS-
PLATZ

JOHANN-FÜRST-
PLATZ

KRATKY-BASCHNIK-WEG

CALAFATTIPLATZ

STRASSE DES
ERSTEN MAI

PRÄUSCHER
PLATZ

NORDPORTALSTRASSE

AUSSTELLUNGSSTRAS

ELDERSCHP.

236 Time Out Vienna

U Nestroyplatz

HAUPTALLEE

CZERNIN-

BRÜCKEN-
STRASSE

LICHTENAUER

PERSPEKTIVSTR.

See
p240

JANTSCH-
LEICHTWEG
WEG

NORDPORTAL-
STRASSE

LAGERHAUSSTRASSE

STRASSE

AUSSTELLUNGSSTRASSE

AUSSTELLUNGSSTRASSE

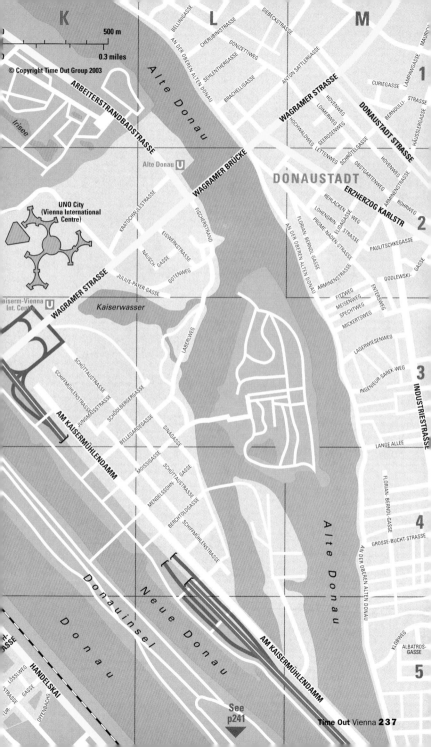

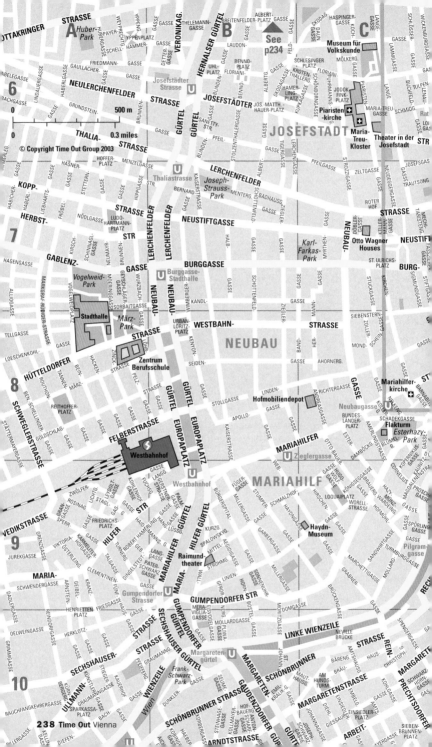

STRASSE

A **Huber-Park**

OTTAKRINGER STRASSE

B

C

ALBERT-PLATZ

See p234

Museum für Volkskunde

NEULERCHENFELDER STRASSE

Josefstädter Strasse

JOSEFSTÄDTER STRASSE

JOSEFSTADT

Piaristen -kirche

Maria-Treu-Kloster

Theater in der Josefstadt

6

0   500 m

0   0.3 miles

THALIA-STRASSE

© Copyright Time Out Group 2003

HERBST-

KOPP-

GABLENZ-GASSE

Vogelweid-Park

Stadthalle

März-Park

LERCHENFELDER STRASSE

LERCHENFELDER STRASSE

Thaliastrasse

Joseph-Strauss-Park

LERCHENFELDER STRASSE

NEUSTIFTGASSE

Karl-Farkas-Park

BURGGASSE

NEUBAU-GASSE

Burggasse-Stadthalle

WESTBAHN-STRASSE

NEUBAU

STRASSE

Zentrum Berufsschule

Otto Wagner Houses

NEUSTIFT

BURG-

7

HÜTTELDORFER

SCHWEGLER-STRASSE

GÜRTEL

GÜRTEL

FELBERSTRASSE

EUROPAPLATZ

Westbahnhof

Westbahnhof

Mariahilfer-kirche

Hofmobiliendepot

Neubaugasse

Flakturm

Esterhazy-Park

Ziegelgasse

MARIAHILF

8

VEDIKSTRASSE

MARIA-

HILFER GÜRTEL

MARIAHILFER-

HILFER GÜRTEL

Raimundtheater

Haydn-Museum

Pilgramgasse

9

Gumpendorfer Strasse

GUMPENDORFER STR

SECHSHAUSER-

WIENZEILE

SECHSHAUSER GÜRTEL

GUMPENDORFER GÜRTEL

Frank-Schwarz-Park

Margaretengürtel

LINKE WIENZEILE

NEVILLE BRÜCKE

SCHÖNBRUNNER

MARGARETEN

ULLMANN

SCHÖNBRUNNER STRASSE

MARGARETENSTRASSE

PRECHTSDORFER

10

ARNDTSTRASSE

ARBEIT-

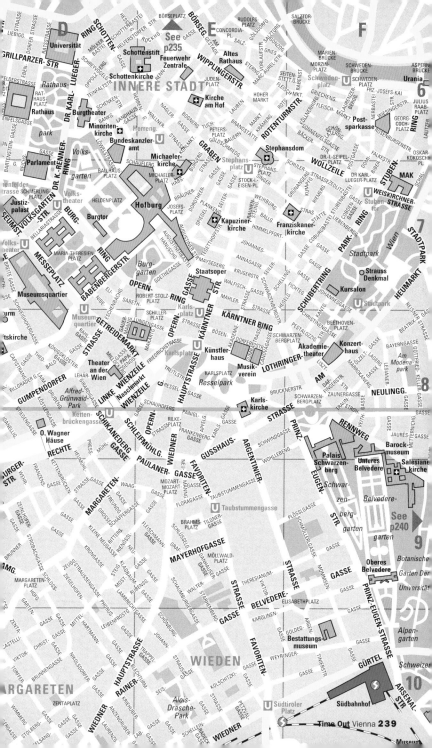

© Copyright Time Out Group 2003

500 m
0.3 miles

K
L
M

See
p237

STRASSE
VORGARTENSTRASSE

HANDELSKAI

Donauinsel

ENGERTHSTRASSE

STRASSE

MEIEREI-

Ernst-Happel-
Stadion

MARATHONWEG

WEHLISTRASSE

ICHMANNGASSE

HANDELSKAI

7

WEHLISTRASSE

TENSCHACHERALLEE

LUST-

ALLEE

HAUS-

Oberes Heustadelwasser

HAUPTALLEE

STRASSE

KLASCHAUWEG

Unteres Heustadelwasser

8

HAUPTALLEE

LANDE

ERDBERGERBRÜCKE

Unterer Prater

Lusthaus ○

9

SCHNIRCHGASSE

MITTLERER

GRABEN

WEG

ERDBERG STR

STRASSE

KAPPGASSE

PARAGONSTRASSE

OSTAUTOBAHN

SIMMERZINGER LANDE

GARTENSTRASSE

GUGL-

U Gasometer

GASSE

DECENTER

STRASSE

10

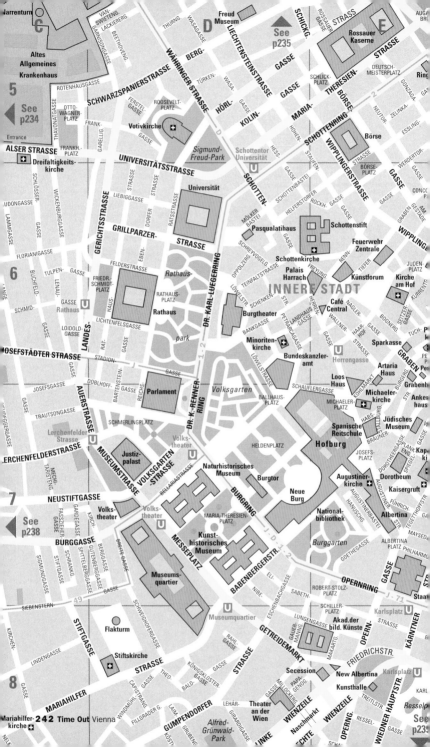

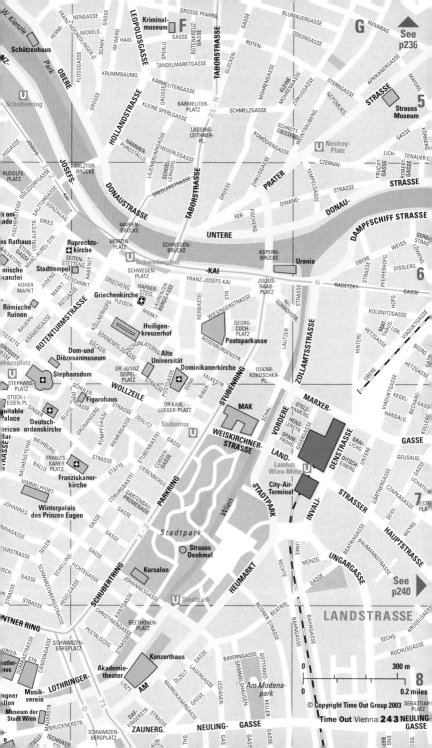

See p236

See p240

LANDSTRASSE

0   300 m
0   0.2 miles

© Copyright Time Out Group 2003

Time Out Vienna **243**

GEMÄLDEGALERIE DER AKADEMIE DER BILDENDEN KÜNSTE IN WIEN
PICTURE GALLERY OF THE ACADEMY OF FINE ARTS VIENNA

The Picture Gallery of the Academy of Fine Arts represents one of Vienna`s hidden treasures, a splendid walk across the history of European painting leads from Bosch`s Last Judgement Triptych to Titian, Rubens, Rembrandt, Ruisdael and G.B. Tiepolo or F. Guardi.
A special section is dedicated to the masterpieces of the Viennese Academy around 1800.

Opening hours: Tues - Sun, holidays 10 am - 4 pm

1010 WIEN, Schillerplatz 3 •Tel: +43 1 58 816 225
e-mail: gemgal@akbild.ac.at • www.akademiegalerie.at

Street Index

Peter-Jordan-Strasse – A2, B2, C2
Petersplatz – E6
Petrarcagasse – D6
Petraschgasse – E3
Petrusgasse – H9
Pettenkofengasse – G9
Petzvalgasse – E10
Pezzlgasse – A4, A5, B5
Pfarrhofgasse – G8
Pfeffergasse – F4
Pfefferhofgasse – G6
Pfeiffergasse – A10
Pfeilgasse – B6, C6, C7
Pfluggasse – D4
Philharmgasse – E7
Philippovichgasse – C2
Phorusgasse – D9, D10
Piaristengasse – C6, C7
Pichlergasse – C4
Pilgramgasse – D9
Pillergasse – A10
Pillers-Dorfgasse – G4, G5
Plankengasse – E7
Plenergasse – A3, B3
Pliwagasse – B10
Plösslgasse – F9
Pöchlarnstrasse – G2
Pokornygasse – D1
Porzellangasse – D4, D5
Postgasse – F6, F7
Posthorngasse – G8
Pramergasse – D4, E4
Prater Strasse – F6, G5
Präuscherplatz – H5
Prechtlgasse – C4
Pressgasse – D8, D9
Prinz-Eugen-Strasse – F8-10
Promenadenstrasse – M2
Proschkogasse – C9
Pulverturmgasse – C3
Pyrkergasse – C1

Rabengasse – H9
Rabenstrasse – F6
Radeckgasse – E10
Radelmayergasse – C2, D2
Radetzkygasse – G6
Radetzkyplatz – G6
Radingerstrasse – H4
Raffaelgasse – E2, E3
Rahlgasse – D8
Raimundgasse – F5
Rainergasse – D10, E10
Ramperstorffergasse – C10, D10
Ranftlgasse – B5
Rasumofskygasse – G7
Rathausplatz – D6
Ratsstrasse – D6
Rauchfangkehrergasse – A10
Rauhensteingasse – E7
Rauscherstrasse – F3, F4
Rebhanngasse – G3
Rechte Bahngasse – F7, G8, G9
Rechte Wienzeile – C9, D8, E8
Rehgasse – H1
Rehlackenweg – M2
Reichsbrücke – J3
Reiichsrathausstrasse – D6, D7
Reindorfgasse – A9, A10
Reinprechtsdorfer Str – C10
Reischachstrasse – F6
Reisner Strasse – F7, F8
Reisnerstrasse – F8, F9
Reithlegasse – C2
Reithofferplatz – A8
Rembrandtstrasse – E4
Renngasse – E6
Rennweg – F8, F9
Rennweg – G9, H10, J10
Resselgasse – E7
Reznicekgasse – D3
Richtergasse – C8
Riemergasse – F7

Rienösslgasse – D9, E9
Riesgasse – G8
Riglergasse – B3
Rilkeplatz – E8
Rittergasse – D9
Robert-Hamerling-Gasse – A9, B9
Robertgasse – G5, G6
Robert-Stolz-Platz – E7
Rochusgasse – G8
Rockhgasse – E6
Rodlergasse – A1
Rögergasse – D4, E4
Rohrweg – M2
Rokitanskygasse – A4
Romanogasse – D3, E3
Rooseveltplatz – D5
Rosenbursenstrasse – F6
Rosensteingasse – A3, A4
Rosinagasse – A9
Rossauer Lände – E4, E5
Rossauerbrücke – E5
Rossauergasse – E5
Rossauersteg – E4
Rotengasse – F7
Rotenhausgasse – C5, D5
Rotenkreuzgasse – F5
Roten-Löwengasse – D4
Rotensterngasse – F5, G5
Rotenturmstrasse – E6, F6
Roterhof – C7
Rotgasse – E6, F7
Rotundenbrücke – H7
Rötzergasse – A5
Routhongasse – A8
Rubensgasse – D9, E9
Rüdengasse – H8
Rüdigergasse – D9
Rudolfingergasse – C1
Rudolfsplatz – E6
Rueppgasse – G4
Rummel-Hardtgasse – C5
Rundweg – J9
Rustenschacher-Allee – H6, H7, J7, J8
Rustenschacherallee – K7, K8

Saileräckerg – A1, B1
Salmgasse – G7
Salvatorgasse – E6
Salzachstrasse – G2
Salzergasse – D3, D4
Salzgries – E6
Salztorbrücke – F6
Salztorgasse – E6
Sandwirtgasse – C9
Sanettystrasse – B6
Säulengasse – C3
Schadekgasse – C8
Schäffergasse – D9, E9
Schallautzer Strasse – F6, F7, G6
Schauflergasse – D7, E7
Schauhofergasse – E8
Schaumburgergasse – E9, E10
Schegargasse – C2
Schelleingasse – E10, F10
Schellhammergasse – A6, B6
Schellinggasse – E7, F7
Schenkenstrasse – D6
Scherzergasse – F4
Schickgasse – D5
Schiffamtsgasse – E5, F5
Schiffmühlenstrasse – K3, L4
Schikanedergasse -, D8
Schillerplatz – E7, E8
Schimmelgasse – H9
Schinnaglgasse – A7
Schlachthausgasse – H9, J9
Schlagergasse – C4
Schleifmühlgasse – D8, E9
Schlesingerplatz – C6
Schlickplatz – E5
Schlössergasse – C6
Schlosshofgasse – D9
Schlüsselgasse – E9

Schmalzhofgasse – B9, C9
Schmelzgasse – F5
Schmerlingplatz – D7
Schmidgasse – C6
Schmöllerlgasse – F9
Schnirchgasse – J9, K9, K10
Schödlbergergasse – K3, L3
Schoellerhofgasse – F5, F6
Scholzgasse – E4
Schönborngasse – C6
Schönbrunner Strasse – B10, C9, C10, D9
Schönburgstrasse – E10
Schönlaterngasse – F6
Schönngasse – J5
Schopenhauerstrasse – A4, B4, C4
Schottenbastei – D6
Schottenfeldgasse – B7, B8
Schottengasse – D6
Schottenring – D5, D6, E5
Schrankgasse – C7
Schreygasse – E5, F5
Schreyvogelgasse – D6
Schrötelgasse – M1, M2
Schrottgasse – H9
Schrottgiessergasse – F5, G5
Schrotzbergstrasse – J5
Schubertgasse – C5
Schubertring – F7, F8
Schulerstrasse – F7
Schulgasse – A3, B4, C4
Schulz-Strassnitzki-Gasse – D4, E4
Schumanngasse – A4, B4, B5
Schüttaustrasse – K3, L4
Schüttelstrasse – G6, H7, H8, J8
Schützengasse – G9
Schwalbenweg – H8
Schwarzenbergplatz – E8, F8
Schwarzenbergstrasse – E7, E8
Schwarzhorngasse – C10
Schwarzingergasse – F5
Schwarzspanierstrasse – D5
Schwedenbrücke – F6
Schwedenplatz – F6
Schweglerstrasse – A8
Schweidlgasse – G4
Schweighofergasse – D8
Schwendengasse – A9
Schwindgasse – E8, F8
Sebastian-Kneippgasse – J5
Sebastianplatz – G8
Sechshauser Gürtel – B10
Sechshauserstrasse – A10
Sechskrügelgasse – G8
Sechsschimmelgasse – C4
Seegasse – D4, E4
Seerosenweg – M1
Sehlenthergasse – L1
Seidengasse – B8
Seidlgasse – G6, G7
Seilerstätte – E7, F7
Seippgasse – H10
Seisgasse – E10
Seitenstettengasse – E6, F6
Seitergasse – E7
Seitzergasse – E6
Sellenygasse – H7
Semperstrasse – C3, C4
Sensengasse – C5
Servitengasse – D4, D5
Seumegasse – B10
Severin-Schreiber-Gassee – A2, A3
Severingasse – C4
Siebeckstrasse – L1, M1
Siebenbrunnengasse – C10, D10
Siebenbrunnenplatz – C10
Siebensterngasse – C7, C8, D7
Siebertgasse – B10
Siegelgasse – G7
Sigmundgasse – C7

Sillerweg – J8
Simmerzinger Lände – L10
Simon-Denk-Gasse – D4
Sinagasse – L3, L4
Singerstrasse – E7, F7
Skodagasse – B6, C5, C6
Slezakgasse – B5
Sobieskigasse – C3
Sobieskiplatz – C3
Sollingergasse – A1
Sonnenfelsgasse – F6
Sonnenuhrgasse – B9
Sorbaitgasse – A7
Spalowskygasse – B9
Sparefrohgasse – F7, G7
Sparkassaplatz – A10
Spechtweg – M3
Spengergasse – C10, D10
Sperrgasse – A9
Spiegelgasse – E7
Spielmanngasse – E1
Spitalgasse – C4, C5
Spittelauer Lände – D2, D3
Spittelauer Platz – D3
Spittelberggasse – C7
Spörlinggasse – C9
Sportklubstrasse – H6
Springergasse – G4
St Johann-Gasse – B10
St Nikolaus-Platz – H8
St Ulrichs-Platz – C7
Stadion-Allee – K7, K8
Stadionbrücke – J8
Stadiongasse – D6
Stadtpark – F7
Staglgasse – A9
Stallburgasse – E7
Stammgasse – G7
Stanislausgasse – G9
Stättermayergasse – A8
Staudgasse – A3, A4, B4
Staudingergasse – E3
Steggasse – D9
Steinergasse – A5
Steingasse – G9, H9
Steinhagegasse – B10
Stelzhamergasse – F7, G7
Stephansplatz – E6, E7
Sterngasse – E6
Sternwartestrasse – A2, A3, B3, C3
Stiegengasse – D8
Stiegergasse – A10
Stiftgasse – C7, C8, D8
Stöbergasse – D10
Stock-i-Eisen-Platz – E7
Stoffelagasse – G5
Stolberggasse – D10
Stollgasse – B8
Stolzenthalergasse – B6
Strasse des Ersten Mai – H5, H6
Streffleurgasse – E3
Streichergasse – G8
Strobachgasse – E9
Strohgasse – F8
Strohmgasse – B9
Stromstrasse – E2, F1, F2
Stropheckgasse – D4
Strozzigasse – C6, C7
Strudlhofgasse – D4
Stubenbastei – F7
Stubenring – F6, F7
Stuckgasse – C7
Stumpergasse – B9, C9
Sturgasse – K5
Stuwer-Strasse – J5
Südportalstrasse – J6
Syringgasse – B5

Taborstrasse – F4-F6
Taborstrasse – G3, G4
Talgasse – A9
Tandelmarktgasse – F5
Tannengasse – A8
Taubstummengasse – E9
Technikerstrasse – E8

248 Time Out Vienna

Advertisers' Index

Please refer to relevant pages for full details

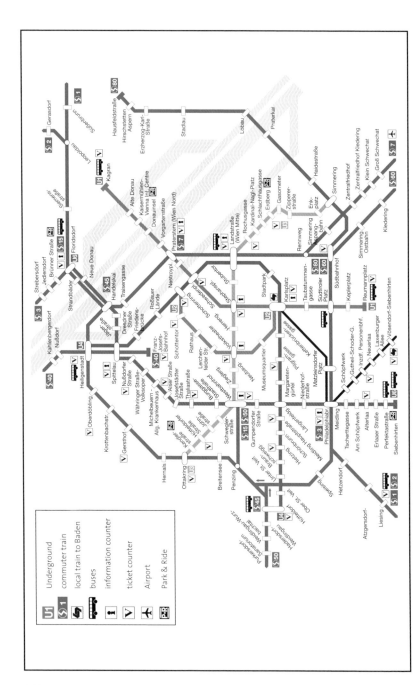